2008
COACH OF THE
YEAR CLINIC
NOTES

LECTURES BY
PREMIER HIGH SCHOOL COACHES

Edited by Earl Browning

COACHES CHOICE™

www.coacheschoice.com

D1334714

ISBN: 978-1-58518-740-9

Telecoach, Inc. Transcription: Earl Browning, Jr., Kent Browning, Tom Cheaney, Dan Haley

Diagrams: Steve Haag

Book layout and cover design: Bean Creek Studio

Special thanks to the Nike clinic managers for having the lectures taped.

Coaches Choice
P.O. Box 1828
Monterey, CA 93942
www.coaceschoice.com

Contents

Contents

MOJO FOOTBALL: *FRIDAY NIGHT LIGHTS*

Odessa Permian High School, Texas

We can see the dedicated football coaches in the room. I have been to the mini-clinics earlier today in the other rooms, and they have all been full. There is some good football talk going on in those rooms. We are big believers in clinics in Texas. We were fortunate enough to have a great year, but we did not win the state championship. We have gone through some changes and have done some good things at Permian High School.

I do not have all the answers, but I have had an unbelievable coaching career in Texas. I grew up in Odessa and went to Permian High School. I was lucky because I graduated the year before they made *Friday Night Lights*. I graduated in 1987. The guys who made all the money on the movie came in after I graduated. Most of the players in that movie were sophomores when I was a senior. The guys in that movie were real. Some of them still live in Odessa.

The movie did a good job of portraying those players—and to an extent even Head Coach Gary Gaines. His first year at Permian was my senior year. We won the state championship when I was a sophomore. My junior year, we went back to the state championship game, and Houston Yates High School beat the snot out of us.

My senior year was Coach Gary Gaines' first, and I was the captain of that team. We lost the last game of the season, and missed the playoffs for the first time in 30 years. It was miserable for him, his family, and a bad time for all of the players on that team. The "For Sale" signs in his yard and all the stuff that went on in the film actually happened. Coach Gaines left Permian and went to Texas Tech as an assistant, and from there back into high school football in Abilene, Texas. He ended up as the executive athletic director for our school district and hired me as football coach at Permian High School in 2005.

Permian has won the most games of any high school in the state of Texas and has won six state championships. The tradition was deep, but the school fell on hard times. Permian went from 1998 until 2006 without making the playoffs.

I do not have time to go into all of the things that went wrong with the program, but they got away from the things that helped get them to the top in the first place. They felt they had to hire a big-time football coach to run the program. They had hired two coaches with winning credentials in the state of Texas. One was from Houston, and one was from Dallas. Neither of them could turn the program around. For whatever reason, the coaches they hired were not a good fit for the school. However, they were good football coaches.

Everyone in Odessa Permian High was shocked when they hired a young coach who had never been a head coach to lead the program. I had never been a head coach. I had been a defensive coordinator for 12 years.

I was in good football programs. I coached in Dallas at Highland Park High School, Temple High School, and Brownwood High School. I started my defensive career as a coordinator at Brownwood High School. Some of you may have heard of Coach Gordon Wood. He was one of the coaches with the most wins in football in the country. At one time, he had the most wins in the country. He won seven state championships at Brownwood. I did get to spend a lot of time with him and learned a lot of football. He has passed away now.

My experience as a young coach was unbelievable. When I went to Permian in 2005, we had 10 football coaches. In a school like that in Texas, the assistants do not stay when they bring in a new coach. Every one of the assistants was let go.

The first thing I had to do was to hire a staff. I brought in an entirely new staff, and we got the program turned around and have been winning for the last two years. That was one reason I got the head job: because they felt I could bring in a staff. We turned the program around immediately. That is what I am going to share with you today in this lecture. In the second lecture, I will talk defense.

I want to share with you the some of the things that are so important in our program. I am a believer in taking care of players. I love high school kids, and I love coaching high school football. We do the best job in Texas of taking care of our kids. I think that is one of the big reasons we are back on track with the program now. Along the way, I have learned some things from coaches who have mentored me who knew much more than I do.

I am sure you have heard some of these things ten thousand times. Coaching is a passion. If you do not have the passion to coach where you are right now, if it is not a passion for you, you are not going to be successful. It does not matter what you know or how smart you are. Players must have the same passion. Passion gets you through the off-season when people are not looking at you.

When I went back to Permian, I had to question my passion about going home. I had just moved my family 10 months earlier for the third time and had one of the best coaching jobs in Texas at Dallas Highland Park High School. They were primed to win another state championship in class 4-A.

When the job at Permian came open, I did some soul searching to consider going back. I had seen Permian get beaten on national TV earlier that season. They were demoralized in that loss to Midland Lee High School, our big rival. I was embarrassed. I had been hearing stories about how bad the kids were, and the fact they did not have any players.

I had just moved my family for the third straight year. To take the job at Permian was not appealing to me at all. I did feel I owed it to myself to go talk with the school people at Permian. That meant I was taking my butt from Dallas to Odessa, which was about a six-hour drive.

To get to Odessa, I went through Brownwood because it was on the way to Odessa. I went in to see Coach Steve Freeman, the coach I had worked for before at Brownwood. There was a power-lifting competition going on at Brownwood that day. I was talking with Coach Freeman, telling him I did not have the passion to go back to Odessa because it would mean I would have to make another move. I told him I did not want to get my brains beat out if the situation was so desperate at Permian.

Steve was giving me some good advice on how to approach the job. As we were talking, another coach from one of the schools in our district came into the meeting. He was at the power-lifting meet. He was the offensive coordinator of one of the teams in the Permian district. They had won 19 straight district games. They had been kicking Permian's lungs in for the past four years.

He asked Steve who he thought would get the Permian head coaching job. Steve was thinking a mile a minute. The wheels were turning in his head. Steve played along with the assistant coach and asked him who he thought would get the job. Then the offensive coordinator said he did not know. Then he went on to say some unkind words about how bad the Permian situation had gotten. The last thing he said was how bad he felt for "the poor Permian kids" in that program. I started getting tears in my eyes. I was so mad about those comments.

By that time, Steve could see I had heard enough. Steve said, "Hey, coach, do you know who's fixing to take the Permian job?" He said, "No, who?" Steve said, "The man sitting right there is going to get the Permian job." The coordinator just turned purple. Now, that stirred the passion in me to say the least. That was one of the reasons I considered going back to Permian. I knew once I returned to Permian, I would have the passion to do the job.

Had I not had that burning passion, I would not have been successful. Two years later, we kicked Abilene's lungs in. It gave me great satisfaction in beating them and breaking their home winning streak. I felt with the help of my assistant coaches, together we could turn the Permian program around.

As I left Brownwood to interview for the Permian job, Coach Freeman gave me something as I went out the door that day. I want to share it with you today. He handed me this poem. If you are in a situation where you are trying to rebuild a program, this may be something you would want to try. It is a poem by Myra Brooks Welch.

This is the story of an old dirty violin that was going up for auction, and no one wanted it. Do you know how many coaches applied for the Permian coaching job when it came open? You would have thought everyone that was looking for a job in Texas would have applied for the job. Do you know how many applied for that job? There were about 10 coaches who applied for the job. Some of them were very good, and some were not.

The thing was, the old violin was sitting up on the shelf, and it was dusty and it had been beaten to death. Not many people wanted to touch the violin.

Steve went on to tell me when the violin is taken off the shelf by someone that cares about it, and they dust it off, and polish it, and tighten the strings, and fine tune it, it will become special again. I took the poem he gave me as I left his office.

The poem is entitled: "The Touch of the Master's Hand."

It was battered and scarred,
And the auctioneer thought it
Hardly worth his while
To waste his time on the old violin,
But he held it up with a smile.
"What am I bid, good people," he cried,
"Who starts the bidding for me?"
"One dollar, one dollar, Do I hear two?"
"Two dollars, who makes it three?"

"Three dollars once, three dollars twice, going for three,"
But, No,
From the room far back a grey-haired man
Came forward and picked up the bow,
Then wiping the dust from the old violin
And tightening up the strings,
He played a melody, pure and sweet,
As sweet as the caroling angel sings.

The music ceased and the auctioneer
With a voice that was quiet and low,
Said, "What now am I bid for this old violin?"
As he held it aloft with its bow.
"One thousand, one thousand, Do I hear two?"
"Two thousand, Who makes it three?"
"Three thousand once, three thousand twice,
Going and gone," said he.

The audience cheered
But some of them cried,
"We just don't understand."
"What changed its worth?"
Swift came the reply.
"The touch of the Master's Hand."

And many a man with life out of tune,
All battered with bourbon and gin,
Is auctioned cheap to a thoughtless crowd
Much like that old violin.
A mess of pottage, a glass of wine,
A game and he travels on.
He is going once, he is going twice,
He is going and almost gone.
But the Master comes,
And the foolish crowd never can quite understand,
The worth of a soul and the change that is wrought
by the touch of the Master's hand

This poem hangs in our coaches' locker room. I told the staff when we first met that we were the Master's hand. We are the ones who could dust off the old violin and make it right again, but it would be a daily process. It is unbelievable what has happened in our program in the last two years at Permian High School.

We had seven games this year where we had more than 20,000 people in attendance. Our football booster club has a budget of over $250,000, which allows us to do special things. This is outside of our athletic budget. This August, our defensive staff is going to Notre Dame for five days. Our offensive staff is going to the University of Oregon for five days. We are spending a lot of time studying football.

I can tell a lot of stories and I have a lot to cover. The next point I want to cover relates to assistant coaches.

Hire Winners

- Character
- Class
- Technical knowledge
- Teaching ability
- Loyalty

Our assistant coaches do teach classes. They do not have the P.E. and study halls as their class. They teach math, biology, history, and computer science. I did not like that at first. I had to hire 10 assistant coaches. I found the best teachers are the best football coaches. Our staff consists of three algebra, three science, two history, and two computer science teachers. All of these subjects are core classes.

If a school is special to you, and you are one of our coaches, you cannot allow anyone to walk through your locker room and not have things right. If you walk by and see towels on the floor, and they do not mean anything to you, then you are probably in the wrong place. I talk about these points with everyone I have hired in our program.

Either you have it, or you don't! I am a firm believer in this point. A coach can coach, or he can't coach. It all comes down to this fact. Does he care or not? There are coaches who draw paychecks, and there are people who take pride in what they do. The good coaches are hard to find, but they are not hard to recognize.

Be patient enough to figure out what to do, but strong enough to make the tough decisions. This is true for the head coach and the assistants. You have to do this tactfully and in a professional manner. Be strong enough to make tough decisions on who is going to play, and how long they are going to play.

Coaches must earn the right to coach a kid hard. We all come in new to Permian. We have some kids who could not lift much in the weight program. We did not have the right to get on him because I do not know anything about him.

After three years, we have raised the kids. Now we know them and we understand their backgrounds. We find the right way to boost them and to pick them up. If we have a few players who are not doing what we think they should be doing in academics, the weight room, on the field, and in other areas, I will get on them because I have earned that right. We do this privately and behind closed doors.

"Bloom where planted" means you better take care of the job you have now. There are always greener pastures. If I am thinking about taking another job, I need to be the best person for that job at the place I am coaching. I may be looking to become the head coach in the school I am an assistant coach in now.

Use your strength as a coach, and refine your weakness. We all have strengths and weaknesses. Think about the weak areas, and work to become better in those areas.

It is important to be a professional coach. This area includes how you come dressed to work, and more than anything, how you speak to each other. We will not prop our feet up on the desk in our coaches' office. We do not put our hands in our pockets. We do not spit in the trashcans.

The way we speak to our kids is important. We will not scream and curse at them. We are going to be professional teachers and professional football coaches. We are going to approach our job as football coaches the same way as the executives in downtown approach their jobs. We are going to do research, be organized, dress properly, and communicate with each other in the proper manner. There are a lot of examples that can help you on how to be a professional. How you speak is important. We say language is an expression of thought. I have touched on this, so I will go on.

One of the worst things a coach can do is to have a great thought and not communicate it. If you do not communicate now, it may be too late. If you have an idea you want to discuss, talk about it with the rest of the staff.

When our staff goes to a clinic, we have a meeting on Monday morning. I ask the assistant coaches to share with us what they learned at that clinic. You never know how a small point picked up at a clinic can make you a better coach. It may influence a player you work with on a daily basis.

In small schools, where coaches work on both sides of the ball, there are some good points to this. I have worked with staffs that did this. We had the responsibility of everything in the program. We had five varsity coaches and four JV coaches. We had four sophomore coaches who coached both sides of the ball. So separation of staff is not all bad.

There are several benefits in breaking the staffs down to work with the kids they coach. There are some negatives to this as well. You never see your family when you have all of the responsibility as a staff. If you are coach on both sides of the ball, weekends are long. We would finish our work on defense about 6:00 p.m. before we even started on offense. As a result, Sundays were horrible.

I decided when I became a head coach I was not going to have the coaches work on both sides of the ball. However, I wanted to make sure to take some of the advantages I learned from those experiences into the two-platoon system.

When we coach on both sides of the ball, we are one staff. When we are on offense, we are all together. When we are on defense, we are all together. As head coaches, with five assistants on each side of the ball, how do we keep this from becoming the blame game? "We need to get more first downs!"

In addition, we hear this: "The offense needs to get some first downs so we are not on the field too long on defense." When an assistant coach starts telling me about these situations, I tell him he had better take advantage of the situations he gets and

to make the best of each possession. I believe if the head coach is a believer in playing great defense, then everything is going to take care of itself. It has helped us so much, because everything we do starts with defense.

When we group players, we always group the defense to go first. The offense has to sit tight at times, but they must understand this. If I were not a defensive coach, I would act like I was a defensive coach. Do I believe defenses win championships? Yes, I do. However, you cannot play good defense unless you have a good offense. I have learned this over time.

We won 13 straight games this year. We won because we caused 35 turnovers. Our offense only turned the ball over three times. If that happens, you are going to win most of your games. We were 50/50 on run/pass. We set several records on offense, and then everyone started telling us we were smart defensive coaches. It was because our offense could score, and they did not turn the ball over.

I took the job at Permian when I was 35 years old. People wanted to know how we were going to handle the pressure. The only pressure I feel is to do the best I can do every day. If we can walk away from practice every day knowing we have done our best, we can look back over the season in July and say, "We would not change one single thing that we did during the past season." That is when football becomes fun.

When we step on the field against any team, the only time we should feel any pressure is when there is a doubt we have been outworked by the opponents going into that game. If we look at them in the warm-ups and it appears they may have done a better job than we did in the weight room, or in other areas, then we will feel the pressure.

We relieve the football pressure outside of the season. When we step on the field, we just take a deep breath. By that time, we know we have done everything possible prior to that game to get the kids ready to go. We can live with ourselves when that happens.

Get on a level playing field with your opponents. If you are not on the same level with the number of coaches, facilities, and in other areas, you need to make changes.

The community will get what the community wants. This is a good message to send to the school board and all of the people who support your program. If we have someone in the community who is bitching about our program, the first thing I am going to ask that person is this: "What are you doing to help our program?" I am not talking about financially. I am not asking for your money. Are you encouraging our kids?

At the first meeting with the players at Permian, I tried to set the tone for our entry to the program. The team was 5-5 before I got there. They had not won a district in two years. When I walked into the room, all of the players were standing in a line with their hands behind their back. There were 200 kids in the last athletic period at Permian. There were 100 kids in the first athletic period. It looked as if they were lining up for a military inspection.

I told them to put their hands down and to relax. When I said that, the reply was, "Yes, sir!" I could not believe what had happened here. I think the people before had worked so hard to get the discipline back that had been gone at Permian for so long. You are looking for that discipline on the football field to carry over to the everyday life, and in the classroom.

I explained to those kids there is a difference in cosmetic discipline and real discipline. Cosmetic discipline is being able to say "yes, sir." At this point, I am not concerned if you say "yes, sir" right now. I want to *see* "yes, sir!" I do not want to hear it; I want to see it. I do not care if you can stand up straight or not. What I want to know is this: when you are in a football game and you are out of breath and you are about to throw up, can you get in a good football stance? Can you take the right step, or are you going to run around the drive block? That is real discipline. It is doing right when it is not easy. It is easy when we are standing around to look disciplined. Do not tell me "yes, sir." *Show* me "yes, sir."

Do not act as if everything is okay when everything is not okay. That is a yearlong coaching point. Do not be afraid to tell the assistant coaches if the players are not doing a good job. As coaches, we do not carry feelings on our sleeves.

Avoid the highway-department drills. If you have people standing around in drills, you do not get much accomplished.

I want to read this to you from Bill Parcells. It is about confusing talent with skill. Bill was asked about a sign or slogan that hung in the Cowboys locker room. The slogan was: "Dumb players do dumb things!"

We all go through this at this time of the year when we are trying to find out who our players are. Parcells said, "People confuse talent with skills. I think talent includes three or four other things besides the ability to run, jump, and catch the ball. One of them is making intelligent decisions and good decisions under pressure. Now, that is a talent." Some skilled players cannot do those things in my estimation.

At Permian, we are going to put the players on the field who are going to make good decisions when there are lots of people in the stands. We do not send many players to Division I colleges. However, we have players who we can put on the field whom we can trust. You cannot just change colors at game time and become something different from what you have been doing all week. You are putting the player with his character that he has been carrying all week long on the field.

If he has been a dipstick all week in school, and you put him on the field, something bad is going to happen to you. We have made that mistake, and it has hurt us before. Our players understand this, and we insist we will not put a dipstick on the field.

Teach toughness every day. One of the things that happened to Permian in their downfall was that they got away from this. They had a kid get paralyzed in practice. I see him every day. He is a paraplegic, and he is in a wheelchair. The player got hurt in practice, and it hurt that coaching staff. It is a big deal in Odessa, and we are still raising money for the player and his family.

However, we feel it is important to teach tackling. You have to do those things to teach them to play the game the way it is designed to be played. If we are not teaching them to be tough, we are putting them in a dangerous situation on game night. It is teaching physical and mental toughness as well.

The number-one motivator is pain. That is physical and mental. If I go through some pain for this football team, I am going to care a whole lot more about the team. If the off-season is easy, and it is like a country club, then I am not putting a lot into the team. If we do not go through some emotional strife along the way, I will not be emotionally tied into the football team and our program.

I talk about the schizophrenic nature of football with our team. We tell our players we want them to be the students who go through the halls with a "yes, sir" and "yes, ma'am" with a smile on their faces. We want them to go to the classroom and do what is right. However, when they put the helmet on, and when they come into the workout room, we want them to be Mr. Badass, but not by what they say or how they strut. We want them to be as aggressive as possible. That is the schizophrenic nature of football. We are trying to teach them to be nice guys, and then to be bad guys, then back to good guys, and swoosh, to bad guys again.

When we can teach players to do that, it will help them later in life. They end up being a CEO of a big company. They know how to treat people. Then when someone does them wrong, they know how to fight back.

We say this before we take the field at Permian every time. We must play mad, but be cold-blooded. If we do not do this, we are going to get beat. We play good teams each game, and it is nasty when we play. If we think Permian intimidates our opponents, we are going to get our butt beat. We have to be a little mad when we take the field. They had better have an attitude when they take that field. At the same time, they have to be cold-blooded. This is the way we explain it to our players: "Snot bubbles coming out of your nose, and a smile on your face. I am a thinking man. I can be mad, and I can be playing mad and hard, but I am still thinking. As the offense breaks the huddle and comes to the line of scrimmage, I am thinking. But, when I get back into my stance, I am mad again. On the snap of the ball, I am reacting."

We have a sign we put on our stadium door so we can see it when we take the field: "Be mad, and play cold-blooded." This is not a dirty or mean term. If you get so mad and want to play dirty, you stop thinking. We want to play tough, but we want to think as well. Thinking is so much a big part of the game.

Permian football is all about attacking simultaneously from all directions. This means our booster club, our student body, our cheerleaders, band, and school community will come at you on Friday Night. This is the term I use to describe our approach to the games today. We are going to attack our opponents from all directions. People love that, I am telling you. That is *Friday Night Lights* for Permian. All of the groups feel they are contributing to the game. They are going to work their butt off to help with the game.

Mind progression is a big part of our offensive and defensive philosophy. It means this: what are you thinking about prior to the snap of the ball? If you do not teach the players a progression of what happens when the ball is snapped, then you are missing the boat.

We move from a mind progression to a teaching progression. I am not trying to trick the players when I am teaching them. I am trying to teach them just as I would if I were teaching them algebra. I am going to build confidence in them because I am not trying to trick them. We teach this way. First it is the what-and-when theory. I will cover this more in the second lecture.

One of the great things that football teaches us is the inner voice:

"Every athlete has an inner voice of pride. It is the voice only athletes can hear, pushing them to the brink of exhaustion, demanding excellence, and condemning failure. Failure, understand, is the driving force behind an athlete. Every athlete has experienced failure, and now trains so they will not experience it again. This inner voice knows the difference between training and exercising. Many athletes stop exercising when they reach a perceived limit, or when it becomes uncomfortable to continue. Only a select few athletes have the heart and desire to train unconditionally. Only a select few push past physical or mental limits, and only a few push past the pain and discomfort. Only a few have the courage and character to understand that training makes them quicker, faster, and stronger, and most important, it allows them to get a mental edge over future opponents. So when failure laughs in my face as I desperately try to earn the respect of that last repetition, it must realize one thing: Each time I train, I not only hear, but I answer to the inner voice."

We talk about the inner voice with our kids. We ask them what their body language is at the time. We are in our indoor sessions now. We are gassing them now. We have three big trash cans available for them if they need them. We let them know it is okay to use them. We let them know we are testing them in the program. If they place their hands on their side, we get on them. They do not do that in the game, at least I hope not. They are not going to play for us and do that. We work them when they are breathing hard and when they are dizzy. We are testing them for the football games. Football games are hard work, and they have to train for the games.

> "What we do today is very expensive because we spend one day of our life for it, and one day of our life is a high price to pay."
>
> 75 years = 27,375 days
> 40 years = 14,600 days
> 16 years = 5,440 days

The average age in America is 75. Think of it as money in the bank. If those are dollars in the bank, are you going to spend each dollar wisely? Each day, we have to spend one of those dollars. If you waste a day, it is a dollar thrown away. You are not going to get it back. We talk about this with coaches and players.

The definition of class to us is this: if I can treat the lowest person in our program with the same respect as I treat the principal of the school, then I have class.

Our number-one concern is to take care of the kids *in every way*. You are some kid's coach and always will be. These are the things that last; the "fluff" goes away. You can win all the trophies you want, but the people are going to forget about the trophies. What is going to matter is the influence you have had on the kids.

The two things that make a great leader:

- Consistently make a high quality decision.
- Secure emotional support of the organization.

Do not forget: people support what they help create. If it is all about you and your coaches, you are not going to get the support of the community. Get as many people involved as possible to help create your success.

When we look at a statue of someone great, we think the person had something we do not have. Think about all of the statues you have seen. We are trained to think only a tiny percentage of us have what it takes to be a hero. Not many of us will cure any diseases or slay any dragons, but every single one of us is destined to be a king, queen, or hero in our everyday, ordinary life. We do not build statues to worship the exceptional life; we build them to remind ourselves what is possible in our own life. Think of this the next time you see a statue. It is not only to honor that extraordinary life. The statues remind ourselves what we can do in our lives.

I promise I will talk on the techniques of football in the next lecture. Thank you for your time.

THE MULTIPLICITY OF THE 3-4 DEFENSE

Odessa Permian High School, Texas

If you want to find out what blitzes are good, ask the offensive line coaches. They can tell you the one they have trouble blocking. If my offensive line coach shows me a blitz they cannot block, I guarantee you we will put it in our scheme. Just about everything that our offense has problems with, we run on defense. I am going to talk about the 3-4 defense. The reason we run the 3-4 is the multiplicity of the defense. If we want to align in a 4-3 defense, we can get into one. That is one of the adjustments and fronts we run. I will try to give you as much as I can in an hour. I will be here until Sunday, and if you want to get into more detail, I can wear you out on defense.

The personnel of our defense is basically 3-4 personnel. We have many linebackers in our program. We do not have the personnel to play at the defensive ends in a 4-3 scheme. We have linebackers all over the place, and we can muster up some 230-pound players, who can play defensive tackles.

This past season was an unusual year for us. We had two big outside linebackers, who were more suited to playing down than up. They were a bit out-of-place at outside linebacker. Anytime we reduced the front, one of them wanted to get down in a three-point stance. We ended up playing the 4-3 defense about 90 percent of the time this year. Both of the outside linebackers were 6'4" and ran 4.7 in the 40. One of them was 250 pounds, and the other was 220 pounds. We had three little linebackers we played inside. They were all in the 5'9" and 185-pound range. They were fast and strong as an ox.

We had three linebackers who could go get the football and two tall defensive ends who could stop the quick passing game. We did not outsmart ourselves and stay in the 3-4 front when it did not fit our personnel. The 4-3 was part of our package, so we played it most of the time. To stay as a basic 3-4 team would have been silly for us. Common sense took over, and we played the front that suited our personnel.

We went five straight games against good teams in our base 4-3 defense. In our third game, we played the team that won the 5-A championship in Texas, and we beat them 30-3. We told the defense not to look to the sidelines because we were not going to give them a defensive call. We played the defense and made our adjustments with our linebackers. There were times when we played eight defenders in the box, but it did not change our calls.

It made us play faster. When you play 3-4 defense, you have to get four-man pressure all the time. That requires you to make all kinds of calls with four different coverages. We played 52 cover 4 in the first game and played so much faster. We were sound getting lined up, but everything was simple for the players. Because of that, they sped up and played five games better than any time since we had been at Permian. After five games, we had to make adjustments back to the 3-4 because teams started to expand their formations.

There are things in our philosophy that every player in our program and every youth-league player and coach knows. They can recite it if we ask them. Everyone on our defense has to be able to repeat this to his coach. We ask them what our philosophy on defense is. They give us the following response:

Mojo Methods

- Get off.
- Control the gap.

- Squeeze the point-of-attack.
- Cross face to the football.

Our number-one goal is to fly to the football and get turnovers. Get the ball back to the offense as soon as possible. Before they play for us, they have to be able to quote that goal. As simple as that sounds, it is everything to football, to defense, and all levels players. "Get-off" has to do with the reaction by the feet at the snap of the ball. "Controlling my gap" is important because every player has to know the gap he is responsible to cover. Gaps in the defense move. When we squeeze, we move in the direction our gap is moving. When we squeeze, we do not turn and run. That is chasing like a dog in heat. We learn how to run laterally with our hips and shoulders square to the line of scrimmage.

Every day, we drill running full speed with our hips and shoulders parallel to the line of scrimmage. We tell them if they are inside the tackle box and are running with their shoulders parallel to the sidelines, they are not the player they used to be. When you see defenders arm tackling, that means they have turned their shoulders.

The last principle is the most important. "Crossing someone's face to the football" is a base principle of defensive football. When we got to Permian, it was the number-one reason for their failures on defense. When we looked at film, we saw defenders taking the easy way out of blocks. It did not make any difference what position; they all had the same problems. Everybody was running around the blocks. If you end up with one defender playing that way, you are playing with 10 on defense. You cannot chase butts. That was the number-one thing we had to fix when we got there.

Our number-one defensive goal is to fly to the ball. We want to cause turnovers and get the ball back as quickly as possible. Our turnover ratio this year was 35 to 3. Our defense caused 35 turnovers, and we turned it over three times. It you can do that, you will win. We beat Euless Trinity the first time because they turned it over four times and we turned it over zero. The second time we played them, we played in Abilene. The wind was blowing 50 miles per hour. Neither team turned the ball over. Playing them was like playing a junior college. They simply ran the ball down our throats. If they had turned the ball over one time, we probably could have beat them. They did not, did a good job, and went on to win the state championship.

We do not have time to do a turnover circuit. In all our group and individual drills, we coach turnovers. In a 1-on-1 receiver drill, if the receiver catches the ball, the defensive back has to strip it before the rep is over. With any drill we do, the defensive coaches are constantly teaching that skill. When we get into a group and team drill, we are not having a desertion on technique and alignment. We do those things in meetings and individual time. When we get into those drills, we are coaching effort and turnovers. Effort, angles, across the face, and turnovers are all we work on in a team drill.

In practice against the scout team, we try to stand the ball up and strip it every play. When we have an incomplete pass in our team drills, the defender closest to the ball runs, scoops it up, and scores. We teach our defense that at the end of each offensive play, the defense will have possession of the ball. We will strip it from the back, intercept it, or pick it off the ground and score. Everyone in the drill turns, sprints to the ball, and continues to score until we blow the whistle. We do not run to the end zone every time, but we are building the mind-set.

If you do not teach it that way, you are not making it a priority. One of the things we emphasize to our players is "mind possession." We want to know what every player on the defense is thinking prior to the snap of the ball. Every player on the defense has a priority. In a 3-4 defense, you have two linebackers aligned over an uncovered guard. If the first thing on their minds is not "inside flow to me," you will not be able to stop the run. They not only have to be thinking that, they are hoping and expecting it to come over their guard. When people run at the bubble, it will look as if we sent the linebacker on a blitz in the B gap.

When he gets in his stance, he is thinking, "Here it comes, here it comes!" If the ball goes somewhere else, he reacts. He is an inside-out player and has to protect the inside. He does not have to outrun the running back on a sweep. We want to tell them what to think prior to the snap of the ball and teach in that progression. It makes no sense to get the corner thinking quick pass as his first thought, and throw deep passes. We have to teach to the emphasis of a particular mind-set and expand from that. We want to teach to build confidence.

We have a teaching progression. We ask the linebacker what is number one on his mind. His response is, "Inside flow to me." The coach tells him he is going to run inside flow to him on "go." We call "Go," and he takes on the block at or behind the line of scrimmage. If he knows what is coming and when it is coming, he will do it right.

What/When Teaching Progression

- What/?
- ?/When
- ?/?

The next thing we tell him is that we are going to run right at him, but we are coming on movement. He knows *what* is coming, but he does not know *when* it will come. The third thing we tell him is that we are going to run isolate or toss at him on "go." He does not know the *what*, but he knows the *when*. The last progression is when he does not know the *what* or the *when*. If you try to trick them right off the bat, they never get as good as they can.

When I was in the sixth grade in Permian, we ran the high school's system. We ran the wing-T offense and the 29 defense with all the terminology. It made a difference for us. You cannot do that today because the offenses have changed so much. During my time in high school in the 1980s, we only played one team that was a one-back team. This is the way we do it now.

4-3 Versus 3-4 at Permian

- Seventh, eighth, and ninth graders learn the 3-4 defense.

- 53 is a front they learn which is one of our 4-3 fronts.
- Sophomore (JV): 75 percent learn 4-3, and 25 percent learn 3-4.
- Varsity: They will have learned both the 3-4 and the 4-3.

We do not have ninth graders in the high school. They all run the 53 defense, which is one of our fronts. The 53 is a reduced front. When we get them as 10th graders, we teach them the 4-3. We have two junior varsity teams at Permian, and they play 4-3 with our terminology. We teach our linebacker how to play over the center and the outside linebacker how to play in the outside bubble. We play quarters and halves in the secondary.

With our two JV teams we do not get out of the 4-3 unless people make us. When we get them at the varsity level, they know the 3-4 and the 4-3. When things happen like they did this year, we do not have to go back and change terminology to get from one front to the other. The 54 and 45 are our two 50 fronts. In the 50-front call, the first number is the strongside, and the second number is the weakside. We do not flip anyone on the defensive line. In the 54, we have a 5 technique strong, a 4 technique weak, and the noseguard is head-up on the center going to the strongside. In the 45, the strongside is a 4 technique, the weakside is a 5 technique, and the nose is going weak. The nose always moves to our 5 side. We have four base fronts.

Fronts

- 54 (3-4)
- 45 (3-4)
- 53 (4-3)
- 52 (4-3)

In our 54, we have two defensive ends in a 5 technique strong and a 4 technique weak (Diagram #1). We have a strongside outside linebacker in a 9 technique on the tight end. The Mike and Will linebacker are the inside linebackers, and they do a flip with alignment. The weak outside linebacker is off the line of scrimmage.

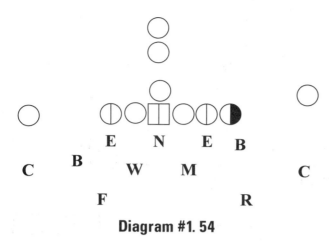

Diagram #1. 54

The 45 front is the same alignment for everyone except the defensive ends. They reverse their alignments.

The 53 is a reduced front with two linebackers (Diagram #2). In the four-man front, we drop one of our linebackers down in a defensive-end position. He plays the backside 5 technique on the tackle, and the defensive end slides into a 3 technique on the guard. The nose moves to a strong shade on the center. The callside is the same alignments.

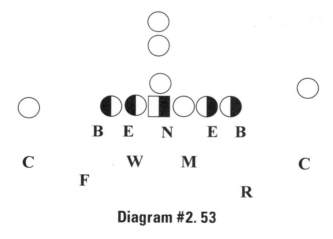

Diagram #2. 53

The outside linebackers have to know how to play a 9 technique and a 5 technique. They also have to play a loose technique on the split end. The defensive linemen have to play shade techniques, and they have to know how to slant. There is no difference in technique in playing a 5 technique or a 3 technique. The alignment is different, but the technique is the same. Once they learn how to slant, they can play the end or the nose position.

In the 54 alignment, we put both the defensive ends in a tight 5 technique on the offensive tackles.

We want the defensive end's inside eye on the tackle's outside ear with his inside foot back. He has a toe-to-heel stagger in his stance. The 5-technique end reads the tackle and is responsible for the C gap. The backside defensive tackle aligns the same as the strongside end. However, his vision key is the offensive guard. He has to see him out of his peripheral vision. He steps with his inside foot and makes a lateral step down the line of scrimmage.

He may have to redirect his second step, depending on the charge of the guard. He cannot let the guard reach him. If the guard is zone stepping for him, his next step has to be outside. If the guard is pulling to the other side, he gets in the hip pocket of the guard and runs. All of our 4-technique players make plays all the time. They come free and unblocked frequently. That technique drives our offensive line coach crazy.

The thing the end has to do is control the B gap. If the tackle can keep him from getting to the B gap, he has to get better. He has to keep the tackle off his legs and get down the line of scrimmage. It may give the tackle a free track to the Will linebacker, but if he does not get reached by the guard, he will make the play.

When we go to the 52 defense, we change our terminology with our front (Diagram #3). The outside linebacker is now a defensive end, the linebacker away from the defensive end is the Will linebacker. The Mike and Will linebackers slide over and become the Mike and Sam linebackers. We play two 1 techniques on the guards and two 5 techniques, or a 5 technique to the open side and a 7 technique to the tight end. The reason we play those techniques is because our offense line coach hates them.

The 1 techniques are tight on the inside eyes of the guards. On film, they look like 2 techniques. That allows the Mike linebacker to play free. He can make a ton of plays. If the tackles come down on the Mike linebacker, our defensive end closes and squeezes inside to the B gap. When the tackles came down, the Mike linebacker ran over the top of their blocks. The ends squeeze the B gap, and the Mike linebacker comes over the top into the C gap. We end up with two defenders in the B gap on some occasions.

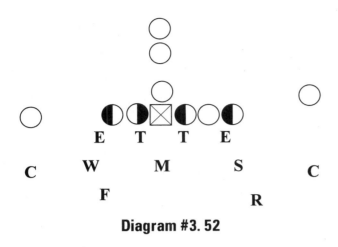

Diagram #3. 52

From this front, we can make a *rope* call and go to the eight-man front. The rope call drops the rover down into a linebacker position. We moved the Sam and Mike into the B gaps and ended up in a 4-4 look. With the defensive end we had this year, we did not need to blitz. That allowed us to rush with four down people and get good at what we did.

The way we teach our blitz package is something you want to see. We have combined the defensive front so they come under the same blitz package. The inside linebackers and outside linebackers must know four things to learn in our blitz scheme.

Blitz Package

- We use a combination of six blitzes to bring pressure from the linebacker position.
- *Inside Linebacker Blitzes*
    - ✓ Plug
    - ✓ Fire
    - ✓ Go
    - ✓ Ax
- *Outside Linebacker Blitzes*
    - ✓ Strong
    - ✓ Weak
    - ✓ Dig
    - ✓ Thunder (Both OLB)

Once we teach them these four things, we have an unlimited amount of blitzes we can run. A *plug* blitz for the inside linebacker is an A-gap blitz to his side. *Fire* is a B-gap blitz to his side. The *go* means to blitz the C gap. If we call "ax," that is the opposite A

gap. On the ax stunt, the nose angles away from the linebacker blitz. That is all they have to know in our defense. We teach them that in the seventh grade.

If the outside linebacker runs "strong," he comes off the edge from the strongside. He is a D-gap contain-rush and force player. He has the pitch on the option. He cannot let anything outside of him. The weak call is the same thing, except from the weakside of the formation. If we call "thunder," both the outside linebackers come. The dig blitz sends the weakside linebacker under the charge of the defensive end into the B gap. We generally run this from a walk-off position. He comes back inside behind the defensive end's outside charge.

Blitz Package

- We can get five-man pressure by calling two blitzes at once.
    - ✓ We can send both inside linebackers.
    - ✓ We can send both outside linebackers
    - ✓ We can send one inside linebacker and one outside linebacker (overload a side).

An example of a combination stunt is *weak Will plug* (Diagram #4). It is a flood stunt to the weakside of the formation. The Will linebacker blitzes the A gap to his side, and the outside linebacker comes off the edge.

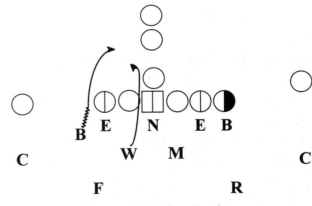

Diagram #4. Weak Will Plug

If we overload one side or the other, we have to do something at the line of scrimmage to help us with the screen. We call "dog" or "hunt," which is a defensive line call. When we blitz, we give those calls to the defensive line. On a dog call, the defensive lineman plays his run technique off the ball. If he reads pass, he drops three steps, squares up, and gets his head on a swivel. He is looking for rocket screens, tunnel screens, and things like that.

If we tell them to hunt, they play run as they normally do. If he reads pass, he settles where he is. Against a team that runs the jailbreak screen and delay screen into the middle, you do not want your defender dropping off the line of scrimmage. In the terminology, we hunt for screens and dog for shallow crossing routes. You can drill these types of things, and it keeps their interest in practice.

Another combination stunt we run is strong Mike go (Diagram #5). This is a strongside overload. We bring the outside linebacker off the edge and blitz the Mike linebacker through the C gap.

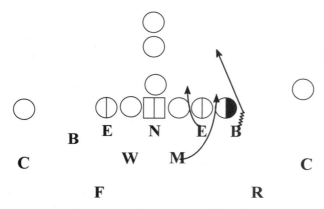

Diagram #5. Strong Mike Go

If we bring the stunt from the 4-3 look, the terminology is the same. This stunt is *52 thunder* (Diagram #6). We bring both outside linebackers on edge stunts.

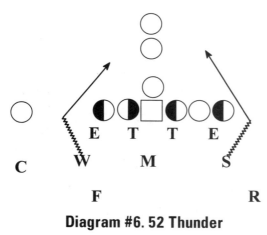

Diagram #6. 52 Thunder

On the fire and plug stunts from the 52, the 1 techniques have to make sure they get outside on the plug blitzes (Diagram #7). If we run 52 *Mike plug*, the 1 technique goes through the B gap, and the Mike linebacker blitzes the A gap.

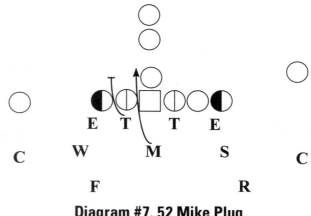

Diagram #7. 52 Mike Plug

If we get sprint-out pass, we like to contain it with our inside linebackers (Diagram #8). It is harder for the fullback to pick up the containment coming from that angle and that speed. All week long, he has been chopping the dummy at the line of scrimmage. For him to adjust to linebacker containment is like two ships passing in the night. On occasion, we bring the strong call for the outside linebacker and bring the inside linebacker over the top of him for contain.

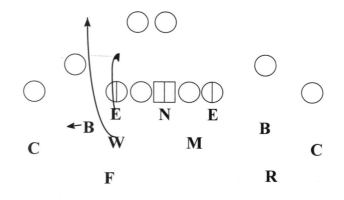

Diagram #8. Will Go

If we bring both the inside and outside linebackers on the sprint-out pass, we normally roll down the corner to cover the flat (Diagram #9).

We let the corner sit down on the out patterns and roll the safety over the top. If the offense gives

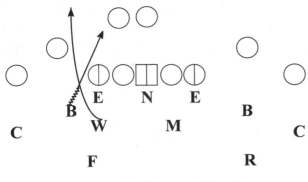

Diagram #9. Strong Mike Go

us full sprint, the corner settles. The frontside safety gets over the top, and the backside corner plays the post in the middle, while the backside safety drops down on the drag.

The last thing I want to cover is some of the things we do with our linebackers. Linebacker play at Permian has been one of the things we have always done well. I want to show you a great tool to teach any concept at any position. You cannot go out of order when you teach these concepts. We call it *CASKER*.

CASKER

- **C**all
  - ✓ I must get the call first from the sideline.

- **A**lignment
  - ✓ I must make a strength call for defense.
  - ✓ Depending on formation, I will be in a 20, 30, 40, or walk alignment.

- **S**tance
  - ✓ Once I get to my position, I must get in a good stance every play.

- **K**ey
  - ✓ Who am I keying from this alignment or particular stunt?

- **E**xecute
  - ✓ Do I have a stunt going on in front of me?
  - ✓ Am I on a blitz?
  - ✓ What coverage do I have?

- **R**ead and React
  - ✓ Once I read my key, I take the steps and technique I learn in practice every day and make the play.

If you need anything that I can help you with, I am willing to send you anything we have. I do not have all the answers, and I am still learning. I will be at every lecture that goes on at the clinic because I love to hear coaches talk about football. I have already learned some new stuff since I have been here. Thank you so much for your attention.

EFFICIENCY OF A BALANCED OFFENSE

Columbus North High School, Indiana

Good afternoon. It is good to be here. I consider Columbus North to be a mid-major in class 5-A in Indiana high school football. We have an enrollment of about 2,000 students. The 5-A classification runs all the way up to 4,500 students. We are proud because three out of the last four years we have advanced to the final four in the Indiana championship playoffs. This past year, we went 12-2 and were six painful points away from playing for the state championship.

I am honored to speak at this clinic. I attended my first Louisville clinic when I was a senior in college. I learned many important things that year. I learned when to hold them and when to fold them. I learned that a walk across the bridge is a good way to clear your head after a hard Friday night. I also learned there was an awful lot of football to be learned.

I had a lot to learn if I was going to become a good football coach, and I still feel that way today. I come before you representing a family of coaches. My father was a lifetime coach and was my college coach. He was the head coach at the University of Indianapolis for 21 years. My two brothers are high school coaches and are in attendance today.

I am here representing Columbus North High School, our players, and our staff. Two things my staff has in common are their passion for the players and a passion for the greatest game ever played. My assistant coaches have played a huge role in the success we have acquired at Columbus North.

We are in an amazing occupation. There are two things I want to share with you before I get to my topic. This job can be consuming. It is easy to get consumed by the job. I would hope you keep your priorities in order. You live by your faith, family, and football. It is vital that we serve as role models to the players who are in our charge. If you let your players see you as a father, husband, and man of faith, your experience will be more rewarding in this noble profession. Relationships are more important than championships.

My topic today is "offensive balance." I am a former defensive coordinator. When I became the head coach, I moved to the offensive side of the ball. We are a spread offense. I learned a lot about the spread offense by trying to defend it. When we took over at Columbus North, we knew we were going to build our program in the weight room. We knew we wanted to establish a physical run-game program. The plays on which we based that scheme were the inside- and outside-zone plays.

We knew that conditioning was going to be a key attribute if we were going to be successful. We felt to be successful we had to be in better condition than the teams we played. Balance in the offense is a must in class 5-A football in Indiana. You do not see teams playing for the title that are all run or all pass. We compete with the top teams in Indiana. We ran for 2,400 yards and threw for 2,469 yards.

Our offense is built around a four-receiver set. However, the engine that drives our offense is our running back. He gets many carries on Friday. The key to the zone game is vision. We do not have a fullback in our offense, but we do have an H-back. He is a tight-end/receiver type of player in our offense. He moves through our formations.

Within our offense, we have a tight end, a split end, and a flanker. On our offensive line, we feel we must have a good tackle playing at the left tackle position. He protects the quarterback's backside. We probably ran to the left more this year.

The first formation I want to show you is the *left* formation (Diagram #1). The opposite set is the right formation. In the left formation, the tight end and the flanker go to the left side of the field. The split end and the H-back are to the right in the formation. The H-back sits outside the right tackle in a one-by-one alignment. This a two-by-two set, but could also be a double tight-end set with one back in the backfield.

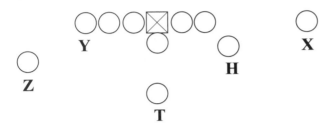

Diagram #1. Left Formation

The *left-wing* formation is the same set for everyone except the H-back (Diagram #2). He aligns outside the tight end in a wing position. That gives us a trips set to that side. We can align him in that position or motion him over from the left formation.

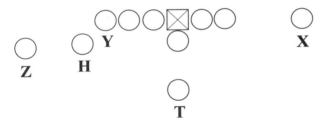

Diagram #2. Left Wing

When we get into more of a passing set, we run *gun left slot* (Diagram #3). The tight end is to the left, and we have a twins-set alignment to the right. We align the H-back in the slot, splitting the difference between the tackle and the split end. The H-back is a hybrid type of player. He is part tight end and part wide receiver. This formation is more of a traditional two-by-two set, but it gives us the power running to the tight-end side.

If we move the H-back to the slot on the tight-end side, it gives us a trips formation to that side. We call it *gun left trey* (Diagram #4). When the H-back aligns, he splits the difference between the flanker and the tight end. The set gives us a double flanker to the left.

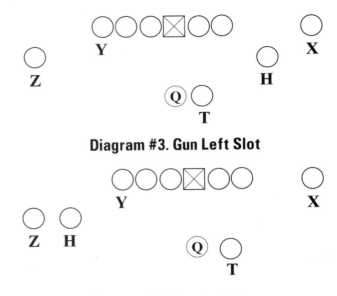

Diagram #3. Gun Left Slot

Diagram #4. Gun Left Trey

What I am going to talk about today is the run and the play-action pass that complements that run. In our offense, we have a three-step game, dropback, sprint-out, and play-action game. I do not want to get into the blocking schemes too much today; however, I want to give you the base rules for them.

The center identifies the zero-technique defender to the zone side of the play (Diagram #5). The playside guard identifies the #1 defender to that side. The tackle looks for the #2 defender. The tight end takes the #3 defender to the callside. On the backside, the guard blocks the #1 defender to the backside, and the tackle blocks the #2 defender that way. However, in this particular set, we like to fold the H-back inside the tackle and block the #2 defender. That leaves the tackle to turn back on the #3 defender.

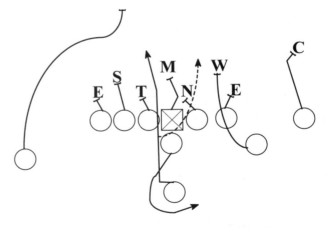

Diagram #5. Zone Blocking Left

The fold block on the backside allows the play to run backside more times than not. The out block by the tackle creates the seam for the running back to bring the ball. In this particular set, the center and backside guard have a combo block for the nose and the Mike linebacker.

The tailback takes an open step and hits downhill at the line of scrimmage, aiming in the A gap. He looks to cut off the combo block. He wants to "bang" the ball to the frontside of the formation or "bend" it to the backside. The quarterback faces out to the left side, hands the ball off, and fakes the bootleg to the right.

We can run the inside-zone play to the weakside of the formation also (Diagram #6). The blocking rules are the same for the offensive line. We block 1, 2, and 3 to the frontside and backside. We can determine against certain defenses that we want to fold block with the H-back on the zone play. If we do, it gives the appearance of an isolation play.

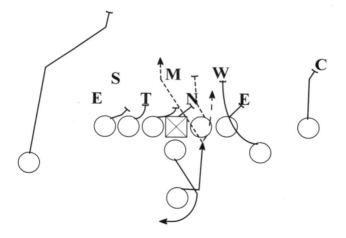

Diagram #6. Zone Weak

We want the ball delivered to the tailback as deep as possible. The tailback cannot rush the play and must be patient. If he gets the ball right behind the offensive line, he has no chance to use his vision. If he is too close to the line of scrimmage, he cannot use his "bang" or "bend" reads. We want the ball delivered deep so the tailback can see the blocks developing.

If we run this play from the gun, we read the backside defensive end. It becomes a read option for

the quarterback. If the defensive end closes on the tailback, the quarterback pulls the ball and runs out the backside.

The companion play to the inside-zone play is the bootleg pass (Diagram #7). We want this play to look exactly like the zone play. On this play, we block the H-back on the backside defensive end. The quarterback should be able to get out to the backside. We want to sell the inside-zone play, and the mesh point is critical.

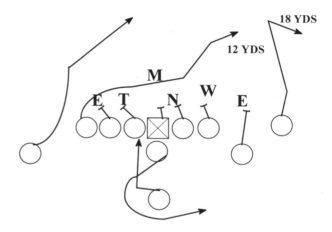

Diagram #7. Boot

The X-receiver or split end runs a comeback pattern at 18 yards. We have several ways to run the underneath patterns. One way is to block the H-back. That makes sure we get the quarterback outside. We can delay block the H-back on the defensive end and release him late into the flat. We can bring the tight end on a 12-yard crossing pattern. We tag the play to release the tight end or the H-back. We never release both those receivers. If we release the H-back into the flat, the tight end stays in and blocks. If the tight end runs the crossing route, the H-back stays in to block.

With the quarterback who will play next year, this play may become more of an option run-throw type of play. The backside flanker runs a post pattern to keep the safety from jumping the crossing route. We do not look back to throw that pattern.

If the quarterback sees an overhang defender playing to the boot side, he still has to sell the run fake. However, he has to get his eyes around quickly because that defender could get in his face in a hurry. If that happens, the quarterback has to deal the ball quickly.

With a right-handed quarterback, you still must run the boot to the left side. You fake the zone play to the right and boot to the left side. The blocking is the same. We tag the tight end or H-back for the underneath pattern. The Z-receiver or flanker runs the comeback pattern. The X-receiver runs the post through the middle to hold the safety in the middle.

When we look at our video on Saturday mornings, if the linebackers are no factor on the boot, we know the fake is good. We can tag and adjust the wide receiver's pattern. Instead of the comeback, we can use a double move and go deep or adjust to whatever the defense gives us. If we want to throw back to the backside post, we tag the play. If we go to a twins set, we bring the Z-receiver to the X-receiver side. The Z-receiver splits the difference between the X-receiver and the H-back. The H-back stays in so the quarterback can get outside. The tight end runs the post on the backside.

An adjustment we make to this play is the "slice" technique by the H-back (Diagram #8). We use the slice technique by the H-back to block the backside defensive end on the inside-zone play. If the defensive end is crashing and catching the tailback from behind, we use the H-back across the set to block him. If we run the boot away from the H-back, the H-back uses his slice path and comes out the frontside of the bootleg. We hope he gets lost running behind the line of scrimmage.

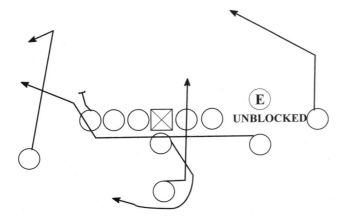

Diagram #8. Boot Slice

The coaching point for the quarterback is to remind him that the backside end will probably be unblocked. He has to get his eyes around quickly and find the H-back in the flat.

The outside-zone play is the complement to the inside-zone play. The more the inside zone works, the tighter the outside defenders get to the play. They start to squeeze inside to cut the gaps to the inside. The outside zone is a quick-hitting perimeter play (Diagram #9). In Diagram #9, we run the play to the H-back side; however, we run it to the tight end equally as well and probably with more frequency.

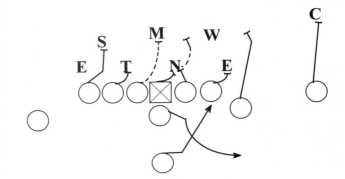

Diagram #9. Outside Zone

The line blocking is the same as the inside-zone play. The H-back to the side of the play climbs to the outside and cleans up the edge so the ball can work outside. The footwork for the line does not change, but the target moves further outside in their technique. The difference in the blocking is we use no combo calls on this play. On the play, everyone reaches and rips through the defenders playing to their outside. We want to take the ball outside the tackle. The quarterback does not boot fake after the handoff. He meshes with the tailback and carries out his frontside run fake behind the offensive tackle.

On this play, the vision of the tailback is the most important thing. If the tailback bangs the ball into the C gap and gets four yards, that is fine with us. If we bounce the play and get the edge, the wide receiver's block is critical. He stalks the defender playing on him. We "bang" the ball inside the tight end's block or "bounce" the ball outside of his block.

We try to run the outside zone with a first-sound cadence. We feel the defense may not be ready to play. This is a great red-zone play, when teams try to close off the inside. We can run the same play with a toss scheme. The blocking is the same, and the tailback still reads the blocks the same way. The reason for tossing the ball is to get to the edge quicker.

We did not run much outside zone from the shotgun set this year, but we can run the play. Instead of meshing the ball in front of the quarterback, the mesh occurs behind the quarterback. This gives the tailback a better angle to attack the line of scrimmage. He is deeper and gets more of a downhill angle coming to the line. If the mesh is in front of the quarterback, the tailback is too flat to the line of scrimmage. This is a good concept.

We call the play-action pass for this play *X-* or *Z-choice pass*. The play in the diagram is the Z-choice (Diagram #10). The Z-receiver has a choice of an out, a post, or a stutter pass deep. If the corner retreats into the third coverage, we want to throw the out cut. We run the out at 12 yards and come back to the sidelines. If we get a low safety or a robber situation, we feel we can get over the top to the post. If we get the corner playing up for the out cut, the stutter (stop-and-go) pattern is a good choice.

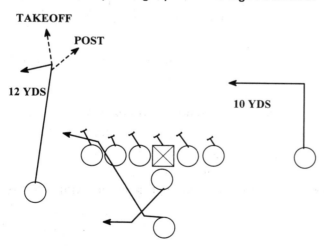

Diagram #10. Z-Choice

We must have a great mesh with the tailback and hope he gets to the flat late. He is a good checkdown pattern for the quarterback. If he gets caught up in the wash, that means we probably had

a good play fake. With the H-back staying in on the backside, we can slide the protection toward the play, which makes it look like the outside zone. On the backside, we run a dig pattern by the X-receiver. If we run the post to the Z-receiver, the post, dig, and checkdown is a good triangle read for the quarterback. If we want to pick on the middle safety, we run the Z-receiver on the out cut and the X-receiver on the post cut.

The last play is our counter gap (Diagram #11). This play is a nice complement to the outside-zone play. The steps for the tailback look like the outside zone initially. The beauty of the play is the naked that comes off the play. We have to run the counter play enough so we can run the naked bootleg. The first two steps of the quarterback and tailback have to sell the outside-zone play. On this play, we pull two blockers off the backside. We pull the backside guard and H-back. The backside guard pulls and kicks out the first man passed the B gap. The H-back pulls and wheels.

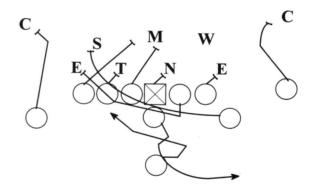

Diagram #11. Counter Gap

The frontside blocking is all down blocks for the offensive line. We run the play like most everyone else. The guard pulls and kicks out on the defensive end. If the defensive end comes down inside and wrong arms the blocker, the guard logs him to the inside. The H-back reads the block of the pulling guard. On the play, if the guard kicks out, the H-back reads the block and turns into the hole and looking for the inside linebacker. If the pulling guard logs the defensive end, he goes to the around the outside and looks back inside for the linebacker.

The complement off the counter gap is the naked bootleg pass. As with every play-action pass you run, the play will not work unless it looks exactly like the running play. In the play, we pull the guard and H-back as we did in the counter gap. The X-receiver runs a drag route to the inside. That does two things. It brings the corner into no-man's land and creates a rub off block on the Will linebacker in the event the quarterback runs the ball. The tight end comes down as if to block the inside linebacker. He bypasses the linebacker and gets across the field to into the hash area at 10 yards deep.

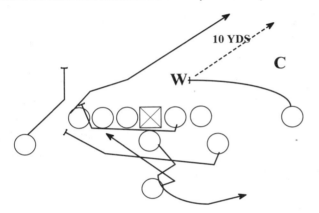

Diagram #12. Naked Bootleg

We look to run the ball first. We want to work on the backside alley player. We put the tight end in the backside safety's spot. If the safety reacts to the line of scrimmage, the quarterback throws the ball to the area the safety left. If the safety hangs in his coverage, the quarterback runs the ball. After the X-receiver runs his rub on the Will linebacker, he comes back outside and runs a late flag route.

I want to share some additional key elements that we carry in our game plan every week. Each week, we carry three to five plays we call "alerts." The offense aligns on the ball, and we get an uptempo play immediately. It could be any three plays, either pass or run. We mostly use this situation after we make a big play. When the defense is licking it wounds and has their heads down, we want to get on the ball and snap it as quickly as possible.

I also think you must have line-of-scrimmage checks. Each week, we want a run/pass check based on what the defense gives us. We either stay with the run or check into the pass, depending on what the quarterback sees.

The thing that is in vogue today is to use a second cadence with that check. We want the defense to declare itself before we call our play. Our regular cadence is "set, go." When we want to use the check, we go to the second cadence, which might be "set, right, 8, right, 8, go." With the second cadence, we directional check the outside-zone play an awful lot. Our formation is a balanced formation most of the time. Since we are two-by-two, we can run to either side. That way, it becomes a check-with-me call. The other thing we check is the choice pattern if we read zero coverage.

In the past, we have used no-huddle the entire game. Last year, we did not use it as much. We do use it as a tempo changer. We use the no-huddle with our "wristband" system. The example you see on the slide has 40 plays listed on it. There is no thinking by the quarterback. We signal the play from the sideline. We call "Band #9." He looks at his band for play number nine.

#9 Left 838 X-Choice 1

The example in the box is what he looks at. He looks at the band and comes up with "L-838," which is a play-action pass. The three digits tell us it is play-action. The "L" means we are in left formation. Eight tells us we are sliding right, faking the outside zone, and running X-choice. Within those numbers is the message telling the X-receiver what route he is running. The single number to the far right on the entry is the snap count. In this example, the snap count is one.

I want to thank you for your attention. I am proud to be able to speak at this clinic, and I wish all of you the best of luck.

FOUR PHASES OF THE OPTION OFFENSE

Colerain High School, Ohio

I want to thank you for coming out today. I am going to talk about the four phases of the triple option. We have been running it at Colerain High School for the last 15 years. During that span of time, we have been very successful with the triple option.

There are some good reasons to run the triple option. The first reason is you do not need many great linemen to run this scheme. So many times, if you have one good lineman, you are doing well. When you run the scoop scheme or veer scheme, there is not much drive blocking involved with those types of blocks. Sometimes, all the linemen have to do is get in the defenders' way to make things happen.

Everyone wants that 6'3" or 6'4" quarterback with the laser arm who can stand in the pocket and pick teams apart. Those types of players are few and far between. In the triple-option offense, you do not need a true quarterback. All you need is a player who can run and make good decisions.

The triple option is difficult to prepare for in one week. If we watch teams during the pre-game warm-up and we see one of the assistant coaches trying to assimilate the quarterback in the option game, we know they have done that all week in preparation for us. When we see that, we know we are in good shape. It is hard for a scout team to simulate the option game with almost no time to practice it.

The triple option is a rarity today in offenses. Teams do not see it as a week-in-and-week-out offense. It takes discipline and correct assignments to play defense against the triple option. Also, with the triple option game, you can control the tempo of the game.

In the triple option, the fullback and the quarterback should be the best ballcarriers. They are the ones carrying the load. The running back and wide receiver must be able to block.

The quarterback must master some techniques to run the triple option. There is more than one way to skin a cat. You have to decide whether the quarterback is more comfortable with the hop or the glide. The first step into the triple option is either a hop step or a glide step. That step puts him into the mesh area. Most of our quarterbacks have been more comfortable with the hop step.

The hop step gets the quarterback away from the center and turns his shoulders to reach back to get into the mesh. He has to reach back with the ball to the fullback to make the ride and read. I will talk about the read later.

If the quarterback pulls the ball, he has to attack downhill. He cannot delay. He must force on the pitch key to react. When he pitches the ball, he uses a basketball pitch.

As the quarterback makes his read, he looks at the jersey numbers of the key. If he can see both numbers of the jersey, he gives the ball. If the defender is flat down the line of scrimmage, the quarterback pulls the ball. If the defender gets depth across the line of scrimmage, the quarterback gives the ball.

The fullback's hands in his stance are two yards from the quarterback's heels. If he steps straight ahead, that is the step for the midline play. The second step is the hard crossover step. We refer to his movement as a "train on a track." His target is the butt of the center, guard, or tackle. If he runs the midline, his track is right up the center's butt. If we run the inside veer, he runs at the butt of the guard. The target for the outside veer is the butt of the tackle. He is a train on a track, and he never leaves that track.

As the quarterback reaches back with the ball to mesh with the fullback, the fullback needs to feel pressure. If the quarterback gives pressure on the ball, the fullback knows he is taking the ball. If he does not feel the pressure, he knows the quarterback is keeping the ball. The hardest thing for the quarterback is to pull and pitch the ball immediately. That happens when both the handoff key and pitch key are stunting inside.

With the running backs and wingbacks, we like to use late and fast motion. That means they do not leave until the ball is about to be snapped. When they go in motion, it is fast. If the running back is in the I formation, he bucket steps to get the pitch relationship. The pitch relationship is about four yards from the quarterback and a half yard behind him. When the running back catches the ball, he wants his shoulders square, and he wants to run downhill as fast as he can.

Our wide receiver must block on this play. We have two blocks for the wide receiver. We call them "cloud" and "stalk." If the coverage is a cover 3 or cover 4, the wide receiver stalk blocks on the perimeter. If we get a cover-2 look, we "cloud" block on the play. On cloud, the split end cracks inside on the safety, and the wingback comes outside to block the corner. It creates a natural alley for the pitch back to run.

In the offensive line, we want to get huge splits. We split three feet or more in the offensive line. We take the defensive line as wide as they will go. If they come back inside, it gives our quarterback a pre-snap read on the defenders as to what his read is. That works to our advantage.

At Colerain, we have a quickside and strongside in our offensive line. Our quickside tends to be not as good as the strongside. We flip-flop our line. That does not mean we always run to the strongside. Fifty percent of the plays we send into the game are check-with-me plays. We have the ability in our offense to go from the midline to the inside veer and from the inside veer to the midline. Linemen need to

know three main principles for the triple option. They must know veer, loop, and scoop schemes in this offense.

If the defender is head-up on the offensive lineman, he loops to the outside. If the defender aligns in an outside technique, we veer block to the inside.

Phase 1 is the midline, which I think is the best play in football. The good thing about the midline play is you do not have to worry about an errant pitch. The midline is a two-man game. We always run this play toward a 3 technique or double 2 techniques. We have four different ways to run the midline play. We call slam, freeze, tuff, or dick 'em.

Responsibilities Versus 40 Front

- Backside tackle: Anchor backside
- Backside guard and center: 2-for-2 on 1 technique and Will linebacker
- Playside guard: Mike linebacker
- Playside tackle: Defensive end
- Split end: Stalk corner
- Playside running back: Inside of tackle's block; block for quarterback
- Backside running back: Pitch phase
- Fullback: Butt of center
- Quarterback: Hop back; reach back and read depth of 3 technique

The backside guard and center double on the 1 technique up to the Will linebacker (Diagram #1). If the Will linebacker is wide enough, the center blocks back on the nose tackle, and the guard goes straight up on the Will linebacker. The playside wingback's track is the slam tag for the play. He goes inside the tackle's block on the defensive end. If the quarterback pulls the ball, he runs through the gap off the wingback's block. However, if the outside linebacker runs outside to take the pitchman, the playside wingback continues on to the safety. He is the lead blocker for the quarterback.

The quarterback has to hop to get out of the way of the fullback, who is tracking right up the center's butt. The quarterback hops out to seven o'clock on the quarterback clock and reaches back

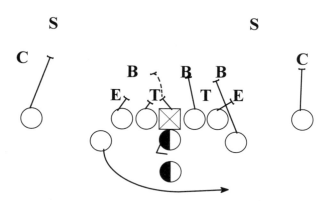

Diagram #1. Slam Versus 40 Front

for the fullback. He reads the 3 technique and pulls the ball or gives it to the fullback. If he pulls the ball, he can pitch it to the wingback going in motion. However, he looks to run the ball behind the wingback's block in the B gap.

We use formations to get the looks we want to run against. The slam play against the 40 defense with a tight end is almost the same. The only difference is the tight end anchors the defensive end, which allows the tackle to block the Sam linebacker. The playside wingback goes inside the tackle's block on the linebacker all the way to the safety. Everything else on the play is the same. If we run the play against the 50 front, the rules are similar.

Responsibilities Versus 50 Front

- Backside tackle: Anchor backside
- Backside guard: Mike linebacker
- Center: Nose
- Playside guard: Mike linebacker
- Playside tackle: Out on defensive end
- Split end: Stalk
- Playside wingback: Inside of tackle's block; block for quarterback
- Backside running back: Pitch phase
- Fullback: Butt of center
- Quarterback: Hop back; reach back and read depth of 3 technique

We traditionally have the most athletic lineman play the center position (Diagram #2). He is not the biggest lineman, but he is the player with the best feet. The kid we had this year signed with Cincinnati.

When we played 50 defenses this year, he did an excellent job on the noseguard. The 50 defenses are slant-and-angle defenses. Something that helps us against a 50 defense is we can formation the front so we know which way they will angle. We run the midline away from the angle of the front. However, we teach our fullback to cut off the center's block on an angling noseguard.

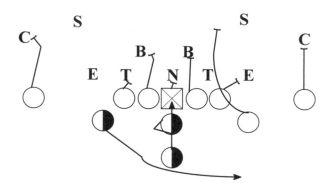

Diagram #2. Slam Versus 50 Front

We play teams that play the 50 defense and always angle to the wideside of the field. We align in a balanced set, knowing they are going to angle to the field and run the midline into the boundary. We run behind the angling noseguard, and the playside tackle cannot get down that quickly to stop the midline. Our splits prevent him from covering that much ground.

The question was: how do we handle the 3-3 stack from the odd front? St. Xavier of Cincinnati runs a 3-3 stack defense. When we play them, we do not run the read midline. If we run the midline against them, we call the give play. We wedge the center and two guards on the nose stack. We block three blockers on two defenders. We get in a double-wing set, release the tackles inside on their outside linebackers, and try to cut the end with our wingbacks. When we play St. Xavier, the only midline we have in the game plan is 40-41 give. It is a keep-them-honest type of play. We do not expect to get many yards on the play. It keeps the linebackers from flying out of the middle.

If we run the slam with the tight end against the 50 defense, it is almost the same blocking. The difference is the playside tackle. Instead of blocking the defensive end, he loops around the defensive tackle and cleans up on the linebacker. That scheme is more of an influence block on the defensive tackle. If the defensive tackle reacts to the tackle loop, the fullback is gone inside.

When we play Sycamore High, they pinch their tackles inside and scrape the linebackers. The loop by the tackle takes care of that scheme also. When the defensive tackle slants inside, the quarterback pulls the ball and steps behind the offensive tackle, looping on the scraping linebacker.

We have run this play from the I formation this year (Diagram #3). With the running back in the I formation instead of the wing position, he has to run his slam technique from the back of the I. We run the play away from the tight end and read the 5-technique tackle to the split-end side. The quarterback reads the tackle, and if he pulls the ball, he follows the running back through the gap. He goes through the same gap and more or less isolates on the safety. Everyone else blocks a hat on a hat.

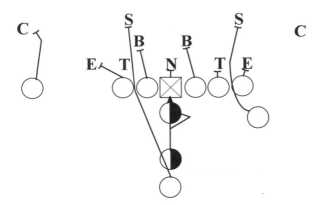

Diagram #3. I Slam Versus 50

The second way we run the slam is a freeze with no motion (Diagram #4). When we start to have problems with the safeties dropping over the top or coming downhill in the box, we want to use that against them. We call "freeze," and we have no motion back for the pitch. We run the play the same way, except the motion back stays in position and goes downfield on the backside safety.

The next adjustment to the midline play is "tuff" (Diagram #5). It is the same play as the slam, except we run a double slam. We bring the playside

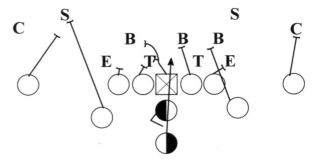

Diagram #4. Freeze

wing through the gap on the safety, and the motioning pitchman comes through the same gap and blocks the linebacker. We got this play from Georgia Southern. The motion back aims for the butt of the fullback as he comes in motion. When he reaches the fullback's butt, he plants and gets downhill in the B gap. That gives us two blockers leading the quarterback.

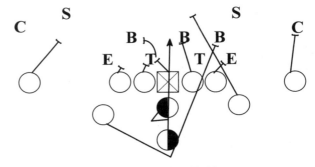

Diagram #5. Tuff

This is probably my favorite midline play of them all. We call *dick 'em* (Diagram #6). When we run the running back in motion, we get the safeties squirming down to the side of the motion. We come in the motion and run the midline away from the motion. The thing you have to do is have a tight end to the side of the play. We block the play with the playside guard and tackle blocking the Mike and Sam linebackers. The tight end turns out on the defensive end. The backside safety is squirming to the motionside to cover for the strong safety coming down to the motionside.

The second phase of the triple option is the inside veer. We want to run the veer toward the 1-technique defender. When we come to the line of scrimmage, we may have to check the play to the other side or back to the midline. That decision is up

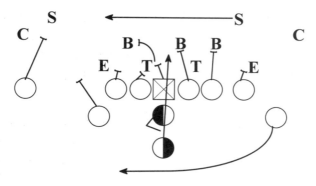

Diagram #6. Dick 'em

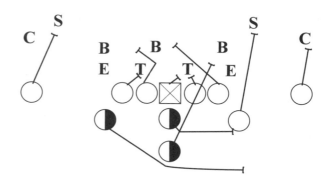

Diagram #7. Inside Veer Versus 4-3

to the quarterback, who must consider the flow of the game and what he sees.

We run two types of inside veer. We run "regular" and "load." The veer we run the most is regular, but we can tag the play with "load." We use the load scheme to run against 4-4 types of defenses. The wide receiver's rules are stalk and cloud. We stalk block cover 3 and cover 4 and cloud block cover 2.

Responsibilities Versus 4-3

- Center and playside guard: Double-team 1 technique
- Playside tackle: Veer to Mike
- Backside guard and tackle: Scoop
- Playside wingback and wide receiver: Stalk versus cover 3 or cover 4; cloud versus cover 2
- Fullback: Crossover step and aim for butt of playside guard
- Quarterback: Hop or glide; read first defensive lineman outside guard (B gap)

The quarterback has to hop or glide to get to the mesh area. We have been fortunate enough to have athletic quarterbacks. We can hop to get off the mesh. If you have a quarterback who is not very fast, you might want to teach him to glide. That puts it all in one motion and makes it smoother.

This is our bread-and-butter play (Diagram #7). We probably run this play 70 percent of the time. We double the 1-technique defender and veer block the tackle on the Mike linebacker. The quarterback reads the defensive end as his handoff key. If the defensive end closes on the fullback, the

quarterback pulls the ball and options the Will linebacker.

If we run the play against the 4-4 defense, we have to make two adjustments in the blocking scheme because there are two linebackers inside instead of one. Instead of the double-team between the center and playside guard, we have a 2-for-2 combo. They have to block the 1 technique and the backside linebacker. Either the center or guard comes off the double-team and blocks the backside linebacker. The playside tackle has to block the onside linebacker. The wingback to that side arcs up on the safety and stalks him.

If the backside linebacker is wide enough to the backside, our center is athletic enough to go directly to him. If we can do that, the guard blocks down on the 1 technique, and the center goes to the backside linebacker. However, the most important thing on the inside veer is to get the 1 technique blocked. You have to get push off the ball on the 1 technique. If you do not, you are in trouble.

In our practice, we are fortunate enough to have two offensive line coaches. We have one to work with the strongside and one to work with the quickside. We work the hell out of the double-teams and combination blocks in practice.

We can tag the inside veer with the term "load." If the 4-4 defenders cheat their linebackers and fly on the quarterback movement, you need the load scheme (Diagram #8). The playside tackle on the normal scheme blocks the playside linebacker. If the playside linebacker flies to the outside, the tackle cannot get him. For that situation, we add the load scheme. The wingback becomes the responsibility for the playside linebacker. The playside tackle goes to the backside linebacker, and we go back to the double-team on the 1 technique. The thing we give up is the wingback's block on the safety. However, if the safety flies downhill, he opens the middle for all the play-action passes.

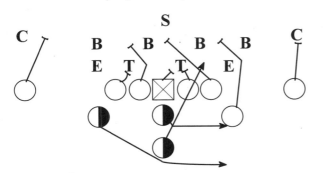

Diagram #8. Inside Veer Load

If we run the inside veer against a 50 defense, we adjust the rules.

Responsibilities Versus 50

- Center: Scoop to backside linebacker
- Playside guard: Reach playside linebacker, or climb to next level
- Playside tackle: Loop to linebacker
- Backside guard: Scoop (cut) nose
- Backside tackle: Scoop to next level
- Playside wingback: To corner (cloud)
- Playside split end: To safety (cloud)
- Fullback: Crossover and aim for butt of guard
- Quarterback: Hop or glide and read defensive tackle for give and defensive end for pitch

The playside tackle loops outside the defensive tackle for the playside linebacker. The backside guard scoop schemes with the center and cuts the noseguard. The backside guard has to reduce his split to get to the nose. The center comes to the next level for the backside linebacker.

If you play a good noseguard, we adjust the scheme somewhat. We let the center scramble block the nose and get into his feet to slow him down. The center bear crawls through the noseguard's outside hip to block him. The backside guard climbs to the next level and blocks the

backside linebacker. If you cannot handle the nose, it presents problems with the scheme. If we have to double-team the nose, that almost releases the frontside linebacker into the play. If he fills hard, we have no shot of the tackle blocking him.

The quarterback reads the defensive tackle and pitches off the end. Good teams playing the 50 defense will have the defensive end feather the quarterback. They want to keep the quarterback running east and west long enough for the pursuit to catch up with him. We attack the inside shoulder of the defensive end and let the quarterback ball fake the pitch to get the end to commit.

In practice, we run an option drill on the inside and outside veer. It helps our offense and defense. We drill our quarterbacks, wingbacks, and wide receivers against the defensive ends and defensive backs. The quarterback gets to work against the feather, and the defensive end gets to work on his techniques. One thing we tell our quarterback when he runs the ball is: once he gets past the second level, cut the play back.

Phase three of the triple option is the outside veer (Diagram #9). The offensive line reduces its splits on the playside from three feet to two or two-and-a-half feet. This play is excellent with an unbalanced formation. To run this play, you must have a tight end to that side. This is an excellent play to run against the 50 defense and the 3-3 stack.

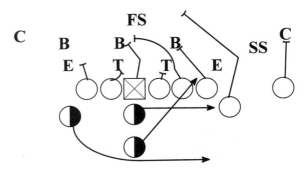

Diagram #9. Outside Veer Versus 4-3/4-4

Responsibilities Versus 4-3 and 4-4

- Playside tight end or tackle over: Veer to Sam linebacker
- Playside guard and tackle: 2-for-2 on tackle and Mike linebacker

- Center: Scoop to next level
- Backside guard: Scoop 1 technique
- Backside tackle or tight end: Scoop to next level
- Playside wingback: Stalk free safety
- Playside wide receiver: Stalk corner
- Fullback: Slide step, aim for the butt of tackle
- Pitchback: Late and fast motion
- Quarterback: Hop or glide wide and reach wide

If we go unbalanced, we flip a tackle to the tight-end position and take the tight end to the two-man side. If the defense starts to load to the unbalanced side, we can come back and run the inside veer to the two-man side.

The fullback takes a six-inch slide step to help him get his width on his crossover step. He aims at the butt of the tackle. This is where the quarterback techniques get tricky. If he is a glide stepper, it is easy. He sprints to the mesh point and glide steps with the fullback. If he hops, he has to get extremely wide in his hop. The quarterback reads the first defender outside the C gap. He pitches off the strong safety. The diagram is our unbalanced look.

If the 4-3 defense moves into an over look to the tight end, the blocking is harder (Diagram #10). If they move the nose to a 1 or 2 technique on the strongside guard and move the defensive end down on the tackle, the tight end's rule changes. The Sam linebacker will move to the line of scrimmage on this defense. On the play, the tight end double-teams with the tackle on the 5-technique defender. The quarterback's give read is now the Sam linebacker.

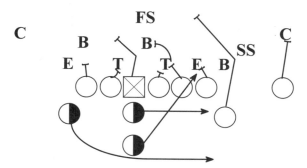

Diagram #10. Outside Veer Versus Over

This play is great against the 50 and 3-3 defenses (Diagram #11). When we get this defense,

we call "corner" or "triple X." The playside guard, tackle, and tight end or tackle over are 3-for-2 on the defensive tackle and playside linebacker. We get a big push on the tackle to the frontside linebacker. The read on the stand-up defensive end is harder for the quarterback. The end can fake coming flat and step up for the quarterback. The read on the defensive tackle is much more reliable. The center, backside guard, and tackle run their scoop scheme for the nose and backside linebacker.

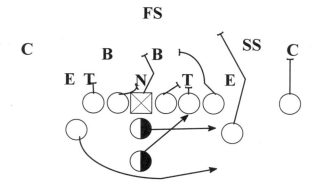

Diagram #11. Outside Veer Versus 50

If the defense moves the noseguard to a strongside shade on the center, the playside guard works with the center on a 2-for-2 block to the backside linebacker. The playside tackle and tight end do the same thing with the defensive tackle and playside linebacker.

This is also a good play against the 3-3 defense (Diagram #12). The playside guard, tackle, and tight end (or tackle over) triple-team the defensive tackle. We want movement back off the ball. The tackle works to control the defensive tackle. The playside guard can slip to the Mike linebacker, and the tight end can slip to the Sam linebacker. The backside linemen and center run the scoop scheme for the stack on the center and backside stack. The wingback blocks the strong safety, and the wide receiver stalks the corner. St. Xavier runs this defense. Against them this year, we struggled running this play. It was not the scheme. It was the talent that St. Xavier had on the field that made it hard on us. We had 13 players sign college scholarships Wednesday, and I can tell you against St. Xavier, they were the best team. They had a hell of a team and a ton of talent.

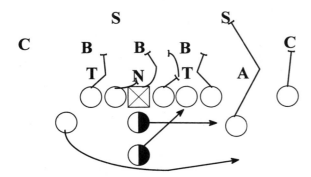

Diagram #12. Outside Veer Versus 3-3

The speed option is phase four of the triple option (Diagram #13). I want to cover this quickly so we can get to the film. We do not run this play much, but it gets you to the edge quickly and uses the fullback as a blocker.

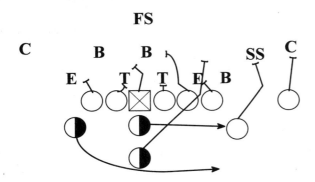

Diagram #13. Speed Option Versus 40 Strong

Responsibilities Versus 40 Strong

- Offensive linemen, running backs, and wide receivers: Block like outside veer up front
- Fullback: Take track of outside veer; Mike linebacker

- Quarterback: "Flash" fake and pitch off defender outside C gap

The quarterback does not read or put the ball into the fullback's pocket. He flash fakes the fullback and pitches off the first defender outside the C gap. The fullback runs an inside-veer track and tries to turn back on the Mike linebacker. If he is blocked, he continues up to the free safety. If the defense is a 50 front, the fullback's path is tight to the double-team on the tackle.

In the film, you see an adjustment I did not talk about in our scheme. If the pitch key comes up on the line of scrimmage and closes hard on the quarterback, we block him. We call it *deuce*. On deuce, the quarterback runs the inside veer. If he gets a keep read, he knows there is no pitch because we have blocked the pitch read. The wingback blocks the pitch read on the play. He is supposed to block the safety. If the safety comes screaming for the pitch, we may score as the quarterback turns up with the ball. This prevents the quarterback from being hit in the mouth as he pulls the ball. It slows down the double crash from the outside.

Thank you, men, for attending today's lecture. I appreciate the questions, and I will be around if you would like to talk further about the triple option. I would like to thank Earl Browning and Nike for giving me this opportunity to speak.

PASSING-SCHEME CONCEPTS

Christian Academy of Knoxville, Tennessee

I am really excited about being here. This past year was my first year as head coach at CAK, and I have been blessed to grow up around football. My dad was a college coach, and I have had the opportunity to be a graduate assistant at different schools around the country.

Today, I want to share some base concepts that we use at CAK. It is nothing that I have invented. It is stuff that I have learned along the way as a G.A. at different schools, and stuff that has worked well for us. I have learned that it is not as much the scheme as it is your personnel, and it is about believing in what you do. At CAK, throwing the football is something that we believe in doing.

We are a 1-A school in enrollment, but our enrollment gets multiplied by 1.8, so we play a 2-A schedule. We are getting ready to get bumped up to 3A in 2009, and we are excited about the chance to compete at a higher level. The thing that I have found that gives us a chance to compete at that level is to put our quarterback in the shotgun at a seven-yard depth, snap it to him, drop back, and throw it. We were 9-3 this past year, with two of those losses to the four-time 2A state champion, who just happens to be in our region.

I am going to take you through four concepts that we like to throw, and at which we have had a lot of success throwing. I will draw them up on transparencies, coach you guys through how we teach them and how our kids run them, and then I want to show film of us running each one. If there is time at the end, I also have our play-action pass series that we like, including some naked plays and other things we ran.

We are predominantly a two-back, three-wide team. We are in the shotgun with split backs.

Sometimes, we will offset the fullback and put the tailback behind the quarterback. We will show some one-back, four-wide stuff, but we are 85 percent of the time a two-back, three-wide team, and we are mainly a dropback team.

The first concept I want to talk about is a curl/flat concept that we run off our sprint-out protection. We like to throw this to our right because our quarterback is right-handed. We call it *Colorado* because I learned it as a G.A. at Colorado, but its universal name is "sprint right option." As I draw these things up, I will just draw a straight line for the offensive linemen and not get into much detail about them.

Our 800/900 protection is our sprint-out, and our quarterback will be in the gun. We want to get the ball to our slot receiver in the flat. We call the slot receiver Y, and we run him on a speed-out route. He has his outside leg back, and will roll the route over on his second outside step after his release. So, if the ball is inside to my left, when my second outside step hits, I want to roll my foot over, come out of it, and get my head around quickly because we are trying to get the ball thrown to the flat as quickly as possible.

Our outside receiver runs a return route. He pushes vertically to a depth of eight yards, and then pushes inside to 10 yards. We tell him to "run the track," as if he is running from the straightaway onto the curve of a racetrack. He keeps sprinting as he runs into and around the curve. As he works inside to a depth of 10 yards, he is reading the inside linebacker. I will start here and draw it up against a 4-4 defense in a cover 3 (Diagram #1).

We are just reading the strong safety. The outside receiver is reading the strong safety as he

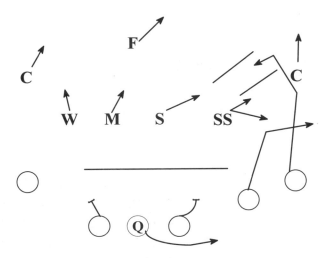

Diagram #1. Spring Right Option Versus Cover 3

works inside. He determines what he is going to do based on how the strong safety is playing. The idea of the play is to get the ball thrown to the flat as quickly as possible as our quarterback sprints out. If we can get the strong safety outleveraged to the flat, that is what we want to throw.

Ideally, that is thrown on the quarterback's third or fifth step. It is three or five to the flat if we have leverage on the flat defender. If he gets depth, or if he is late chasing the flat in cover 3, we want to take the flat.

If the flat defender has gobbled up this flat route, then our Z-receiver will read him widening and settle right inside him. Third to fifth step to the flat, and if our quarterback does not like the flat route because there is a lack of separation, then we want to throw the return route to the Z-receiver on the quarterback's fifth to seventh step. In an ideal world, then, it is third to fifth step to the flat, or fifth to seventh step to the return route. It is a great play against cover 3. We see a lot of zone coverage, and we just read the flat defender in cover 3.

As soon as Z gets inside, he wants to settle, but when we sprint out, we see the inside linebacker pushing hard to where we are sprinting. Our Z is taught to maintain the window between these two linebackers, so as the strong safety takes away the flat, and Z has not gotten the ball yet but sees the inside linebacker pushing toward him, he will simply slide away.

The same read holds true against cover 4 (Diagram #2). Against a 4-3, cover-4 defense, it is the same read for the quarterback. I teach our quarterbacks to read the coverage contour pre-snap. If they read a soft corners, outside leverage, one-safety look, we assume it is cover 3. If they see a two-safety look, but there is not a deep umbrella, we know that is cover 4. Cover 4 is susceptible in the flat, so we know that we are probably throwing in the flat against that coverage. It is the same read, but now it would be the Sam linebacker instead of the strong safety.

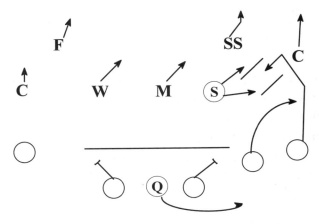

Diagram #2. Sprint Right Option Versus Cover 4

We have also had a lot of success running this play into man coverage (Diagram #3). If we read bump coverage pre-snap, the route by Y does not change, but we want to get the strong safety working vertically to create some separation, so we really drive off hard, then roll over on the second outside step and get our head around. If we get separation, we will take the throw to the flat.

If we do not have separation, we are working to Z. If we have a bump corner, whether cover-1 press or cover-2 man, we want to get the corner on our inside hip so we can "narrow and slip." We will narrow him inside to get his hips working to the inside, and then we slip him back outside. Then, we are vertical to eight yards with him on our inside hip. Next, we whip him in to 10 yards, pivot, and come back outside, and we have lost him. That is how we run it against man coverage.

Also, if it is cover 3 or cover 1, and it is a soft corner, but Z feels the corner on his outside hip, we

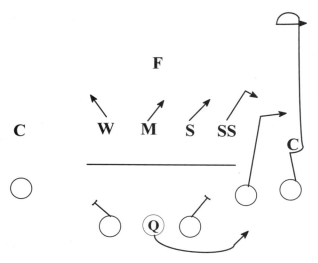

Diagram #3. Sprint Right Option Versus Man Coverage

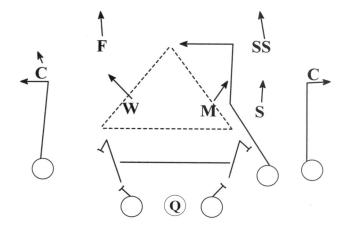

Diagram #4. Double Out Versus 4-3 Cover 4

will whip that and turn it back outside to try to create some separation. Further, if it is man coverage, it may take the quarterback a little longer than third to fifth step to flat, fifth to seventh step to Z, especially to Z, because we have to give time to create separation.

Finally, it is not a great play into cover 2. We have had to throw it into cover 2 because sometimes teams will disguise cover 4 and play cover 2. If we see that, we have a couple of ways to make it work, and I have it on film to show you. First, we still read the outside linebacker. We are sprinting out, running the flat with Y and the return with Z. In the cover 2 that we see, sometimes we can move the outside backer to the flat when we sprint out, and we can still get the Z inside him. If the linebacker stays inside, we will still throw to the flat if the cornerback is still retreating. If the corner is flatfooted or reacting up, our Z reads the linebacker staying inside, and he will stay outside and work the window between the linebacker and the corner. It is not great against cover 2, but you can make it work if you have to. It is best against cover 3, cover 4, or man. (Film)

The next concept is our double-out package. We had success using this concept, and you can actually read the play two different ways. We run it predominantly out of our two-back, three-wide set (Diagram #4). I will start out and draw it up against a 4-3, cover-4 defense.

The very first thing we look for in this play is the out route to our backside receiver. Our two outside receivers cut their splits down and run 10-yard square-outs. Our backside receiver cuts his split down to nine yards from the tackle, and the wide receiver on the slotside cuts his split down to 12 yards from the tackle. The slot receiver cuts his split down to five yards from the tackle.

The slot receiver will inside release, push vertically to 10 yards, and run a hunt route. He is "hunting" for the window between the Mike and Will linebackers. If it is zone coverage, he will settle in the front of that window. The backs will check release and sit down one yard outside the tackle. That is our quarterback's picture once he takes his drop.

This is a dropback protection, so it is our version of what would be a five-step drop if we were under center, which we are not, so for us, in the gun it is a three-step drop. We call it a "quick three and close."

If we have a clean box on the backside, we want to throw to the out route there. A clean box means there is no outside linebacker. Nothing outside the box prevents us from throwing that out route to our X-receiver.

If we have a dirty box, which might be another defender out there or maybe a wide attitude by the Will linebacker, then we are going to work the field. We would try to work the out route to the Z-receiver instead.

If the quarterback likes the look on the backside, he will try to work the out route to the

X-receiver. If the linebacker skates underneath the out route, the quarterback comes off the out and reads this middle triangle, from dig to checkdowns. It would be: one to the out, two to the Y, and three to the checkdowns.

If we want to work the field instead, then we just read the outside linebacker on that side. If he drops with depth and does not defend the out route, then we go ahead and take the out route to the Z-receiver. If he skates underneath the out route, we are back to reading the middle triangle.

That is the play into cover 4. Against that coverage, we will throw the out route to the X-receiver most of the time, because most of the time it gives us a clean box backside.

I want to draw it up against cover 3 and explain what happens with the middle triangle inside (Diagram #5). In this look pre-snap, I know I am off of the backside route because the linebacker is outside the box on that side, so our quarterback knows he is reading the linebacker on the slotside of the formation.

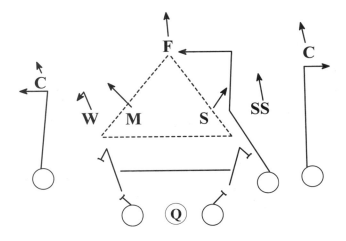

Diagram #5. Double Out Versus Cover 3

If he drops with depth and does not drop underneath the out route, then that is what we are going to throw, but if he skates underneath the out route, we come back and read the middle triangle, where we would have a 3-on-2 advantages. Against cover 3, that match-up is good enough that, at times, we will not worry with the out routes, and we will just read the middle triangle. We read it from

Y to the two checkdowns, based on how these two linebackers play.

If they drop for depth and then react up, we know we have our Y-receiver right behind them. If the Sam linebacker drops for depth underneath our Y-receiver, we check it down to the back on that side, and if the Mike linebacker drops for depth, we check it down to the back on that side. That actually makes it two plays in one. We can read outs to the middle triangle, or we can just read the middle triangle.

That is how we run it against cover 4 and cover 3. If we see cover 2, we will not convert routes on the outside. We know that we are off the out routes, and we are just going to read the middle triangle.

If we see man coverage, such as cover-2 man, then we get the bump corner on our inside hip. We can either speed release him to the outside or narrow and slip him, push vertically, quick burst at 10 yards, and come out of the route and lose him on the outside break. Then, of course, the route by the Y-receiver has to stay on the move. The Mike and Will linebackers gobble up the check-release routes, and we can throw the dig route right behind them. (Film)

We throw enough out routes that corners will start jumping them, so we will call out-and-up routes. When we run our out route, we give a quick burst and come out flat, so on the out-and-up route, we just fire our feet, turn our shoulders, and then get back out of the route upfield wide. The quarterback will take his "quick three and close," and then pump fake the out route. On the pump fake, he will take his front hand off the ball because that makes corners come up. We take our front hand off, reset, and then throw the deep ball.

The next concept we throw is our smash concept (Diagram #6). We can run it out of a two-back, three-wide set, or out of one-back, four-wideouts. The concept does not change, but the picture of how we run it does. If we run it out of our two-back, three-wide set, we put our slot receiver on and our outside receiver off. I will draw it up first against cover 2.

We run the Z-receiver on a whip route. He gives a quick footfire, works in to a depth of three yards,

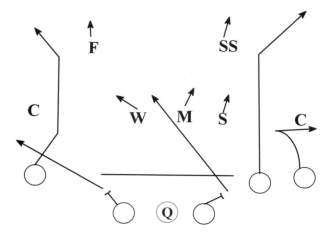

Diagram #6. Smash Versus Cover 2

and then comes back out flat. The slot receiver will outside release the Sam linebacker, go vertically past 10 yards, stick, and then come out of the stick at 45 degrees.

Our split end on the backside cuts his split down to six yards, releases inside to three, vertically past 10, and then back to the corner. We then check release the back into the flat. This gives us a smash concept on both corners. Our fullback just sits down over the center.

We want to pick the side with the best safety leverage, that is, the side where the safety is tucked further inside the corner route. In cover 2, we are reading the corner. If he bails out, we will just throw the whip route. If the corner is softer than the vertical stem of our slot receiver before he sticks, we throw the whip route.

If the corner reacts up on the whip route, we throw the corner route. If the corner chases the whip route inside, that clears up the quarterback's read immediately, and he goes straight to the corner route. If the corner sinks but then stops, we have to make a decision. If we have him outleveraged but he is still sinking, we will go with the whip route, but if we have him outleveraged and he is flat-footed, we will throw the corner. The same concept works backside. Now we are just high-lowing this cornerback, but the same rules apply.

We give our quarterbacks catch points on the corner routes. We tell them the catch needs to be made 18 to 20 yards from the line of scrimmage. If

we stick past 10 yards and come out of it at a 45-degree angle, we should catch the ball at 18 to 20 yards, about two yards outside the wide receiver's alignment. If we are throwing to the boundary, the catch should be made over the X-receiver's original alignment.

The other way we throw this is out of a two-by-two alignment, and now the routes are the same on both sides. It is just a different look. That is how we throw it into cover 2.

If our quarterback pre-snap reads a cover-4 contour, he will cut his drop short and just try to throw to the whip route. When we read a soft corner, we cut our drop short and get the ball to the whip route.

If we read cover 3 pre-snap, it is really a bad play there, and we would want to check to something else. If we went ahead with it, we would be off the corner route, and we would work whip to checkdown based on the outside linebacker.

This is a very good play into man coverage. Our man-beater on this play is our corner route. When we see bump coverage, the Y-receiver will narrow and slip the outside linebacker, release back vertically with him on his inside hip, lean him inside, stick, and create separation. The catch point is the same. That is how we throw smash. We do not like it into cover 3, it is good into cover 4, and I like it a lot into cover 2 and man.

We have one complement to smash that I want to show you (Diagram #7). We will "nod" the corner and run a skinny post off this. Sometimes, we will see a cover-2 contour with the safety aligned outside our slot receiver. We would have to cross his face if we are going to run the corner route, so we can check to a "nod" route, "nod" to the corner route, and run a skinny post, hopefully for a touchdown.

If we make that check, we call it a "one throw." That means we are throwing it "on a rope." For us, a "three throw" is a deep ball, and a "two throw" is in between. Our corner routes are thrown in 1.75 seconds, which is a little less than a two. Our "nod"

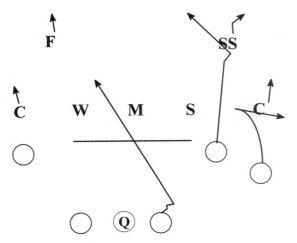

Diagram #7. Nod Versus Cover 2

route is a "one throw," which is 18 to 20 yards "on a rope." (Film)

I want to take you through our four-verticals concept, which we run two ways. We run it out of either a two-by-two or a three-by-one set. It is determined by where the ball is on the field. On the hash, we run it out of a three-by-one set, and toward the middle of the field, we run it out of a two-by-two set. I will draw it up both ways.

This is our two-by-two formation (Diagram #8). Whether it is cover 3 or cover 2, we are trying to get a 2-on-1 on a safety. I am showing it in a 4-4, cover-3 defense. Here, we are trying to get a 2-on-1 into cover 3 with our two inside verticals. We read the safety and throw to the one he does not cover.

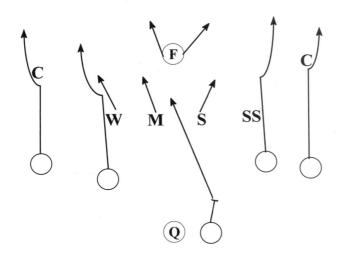

Diagram #8. Four Verticals Versus Cover 3 Out of a Two-by-Two Set

On the outside, we get nose-to-nose on the corner. We attack his technique, step on his toes, stick, and then get outside the numbers. That will take the corners out of the play.

Against the one-safety look, the landmarks for the two slot receivers are the hash marks, and they will take an outside release. Whichever vertical the safety takes away, we will throw the other. The catch points are at 18 to 22 yards, and it is a "one throw." We are trying to work it in between the safety and the corner, and on top of the linebackers, and we will throw it "on a rope." If linebackers are carrying the vertical routes, we will just check it down to our back over the center. We read it inside verticals to checkdown against cover 3.

We can also run it out of a three-by-one set (Diagram #9). It is still the same read for the quarterback. The wideouts still work nose-to-nose, step on his toes, and outside the numbers. The inside slot receiver takes his best release and works across to the opposite hash. The outside slot receiver works down his hash, and we 2-on-1 the safety. Again, if linebackers are carrying vertical, we will check it down over the center.

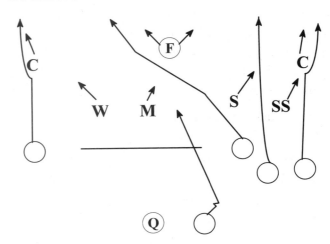

Diagram #9. Four Verticals Versus Cover 3 Out of a Three-by-One Set

Into cover 2, we will pick one of the two half-field safeties and go 2-on-1 on him (Diagram #10). It is the same concept as against the middle safety in cover 3. Most of the time on this, we want to work the field because against us, the field safety will be

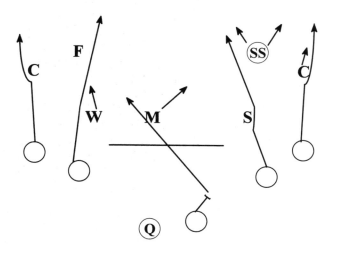

Diagram #10. Four Verticals Versus Cover 2 Out of a Two-by-Two Set

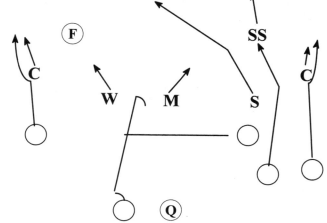

Diagram #11. Four Verticals Versus Cover 2 Out of a Three-by-One Set

head up to outside our slot receiver, and we want to work inside if possible.

Again, our wideouts have exactly the same rule as before. Our slot receiver to the boundary is down the hash, and our slot receiver to the field will adjust his landmark to two yards inside the hash. That way, we get more of a horizontal stretch on the safety.

If the safety works off the hash, or gets depth and gives us the inside throw, that is what we want to take. It is a "one throw" at 18 to 20 yards. If he stays inside or chases inside, we are working outside. If the read takes us inside but the linebackers are carrying, we will just check it down.

Of course, the same things apply if we are in three-by-one against cover 2 (Diagram #11). We are just going to pick a safety and 2-on-1 him. I like throwing it into cover 2 out of a three-by-one set and reading the backside safety. The safety tends to come off the hash to help with the wide receiver over there, and we have our Y-receiver working the void across the field.

The last thing we like to do with this is against a team that is going to play us in man coverage (Diagram #12). Here it is against cover-2 man, and we can see that we have man coverage. We clear with our four receivers against their two safeties and their four underneath man players, and tag the play with the term *Oscar*.

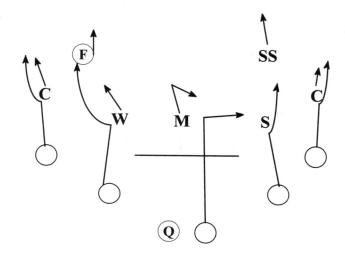

Diagram #12. Four Verticals Versus Cover-2 Man

Our tailback will free release, and we have him on a linebacker who wears high-tops and ankle braces, and we are running an option route on him. If we see man coverage, we can tag the four-verticals play with Oscar, and we have our tailback 1-on-1 against a linebacker. (Film)

I hope that this will help you with your offense. I will be here for any questions you may have. Thank you.

BUILDING A CULTURE OF CHAMPIONS

Christian Brothers Academy, New York

The most powerful person in most communities is the head football coach. It is not the priest, the mayor, the cops, or the superintendent—no one is more powerful than the head football coach and his assistants. As football coaches, you hold the kids in the palm of your hands. Think about this statement. Every one of those kids is someone's son. The way you love your own kid is the way they love their kid.

There is nothing worse than a coach getting so wrapped up in the task that we forget our job. Are you ready for this? Those kids want to be you! They want to be you. Wow! You talk about responsibility; this is big. The kids want to emulate the coach. "I give you my son, and he wants to be you?" No wonder those parents are such a pain in the butt. It is not just when you are on the field calling a play, but when you are in the bar at the Marriott as well.

Think about this situation. I work for a national company and speak at schools all over the country. We are the richest country in the world. Just think about this next statement. Before we leave here today, over 700 kids will be arrested for drug abuse. Over 400 babies will be born into poverty. Approximately 150 kids will report physical abuse in their home before we leave this meeting today. Two teenage kids will commit suicide before we leave here today.

There are over 2.1 million battered women in this country. That means someone's wife and someone's mother is beaten by a male in her family. Are you ready for this, coaches? The day with the most 911 calls on assaults occurs on Super Bowl Sunday. We do have a lot to be proud of in the U.S.A., but we also have a lot that we need to fix in the U.S.A.

I believe coaches are the last bastion of discipline, the last bastion of integrity in this country. I know because I was an administrator, and I know what is going on in the schools. You are the defenders of faith. It is a huge responsibility, and we have to jump on it.

I was asked to speak in Pittsburgh. They had 1,100 coaches sitting in the room when I spoke. My topic was "Creating a Culture of Champions." I got up and started talking. I said to them we do not talk about winning and losing at our school. We talk about discipline, work ethic, commitment, loyalty, and compassion. As soon as I said that, 1,099 coaches put their pens down and quit writing. I had to swear at them. "Pick the damn pen up. You are missing the most important part of the clinic."

I have coached a lot of great athletes. However, the fact is, some of your greatest teams do not necessarily have the greatest athletes. The best teams are those with the best character and chemistry. What we mean is you win with character and leadership. If you want to win, and win consistently, and do something significant in your community, create men of character and create leaders. That is what we need to do.

I have schools call me to visit with their coaches to see if I can assist them in building a winning program. As soon as I talk with the coaches, they start telling me what they are going to do to win big. That is their answer. They are going to win. They are going to line up against the opponents and win. What happens if they do not win? What if they do not win? Is that all they are going to promise the kids?

That is when I ask them what their vision is for the program. Our first meeting with our team is in March in the cafeteria, and not in the gym or weight room. We give them a sheet of paper and ask them to write down what our vision should be for the coming season. What do we want to be known for in the community? I know most of them will say they want to win a state championship. What else do they want to be known for? We need to make it so much larger than winning. When you do that, you have them right there. It has to be about family, commitment to each other, and whatever you make it. At our place, we want to be known as the hardest working, classiest, tightest knit family in the Northeast.

I get upset with the team when they do not include other issues except winning. "Why do you want to limit your vision? Why do you limit the area to the Northeast?"

I spoke in California, and they asked me if I was from Christian Brothers in Syracuse, New York. I assured them I was. I value coaches, and I go places to hear other speakers. I went to De La Salle High School in California to hear their coaches speak. They won 136 games in a row without losing a game. I do not care if you are playing a game of checkers—that is an unbelievable winning streak.

I went to visit with the coaches to see why they were winning so consistently. The kids said the most important thing they did was to get up in front of the team of seniors on Thursday night and tell them what they were going to do to help the team win the game the next night. I asked about the X's and O's. They went on to tell me they have a meeting on Friday morning in the chapel. They cannot leave the chapel until they hug everyone and tell them they love them. When is the last time you had your kids stand and tell their teammates they love them? When they do that, you will win. You will win!

I am going to talk about leadership. This is what I used to do for my captain. I would take my best football player, and because he was a stud player, I made him my captain. What is that all about? He does not know anything about being a leader. He does not know anything for having passion for someone else, or helping one of his teammates.

My captains do not even have to see the field. I have found every kid on the team loves the captains now. They love them because character is being rewarded, and not because the captain is 6'6". Their work ethic is rewarded. I tell the captains I need for them to be leaders. None of them tell me they do not know how to be a leader. Not many players want to be a captain on our team because the players know what I expect. You have to help the players become leaders. It is a huge responsibility.

The first thing you can do to help the kids is to talk to them about attitude. The power of a positive attitude is important. I want to give you several reasons for this. It sustains you in your quest for your goal. How many of you have goals for your team? How many of you have the goals written down? If they are important, you should have them written down. My kids write them down on those 3-by-5 cards. "We are going to be the hardest working team in the Northeast." I ask them how we are going to accomplish this goal. It is amazing the goals they come up with. I tell them to write the goals down and note how we can obtain the goals.

Next, I ask them to list their individual goals. I ask them to write the goals down. We ask them to put the goals in their playbook. We ask them to put it on their mirror, and in their room at home. We want them to put the goals everywhere they can see them. They have to be able to see their goals.

I am not a teacher. I am a storyteller, and I want you to hear this one. Attitude is the power of positive thinking. I was a hotshot coach because I had coached seven consecutive championships and I was only 29 years old. "Look at me!" I was in my office with my feet propped up on the desk, and I just knew the whole world revolved around me.

One day I was in the hall, and I looked up and saw the fattest kid I had ever seen. He was 5'10" and 395 pounds. He approached me and said, "Coach Cas, my name is Trent Patterson, and I would like to play football." I looked at him and said, "If you want to play football, you would have to lose 100 pounds and then come to see me." I turned and walked away from the kid. I turned my back on the kid.

I had been in coaching for nine years, and I was selfish, arrogant, and I was a jerk. If I were Trent Patterson, I would have thought, "Coach Cas is a jerk." But he did not do that. He was a 14-year-old kid. Your kids need to hear this story. He was only 14 years old, but he changed my life. He was only a freshman who did not know anything.

The next day Trent came to me in the cafeteria. He said, "Coach, can you help me lose those 100 pounds?" I said, this is it. You talk about having a good attitude. He wanted to play football so bad, and his coach told him no. The coach told him *no*! Have you ever told your kids they could not do something? Be careful what you say.

I took Trent to the school nurse and asked her to help Trent. He lost 95 pounds in one year. That is determination. That is work ethic, and that is commitment. He came back to me, and he was loyal to me and told me he wanted to take his physical for football. He passed the physical. It was the first time he had passed his physical.

I told him he had to lift weights and that he would have to run before he could play football. He could not run a lap. He used to walk around the track. He would move his arms and shuffle his feet as he walked. We called it the Patterson shuffle. Everyone used to laugh at him except me. Now, I was his disciple. The coach was following him. He finally got to the point where he could run.

Then I told Trent he had to get flexible to play football. He became a black belt in karate in three years. I told him he had to get strong. He put the shot 64 feet, which set a state record.

He came to me and said he wanted to play Division I football. He was 5'10" and 280 pounds. Who was going to give him a scholarship? No one! I called everyone I knew, and a lot of people I did not know. On the day before National Signing Day, the University of Alabama called and offered him a scholarship. He started for Alabama on an offensive line that was 6'4", 6'3", 6'4", 5'10", and 6'2". He played from 1987 to 1990 and played for a national championship. This is a positive attitude. His attitude sustained him.

This story had a big impact on my life. Kids need to know they are leaders now. You can tell the players on the varsity that the young players in the seventh and eighth grades want to be like them. They are leaders now. They can change people's lives now, and they can change your life if you open up.

Here is the progression we use. First, what is our vision? Have them write down their goals. Have them look at these goals all of the time. Here is the key: we have to develop the process of how we are going to meet our goals. If our goals are to be strong, we have to decide how we are going to become strong. We may have to lift weights four days a week to become strong. If our goal is to become fast, we must do agility drills, plyometrics, and all of the other drills to develop speed.

We must follow up with the process for our goals. We tell our players to fall in love with the process of meeting their goals. We tell the players they can forget about their goals if they will fall in love with the process. They will get to the goal if they can follow the process.

The next point is the kids must take 100 percent responsibility for their actions. They must take credit for their actions.

Here is the last point if you want to be a champion. This is the last point in the process the kids must understand: "You must want the success more for the others than for yourself." You must be more for the others than you are for yourself.

I want to get to the topic of leadership. I will not deny the fact that we have some good athletes. We played New Rochelle for the state championship. Ray Rice was at tailback, and they had five other Division I athletes on their team.

I am going to talk to you about character and positive attitude. I do not lie to our kids. They had six Division I athletes on that team. Three of them are starting at Rutgers now. Going into the state championship, I told our players the team was better than we were. We must find a way to beat them. "Here is your plan to win the game. We are going to play fast, and run the no-huddle on offense, swarm them on defense, and we are going to stay positive. Some things may go against us, but when they stop to take a breath, we are going to be good enough to make a play. If we can wear them down, we have a chance to beat them. We can win the game in the last three minutes of the fourth quarter." We had never been behind all year.

The half ended, and we were down 14-7, having given up a touchdown to them in the last minute of the half. I went into the locker room and told the players we were going to stay with our game play. We kicked off, and nine plays later, they were in the end zone again. Now, we were down 14 points. As we came off the field after the extra point, my 1-technique 184-pound guard came by me and said, "Coach, we have this team right where we want them." Three other kids came by me and said, "Coach they are getting tired, we are going to get them." I almost started to cry. They believed they could win. I did not believe we could win, because I was looking at the scoreboard. They believed! We caught them by the end of the third quarter. With two minutes in the fourth quarter, we went ahead. We scored from 29 yards out and won the game.

We won even though that team was better than we were. We won because the players believed they could win. You cannot go out and say, "I am going to turn this program around, and we are going to win. We are going to run the spread offense and the 4-3 defense." It is not going to happen that way. First, you need to build character, attitude, and leadership. Leadership is a critical part of winning. You can look at the teams you felt could have been great, and you say, "We did not have any leadership." You have to help the players become leaders.

Here is the first thing the players need to know: leadership is not standing up and making speeches. Leaderships is an attitude of service to others. "Do you want to be a leader on this team, kid?" He replies, "I do not know how to be a leader." My response to him is this: "Help someone on the team." I will help the players with all of the words and all of the techniques, but they must help someone.

We were five minutes from leaving the locker room for the state championship game, and the officials came up to me and said, "Coach, Cas, every one of your footballs are illegal." I said, "How could a football be illegal?" They replied, "There is not enough air in the balls." I went running around the stadium looking for an air pump. I was supposed to be talking to my team to get them ready to go on the field.

When I got back to the locker room, every one of the players were crying. I asked the defensive coordinator what had happened. He said, "Greg just spoke to the team." I said, "He speaks to the team every game." He said, "Coach, Greg had it written on the cards." I said, "He had *what* written down?" We had 53 players in the dressing room. "He read out what each of those individual players meant to him in his life. He went over every kid and every coach and told them what they meant to him. He finished with the comments that he was going to give it his all because of it was for them."

I decided not to mess it up, so I said, "Anyone else have anything they want to say?" Another great leader stood up. Now, you have to understand the situation with him. He had no father figure. He had problems at home. He had to go to the library every day when he was an eighth-grader so he could get into our school. His home life was so bad he had to move out of his home to go to our school.

When he graduated and received a scholarship to go to a Division I college, he said the one thing he was proud of was the fact that he did not miss one day of school in the four years he played for us. He stood up and said, "I want everyone in this room to know I love you all. This is my family, in this room. I love all of you like my own brother. I am going to play as hard as I can, so *you* win!" It was not so *we* win; it was so *you* win. After that, I gave the greatest speech of my career. I said, "Let's go!" We beat a team that we had no business of being on the same field with. Leadership is about service to others. Do not select your captains to get up and make speeches. They have to help others.

How are we going to go about helping others? How are you going to help a kid? The first thing I always tell them is to know the importance of leadership.

We had won several games in a row, and the school wanted us to wear t-shirts with some catchy words on them to indicate the winning streak. The players came to me with the idea of getting shirts with "Main Event" on them. We got the t-shirts, but I would not give them to the players. I stored them in the equipment room.

We went out and won the next game on Friday night. I called them in on Saturday morning and passed out the t-shirts. I told them this was the deal. Anyone can be the Main Event on Friday night. You need to know this. You are the Main Event on Saturday afternoon at the mall, and you are the Main Event on Sunday, and Monday night, and on Tuesday, and in school on Wednesday, and at lunchtime when people are picking on the fat kids. You are the Main Event then, and you have to be the leader all of those times. It is a critical thing for those kids to understand this at all times.

There are ways to teach players to believe. First, is to model the way. Leaders are made, not born. Leadership is a learned behavior. Anyone can be a leader. They have to learn it. They have to find it, and they have to work hard to accomplish leadership.

If you want loyalty, give loyalty. If you want compassion, give compassion. If you want affection, give affection. If you want honesty, give honesty. If you want integrity, give integrity. Model the way.

The second point is to inspire a shared vision. How many of your kids tell you, "I do not think I can do that." Someone had to be inspiring them. "Here is the vision, men. We can be the greatest team in our school history." Inspire a shared vision.

The third point is to challenge the process path. If you find something that is holding the kids down, change the process for them. Help those kids find a way. Help them become leaders. Do something to help them. You may take the whole team, go to the rescue mission, and feed the poor. Go to church on Thanksgiving, and hand out turkeys. Find something the kids can do so they can say something good about themselves. Change the process for them. Encourage the heart. You must be careful when you encourage the heart. You will be surprised what kids can do.

In my first year of coaching, I had the philosophy of "You cannot make chicken salad out of chicken manure." When I first started coaching, we would pick out the smallest player on the defensive side of the ball and run at him. It took me several years to learn we had to change that policy. Why do you think that small kid is on the field? He is good, or he would not be on the field with the big guys. Some of those small players have worked hard to overcome their size and do a great job. We have learned to avoid them.

We have had several players with limited size who have worked hard to overcome their disadvantage. I had one player that worked out in the weight room as long as the place was open. Some of the assistant coaches make jokes about the dedication that player had. They would tell me he had been arrested. "You are kidding? Why did he get arrested?" They would reply, "It was 4:00 a.m., and he was in the local health center working out with the lights out." We are in the process of building men. We are not in the game just to build football players.

Write this down. You are going to have someone in your family read what you write because they are going to eulogize you. Just write down one thing you would want them to say. Write down what you would like them to say. Next, write down what you would want some friend of yours to say about you. Last, think of someone from one of your former teams whom you have coached, and write down what you would want that person to say about you. Write down one thought on each of these situations.

Here we go. Now, do not be embarrassed if I call on you. Coach Jones, what was one thing you wanted people to say about you? "That I was honest." Next, Coach Smith, what did you write down? "I cared about others." Next, "I was dedicated."

Not one person said they were the richest man in the community. Not one person said he was the most winning coach we ever had. Not one person said that he taught me how to run for a touchdown, or he taught me football techniques.

If you want to be a caring person, give caring. If you want to be considered honest, give honesty. If you want to be considered loyal, give loyalty. I think I have made my point.

We already want to be significant. The problem is the alumni, the fans, and everyone connected to the team wants you to go out and win. You have to go out and win. No, you don't! But, you will be a character if you develop character anyway. You will be a winner if you develop character as you coach football. You have a chance to win with character.

One additional thing I would ask you to do would be to draw a square and a circle. Now, write down the name of one coach in the circle who uplifted you, who respected you and assisted you, or helped you become what you are today. Write that down in the circle. Next, write down a name of a coach in the square who berated you or belittled you. It could be a coach who did not have time for you, or did not give you the values we talked about.

Everyone in this room can write down a coach's name in the circle. The question is: where do you want your team to write your name, in the circle or the square? They are going to put it in the circle or the square, one of the two.

You have a chance to be significant in the lives of the kids you work with. You are the single-most important asset in our entire nation. You are the last bastion of defense. Are we men enough to look our kids in the eye and say, "I do not care if we win this game, but here is what I care about. Are we going to go out, play together, and stay together to the death? Can we love each other enough to stay together to the death? If we are short on the scoreboard, I do not want to see a single player standing. Make them kill us all."

If we get commitment like that from your kids, and loyalty like that, you have a chance to win every game. God bless all of you, and good luck.

THE 4-3 DEFENSE WITH 3-4 PERSONNEL

Prattville High School, Alabama

It is great to be able to talk to you today about the 3-4 defense. I want to give you a little history of our program at Prattville. I came to Prattville nine years ago. We are a 6-A high school, which is the biggest division in the state of Alabama. We have about 120 players in our program. At Prattville, we are 107-11 over those nine years, winning the last two state championships and finishing second four years ago. My father was a great high school coach and gave me a great jumpstart. He reminded me to stay humble and keep working every day. It is hard to imagine how anyone could get arrogant in this profession. There are so many great coaches and teams out there.

We did not invent nor do we own the things we do in our program, but we hope to execute them and player harder than our opponents. We all know the scheme is just a small part of being successful on defense. However, the scheme is what we will talk about today. The key to our defense is multiplicity.

I visited the University of Miami almost 20 years ago to learn about the 4-3 defense. This is still the basis for many of the things we do today, but we had to evolve as the offenses evolved. We started mixing in a three-down front in the mid '90s. We used the three-down front as a mixer on passing downs, to blitz, or against four-wide-receiver teams. We are seeing so many spread teams today that we decided to keep another linebacker or nickel back on the field and become a 3-4 team. We now had to mold this defense back to our 4-3 concepts. We feel we are better suited to play against spread teams. We are more versatile from the ability standpoint, and we can cover all of the multiple formations we now see. We were concerned about two-back teams running the ball at us. I am going to talk today about defending two-back teams out of a 3-4 defense.

Before I get to the X's and O's, I want to talk about some other things. I believe you need to have a philosophy and some defensive goals. Our first goal on defense is to win. We feel we have a chance to reach that goal if we shut out the opponent. We had seven shutouts this year, and in past years, we have had at least five a year. I believe that happens because we talk about it.

We talk about playing four quarters and finishing a game. We want to take the ball away from the offense. Our goal is five takeaways a game, but we want at least three. In addition to takeaways, we want to score on defense. This is something we talk about and practice in our drills. It is our objective to get off the field and give the ball back to the offense.

We do not want to give up the big play. We do not want any run or pass over 25 yards. That leads to how you practice pursuit. We want to give up less than 200 yards of total offense. We feel that is a good number for high school football. We also set specific goals for personnel. If we play a team that has a great back, our goal would be keeping him under a 100 yards rushing.

We want to be three-and-out 50 percent of the time. We want the defense to get off the field. Third down is the money down, and it is when we want to perform.

The first thing in our defensive philosophy is to be in top condition. We are going to outwork our opponent. There are ways to make defense fun, but our players have to believe they are in better shape than the opponent. We must see a difference in the third and fourth quarters. You need 11 players running to the football. The more depth you have, the better your team.

This was probably the best defense we have had. We had three players to play two positions. When we substituted, there was no drop-off in talent. We had three inside linebackers instead of two. When we substituted for one of the starters, the replacement was just as good. We did not have great players, but they all were about the same in talent.

We want to swarm and be sharp. That is how we break the huddle. The huddle is not what it used to be. The huddle is not as important as the concept of how we break it and the mind-set that comes from the break.

We want to be more physical than our opponents. I do not care what type of offense we play; we want to be more physical. We want to enjoy contact and coach physical. Obviously, we have to coach that part of the game in a smart way. We feel being physical goes back to the weight room.

I have been talking about assignment and execution for years. I remember what Bill Arnsparger said the first year he went to the San Diego Chargers. They found in a two-game period, the defense lined up or missed an assignment 80 percent of the time. That was an NFL team. You know how important it is in the high school game. No matter what we call, we want to run it correctly.

You have to execute your assignment. That goes back to pursuit and tackling. Any defensive team must have great pursuit and tackle well. We practice and talk about it all the time.

You have to play defense with great pride. We know the offense will get all the headlines, but at Prattville, we are known for our defense. We want to develop confidence and not cockiness in our program. If you get cocky in this game, there is something wrong with you. We gain confidence when we know what to do. We get that from video study and hard work in practice.

We practice sudden-change situations every week. We do not allow our players to drop their heads when something bad happens. We do not allow them to throw anything coming off the field or on the sidelines. I do not want to see a cup thrown down when a turnover occurs. It is the defense's job to go out on the field and play defense. We tell our defense this is the opportunity to show everyone what you are made of.

We huddle on the sidelines before we go on the field after a sudden change. We do not run on the field as individuals. We want to make sure they get the call, get their heads up, and chill out before they go on the field. We huddle up and tell them that their backs are against the wall and to go show everyone what they are made of. After that, we swarm onto the field.

The first thing the defense has to do is get the call. There are no secret weapons in the game. It does not matter what the coaches know; it is what the players know. Opponents have tendencies because those plays work for them. If a team does not have tendencies, they are not very good. They have down-and-distance and field-position tendencies. We want to know what they do when they are backed up and what they do when they are going in. Defense is all about the opponent.

The defense is 3-4 personnel in an Eagle front. We play a single-gap defense. We have to identify our players in the 3-4. Our Sam and Jack are the outside linebackers and must be very versatile. They are what everyone refers to as "hybrid" players in today's football. They are part linebacker, lineman, and defensive back. When we started, the Jack was our rush end.

We ask them to line up over a tight end, play a slot receiver, blitz the quarterback, or play in the box. We look for good athletes who are physical. We can play left and right, but they are interchangeable. We usually flip them if one is better against the tight end. We found if we flipped the defender, they got more reps in a specialized technique. They are basically D-gap players.

The Mike and Will are the inside linebackers. They can be interchangeable as well, but our Mike linebacker should be the better box player. We want all of our linebackers to run, and we will definitely sacrifice size for speed. They have to be strong to handle the running game, and of course the weight room is a big factor. Our defensive ends must have good feet. We play with different body types and try to fit their strengths, but we sacrifice size for speed and quickness.

Our nose can be the bigger player on the defensive line. He must get off blocks and create problems inside. He cannot be single blocked. This holds true for both defensive ends. The nose has a number of alignments, depending on the scouting report. We can play him in a normal alignment to the strongside shade of the center to a 2i technique on the guard. If he is in the shade position, he can tilt and angle in at the center.

Our corners must be able to play man-to-man first. We play many coverages, so they must be versatile. The more physical they are, the better, but they are cover people first. Our safeties may be the most important players on our defense. We ask them to do so many things. They must be great on deep balls, help in the box, play some man coverage, and be great tacklers. The strong and free safeties have some different responsibilities, but we try to make them interchangeable. We want the safety who covers better at the strong safety and the better tackler at the free safety.

When we align our defense, we make our calls according to the personnel we see on the field. However, you must be able to adjust to all formations. The important things for our defense are our fits off these formations.

The first alignment is against a pro set with two running backs, a tight end, and a wide receiver to each side (Diagram #1). We call the tight end as our strength. We can play left and right with our outside linebacker, but I want to show the flip-flop technique we use. We match the corners on the wide receivers. They play press alignment on the receivers. The strong safety goes to the tight-end side, and the free safety plays to the split-end side. If the defense trades the tight end, they can play left and right.

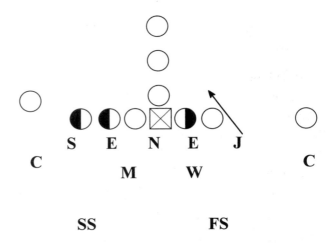

Diagram #1. Base Versus Pro Set

The down linemen move to the tight end as well. The strongside defensive end aligns in a 5 technique on the outside shoulder of the offensive tackle. The backside end slides into a 3 technique on the outside shoulder of the offensive guard, and the Jack linebacker plays a loose 5 technique on the offensive tackle. From this formation, we can play a variety of coverages. We can play cover 2, cover 3, two-man, or man-free coverage.

The first coverage I want to talk about is man-free coverage. The corners lock man-to-man on the wide receivers. The strong safety has the tight end, and the free safety is free. The Sam linebacker has the flat to the strongside. The Mike linebacker has the strongside curl, and the Will linebacker has the flat to his side.

The strong safety plays the tight end (Diagram #2). If the tight end comes vertical, the strong safety takes him deep. If he goes to the flat, the strong safety releases him to the Sam linebacker. If he comes underneath and crosses, the Will linebacker takes him. The strong safety on the cross or the flat sinks into the middle low hole. The strong safety is the eighth defender in the box. He is important in the run support.

The free safety aligns at 10 yards on the offensive tackle to his side. He reads the end man on the line of scrimmage. Once the tackle shows pass, he pushes to the middle of the field immediately. The only thing that will bring the free safety to the line of scrimmage is an option or an off-tackle play. He reads

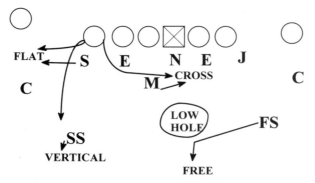

Diagram #2. Low Hole

the down block of the offensive tackle and attacks downhill. He becomes the ninth player in the box.

If the offense goes to a twins set with both wide receivers to the same side, we play it exactly the same (Diagram #3). The strong safety plays on the tight-end side and reads the tight end. The strong safety plays at safety depth. If the tight end runs an arrow route to the flat, the Sam linebacker takes him. The linebacker drops do not change. We bring both corners to the same side because we want to always look like man coverage.

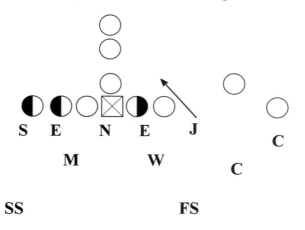

Diagram #3. Twins Set

Our defensive line is an attack-read scheme. In this particular front, we play single-gap responsibility. We tilt our Sam linebacker so he can see inside. Our Jack linebacker comes hard off the offensive tackle's butt. The alignment of our safeties is crucial to our defense. They disguise many of the different coverages we play. They cannot get too tight or wide so that they do not take themselves out of the play. They have to play off the people in front of them. They work with the

linebackers for their fits and reads. The safety makes the linebacker right. If the linebacker gets too wide, the safety fits inside of him. If the linebacker bounces the ball outside, the safety fits outside.

The safety must watch the split of the wide receiver for a possible crack block. If the wide receiver cracks on the safety, the corner gives a call for the crack and replaces the safety in his responsibility.

If we get long motion out of the backfield, we have a few different answers (Diagram #4). We can take the running back with a safety and lock our Sam linebacker on the tight end. We can change the cover or make a back call. If the running back comes to the weakside, the free safety drops down in coverage and picks him up. The strong safety on the snap of the ball becomes the free safety in the middle, and the Sam linebacker takes the tight end.

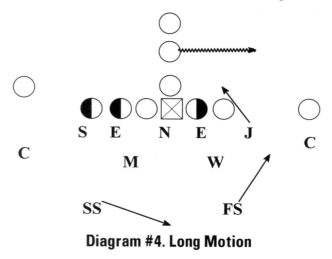

Diagram #4. Long Motion

If the motion goes to the strongside, the strong safety widens with the motion and takes it man-to-man. The Sam linebacker still has the tight end man-to-man. In both situations, the safeties made the adjustments to the motion. Because the safeties make the adjustment, we can keep the box intact. We can play the same adjustments against one-back teams.

When you make these adjustments, you have to know what the offense is trying to do. Are they in the spread to run or pass the ball? Do they use their motion and spread packages to get your defender out of the box?

If the offense comes out of the I formation with a weak or strong set by the fullback, we adjust (Diagram #5). The offense is trying to gain an advantage to the weakside by outgapping the defense. If we have the strong safety on the tight end, we check out of the coverage. The free safety rolls down into the box, and the strong safety rotates into the middle. The Sam linebacker takes the tight end man-to-man. If the offense uses short motion to get the fullback into those positions, we adjust the same way.

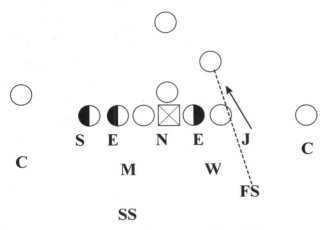

Diagram #5. Strong or Weak Set

In the twins open set, there is no tight end on the field (Diagram #6). If there is, he is in a split position or in the backfield. We play this formation a few different ways. Since the strong safety has no tight end to cover, we check the coverage to quarters coverage to the twins side of the formation. Everything else stays the same. The Sam linebacker has the same responsibility from a wider alignment.

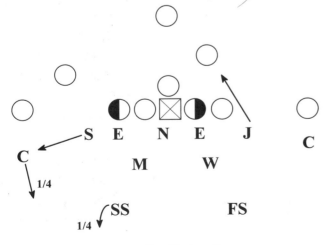

Diagram #6. Twins Open

The quarters coverage played by the corner and strong safety is a pattern-read coverage. The corner reads the outside receiver and has him on all deep routes. The strong safety reads the slot receiver and takes him on all vertical routes. If the slot receiver does not come vertical, the Sam linebacker plays him in the flat zone. The strong safety looks to the wide receiver and doubles with the corner on the any inside route run by the wide receiver. He plays under the curl and dig routes, and helps the corner on the post route. We will play two-man, man-free, cover 2, and cover 3 based on what the offense is doing.

We can play the two-tight-end set two different ways (Diagram #7). We can substitute a player, or we can play it with the regular personnel we have on the field. If we do not change personnel, we walk the corner up to a one-by-one alignment and play a crash technique. If he gets any run his way, he attacks off the butt of the tight end and blows up the play. He spills the ball to the outside with the Will linebacker coming over the top. The Jack linebacker moves out to an inside-shoulder alignment on the tight end and slants hard off the butt of the offensive tackle. He wants the angle to be tighter than from the normal alignment.

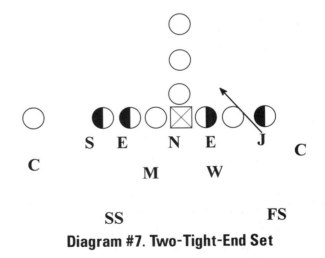

Diagram #7. Two-Tight-End Set

The Will linebacker has the flat to that side, and the free safety has the half coverage to that side. The corner does not have pass coverage on this adjustment. We can also play the free safety in the crash technique and let the corner play the half converge. If the tight end goes deep, the free safety picks him up. If he goes to the flat, the Will linebacker plays him. Everything else in the defense remains the same.

When you make the adjustment to this set, you must ask yourself whether the offense is a true two-tight-end team or uses the split end in a tight-end alignment. If they are a true two-tight-end team, we bring the additional defensive lineman in the game. He replaces the corner and plays in a 1- or 2-technique alignment inside.

From this set, if we get inside isolation play to the strongside, the strong safety is the eighth man in the box (Diagram #8). When he sees the tight end base block, he attacks the B gap. The Mike linebacker fills the B gap as big as he can. He needs to make contact off the offensive side of the line of scrimmage. He pushes the ball to the safety. He does not want the ball to come back inside of him. He wants the ball outside of his fit. If he lets the ball back inside of him, there is no help.

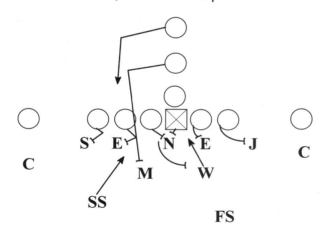

Diagram #8. Strongside Isolation

The Will linebacker has responsibility for the backside flat or the back out to his side. You cannot fast flow the Will linebacker to the strongside and make him responsible for the backside flat. In the running attack away from the Will linebacker, he is the backside A-gap player, which is the cutback lane.

If the offense runs the isolation play to the weakside, they will combo the nose up to the Mike linebacker (Diagram #9). The Mike linebacker is fast flow to the weakside and fills downhill. We want our inside linebackers with their heels at five yards.

We stem with them, but we want them to be at their spots on the snap. The free safety must be aware of the play-action pass. He pats his feet and checks for pass before helping on the run. The Will linebacker attacks the lead blocker on the offensive side of the line of scrimmage and spills the ball to the inside. He cannot let the ball go outside of him. He spills the ball back to the Mike linebacker. If the ball breaks backside to the B gap, the strong safety is the cutback player.

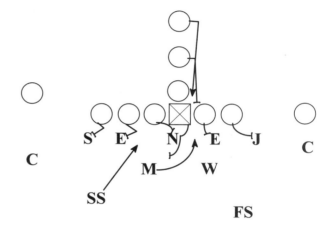

Diagram #9. Isolation Weak

The veer option is a tough play to defend (Diagram #10). The Jack linebacker must close off the dive to the fullback. He is two yards behind the tackle and flat to the line of scrimmage. The Will linebacker scrapes across and takes the quarterback. The free safety pats his feet and goes from quarterback to the pitch. The corner has play-action pass. The Mike linebacker scrapes across and helps on the fullback. We hope our Will linebacker can get over the top of the tackle for the quarterback. When defending an option play, everyone must play his responsibility.

Offenses like to run the power-G play to the tight-end side (Diagram #11). However, we play it the same whether it is strong or weak. The offense will combo block with the tight end and tackle on the defensive end and Mike linebacker. The frontside guard blocks down on the nose, and the center blocks back for the pulling guard. The fullback kicks out the Sam linebacker. We tell the Mike linebacker to scrape over the top and let the Will linebacker cover the B gap.

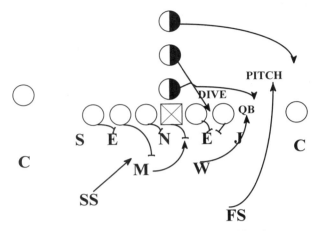

Diagram #10. Veer Option Weak

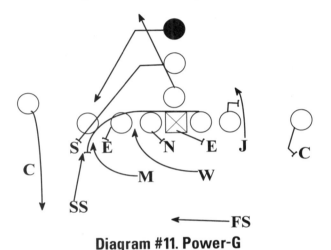

Diagram #11. Power-G

The Mike linebacker matches the angle of the fullback. The Sam linebacker attacks the fullback down the center of his body. We want him to blow up the fullback. There are two things we want to see happen. We want the ball to stop and go deep to the outside or stop and cut back inside. If he goes flat, he gets pinned, and the ball will get to the outside quickly. We used to wrong the fullback's block, but the fullback wrapped the Sam linebacker inside and the running back came immediately to the corner.

The Mike comes tight and scrapes off the Sam linebacker. The strong safety fits off the Sam and Mike linebackers. The strong safety follows the play to the line of scrimmage. He sees the tight end coming to the block on the Mike linebacker. If the tight end does not block and releases on the pass, the strong safety has to read that play. That gives him two things to do, but he can do it. The free safety comes over the top and comes late to the inside.

We tell the Jack linebacker he has the reverse on plays away from him. We want him to go meet the reverse runner instead of waiting for him to come to him. What we do not want is five players holding for the reverse on the backside and six defenders on the frontside playing the power.

The Will linebacker is playing the ball from the inside out. He is the cutback defender should the ball break back inside. We play the same way to the weakside. The Jack linebacker blows up the fullback's block, the Will linebacker comes over the top, and the Mike linebacker is full flow, playing inside out. The free safety follows the play to the line of scrimmage.

We use single movement in our defensive line. These are individual movements for the defensive ends and the nose. The *gap* move is for the strongside defensive end. He takes a lateral step and penetrates the B gap. *Tag* is the same stunt for the weakside defensive end, except he goes from the 3-technique alignment into the A gap. The *nasty* is a stunt for the nose. He penetrates the strongside A gap any way he chooses. He can rip through or swim through based on what is successful for him.

The *stab* is a two-man stunt between the Sam linebacker and the defensive end (Diagram #12). The end goes first and rips through the C gap. The Sam linebacker is tilted on the tight end and comes off the defensive end's butt and into the B gap. The nose on this stunt runs a nasty movement into the A gap to that side.

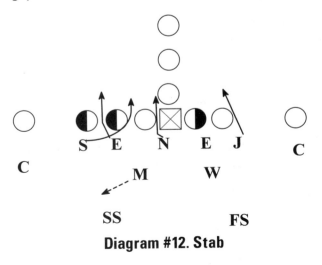

Diagram #12. Stab

The stab stunt is the Sam linebacker in the B gap. That is an "S" for Sam and a "b" for B gap. The *stick* stunt is the Sam linebacker through the C gap. The *sad* stunt is the Sam linebacker through the D gap. That is the way we call our stunts. On the stick, the end runs his gap stunt. On the sad stunt, the defensive end takes the C gap. When we send the Sam linebacker on a stunt, the Mike linebacker takes the pass responsibility for the Sam.

We call the other stunts the same way. On the *mash* movement (Diagram #13), the nose moves to a G alignment on the guard. He moves across the guard's face and into the B gap. The Mike linebacker comes behind him into the A gap. The "m-a" in mash means Mike in the A gap.

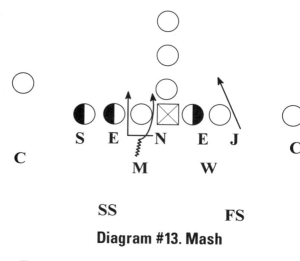

Diagram #13. Mash

The other Mike linebacker stunt we run is *mob*, which sends the Mike linebacker through the B gap. On the mob, the defensive end penetrates the C gap. On the *Mitch* movement, the Mike linebacker blitzes the C gap, and the defensive end run his gap charge into the B gap.

When we run stunts to the Will-linebacker side, we use "W" word stunt. *Wham* sends the Will linebacker on an A-gap blitz. When we run this stunt, the nose has to pressure the center in the strong A gap to keep the center off the Will linebacker. The defensive end has to work hard in the B gap to make sure the protection does not pass someone off on the linebacker. *Web* puts him into the B gap. The *Waco* becomes a three-man movement (Diagram #14). The end and Jack

linebacker take lateral steps and penetrate the gaps to their inside. The end goes through the A gap, and the Jack linebacker takes the B gap. The Will linebacker shuffles and comes outside in the C gap.

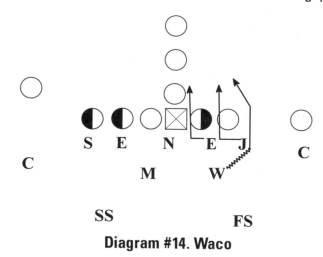

Diagram #14. Waco

We run a zone-blitz scheme with this defense. We call *Eagle 4*, and run a zone blitz (Diagram #15). The Sam linebacker who normally plays the tight end comes off the edge on a blitz. We get line movement away from the tight end. The defensive ends and nose take the gaps away from the tight end. The backside end has the containment to that side.

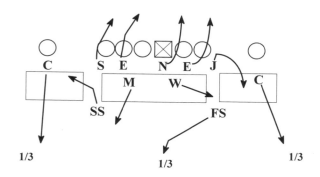

Diagram #15. Eagle-4

The Jack linebacker drops into the backside flat. We have three boxes of coverage underneath the zone blitz. They go from the flat to the curl on the strongside, from hook to hook in the middle, and curl to flat on the backside. We use a press-bail technique on the wide receiver. The corners align in a press cover on the wide receivers and bail out to cover the deep third. The free safety covers the middle third. The strong safety rolls down and plays the flat-curl zone to the strongside. The Mike and Will linebacker play hook to curl in the middle, and the Jack linebacker plays the flat to curl zone in the weakside zone.

The change-up with this zone blitz is *Eagle 4X* (Diagram #16). This is the same movement with the exception of the strongside end and nose. The nose goes across the guard's face into the B gap. The defensive end runs a double-stick movement into the weakside A gap. He comes flat to the line and turns up around the center.

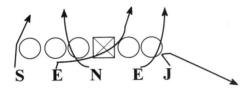

Diagram #16. Eagle 4X

When we run our max blitz, we bring both the Mike and Will linebackers (Diagram #17). We are in zero coverage in the secondary. As the Mike and Will blitz, they are attacking the back as they come through the gaps. The Mike linebacker goes first, and the Will goes second. Mike goes through the weakside A gap, and Will comes through the strongside B gap. We fill all the gaps on the rush.

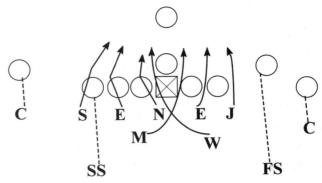

Diagram #17. Max Blitz

With the blitz scheme, we run twist moves between the ends and nose. In one stunt, the end goes first and the nose comes around. The second stunt sends the nose first, and the end comes under. We can work it to both sides of the defense. When we game plan, we include one max blitz and one zone blitz for each game.

I appreciate you having me. I will be around, and we can talk some ball.

Andrew Coverdale

ESTABLISHING THE ALLEY SCREEN PASS

Trinity High School, Kentucky

Today, I am going to discuss a topic that has been very good for us over a number of years. I used this package when I was at Castle High School in southern Indiana. There were a couple of years where all we could do was to throw this pass. It has also been good to us since I returned to Trinity High School in Louisville. We call the pass our alley screen pass.

There are different places where the screen pass can hit. It is not a screen pass that takes place on the numbers, or necessarily a screen pass that takes place over the tackle box. It is a screen pass in which we are trying to create an alley, starting about six yards off the leg of the offensive tackle. We are going to build an alley of blockers with our frontside guard, center, backside guard, and receiver kicking out to create a funnel for our receiver to work through.

The play originated at the University of Toledo. Several years ago, we visited with Rob Spence who was at Toledo at the time, and who is now at Clemson. What Rob Spence did for our screen game was to provide us with a tangible understanding of the play. He gave us landmarks. He detailed specific things that we could coach, rather than telling the players to run to the alley and to hit anyone in the alley. He gave us ways to solve our screen game.

At this point, this is a legitimate attitude play for us. It is not an accessory play. We feel that this play makes everything else go for us offensively. We have a reputation of being a passing team. In reality, however, we are a balanced offensive team. Last year, we were very close to being 50-50 on the run and pass.

If the defense is going to load up against our running game with certain types of run blitzes in the interior of our core, this play is a great answer. If the 5 techniques are going to get in a jet stance and rush up the field, this pass is a great answer. If you are going to pressure our passing game with pressure off the edge, and use secondary rotations, this play call is an answer. This pass is something we are going to look to establish early in the game, as opposed to calling it when we have to call it. We are going to rep this play enough, where we feel we are going to be effective with it against almost any defense.

There is a time commitment on the play. We find teams trying to stop this play as one of the four plays they try to stop against us. Our view is it is okay because it takes away from the defensive pass rush, and other factors that they might otherwise like to do defensively in a game.

There are positive residual effects we can talk about as we install this play. It takes time to develop. We do not throw other types of screen passes. We employ this concept and dress it up in a lot of different ways, but we use the same rules all of the time. This is our number one screen-pass concept. We also have a slower developing throwback screen that we use. We rep these plays a number of times. We utilize those two concepts as our screen package, rather than using six or seven different elements.

At this point, I would like to give you the basic rules of the alley-screen route and detail as much technique as I can in the time span I have. Regardless of what your offensive structure is, I think this scheme can be a positive addition to your offense.

Diagram #1 illustrates what the play looks like. Initially, I'd like to show you what we are trying to establish and then go over some relevant coaching points regarding the play. Finally, I would like to cover the responsibilities of each position in order to give you some insight into what we are trying to do on the play.

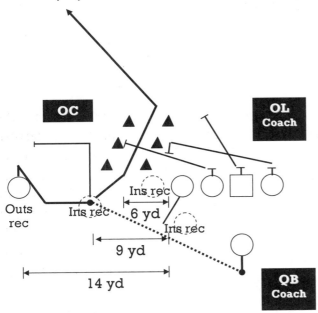

Diagram #1. Alley Screen Big Picture

My primary goal today is for you to have an idea and insight into what this play is about when you leave here. Subsequently, you can research the play and discuss the play with your staff to a point where you feel you would be able to coach the play successfully and address any problem that might otherwise come up on the play.

The underlying concept of the play is to create an alley. As much as we can, we are always going to talk to our kids in terms of pictures. If a player can get a picture of what is supposed to occur on the play, he can see what we are trying to do. At that point, he should be able to see himself in the picture. We hope all of the techniques that we give him will make sense. We want him to have something to which to attach the techniques on the play.

The "picture" of the alley screen is fairly straightforward. Almost every coach, at one time or another, has seen Vince Lombardi with his chalk talk, where he talks about sealing on the 28 sweep play, with Paul Hornung running the ball. He talks about sealing in the alley. On the alley screen, we are doing the same thing, except it involves a little different setting.

The alley starts six yards from the tackle. We name all of the parts of the play. The area where the receiver is going to receive the pass is the junction point. This point is six yards from the tackle (Diagram #2). This designated area is an important point for us, one with which we are very exacting for several reasons.

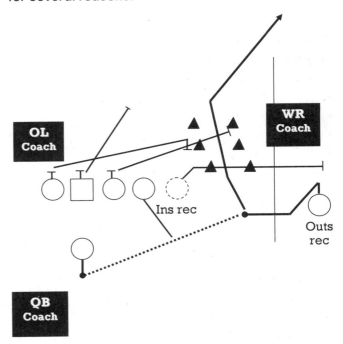

Diagram #2. Alley Screen Junction Point

We create an alley that is protected by four players. The first man to protect the area is the receiver who is inside the intended receiver. He protects the upper outer edge of the alley. The frontside guard seals and protects the lower edge of the alley. Our center walls-off (protects) the inside middle edge of the alley. The backside guard protects the lower inside edge of the alley. Collectively, these four players know how each of them relates to the alley. In turn, their technique arises out of their interrelationship.

We made one major change to our screen seven years ago, which involved our center and tackle. We deep-set the onside tackle, as opposed to having him in the actual screen, in order to have a consistent play. We do not want the 5 technique to come across the line of scrimmage and bat the screen pass down. When we were pulling the onside tackle on the play, we could not effectively control the defensive tackle on the playside. We give up that onside tackle as a lead blocker and create the alley in other ways in exchange for getting more predictability out of the 5-technique tackle.

Before we teach an assignment or teach the play, we want all 11 players to know both what the alley is and what the junction point is. In reference to the tackle, we also want them to know what the window is.

Our last two quarterbacks were 5'9" and 5'8". A few years ago, we had a 6'4" quarterback who was very good. In reality, however, all of our quarterbacks have been able to execute this alley screen play, regardless of their height. We believe that the primary reason for this is that we create a window for the quarterback to throw the ball in with our onside tackle. Using the tackle to control the rush of the 5 technique, we create a lane into which the quarterback can throw.

The aforementioned are the starting points for our alley screen. These factors provide the basis of where we begin our thought process regarding the play.

Next, I would like to discuss the way we introduce the play to our players. This information can provide you with an advance warning of some of the problems you might face involving this play. In turn, I would also like to give you some ideas that could help you correct the problems that might come up.

The first point I'd like to make is that alley screens are the ATTITUDE plays of our screen game. All factors considered, the alley screen may not sound very physical. It is, however. In fact, we also have an attitude run, which is our wide-zone play, and an attitude pass, which is our semi-sprint flat route, in addition to our attitude screen. On all of three of these plays, we execute the details and MAKE them work, no matter *what* our opponents try to do to us defensively.

The fundamental precept behind all quick screens is to *divide the defense* with our blockers, creating an "alley" in which to run, and attack it

with fast guys running into that space, thereby forcing slower defenders to chase it from inside out.

Next, I'd like to discuss two screens that we utilize—one version, which involves throwing to a two-receiver surface, and a second version that entails throwing to a three-receiver surface. Both screens have simple, almost identical rules that allow us to execute them against any defensive scheme we see, while at the same time giving us the ability to get the ball in space to any of our five eligible receivers.

These plays are a viable *threat* for us on any down and distance and on any part of the field, especially base downs, second-and-long situations, and third downs where we expect blitz. As a result, our entire passing game is better because the pass rush is discouraged.

One of the critical factors we stress concerning this play is the fact that we can feature different players from year to year in the play, depending on their ability. As such, we have a system for calling the alley screen that is flexible enough to get any of our five eligible receivers involved in catching the screen. We never know who the featured receiver is going to be from year to year.

Alley screens offer a number of benefits. For example, alley screens of all types are excellent ball-control plays against zones. They are also an effective tool for attacking blitzes. In addition, they are *always* one-to-two missed tackles away from going the distance. Our quarterback has the capability to check to this play if he sees the blitz coming, which indicates how strongly we feel about utilizing the play against the blitz.

The following question points out the underlying value of executing the alley screen play. On third down-and-eight to go, what are your chances to gain the first down? If you're fortunate, you may have a special quarterback and special receivers. On most years, however, you are not going to have those special players. What are your chances of all five of your linemen to execute pass protection for 3.2 seconds, get all of your receivers split correctly, and get them to run their proper depths, working to the holes of a zone defense, and have the quarterback show enough poise to stand in the pocket under pressure, get through his progression, and complete the pass?

We had a good quarterback this year, and our percentages of accomplishing the aforementioned was less than 50 percent. Similar to most teams, we were not very good in third-and-eight situations.

In most cases, I believe that our percentages would be better on the alley screen to get the first down on third-and-eight than it would be on a dropback pass.

The key point to note about the alley screen in this situation is that it is not a give-up play for us on a third-and-eight. As such, this play makes a lot of sense for the world in which most of us live. When we employ it, the defense had better hope that they are blitzing in the right area against the play.

With regard to the alley screen, there are certain things that you should know as a coach. Similarly, if you want your team to effectively execute the alley screen, there are certain factors that you should emphasize to your players. First, the pass is an easy completion, but in some ways, it is a hard throw. The quarterback cannot just complete it or throw the pass to any guy. It involves a very specific kind of throw with a specific level of finesse. Furthermore, it has to be thrown to a specific spot. The quarterback must be accurate on the throw. He has to be able to throw the ball exactly where he needs to put it, and precisely when he wants to put it there. Doing this takes a ton of reps. As such, the quarterback must follow his routine on all screen plays, which is one of the keys to the success of the play.

Keys to a Successful Play

- The quarterback gets on his toes and helps the screen receiver by throwing him a chin-high ball into the funnel.
- The screener and inside blockers align with correct spacing.

- The inside blocker charts his course with a pre-read and his eyes, times his block with the catch, and makes his man run under by attacking the high shoulder.
- The screener uses correct line of scrimmage footwork, catches the ball at the "junction point" at 85 percent speed, gets into the funnel (or alley), and finds his cut-read off the center's block.
- The frontside tackle uses a convincing pass set to create a "window."
- The center and frontside guard set correctly to an edge, and run full-speed courses that are led with their eyes.
- The backside guard cleans up, spying the defensive lineman with effective ambushes.

It should be noted that the term funnel is the same as the term alley. The receiver cannot have a pass on his backside hip. He cannot have a pass thrown to him that he has to strain to catch. The quarterback must throw the ball in a way that keeps the receiver in his timing and the flow of the course he is running to make the screen pass time up correctly. The ball should be on the receiver's chin, leading the receiver into the alley. The quarterback should have to get up on his toes to make that throw. In reality, he will have to make a lot of throws under duress.

Exact spacing is critical on the play. Players have to be at certain spots at certain times. The blockers should be engaging their man just as the receiver gets the ball. We do not want them to engage either early or late. The blockers should engage their man just as the screen receiver gets to the proper spot.

The man inside the screen man needs to line up five yards away from him. The screen man lines up 14 yards off the offensive tackle. We do not have our receivers go out and count off 14 yards as they come out of the huddle. What we do is teach them how to use certain landmarks on the field. We use these landmarks to help our blockers to get on the defenders at the correct time, so exact spacing is critical.

The man blocking for the screen receiver must do a great job with his eyes. He must understand the type of block he must employ on the play. We can execute the play against press corners. A unique technique is required by the man who is blocking for the screener. To a great degree, the success of the blocker involves his eyes and pre-snap recognition.

One factor that everyone must understand concerning the play is that if each player does his job correctly, it will make the job of the man inside of him much easier.

Another important factor involving the play is that the screener must use correct footwork in order to help the man blocking for him to execute his block. The blocker protecting the screener must do a good job against the man over the screener before he sets up to block in order to set up the block for the onside guard. On and on it goes down the line.

Proper timing is also essential for the screener. He has to hit the junction point when he is supposed to hit it. He has to time it with all of the blockers. The way he does this is by running 85 percent speed, which should get him there at the right time.

One of the problems we sometimes have with our receivers is them not being physical enough. Almost every coach has encountered this problem with their players. Almost no receiver likes to go into traffic.

As such, we rep the play a ton of times against air. We try to give our kids some confidence that they can make the catch on the play while running at 85 percent. All factors considered, good things are going to happen when they can do that. If you run the play live the first day, and the receiver gets stung by one of the defenders who is otherwise slow to react on the play, the receiver will not catch the pass. In fact, he may never catch it again. Consequently, you should practice against air, before you go live on the play.

Another reason we practice the play on air is to establish the proper timing and rhythm of the play. We work on getting the other players to the right places. Then, we start adding rip bags, and then

defenders on the play. The receiver has to trust the value of running at 85-percent speed into the alley. He cannot tiptoe into the alley.

The frontside tackle must use a convincing pass-set to create a "window." The frontside guard and center must take a great set. When our pulling linemen, especially the center and frontside guard, have to convince the defenders over them that they (the offensive linemen) are beaten. We need to do a better job this next year because more and more teams are doing a better job of reading with their defensive linemen.

The pulling linemen must set the correct edge on the play. They must allow penetration by the defensive linemen. They must get out into their pull course on time. If they get too tangled with the defensive linemen, they are not going to get out on time, and the defensive linemen are not going to penetrate on the play.

Another potentially troublesome factor on the play is the fact that the players must run full speed to space on the screen, which is the most difficult thing that the offensive linemen have to do on this play.

The play can be varied in a number of ways. Because we have a good running back, we are starting to marry the play to a swing screen on the frontside. In this instance, the alley part of the screen is our second read. We are getting the ball to our running back early if we can. Another thing we have done on the screen is to fake a running play to hold the linebackers and defensive linemen to allow our linemen to get into the alley and get fit up on the defenders.

Next, I'd like to review the technique for each position—position by position. Coaches must commit practice time to working on these techniques in order to be successful. On Monday, we hit all of our screens five minutes each (Diagram #3). Doing so gives us a 15-minute screen period on air.

On Tuesday, the first thing we do for five minutes is a team takeoff period. At this point, we conduct all of our alley screens against bags,

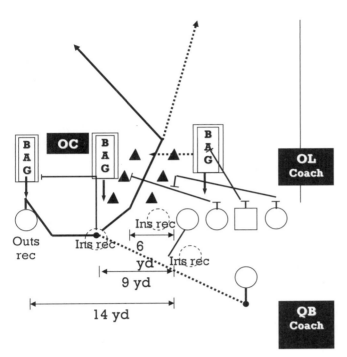

Diagram #3. Alley Screen L vs. Bags

against the look we are going to see that week (Diagram #4). During practice that day, we rep the five best versions of our alley screen against the defensive scheme of our next opponent. This step gives us live work on the play on Tuesdays.

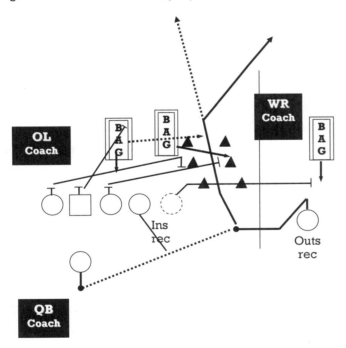

Diagram #4. Alley Screen R vs. Bags

If we do not like where we are with the play, we can rep it again on Thursdays. As such, we hit the

play two or three times during each week. We feel we must spend this much time on the play for the timing to be as precise as we want it.

As mentioned previously, we employ two versions of the alley screen. The first is to a two-receiver surface, and the second one is to a three-receiver surface.

The two-receiver screen always goes to the outside receiver. If you have a twin set, or an outside set, the outside man is going to get the ball. The blocker for the screener does not always have to be the slot receiver. It could either be a tight end or a back. You can give the play different looks. In a pro set, the screen could be thrown to the Z back with the tight end blocking for him.

The three-receiver screen can be thrown either to the outside or the middle receiver. We tend to throw this pass to the wide side of the field, but not always. We tend to throw the two-receiver screen to the boundary, but not always. We can throw both screens to either side of the formations and to either side of the field.

If you are the outside receiver to the callside, you are getting the screen pass. The receiver is 14 yards from the tackle. Ideally, we would like for him to be off the ball, although he does not have to be. We do not want to give anything away. All things being equal, however, we would like the screener to be off the ball. What does 14 yards from the tackle mean? If the ball is in the middle of the field, 14 yards from the tackle is going to be in the middle of the numbers on the field. If the ball is on the far hash mark, and the receiver is on the wide side of the field, the 14 yards will place him two yards outside the hash mark.

If the receiver is on the short side of the field, we tell the receiver we want him three to four yards from the sideline, which will give us the spacing we want. This system of spacing makes it easier for him to work off the landmarks in the heat of a game, rather than try to figure out what 14 yards looks like in the heat of a game.

The receiver's footwork is based on what he sees from the cornerback. If the corner is off, meaning six yards deep or deeper, he is going to take one giant step and then come back to the funnel. If the receiver is working against a press corner, he takes three quick steps and gains width on those three quick steps. The quick three steps will get him to the same spot as one giant step gets him.

We use different footwork on the play in order to make the block of the inside man easier. If the block is against a press corner, he needs to turns the hips of that press corner. We do not want a press corner who can sit and look at a block coming, and take on the blocker and beat him to the spot to which we are throwing the ball.

He must sell the fade route with his three steps. The tighter the corner is, the wider the receiver must get on those first three steps. He must be convincing with his head and shoulders. There has to be a lot of movement, but not much ground covered, on those first three steps.

After the receiver makes his initial three steps, he comes behind the line of scrimmage back to the ball. He is running at 85-percent speed (Diagram #5). When he arrives at the junction spot, the ball should meet him and take him into the funnel or alley.

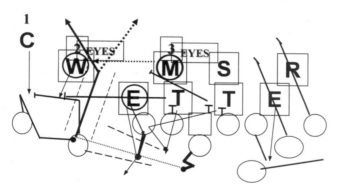

Diagram #5. Alley Screen—Two-Receiver Side

We have encountered several issues on the play that are interesting. For example, we had one receiver who did not want to run his route flat. He would always get up the field before he caught the ball. He ended up ahead of his blocking, which screwed up the timing on the play. Another issue occurred when the receiver was not able to get to the funnel fast enough. He would run at half speed. As a result, he did not end up in the proper

relationship with the blocker when he caught the ball.

The slot receiver on the play should be split five yards inside the screen man. His responsibility is to block the man over the screener. In the two-man receiver version, that defender is always the cornerback. The block should be made when the screener catches the ball.

If it is a corner who is playing off the receiver, the blocker should push at the corner as long as he can. He wants to soften the alley defender as much as possible. If the defender is an off-corner, the blocker should work upfield to his upfield shoulder. The shortest path for the corner to tackle the screener is over the top, which is why we want to stay on the corner at the top of the play. We coach the blocker to lead with his eyes.

If the corner is pressing, we engage the man and look at him to get him to follow the blocker. If he follows the inside receiver, it will widen the alley for the lineman who is coming to block him. The thing we must accomplish with the inside receiver is to get his helmet between the corner and the screen receiver. Otherwise, the corner can get behind the screen man and follow him to the alley and blow up the play. Another way to say the same thing is to tell the blocker to rub shoulders with the screener, which will assure that the corner does not get inside the blocker to the screen receiver.

The frontside tackle has the window block. As such, achieving the proper splits is essential. If we are too tight, it makes it hard for the defensive line to penetrate the way we want them to. In this instance, we take a yardstick split, which we call *whopper* splits. A problem we had with this terminology is that our right tackle insisted that he did not eat junk food. As a result, we had to call them *Subway* splits. Our normal split is two feet. On occasion, we may have overcompensated on the splits.

You want the offensive tackle to have a healthy split. You want him in an upright stance, because that indicates pass. He must be committed. We tell him he has French army rules. What does the French army do best? They know how to retreat and back up. We want the tackle to back up as quickly as he can, just like the French army.

On the other hand, if he is a good tackle, he wants to sit on the line and engage the defense. We do not want that to happen. He wants vertical kick in a hurry. We want him to get in three vertical kicks back, before he engages the defender, which is his goal. By doing that quickly, the defender will tell him what he is going to do by that time. He is trying to create a window. He kicks for depth, with urgency. Doing so will entice the defender to get up the field to create the window we want.

If the defensive end crosses the face of the onside tackle, or if he just sits on the line, the tackle gets out of the kick slide, and goes after the end with his outside arm through his ribcage and protects that window by crushing him down inside. The most important aspect for the tackle is the window.

If the defensive end comes to the tackle, he takes his three steps, and then with his inside arm, clubs him up the field. This scenario takes the defensive end beyond the window. It also gives the quarterback the throwing lane we want. If the defensive end goes upfield, we club him on the third kick. If he sits or crosses the tackle's face, the tackle drives him inside.

The tackle adheres to the same rules that all linemen have. If he has a down lineman over him who "quicks" out or zone drops, then all of the other rules are off. We have no window, no pull, no nothing. In this instance, his rule is to go get the defender who just "quicked" out of the line. We want to get a hat on that defender, who will be the most dangerous man to the screen.

While we do not see a lot of true fire zones, we don't wait until we play a team that runs the fire zone before we put the rule to counter it into our screen package. In fact, we put such a rule in from the very beginning and rep it sparingly.

Two things happen when the defense drops a man off the line. First, that man becomes the most dangerous man to the screen play. Second, if the defense is dropping a man, the defense will usually have a man blitzing to replace the man who dropped off the line. We can let the blitz man go. Good things will happen if we can put a hat on the man dropping off the line.

The frontside guard and center are going to use the count system. We count from the outside to the inside. The corner is always number one, the outside linebacker or safety is number two, and the next backer inside (the next person who is not in a down stance) is going to be the number three man.

The guard sets the outside edge of the alley by kicking out the number two man. The center sets the inside edge or the alley by sealing or running the number three defender by the alley. These rules help us, because they hold up against all kinds of different defenses.

The most important factor for the two players setting the alley is to take the correct set. This step requires the most work. You must play on one edge or the other of the defensive lineman. If the defender gets down the middle of the guard or center, he is going to gobble them up. That situation makes it impossible to release, and it is impossible for him to penetrate if he is splitting the blocker.

In general, we like the blockers to set to the nearest edge of the defensive lineman. The defensive lineman should not be allowed to play down the middle of the blocker. Having depth off the ball helps in this situation, especially against slanting linemen.

We only set for one count. It is one thousand—and we are gone. It is fast. Once we set, we pull flat on a full-speed course for either the number two or number three defender, depending on whomever the blocker is assigned.

In this regard, several problems can arise, For example, you only want one blocker on any down lineman. The center and guard must talk with each other. It does not matter who is right or wrong. At times, they both treat the A-gap tackle as their man. If that happens, we have two players punching one defensive lineman, which keeps that defensive man from penetrating. As a result, that tackle is a threat to ooze back into the alley. The blockers must communicate with each other.

If an uncovered lineman is not setting off a defensive lineman, he should open to the side where there is more open air so that he does not become tangled. If the center cannot get his head by the number three defender, he should try to run his head by the alley. His eyes are key. When players miss blocks, it is usually because they are not flat enough.

The backside guard has a one-count ambush. He sets inside the defensive lineman over him, regardless of the technique the defender is in. He takes a one-count block, turns his back to the line of scrimmage, and sprints to a front corner of the alley. He wants to meet any defensive lineman who tries to ooze outside. Tempo is the key in this instance. He should not look around for someone to block, until after he has established his position on the front edge of the alley.

The other tackle has a window set, just like the frontside tackle. Both window sets are the same. The backside receivers try to get into the touchdown alley. Occasionally, we call mirror and fake the screen one way and throw it back to the other side.

If a play is called where the running back is not involved, he swings to the opposite side of the play. We say swing with urgency.

The quarterback uses a straight drop, with small steps. It is really a three-step thought process. We want the running back and quarterback to control the number four defensive player. We have the quarterback either fake or look at the swing back, in order to distract the number four defender and make him a non-factor in the play.

We want the quarterback to have a rhythm in his head and throw the ball on rhythm every time. The only way to do that is through reps, reps, reps, and more reps.

Although we run the play out of the shotgun set, the play can be executed with the quarterback under the center. The quarterback takes three steps under control when he is in the gun. He gives

active eyes to the swing back. If he uses a pump fake, it must not slow him down on the play. The minute he gets on his third step, he gets up on his toes, and simultaneously releases the ball. He cannot get up on his toes and then load to throw. By then, it is too late.

The throw should not be a line drive. Rather, the throw should have a little touch. There is a small hump on the ball. The quarterback should lead the receiver up into the funnel. We do not want to slow the receiver down with a pass below his waist or a ball thrown to his back shoulder.

From the screener's standpoint, we want to be very precise. We want him to read the defender, and then get up in the alley, and immediately jump back outside and get to the sideline, which is where the clean air is going to be. We want it to be clear to the receivers that we want them to get up in the alley and then to get back outside and down the sideline. This is where the big plays are going to happen.

Next, I'd like to discuss the three-receiver alley screen. Everything is almost exactly the same for this screen play as for the two-receiver version. If we do not make a special call, the screen is going to the middle receiver (Diagram #6). The screen's split is still 14 yards from the tackle. The landmarks are the exact same. An outside receiver who is not called into the screen should maximize his split and block the corner.

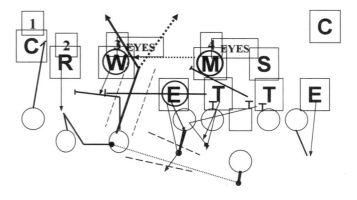

Diagram #6. Alley Screen—Three-Receiver Side

The only thing that changes in the three-receiver alley screen version is that one is added to the numbers our linemen are blocking on the play. In this instance, the guard is going to kick out the number three defender, and the center is sealing the number four man (the Mike linebacker). We expect the quarterback to control the number five man (the Sam linebacker). By adding a third receiver, we are going to get an additional defender in the area.

The two- and three-receiver screens change by game plans. In some years, our slot backs were our best receivers. In those instances, we used more three-receiver versions. When our best receiver is an outside receiver, we employ the two-receiver version.

We do not block blitzing backers or deep backs on the play. We let them go, which is what we want. We love the defense when they blitz from depth. All the other rules hold up.

The play can be executed from several different formations. When you set the play up, you should make sure that everyone has a chance to be the man who receives the ball on the screen. Keep in mind that the best screen man may not be your best receiver. We give different players a chance to get a feel for this play. You may be surprised. You can create formations that get the best screen man the ball. Fortunately, achieving this objective is not complicated.

At this point, I'd like to show some film that illustrates the points that I have been trying to make. The way we drill this play is one of the best things we do. We want to build the components of the screen bit by bit. We want to develop an environment where the players have confidence and gradually acquire the skills and techniques required to run the play successfully. Running the plays against air has allowed us to gain a couple of things. For example, we get a lot of reps real quickly. It has also enabled us to get a look at different players doing different things. It has helped us make the whole alley screen visual for the players. When we set up the drill, we have bags set up for the alley. We use different color cones to designate where the junction box is and where the spacing should be for the receivers on the field.

We want the bags and cones to create a picture that our players can grasp and have stay with them. They must understand where they have to go in relationship to different people. We set the play up on different hash marks so they get a feel for the different landmarks. One thing we did that helped us this year was to conduct a drill walk-through before practice, in which we worked on both types of the alley screen.

A few years ago, I discovered that I was spending too much time in practice telling everyone who was on offense, who was on defense, and how the demonstrators were to perform. Subsequently, we started having drill walk-throughs in pre-practice. In these exercises, we walked through each drill we were going to use in practice and let the players know what we wanted on each drill. That saved us a lot of time in practice and enabled me to stop wasting my players' time.

Thank you for your attention today. Please contact me if I can help you in any way.

NUTS AND BOLTS OF THE 3-4 DEFENSE

Pike High School, Indiana

My name is Derek Moyers. I am the head football coach at Pike High School. It is a pleasure for me to be part of this clinic. When asked to speak, I was told to speak on our defense. I do not coach our defense, so I brought my defensive coordinator with me. He will give the lecture today on the Multiple 3-4 Package. Let me introduce Coach Pat Echeverria.

PAT ECHEVERRIA

We play what we call a 3-4 defense. We call it that because our defensive ends like to be called linebackers. When I started out, I ran a 4-4 defense, which evolved over time into more of a 50-front philosophy. Today, I'd like to discuss the nuts and bolts of our defense.

As the following six key factors illustrate, our defensive philosophy is relatively simple.

PHILOSOPHY

- Hustle and attitude
- Tackling and technique
- Play within the defense
- Get the ball back to our offense
- Take away our opponent's best plays
- Score

Every defense must have hustle and play with an attitude. When we coach tackling, we like to drill it in a game-type situation. We want our players to know their responsibilities and the responsibilities of the people around them. I think one of the most important things you can do for your defense is to explain why they have a responsibility. If you coach a player to keep outside leverage, but he does not know why, you compromise his ability to be an effective football player. When we talk about leverage, he needs to know why he is playing that way and where his help is.

We want to get the ball back for our offense. We want to turn the opponent over or hold them on third down. We want as many "three-and-out" situations as we can get. Given the fact that our offense averaged 30 points a game, we want them with the ball as much as possible. We want to turn "take-aways" into scores.

Our players know through the scouting report and film study what the opponent's best plays are. We practice against those plays and come up with stunts to stop them. Football is the only sport I know where the defense can score. We want to take advantage of that fact. In fact, we turned the opponents over 35 times this year. Defensively, we scored two touchdowns and two safeties this year and had four or five touchdowns called back by penalties.

My beliefs as a defensive coordinator are fairly straightforward:

- Be demanding about effort and hustle
- Coach your athletes to be football players, not robots
- Be multiple in looks, not in techniques
- Do not allow quick scores
- Play zone coverage
- Get inside the head of the offensive coordinator
- Do not let the offense control what you run

If a player does not put forth the expected effort, he will not play. I want each player to know his assignment. At the same time, however, he has to think about situations within a game. We do not want a mechanical player; we want an athlete who makes plays. We can constantly change the front, but the techniques in that front have to remain consistent. If an offense scores on us, it has to be after a long drive. We do not want to give up a quick score, because of the mental impact that it can have on our attitude.

I like zone coverage. My background is in that type of scheme. I have been at schools that did not have the talent we have at Pike High School. I was anxious to see how we played this defense when we had talent. While the principles are the same, the coverage is better when you have talent.

We play the defense that we call from the sidelines. I do not let the offense force me out of a defensive call. This approach instills confidence in our players. It does, however, require mental capacity to make the necessary adjustments to check out of a stunt. Although we adjust to the way the offense plays during a game, we do not let them run us out of a defensive call.

We run the 3-4 defense because it gives us flexibility in personnel and alignment. You can play this defense with 11 players whose weight averages 180 pounds. In fact, I played this defense when I was coaching AA football with a 5-3, 130-pound middle linebacker.

You can play the defense with a variety of players when you play with four linebackers and four defensive backs. The alignment and adjustments are very simple. The safeties and outside linebackers are our primary adjusters. In our system, we do not adjust too much. In the 3-4 defense, slanting and blitzing cause confusion for the offense. I played offensive line in college at DePaul University. The main reason I got out of the 4-4 defense was to play with a four-deep secondary. I wanted to play cover-2. I think cover-2 is great against passing offenses and gives you good support on the run.

For communication, we name most of our defenders (Diagram #1). Certain players travel in our scheme, depending on the formation. We can better identify the positions by naming them. We play a fox, nose, tackle, end, Sam, Mike, and bandit. In the secondary, we have two safeties and two corners.

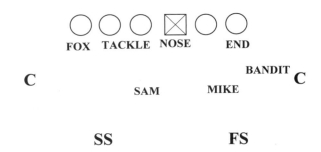

Diagram #1. Defensive Alignment and Names

When we set our front, we set our personnel to the field or bench. The fox, tackle, Sam, and strong safety always go to the wideside of the field. We want to put our best players to the side of the field that is harder to defend. If the offense wants to run into the bench, we have an extra defender to that side. The defender is the sideline.

We make our strength call to the more-receiver side. If the formation is balanced, we declare the strength to the field. We can change either of those calls by a huddle call, if needed. We can mix up the calls depending on the offense we play. If the opponent is a strong running team, we can put the running strength to the tight end and the secondary to the multiple-receiver side.

When we number our techniques, we start at the center and go outside each way (Diagram #2). On the center, are two shade techniques and a zero. Moving outside, we number numerically from the inside shoulder of the guard to the outside shoulder of the tight end. The difference occurs at the tackle where the inside shoulder is four, the head up is five, and the outside shoulder is six. The end techniques are seven, eight, and nine. As a result, the head-up position on the tight end is an 8-technique.

Diagram #2. Defensive Numbering

If we call "55 strong whip-2," that tells us a number of things. Fifty-five is our front. Strong indicates the stunt or slant of the defensive line. We can slant strong or weak, field, or bench, and tight or open. As a result, we have six different ways to move the front with the same technique every time.

You have to coordinate the blitz with the front movement. If the slant is strong, we blitz from the weakside. If the slant is weak, we come off the strongside. The "whip" in the call is a blitz from the weakside outside linebacker. The number two is the coverage.

The first number in "55" goes to the strongside defensive tackle, which we call "tackle." The second number in the call is for the weakside defensive tackle, which we call "end." The tackle and end in our terminology are our defensive tackles. The number "55" puts both defensive tackles in 5 techniques or head-up on the offensive tackles.

In a "55" alignment, the nose aligns head-up the center. As long as the numbers are the same, the nose is in a zero technique on the center. If the numbers are different, he shades the center to the side of the biggest number. For example, if the defense were "63," the nose would shade the center to the tackle's side, since the tackle is the first number. If the number were "36," the nose would shade toward the end. You can run any variety of fronts with this numbering system.

The outside linebacker also aligns from the numbers. The smaller the number, the more the outside linebacker tightens up his alignment, unless we call "stud," which I will talk about later.

In our defensive front, we use a head-up alignment 90 percent of the time. This set-up keeps the offensive linemen from knowing which gap the defender has. We line up one or two feet off the ball. That distance off the ball provides us with a better angle in the slant. It also gives us time to redirect before we make contact with the offensive lineman. Because we are off the line, we can flinch and not be offsides. This factor is particularly important if you are playing with smaller defensive linemen. Being off the ball helps the defenders use their quickness.

We employ two types of keys—a visual key and a pressure key. The visual key is what the offensive linemen see once the offense snaps the ball. The visual key is what the defender attacks off the ball. The pressure key comes from an adjacent offensive lineman, for example, a down block from outside the defender's position. In a slant technique, the defender's visual key is the man he slants toward, while his pressure key is the man he leaves. He feels the pressure key and sees the visual.

Our defensive linemen utilize two techniques. We play straight and slant techniques. On the straight technique, we play through the outside number of the offensive linemen. We are always heavy to one side of the offensive linemen. We use a six-inch step with the foot on the side of our gap. We fire the hands into the blocker's chest and armpit.

In our slant technique, we want to get to the hip of the next offensive lineman. We do not tell our players to slant to a gap because that allows the defensive lineman to be cut off. If the defensive lineman thinks gap, he does not get far enough into the gap. He has to think about the hip of the offensive lineman, so he gets into that gap. In the slant technique, we use a six-inch step at a 45-degree angle to the next gap. We step with the gap-side foot. We want to rip-and-step with the opposite arm and foot on the second step. We can slant from either a head-up position or a shade position.

The outside linebacker is a hybrid player—half-defensive lineman and half linebacker. He aligns in a two-point stance, with his outside foot slightly back. He steps with his inside foot and keys through the end man to the near back. He forces all run plays back inside or deep, bouncing them to the outside. He plays the counter and bootleg on plays away from him. He never runs straight up the field.

The "fox" linebacker plays to the tight-end side of the formation. Against the tight end, he aligns with his inside foot on the outside foot of the tight end. He jams the outside number of the tight end and closes on the down block. He takes on all blocks with his inside arm and shoulder. The "bandit" linebacker plays to the open side of the formation or away from the fox. He loosens his alignment, plays off the line, and stems inside to outside. We play against the spread offense every day in practice. The "bandit" linebacker has to disguise where he is playing. He moves around between the receivers and the offensive tackle in order to disguise what his assignment is. He plays all blocks the same as the "fox" linebacker.

The middle linebackers align on the outside shoulder of the offensive guard, four-to-five yards off the line of scrimmage. The Mike linebacker aligns to the open side of the formation or away from the tight end. The Sam linebacker aligns to the strongside of the formation. Both linebackers key through the guard to the backfield. Their key can change, based on film study and the scouting report. They always have to know if the guard pulls or pass blocks.

The most important thing the linebacker must know is where the front goes. His gaps will change, based on the direction and call for the defensive line. He has to know which gap his tackle is supposed to fill. His fit is where the defensive tackle has slanted.

When the ball goes away from the linebackers, they stay behind the running back, playing for the cutback in the A-gap. They play over the top of all blocks at them. They cannot go under blocks. We never want to overcoach the linebackers. If you do that, you turn them into robots. We want them to make plays. We try to let them be football players and learn their fits through repetition.

If we play a "55-strong," our tackle and end align head-up on the offensive tackles, while the nose is head-up on the center (Diagram #3). We anchor the tackle and have him play with a straight technique. The nose and end defenders run a slant technique toward the tight-end side. If the tackle slants to the tight end and is washed to the outside, we'll have a tremendous gap in the B-gap. We decided to keep the tackle in a straight technique to help the linebacker.

The Sam linebacker knows the tackle plays heavy in the C-gap. On action toward him, his gap is the B-gap. On flow away from him, his gap is the weakside A-gap. The Mike linebacker on flow away has the weakside A-gap, and on flow toward him, he fills into the C-gap.

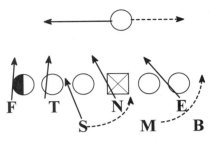

Diagram #3. 55-Strong

Another defensive movement we use is "55 pinch" (Diagram #4). On this movement, the tackle and end start out in 5 techniques head-up on the offensive tackles. They both slant inside to the hips of the guards. The nose plays a straight technique on the center. He does not have two gaps. Rather, he fights the pressure of the center. If the center turns him, the Mike or Sam linebackers play the A-gap on flow away. The Mike and Sam linebackers read the flow of the backs. They know that on flow to them, they are C-gap players. On flow away, they play A-gap away.

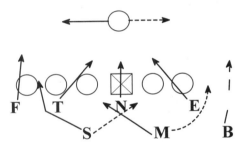

Diagram #4. 55-Pinch

We did not play much shade defense this year, but the following is how we get into it (Diagram #5). This defense is "63-whip." We played this defense against teams that unbalanced their line. Instead of shifting a whole man, we shifted a half-man. The down linemen play straight technique all the way across. The bandit cheats up and comes off the backside edge. The Sam and Mike linebackers play in the gaps not taken by the linemen. The Sam linebacker on flow to him plays the B-gap. On flow away from him, he plays the weakside A-gap. The Mike linebacker on flow to him has C-gap. On flow away, he plays the A-gap to his side.

This next defense is one of my favorites. The defense is "33-stud" (Diagram #6). The "stud" call

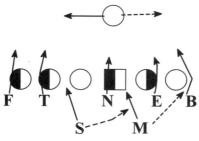

Diagram #5. 63-Whip

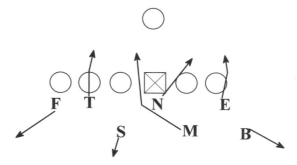

Diagram #7. 55-Switch

tells the strong safety he plays as a linebacker. I like the defense because it covers every alignment and frees the Sam and Mike linebackers. The defensive tackles move into 3 techniques to each side. The bandit comes to the line of scrimmage and comes off the edge. The safety drops down into a 7 technique on the tight end. We probably would play cover-1 coverage with this defense. Cover-1 for us is a man scheme.

have a two-tight end team or a power two-back team, we use this defense. The nose plays a straight technique, with the ends and outside linebacker pinching their inside gaps. We use this stunt in short-yardage situations. The Sam and Mike linebackers have to know they are responsible for the D-gaps. If the ball starts moving to the perimeter, they have to get there in a hurry.

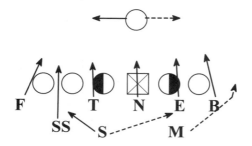

Diagram #6. 33-Stud

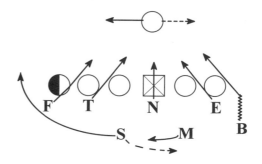

Diagram #8. 55-Jam

If the offense came out with a spread formation, with four wide receivers and one back, the Mike linebacker and strong safety are the adjusters in the defense. They are the defenders who come out of the box to play the slot receivers.

If we run a "55-switch," the Mike linebacker and the nose switch responsibilities (Diagram #7). The purpose of this blitz is to overload one side against a strong running team. The crossing motion in the stunt confuses the blocking scheme of the offensive line. It is a good run-and-pass stunt. The offensive line has to account for the Mike linebacker in their pass protection. We are sound on the run and have seven defenders in pass coverage. This blitz allows you to get a player to the weakside flat zone quickly.

The "55-jam" provides a good movement against inside running teams (Diagram #8). If you

The "55-cross" is a cross-stunt between the defensive tackle and end and the outside linebackers (Diagram #9). The tackle and end go first on an outside slant through the hip of the tight end. The tackle has to fight through the block of the tight end to get to the outside. If there is no tight end, he gets penetration across the line and turns quickly back inside. The outside linebackers take lateral steps and fire hard into the B-gaps. This stunt is good against the inside running game. It is not so effective against an outside running game, but it holds up well against the pass. We look for penetration from the tackle and end on the outside-slant move. We want them to get upfield as quickly as they can. Once they get to the outside, they turn back to the inside.

The nose plays a straight technique, and the Sam and Mike linebackers play the "cross" like the

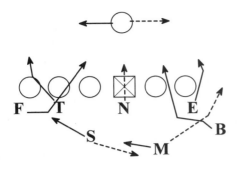

Diagram #9. 55-Cross

"jam." The stunt takes the B-gaps and C-gaps. In other words, the linebackers fill outside on flow toward them. On flow away, they must check the A-gap as they flow. This stunt is a good disruptive technique against a pass-protection scheme.

The "55-scrape weak" is a slant away from the tight end by the tackle and nose (Diagram #10). The end to the weakside plays a straight technique. The Sam linebacker plugs his C-gap immediately. This stunt brings a different player off the edge. On occasion, we also bring the "fox" linebacker on a C-gap slant in this stunt. If we bring the fox into the C-gap, we scrape the Sam linebacker in the D-gap. If we put the fox into the stunt, we have four rushers coming off the strongside.

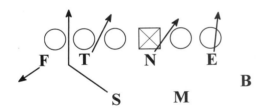

Diagram #10. 55-Scrape Weak

The "55 crash" stunt (Diagram #11) involves my favorite look of all time. I used to be scared of this stunt. This a great stunt to run from the hash mark. It is good if you are a big cover-2 or press man-coverage team. The offense never sees this player coming on the blitz. On "55-crash," we bring the corner off the edge. We like to bring the boundary corner to the outside off the edge. The bandit goes inside the offensive tackle through the B-gap. The end spikes two gaps into the weakside A-gap. The nose slants through the inside hip of the strongside guard, and the tackle plays straight in the C-gap.

The corner times his blitz and comes off the edge. If it is a running play, he blows it up. If it is a pass play, he is probably running clean. We can bring the stunt from the field or boundary. It is better coming from the boundary, because of the distance the corner has to go to get to the quarterback. He can wait longer before he moves, which disguises what he is doing.

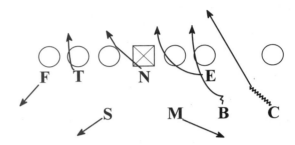

Diagram #11. 55-Crash (Field or Boundary)

Teams that run the ball to the boundary have to block the corner. This stunt was good for us. We bring the bandit linebacker on the stunt, and the fox linebacker drops into coverage.

When we play option from this defense, we do not give the defender a particular part of the option game as his responsibility. We assign gaps, rather than players to option responsibilities. The A- and B-gap players—usually a defensive lineman and an inside linebacker—have the dive back on an option. The C-gap player is responsible for the quarterback. He could be an inside or outside linebacker or the safety on some kind of change-up stunt. The D-gap player is responsible for the pitch. As a general rule, this defender is a secondary player or an outside linebacker.

If two players exchange a gap in a stunt, they also change the responsibility that goes with that gap. On the "scrape" stunt, the tackle starts out as a C-gap player, but stunts into the B-gap. He then has the dive back on the option. The Sam linebacker on the "scrape" stunt starts in the B-gap, but scrapes into the C-gap. He then becomes responsible for the quarterback. This adjustment allows the defense to align in multiple fronts and stunts, while keeping the assignments simple.

We have to make some of these exchanges on the fly. For instance, if the outside linebacker is responsible for the quarterback and the tight end blocks him, this defender will have trouble taking the quarterback. The safety who is responsible for the pitch sees the situation and takes the quarterback, while the outside linebacker works outside and takes the pitch.

We also have a stunt called "killer," which involves the same situation as the scrape stunt. On the "killer" stunt, the outside linebacker fakes having responsibility for the quarterback and runs to the pitchman. The safety fires inside on the quarterback and kills him. It is a change-up stunt on the option.

This adjustment is good against teams that run the option with the intention of pitching the ball quickly. They do not intend for the quarterback to carry the ball. They want to force the linebacker to take him and pitch the ball quickly, so they have a toss sweep. This stunt works well against teams that do that. We take the pitch away immediately and force the quarterback into a situation where he is facing a sure-tackling, hard-hitting safety.

There are several important factors to do when defending the spread offense. When playing against spread teams, you should not change your system. How we defense the spread depends on the ability of our opponent's quarterback. We have to know if he is a runner, passer, or both. This information will affect how we play our linebackers. Playing the 3-4 defense against the spread gives you the flexibility to play between eight to five defenders in the box without many adjustments.

We can walk the outside linebackers outside on the slot receiver or keep them close to the box. They can walk in and out until the offense snaps the ball. The safeties have to move around in the secondary to disguise where they will be when they snap the ball. We want the quarterback to call an audible so late that he cannot change the play when we move. We want to show man coverage and play zone. We want to show blitz and drop. We want to show blitz and blitz. We want to make the quarterback guess as to what we are actually going to do.

We want to put pressure on the quarterback. We want to blitz him and make him throw the ball quickly. Fortunately, for defensive coaches, there are not many Tom Bradys in high school football. Most high school quarterbacks cannot drive the ball for a score by throwing short passes. If you can take away the deep ball and pressure the quarterback, you have a chance to make him make a mistake. When he has to make decisions under pressure, he will sometime lose his poise. Most quarterbacks are impatient, when it comes to throwing the short ball.

I want you look at the following film so that you can see some of these things that I have discussed today in action. I appreciate the opportunity to speak here today. If we can do anything for you, please contact us at Pike High School.

TACKLING CIRCUIT AND LINEBACKER DRILLS

West Deptford High School, New Jersey

It is a pleasure to be here today. If you want to be successful in your football program, you must concentrate on your defensive scheme. If you are not strong defensively, it will be a long night. I do not like games that end up 48-42. I also do not like games where the defense stays on the field all night. As a result, we try to play great defense. We work our tails off in the off-season, and we emphasize defense.

Defensive personality determines the character of a football team. The defense must establish the tempo of a football game. The defensive staff must coach with a sense of urgency. The have to coach every snap in a game. You also need to coach every single play in practice. On every play, the coach should have something to say to some player. If the defense takes one snap off, that may be the one time the offense gets a big play. Your coaches must have enthusiasm, energy, and emotion (the three E's).

The defense has to be prepared and well organized and have a plan with objectives. You have a master schedule for every practice, but each position coach must have his own schedule of what he wants to get done in his drills. A head coach can tell right away which coaches are prepared and which ones are flying by the seat of their pants.

The defense should employ a variety of drills and, in those drills, should promote intensity and enthusiasm. As a linebacker coach, if you are not enthusiastic, you cannot expect your players to be.

The assistant coaches have to be successful communicators with the other position coaches. The defensive line coach, the secondary coach, the inside and outside linebacker coach, and the defensive coordinator must be able to work together. If conflict occurs, it must be resolved in the coach's office—never on the field. If something potentially negative arises on the field, it should never become a confrontation between coaches in front of the players.

When we run drills, we fit the drills to the individual needs of the players. We never run drills for the sake of running a drill. Drills must have carryover value to the game. You should see on the film what you are coaching in practice.

When you coach linebackers, you have to emphasize the use of the eyes. We want the linebackers to use their eyes. After a play, the coach will ask the linebacker what he saw on the play.

We used to feel the less time we spent on individual drills, the more time we could spend on the team drills. In reality, we no longer believe that. What we do in week one of the season, we do in week 15. We want to concentrate on the fundamentals and continue to teach them throughout the season.

The most important thing for any defense to do is tackle. Every defense must master the fundamental skill of tackling. When you do not tackle well in the game, it is undoubtedly because your players are not adhering to the fundamentals involved in sound tackling. To correct those problems you have to go back to fundamentals. You have to tackle every day. The day before a game or when you have many injuries is not the time to slack up on your effort devoted to tackling. You can tackle every day without getting anyone hurt. The fundamentals of footwork and positioning involved in tackling do not change in a full-speed tackle or a non-contact tackle. As such, you can practice tackling without taking anyone to the ground or without hitting.

To play linebacker, you must learn block destruction. You have to defeat blocks and get off them to play linebacker. You have to play smart and know your alignments, assignments, and responsibilities.

On defense, your players can never show weakness. If they show weakness, they have to go to the offensive side of the ball. The fact that the defense can never show weakness has to be taught and receive the proper emphasis in practice.

Coaches should not prejudge their players by appearance and size. How many times have coaches looked at a 6' 2", 215-pound player who can run 4.7 in the 40 and bench 345 pounds as a perfect fit at linebacker. We look at a 5' 8", 170-pound player who works his butt off in the weight room as a player who cannot play. In reality, when the two players get on the field, everyone discovers the big player cannot play a lick and the little player makes all the plays. The point to remember is that coaches should never count a kid out because of his size.

You must coach defensive situation in practice. Your players must understand *down-and-distance* and how it relates to the defense. Coaches should not work their defense from the middle of the field all the time. Rather, they should work from the *hash marks* in practice.

We are a field defense. If the ball is on the hash mark, that determines what we do defensively. We want to use the boundary as the 12th defender. We want to force the offense to run or pass the football into the boundary. Because we need to practice that, the practice field needs to be marked with hash marks.

In the high school game, 75 percent of the time the snap comes from the hash marks. Some officials in high school place the ball in the middle of the field even if the ballcarrier was tackled on the hash mark. In our pre-game conference, we want to make sure if the ball is downed on the hash mark, it stays on the hash. We do not want the official to pick the ball up and move it three feet inside the hash marks. Having the ball on the hash marks dictates where our safeties align.

Coaches must teach "*sudden-change*" situations. To be successful in a sudden-change situation, you have to prepare for it in practice. Sudden change is a mental thing for the defense. They cannot become frustrated with the offense. They have to go on the field and play defense. That is how you have to approach it. They have to learn to deal with sudden change.

Defensive football is a game of field position. The team that wins the *field-position* battle has a better chance of winning. The most important statistic to a football team is wins and losses. However, the next most important statistic for the defense is *turnover ratio*. If we can turn the ball over, we give our offense the short field and an opportunity to score. As a result, we teach stripping the ball and going for the interception. Defensive study is all about the other team. Defenses should know their opponent's *tendencies* and practice against them.

Our defensive philosophy is relatively straightforward:

- Stop the running game.
- Control the passing game.
- Prevent the big play (20 + yards).
- Keep the defense simple.

The linebackers are the focal point of the defense. They are the leaders in the weight room. They are the players who play with passion on the practice field. They are unselfish. They have to be the toughest mental and physical players on the team. They are the heart and soul of our defense. One of our linebackers plays fullback on the offensive side of the ball and has the personality that fits that position.

A linebacker must be physical enough to take on the lead blocker. He also has to be quick enough to fill the alley on the option and zone play. In addition, he has to be able to drop into a zone and play some man coverage.

A linebacker must also be a great communicator and must be vocal. He has to set the defense and get everyone in the right call. He must be able to recognize offensive techniques and must be able to react to what he sees. He makes all of the audible calls.

A linebacker also has to be a great tackler. He must get up the field and play downhill. He has to be able to attack the line of scrimmage at the proper angle. To make great tackles, he must use proper angles to the line of scrimmage and play from the inside out. However, he must be able to read the offensive situation. He can be all the things you look for in a linebacker, but if he cannot read, he will not make plays. He has to read the offense and understand what he sees.

We have specific characteristics for our linebackers. The Sam linebacker is the strong inside linebacker. He must be the defensive leader. He aligns to the tight end. We want a big physical player at this position. He has to be tough, instinctive, and a plugger on our defense. He has to take on the lead block and stuff the blocker. He calls the defense and makes all the adjustments and audibles. He establishes and maintains confidence in the huddle at all times. The linebacker is "the man" on the defense.

The Will linebacker is the weak inside linebacker. He has the same characteristics as the Sam linebacker, but has more quickness and plays in more pass coverage. He is the better blazer runner of the two linebackers, because of his ability to run through creases in the offense. He has to cover the number-two pass receiver to the backside of the formation.

The first thing we do after school, before we get on the practice field, is have a group meeting with the front five and the linebackers. We want the players to settle down from the regular school day and start to get in the proper mood to practice football. We have our film sessions before practice, instead of after practice. That way when we finish practice, we can go home. The first thing we go over is defensive adjustments. We then go through formation recognition and talk about the fronts and blitzes we will use.

After the meeting, we go to the practice field. The first period on the practice field is our team warm-up period. During that period, we stretch and do our individual agilities. The second period is a special-team period. We have a group period, followed by a team period. During the group period, we work with the individual specialists. During the team period, we work with the team concept of the game.

From there, we go into our individual periods. We spend 55-60 minutes in our individual drills, such as:

- Agility bag drills
- Form-tackling period/tackling circuit
- Specific-position movement skills and drills
- Block-destruction period/Iso drills

READ/KEY PERIOD

- Pass drop technique/ball drills
- Group (front 7) vs. inside run
- Group (W/DB's) vs. outside run

We come together in a group period and work the pass-skeleton drill. The defensive backs and linebackers work against the backs and receivers. After we do our group work, we come together in a team period. During this period, we stress down-and-distance and defensive situations. We stress takeaways. We do not spend much time on our team drill. At the end, we do the team-pursuit drill, which addresses functional conditioning.

We have a tackling circuit, which we utilize on a regular basis. During this circuit, we divide the team into four groups and rotate clockwise every four minutes. The drill can either be conducted live, as a contact exercise, or we can control the speed at which we perform the drill and make it a form or non-contact exercise. The drill involves four stations, and we spend 20 minutes practicing tackling.

The first part of the drill is a "mat-explosion drill." During this drill, we put the tackler and ballcarrier one yard apart (Diagram #1). The tackler explodes into the ballcarrier, shoots his arms, runs his feet, and finishes the drill. We have a tumbling mat on the ground. The tackler explodes into the ballcarrier, using his techniques, and drives him to the ground. The tumbling mat keeps everyone from getting hurt.

The next drill we perform is the "eye-opener drill." In this drill, we align four tube dummies on the

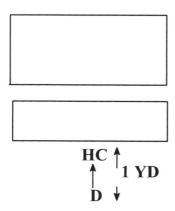

Diagram #1. Explosion-Mat Drill

ground, two yards apart (Diagram #2). The ballcarrier faces the tackler at running-back depth from the dummies. The linebacker is at linebacker depth from the dummies. The ballcarrier runs to the dummies and chooses one of three lanes in which to run. The linebacker mirrors his movement and keeps an inside-out relationship with the ballcarrier, until the back makes his choice of lanes. The tackler enters the lane and makes the tackle, using contact, shooting his arms, and following through with his feet.

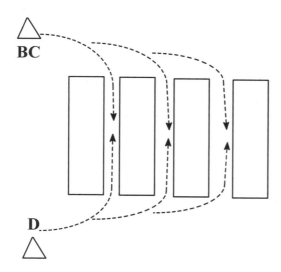

Diagram #2. Eye-Opener Drill

Next, we do the "sideline tackle drill." In this drill, the linebacker and ballcarrier align 16 yards apart, eight yards off the sideline (Diagram #3). We set a cone up on the sideline. The ballcarrier runs to the cone. The tackler mirrors the movement of the ballcarrier. The ballcarrier runs straight to the cone and does not fake or evade the tackler. The tackler

takes the proper angle and gets his head into the outside breastplate of the ballcarrier. He shoots his arms up and through the ballcarrier and runs his feet. He comes across the ballcarrier, lifts him, and runs his feet through the tackle.

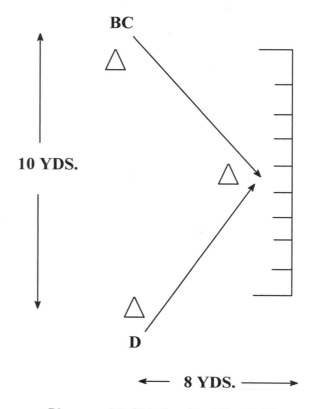

Diagram #3. Sideline Tackling Drill

The last station in the circuit is the "open-field tackling drill." In this drill, we lay a tube dummy on the ground, with a cone one yard from the end of the dummy (Diagram #4). The tackler is on one end of the dummy, while the ballcarrier is on the other end. They are five yards from the cone. The ballcarrier starts, and the tackler reacts to his movement. When the ballcarrier reaches the cone, he must chose one side of the dummy or the other. The linebacker reacts and starts his run up to the cone. When he reaches the cone, he mirrors the direction taken by the ballcarrier. He redirects his movement and makes the tackle, using good tackling techniques.

When we teach linebackers their reads and keys, we start in classroom meetings. We use the chalkboard and talk about the reads and keys. In the pre-practice session, we talk and walk-through the techniques. In practice, we *rep* the techniques.

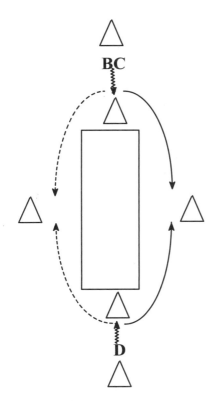

Diagram #4. Open-Field Tackling Drill

Our keys may vary, from week to week. Our base rule for the linebackers is to key the near triangle. As coaches, we must find great keys for the linebackers, because doing so can build confidence on the field.

- Guard—Beat the guard first; see and react off the guard for a directional six-inch step
- Back(s)—Determine the flow of the back(s), which gives direction of point of attack (POA).
- Ball—Define the POA; locate and fill.

We use a linebacker-read drill to teach proper steps and rips moves (Diagram #5). In this drill, three or four offensive linemen are positioned in a drill, facing the coach. The linebackers align on the linemen at linebacker depth, with their backs to the coach. The linemen can do three things: base block on a linebacker; reach to their outside; or scoop to the inside. The coach tells the linemen what to do. The linebacker has to react to the movement of the offensive linemen, protect his gap, play his technique, and rip through the block. All the linemen run the same scheme, and the linebackers react to their keys.

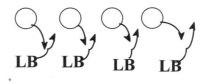

C

Diagram #5. Linebacker Read Drill

We utilize many bag drills in our indoor program. In the fall, we employ them in our individual periods. We do not perform all of the bag drills at our disposal every day. As such, we periodically change them up so we do not bore the players. During these drills, we line up five dummies on the ground, one-yard apart. Whatever movement you have a linebacker do, there must always be a finish to the drill.

We use a blocking shield that is held by the coach or a manager for the linebacker to rip through. We roll a ball in the drill, so the linebackers can practice scooping and scoring. We can also incorporate throwing a pass in the drill and let the linebackers practice making an interception. We do not let them walk out of a drill. Instead, we make them explode and do something football related to end their movement drill.

The first bag drill we use involves having the linebackers running full speed forward over the bags. A manager with a hand shield stands five yards from the last bag. The linebackers move across the bags, hitting the spaces in-between the bags with one of their feet. When they reach the shield holder, they perform a rip movement on the dummy. We run in both directions, so the linebackers can practice ripping with both arms. They rip with the right arm going down and the left arm coming back.

In the second drill, the linebacker aligns with his shoulders perpendicular to the dummies (Diagram #6). He runs over the dummies, staying low and keeping his shoulders square. When he reaches the last dummy, he sprints downhill, toward the dummy holder. On all these drills, we go up and back. That way, they have the opportunity to work with both arms on the rip technique.

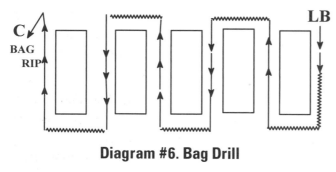

Diagram #6. Bag Drill

The next drill we perform is a weave drill. In this drill, the linebacker starts at the end of the first dummy. He runs forward to the other end, shuffles to the next alley, and backpedals through that alley. He repeats the weaving motion until he gets to the end. When he gets to the end, the last dummy is setting at an angle to the outside. He sprints down the angle and rips through a dummy.

The next drill we perform is very similar to the weave drill. The difference is the player never comes out the end of the alley. He runs to the end of the first dummy and backpedals back through same alley. He then shuffles to the next alley and goes up and back in the alley. He continues through all the dummies and fires upfield. The coach then hits him with a pass for an interception.

In the next phase, the player starts facing the dummies with his shoulder square to them (Diagram #7). He shuffles around one end of the dummy and down the next alley. When he reaches the end of that dummy, he shuffles forward and down the next alley and repeats the movement until he goes through all the dummies. When he comes out of the last dummy, he rushes the passer. When the coach pulls the ball up, he gets his hands up to knock down the ball.

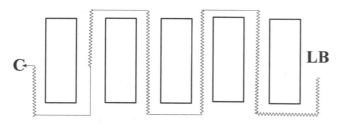

Diagram #7. Lateral Shuffle Drill

On the next drill, the linebacker runs across the bags, facing the coach (Diagram #8). The end bag is set at an angle to the inside. When the linebacker reaches the end bag, he fires down the angle at the coach, who then rolls out a ball. The linebacker scoops the ball and scores.

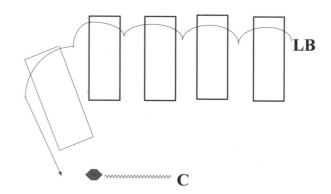

Diagram #8. Bag Drill Scoop and Score

We also perform a low-block drill with the five dummies. In this drill, the linebacker aligns at linebacker depth (Diagram #9). He attacks downhill at the first bag and pushes down on the bag as if playing a low block. He then shuffles down the line of dummies, pushing each dummy. When he gets to the last dummy, he sprints back over the dummies. At the end, the coach rolls out a ball. The linebacker scoops the ball and scores. As noted previously, we go both ways on each drill.

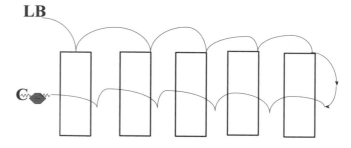

Diagram #9. Low-Block Drill

The next drill we have our linebackers perform is a "three-bag scrape" drill (Diagram #10). In this drill, the linebacker aligns at linebacker depth from the dummies. On movement, he scrapes to the middle dummy. The coach is on the other end of the dummy with a ball. He motions one way or the other with the ball. The linebacker fills on the inside or outside of the middle dummy, according to the direction given by the coach.

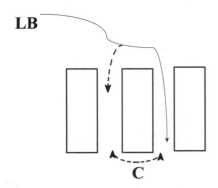

Diagram #10. Three-Bag Scrape Drill

To teach our linebackers how to change direction, we use a "five-yard N drill" (Diagram #11). In this drill, the linebackers align on a yard line. On the snap of the ball, they backpedal for five yards. When they hit the line, they plant their foot and sprint five yards at a 45-degree angle. When they hit the next yard line, they plant their foot and backpedal for five yards, and then plant and sprint forward at a 45-degree angle. They continue the drill to the end. At the end of the drill, they sprint out of the drill, and the coach hits them with an interception. Each linebacker's pattern in this drill is in the shape of the letter "N."

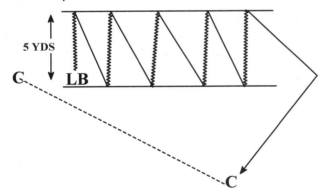

Diagram #11. Five-Yard "N" Drill

We use three dummies in another redirect drill. In this drill, the dummies are positioned two yards apart. Two linebackers set up in the two lanes formed by the dummies. They get in the middle of their alley. The coach stands five yards from the end of the dummies, facing the linebackers. The linebackers get in a good linebacker stance. The coach gives them a direction movement. They move in the direction the coach points, rapidly shuffling their feet. When they get to the dummy, they tap it

with their hand and shuffle the other direction to the other side. They repeat their movement, while moving toward the coach. When the coach pulls the ball up, they sprint out of the drill.

We also do a similar drill, using two dummies. In this drill, the dummies are placed three yards apart. The linebackers stand on one side of the dummy, on the same side of the dummy, to prevent them from running into one another. On the coach's movement, they step across the dummy, with both feet moving one at a time. As soon as they get both feet on one side of the dummy, they repeat the movement the other way. They want to move as rapidly as they can. When the coach lifts the ball, they sprint out of the drill.

The next drill we perform is a linebacker read-and-fill drill (Diagram #12). The coach uses cones to indicate the positions of the offensive linemen. At the C-gap, he places two dummies on each side of the center. The coach has four options available to him. We do this in a progression. He gives a B-gap read, a C-gap read, a counter read, and a pass drop. As they move, they work their fills, according to the coach's instructions. The coach develops hand signals to indicate fills the linebacker should execute.

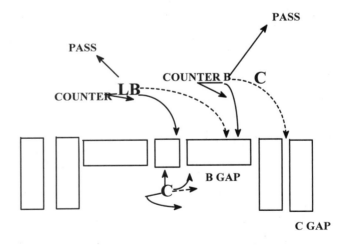

Diagram #12. Linebacker Read-and-Fill Drill

To teach linebacker movement, we utilize a five-by-five mirror drill. The linebackers align opposite one another, in a five yard-by-five yard square. We designate one of the linebackers as the ballcarrier. In this drill, the ballcarrier moves from side to side and forward to backward within his five-yard square. The linebacker mirrors the movement of the back.

When we first start to teach tackling, we use a fit drill. In this drill, we put the ballcarrier and tackler in a fitted-up position. On the coach's command, the tackler shoots his hands up and through the ballcarrier. We carry the movement one-step further by using the lift and follow-through.

From that progression in the fit drill, we next perform the "two-step drill." We do this drill in three phases. We align the tackler one yard away from the ballcarrier. On the coach's initial count ("one"), the tackler takes his first step. As the coach says "two," the tackler takes his second step, which puts him in the fit position. In the second phase of the drill, the tackler takes the two steps and shoots his arms up through the ballcarrier. In the third phase of the drill, the tackler takes his two steps, shoots his arms, and runs his feet in the finish of the tackle.

We perform the same two-step drill when we teach angle tackling. The process is the same. The progression of the tackle is the same. The only difference is the first step—instead of being a straight-ahead step, it is on an angle.

You can practice angle tackling with a non-contact concept. Everything is the same as with the sideline drill in the tackling station. The difference involves the fact that as the tackler gets to his gather position, he throttles down and goes behind the ballcarrier, simulating the arm-shooting movement.

My time is up. I appreciate your attention.

RUNNING THE JET, GUT, AND TRUCK SERIES

Murphy High School, North Carolina

We are a wing-T team that employs all of the nuts and bolts of that system. We run the jet, gut, and truck series and the entire passing game off those plays. We believe that this philosophy provides an effective way to attack teams that overload the box with defenders.

The jet-gut series is a combination play, wherein every time you run the jet play, you block the gut play to the backside. When you run the gut play, we block the jet play to the other side. Doing so gives us repetitions on blocking the jet play in practice. If you miss the jet handoff, you can run the gut play to the backside. Furthermore, you can automatic from one play to the other any time you want.

We are a single-A school and have players playing on both sides of the ball. As a result, we do not have as much time to work on our offense, as we need or would like, because we have to split our practice time to work on offense and defense with the same people. This type of play gives us repetition on two plays at once, which is why we run the wing-T. There are five plays in the offense we use. What we do, we do well.

After we install this play in August, we spend 15 minutes on Tuesday running this play. Wednesday is our offensive day, but we use 15 minutes of Tuesday to time this play. Tuesday for us is a defensive day. You cannot run the jet-speed series unless you have some speed. No one should take a bunch of kids who are slower than smoke off dog-doo and think that they are going to run the jet series. It is not going to happen. Coaches should always remember it is the Jimmys and Joes who make the jet series go—not the play.

At this point, I'd like to discuss the first play in our playbook—the jet/gut to the split-end side.

The following list details the responsibilities of the players, by position, on the play:

SPLIT END JET/GUT 27/28

- TE—seals to FS
- PST—blocks the first man past the 3 technique
- PSG—pulls and seals the onside LB's alley
- C—nose, backside 1 technique; onside 1 technique
- BSG—covered block back; uncovered gut
- BST—guard covered gut; guard uncovered scoop through the 5 technique
- QB—reverse pivots (180 degrees) and steps and hands the ball in the B-gap to the FB
- FB—aligns five yards deep; runs midline
- HB—blocks the second man past the 3 technique
- WB—flat motion sprints; reads the HB's block
- SE—man on; *crack* (SE & HB)—cracks the PSG's kick-out the widest man; *switch* (SE)—cracks the HB's kick-out

The fullback aligns at five yards deep on the jet play. For timing purposes, we back him up one yard on this play from his normal depth of four yards. You may have to adjust the depth, depending on the speed of the fullback. We tell our players any time we run a play to cheat for success. If a back has to block the end and cannot get to him, he moves up a half-step to get to him. We want to put our players in a position to be successful.

The center's rule is head-up—backside, and onside (Diagram #1). If he is covered, he blocks the man on him. If he is uncovered and the backside guard is covered, the center block back. If your rules do not hold up, we tell them to block HIM. We do a lot of HIM blocking. The tight end goes across the formation and seals the free safety. The wingback comes in sprint motion as hard as he can. We do not feel that an unblocked 3 technique can make a play on the wingback if the wingback sprints as hard as he can. The quarterback reverses out at 180 degrees to the playside A-gap and hands the ball off in the B-gap. The wingback gets the ball and reads the block of the halfback.

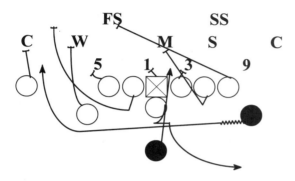

Diagram #1. Split-End Jet/Gut

We do not run a double-wing set with two split ends. We utilize a wingback and a halfback. The wingback travels with the tight end, while the halfback goes to the split end. The 20s are plays to the wingback, and the 40s are plays to the halfback. We do not run double splits and always have a tight end.

All reach blocks must start with a six-inch flat step and then work to the outside shoulder of the defender. This effort does not have to result in a tremendous block. All the blockers have to do is get in the way. The halfback has the same technique. If the Will linebacker continues to widen, the wingback turns into the alley. The playside guard pulls into that alley.

To the backside of the play, we run the "gut" play. The quarterback turns back to the fullback after he gives the ball on the jet or turns back and gives the ball on the gut play. The fullback runs the midline. The fullback usually reads the block of the center, while always starting to run at the midline.

You can change your perimeter blocking by cracking with the spit end and halfback (Diagram #2). If you crack with those players, the guard kicks out the corner. We can also switch the split end and

halfback blocks. If we have a switch call, the split end cracks on the linebacker, and the halfback kicks out on the corner.

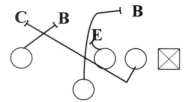

Diagram #2. Crack on the Perimeter

One factor that helps us execute this series is the empty set, which adds an element of confusion to the defense, particularly if they are a man coverage team. With the empty backfield, we still have the gut play, because the quarterback can run the play. All he does is reverse out, fake the jet, spin back, and dash into the hole.

The jet/gut to the tight end is a companion play to the previous play. The play is called 48/47. the following list details the responsibilities of the players, by position on the play:

TIGHT END JET/GUT 48/47

- TE—blocks the second man past the 3 technique
- PST—blocks the first man past the 3 technique
- PSG—pulls and seals the onside LB
- C—nose; backside 1 technique; onside 1 technique
- BSG—covered block backside; uncovered gut
- BST—guard covered gut; guard uncovered scoop through the 5 technique
- HB—motion sprints, reads the block of the WB
- WB—blocks the third man or the second man past the PST
- SE—blocks the FS, loads man on unbalanced

The rules are similar to the split-end jet/gut play. The tight end, playside tackle, and wingback block defenders one, two, and three past the 3 technique. If the 3 technique makes the play on the jet sweep, you have a slow-ass runner. The offensive line is off the ball as far as they can legally be. We do not think the 3 technique is a threat to the jet sweep when he's left unblocked. Teams that play us know that if they penetrate their 3 technique and try to stop the jet sweep, we will trap their head off. The trap is one of our favorite plays.

In 1987, with those five plays, we scored over 700 points, which is a North Carolina state record. I could tell you that we did it with very little talent and no coaches, but I lie a lot also. That year we had great players.

The tight-end jet/gut can run from the spread offense, as well as from the wing-T (Diagram #3). On this play, we can bring the split end over and get into an unbalanced formation. That takes care of the unblocked corner. That alignment is called a load scheme.

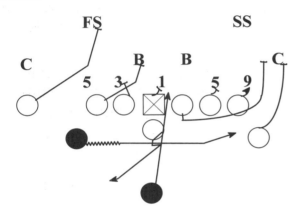

Diagram #3. Tight-End Jet/Gut

On the jet, we snap the ball on the second sound. We work on the timing every day. We call the audible twice and follow that with "set-hut." The hut is the snap count. You practice the timing through repetition. We can also put the fullback into the jet sweep to the tight-end side (Diagram #4). If we do that, we like to put him in an offset toward the tight end. When the fullback blocks on the sweep, the quarterback becomes the gut runner.

Truck plays are reverses off the jet series. We run the truck series both toward the tight end and away from him. The following list outlines the responsibilities of the players, by position, on the tight-end truck 48/47 play:

TIGHT-END TRUCK 48/47

* TE—gap down, reaches
* PST—gap down, pulls and logs

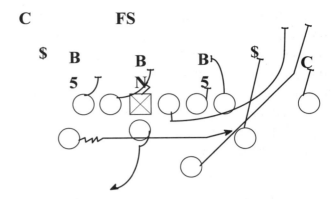

Diagram #4. Unbalanced FB Lead

* PSG—pulls and read blocks on the DE
* C—nose; backside 1 technique; frontside 1 technique
* BSG—pulls and reads the block of the PSG
* BST—scoops the 3 technique area
* QB—reverse pivots, fakes a step, and hands the ball to the second back
* FB—seals the onside 1 technique to the LB
* HB—steps back with his inside foot, runs flat, and reads the block of the BSG
* WB—flat motions and fakes jet
* SE—blocks the FS to the playside nickel

If we run to the tight end, the jet back fakes the jet sweep (Diagram #5). The truck back takes one step back and runs flat to take the handoff, while reading the backside guard. We want to make sure we seal the playside 1 technique to the inside, which we do with the center and fullback's block. The tight end rule is gap down inside. If there is no defender in the inside gap, he reaches.

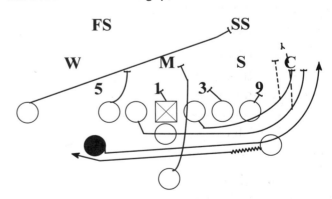

Diagram #5. Tight End Truck

83

The playside guard pulls and reads the block of the tight end. If the tight end is blocking down, the guard is going outside. If the tight end is blocking out, the pulling guard turns inside his block. The fullback's depth on the truck series reduces to three and a half to four yards. He has to seal the onside 1 technique. The backside guard pulls and reads the block of the playside guard. If the playside guard kicks out, the backside guard turns inside his block. The halfback cheats back off the ball to give the wingback room to get inside of him. The wingback drops steps and comes straight across the formation to fake the jet sweep.

The quarterback fakes the jet sweep and hands the ball to the halfback. The halfback reads the block of the backside guard. If the backside guard turns inside, the halfback follows him inside. If the pulling guard goes outside, he follows him there. One of the keys to coaching the running backs is to not overcoach them. If they have speed and instincts, they will find the hole. Just point them in the right direction and let them play.

When we run the truck series to the split end, the blocking does not change too much (Diagram #6). If the playside guard has a 3- or 2-technique aligned on him, he pulls and logs the defensive end. If he is uncovered, he pulls and kicks out the force defender. The backside guard reads the playside guard and blocks either inside or outside off his block. The split end has what we call a "slow-crack" block. Because it takes some time for the reverse to come to him, he takes his time on the crack block.

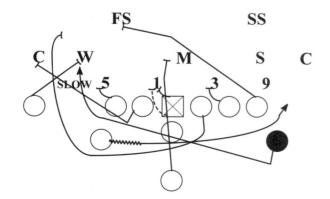

Diagram #6. Split-End Truck

The remainder of the play is the same, with regard to the reads for the wingback. He reads the backside guard for his cuts. The fullback has to seal the onside 1 technique or the linebacker. If the playside guard is uncovered, the fullback fills in for the linebacker on that type of defense. If the guard is uncovered, the tackle is covered. As such, the tackle's rule is to reach the defender on him. If the guard is covered, the tackle blocks down, and the fullback has to secure on the 1 technique.

With regard to the path of the running back on the jet sweep, we do not teach him to bubble back when he receives the ball. We teach him to get away from the trash at the line of scrimmage, and he instinctively bubbles back from the line of scrimmage.

We have two passes that we employ off the jet motion—the keep pass and the bootleg pass. We run the keep pass by snapping the ball when the jet back is just past the playside B-gap.

The following list details the responsibilities of the players, by osition on the right 35 keep pass play:

RIGHT 35 KEEP PASS

- TE—runs a cross route at 10-12 yards
- PST—reach man blocks on anyone
- PSG—reach man blocks on anyone who shows; if no one, blocks back
- C—reaches playside or anyone who shows; if no one, blocks back
- BSG—lead steps in and hinges back
- BST—lead steps in and hinges back
- QB—opens to the WB, fakes jet, and rolls to the playside
- FB—blocks the first man outside the PST
- HB—wide steps up five yards and breaks, angling out to 22 yards
- WB—jet motions, flat two-to-three yards
- SE—outside releases and runs a streak pattern

We call our pass protection scheme "60." To the playside, everyone reaches a half-man to the outside (Diagram #7). To the backside, we lead step in and hinge back to the backside. We snap the ball as the wingback gets to the B-gap. The quarterback fakes the jet and rolls in the direction of the jet motion. He looks onside and works his way to the backside.

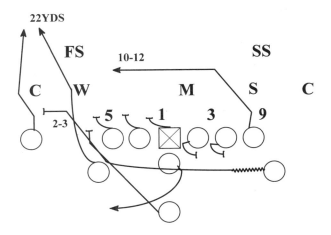

Diagram #7. Jet Motion Keep to SE

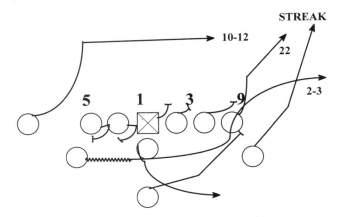

Diagram #8. Jet Motion Keep to TE

The split receiver runs a streak pattern to take the top off of the coverage. The halfback runs what we call a "22." He runs up the field for five yards and breaks angling for the sideline going to a depth of 22 yards. The wingback fakes the jet sweep and goes into the flat at a depth of two-to-three yards. The tight end runs a cross from the backside at a depth of 10-12 yards.

The quarterback has a number of options on this pass. The quarterback takes the ball to a depth of seven yards. We are not too depth-conscious with the quarterback. He takes three good steps to his set point. We want him to work outside to help our protection scheme.

We can run the pattern to the tight-end side, although we do not like it (Diagram #8). We have no wide receiver to get horizontal stretch to start the play. The streak pattern has to come from the wingback, who is off the line of scrimmage. The tight end runs the 22 pattern, and the halfback runs the two-to-three yard flat pattern. We have to make sure he does not get deeper than three yards. If he does, he messes up the spacing on this play. The split receiver runs the crossing pattern at 10-12 yards. He has to cut his split somewhat to get into the play.

We run bootleg-pass routes off the jet motion just like boots from the regular wing-T set. As result, all pass routes are kept consistent and easy to install. In addition, we like to run jet boots from the empty set, especially against man coverages. No matter where your players are, they run the same route on these plays.

The following list details the responsibilities of the players, by position, on the right 48/47 jet boot plan:

RIGHT 48/47 JET BOOT

- TE—runs a cross route
- PST—checks threat to 3 technique down; no e technique, execute 3 big-on-big
- PSG—checks threat to 1 technique down and 2- or 5-technique down
- C—fills for the pulling guard
- BSG—pulls to the DE or the first threat
- BST—scoops to 3-technique area to lead step and hinge back
- QB—fakes the jet and runs the boot
- FB—checks the gap for the onside LB; releases to the flat
- HB—fakes the jet and checks the first man outside the BST
- WB—steps flat and runs a post route
- SE—runs a post-corner route

The split-end route on this play can change from week to week, depending on what the defense does (Diagram #9). Diagram #9 illustrates the split end running a post-corner route. His pattern is a game-plan type of adjustment. The tight end runs his pattern at 12-15 yards deep. The fullback checks the onside LB. He fills in the 3 technique area. If the B-gap is open, the fullback runs through the gap and does a five yard flat pattern. If the guard is uncovered, the B-gap is open, except the linebacker can blitz through that gap, which is why he checks before he releases to the flat. If the guard is covered, the fullback finds the linebacker. If he is gone, he finds a seam and gets into his flat pattern.

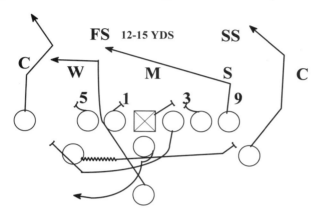

Diagram #9. Jet Motion Boot to SE

The quarterback runs the jet fake and runs the bootleg, with the pulling guard in front of him. He sets up at six-to-seven yards.

The bootleg to the tight-end side has the same patterns in the right 27/28 jet boot play. The following list details the responsibilities of the players, by position, on this play:

RIGHT 27/28 JET BOOT

- TE—runs a corner route
- PST—checks threat to #3 down; if no #3, executes big-on-big
- PSG—checks threat to #1 down
- C—fills for the pulling guard
- BSG—pulls for the DE or the first threat
- BST—scoops to #3's area; lead steps and hinges back
- QB—opens to the WB; fakes 27 run boot
- FB—checks the gap of the onside LB; releases into the flat
- HB—steps into the flat and runs a run post route
- WB—fakes the jet; blocks the first man outside the BST
- SE—runs a cross route at 10-12 yards

The quarterback runs the same action, coming to the tight-end side (Diagram #10). As he sets up behind his pulling guard, he has the same three patterns in front of him. He looks low-to-high in his reads. When the split end has the cross pattern for the bootleg to the tight end, he cuts his split down, which gets him to the frontside quicker and makes him a target for the quarterback. We can change the patterns and let the halfback run the cross, and the split end run the post. The split end reduces his split on other plays so that he does not a tip the defense. He also reduces his splits if he has to crack on a defender. It is not something the defense can see and realize that we are running the bootleg. We adjust the split end as part of our game plan.

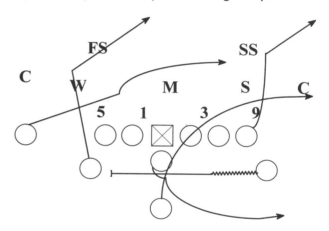

Diagram #10. Right 27/28 Bootleg to TE

We like to throw the bootleg pass from the empty. No changes are made in the patterns we employ on this play. The fullback's pattern is still a five-yard flat pattern. If he lines up to the split end, he goes in and comes back out at a depth of five yards. If he lines up to the tight-end side, he comes across the formation, also at a depth of five yards. We still have the jet motion and fake. The blocking rules for the offensive line do not change. It is an effective play against man coverage.

The blocking rules on the empty set are straightforward. If the onside linebacker rushes, the pulling guard's rule is to pull for the defensive end or the first threat. If the linebacker blitzes, the pulling guard blocks him. If the defense brings a maximum blitz to the side we run the boot, the quarterback has to get rid of the ball quickly. The guard blocks the linebacker on the blitz, and the quarterback has to throw off the defensive end. We are weak on our protection in the B-gap, but the defense has to guess right to be successful.

One of the key blocks on the bootleg is the back who fakes the jet sweep. He has to protect the quarterback's backside. You never want your quarterback to be hit in the back. He can see the pressure to his frontside and throw the ball. However, he cannot see what is coming from behind.

In my talk to you today, I've tried to emphasize the fact that the jet-gut and truck runs with the keeper plays and the bootleg passes are great packages for us—plays that can complement any wing-T offense. It was my pleasure talking to you, and I thank you for your attention.

BLOCKING ESSENTIALS FOR THE OFFENSIVE LINE

Edgewater High School, Florida

Today, I am going to talk offensive line play. I have been a head coach for 25 years and have always coached the offensive line. The offensive line is the position in football that requires the most technique and motivation. You usually deal with players who are a bit different as far as their makeup, both physically and mentally.

The offensive line is a great position to coach. There is always something you can do every day in practice and games to improve their performance.

The first thing I want to talk about is pass protection. The following list details a number of base fundamentals in pass blocking for an offensive lineman:

Base Fundamentals

- Get out of stance and locate the defender.
- Keep leverage on the defender.
- Use your eyes to locate the defender and employ proper hand placement once you do.
- Base footwork on the called protection.

The first thing the lineman has to do is to get into a proper stance. You must have a stance that allows the lineman to get out of that bent-over position and locate the defender. In that regard, it is essential that the lineman can get out of his stance quickly. Once he gets out of his stance, he has to stay low and locate the defender. The most important drill we do every day involves that skill. The faster the lineman gets out of his stance, the faster he can locate his target, and the easier his block will be.

The second factor we emphasize is keeping leverage on the defender. In other words, the offensive lineman has to be lower on contact than the defender. This requirement is a problem in high school because the offensive linemen are generally bigger than the defenders they block.

We have to constantly talk to them about using leverage, with the proper bend in their hips and knees. You have to talk to them about the angles in their knees and ankles, which is a part of pass protection you can teach daily without pads. Although it is a relatively simple thing to do, it is tremendously important in pass protection.

The third factor we emphasize is where the eyes and hands should be placed on the defender. As a pass protector, you have to keep your head up and locate the defender with your eyes. If he loses eye contact on the defender, he probably loses his block.

The lineman's hand placement on the defender is also an important factor. In pass blocking, having good hand placement is paramount in being successful. Keeping your head up and using good eye contact and hand placement makes the block easier to achieve.

You can work on the aforementioned techniques every day in practice without pads. This approach makes the physical part of playing in the offensive line easier.

The last basic fundamental of blocking that we emphasize is the footwork involved. There are so many drills you can do with an offensive lineman that teach footwork. We use three primary drills to work on footwork and hand placement. These drills are designed to make our linemen better pass protectors.

The first drill is the "box drill." In this drill, we line up four cones in a square, six to ten yards apart (Diagram #1). The lineman starts in a stance at the first cone. He breaks out of his stance and runs forward to the second cone. He slides in a shuffle from the second to the third cone. Once he reaches the third cone, he then backpedals to the fourth cone. To conclude the drill, when he gets to the fourth cone, he then does a carioca or hop to the first cone. We perform this drill on an ongoing basis to improve all of the footwork that they will need to be good pass protectors.

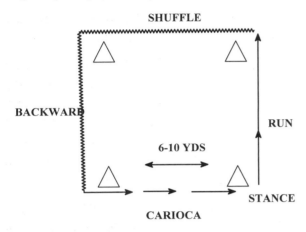

Diagram #1. Box Drill

The second drill we utilize in our protection scheme to teach our players to take the proper angle is the "angle drill" (Diagram #2). In this drill, the offensive linemen start in their stance and locate a defender from 18 inches to two yards outside of them. We stress the importance of making the backward step with the outside foot. This footwork allows them to keep leverage on the defender and scoot back to prevent the defender from making an outside move to the inside of the blocker, which is something we do not want to occur. If the blocker loses the defender, we want to lose him to the outside.

Diagram #2. Angle Drill

The angle drill is designed to teach the offensive linemen the importance of not over-extending. It teaches them to keep their body underneath them, which will keep the defender from giving them an inside move, which is the closest way to the quarterback.

The third drill we employ is the "punch drill," which I am sure everyone uses. There are a number of different ways to teach this drill. We use bags, hand placement, and weights. The basic technique involved in the drill is for the linemen to keep their hands tight to their body, with their thumbs inside. The point we stress involves the lineman's head. When the lineman shoots his hands out, his head must go back. This movement is like a rocking-chair motion.

A situation in which the lineman's head and body go forward as he extends his hands is the easiest way for the defender to get by him. We perform these drills, which can be done without pads, almost every day.

The last factor that I would like to talk about involving pass protection are the following four basic coaching points in this regard that we emphasize with our offensive linemen.

Coaching Points of Emphasis

- Know the protection that is going to be used for the play called.
- Never cross your feet.
- Try to keep one foot on the ground at all times.
- Always keep your helmet upward and away from the defender.

The lineman has to know what the protection is for the play called. He has to know what direction the quarterback is going. It is important to keep the protection as simple as possible, so your players can get the maximum number of reps.

The offensive lineman should never cross his feet over when he makes contact with a defender. If the offensive lineman crosses his feet, he has no power in either foot. The offensive lineman has to keep power in his legs, by keeping one foot stabilized on the ground at all times. Even though the feet move on protection, it is essential to keep one foot in contact with the ground. If both feet are off the ground, the blocker has no power in his block.

The last point of emphasis is to keep the helmet up away from the defender. In order to keep the head back, you have to work on it in the punch drill. The defender should be required to try to turn the entire body of the blocker, instead of being able to grab the back of the blocker's helmet.

In the remainder of my presentation today, I would like to talk about four blocks we use on a continual basis in our program: base, reach, gap, and cutoff. For a player to play in our program, he must understand these four blocking schemes and the fundamentals that are involved to successfully accomplish the blocks.

Base-Blocking Fundamentals

- Stance
- Explosion
- Hip drive
- Leg drive

The first thing you have to do in the base block is to get the players in a proper stance. In the stance for the base block, we use heel-to-toe stagger. However, the taller the player, the more elongated the stagger might be. High school linemen have a hard time staying in a parallel stance because of their lack of flexibility in their hips. When they stagger their feet, it allows them to get down into a stance with some flexibility and power in the hip joint.

We use a three-point stance and want the down hand with all four fingers on the ground. We do not want an enormous amount of weight on their hand on the ground, but at the same time, we do not want them back in their stance. This factor is a critical area about which the offensive line coach needs to constantly remind his players.

In the stance, we want the off-hand cupped on the outside of the knee. It should be cupped on the knee, so the lineman has it in a position where he can use it. It should not be dangling in front of him. It should be where he can punch or fill with his other hand.

The most important factor in blocking is to get out of the stance and explode into the block. The secret is to come out of the stance under control. Doing so keeps the blocker from overextending. If the blocker overextends, he probably will fall down. We try to sell the players on the need to stay on

their feet and in front of the defender to accomplish the block.

An important facet of the base block is the hip drive. Many of the things you do in the weight room and on the field are constantly trying to develop the hip drive. The hip drive is responsible for the power you get in the blocks. Although it is a constant battle, you can develop much of the hip drive with a series of drills, which I will explain later in this presentation.

The leg drive is the fourth element of the base block that we emphasize. This factor is something you can work in numerous drills. The most important aspect of the leg drive is to keep a wide base. If the lineman gets foot-to-foot or gets his feet too close together, chances are he will lose his balance. If he is falling down, he will not make the block.

When working on the base block, we like to use four different drills, which can help our linemen improve their fundamentals.

Drills for Improving the Fundamentals of the Base Block

- Board drill
- Lunge drill
- Arm-extension drill
- Leg-drive drill

The first drill we utilize when working on the base block is the board drill. We use a board that is 12-to-16 inches in width and four-to-five feet in length. We put the offensive blocker at one end of the board, with the defender in the middle of the board. The blocker comes out of his stance, fits into the block, and drives the defender off the board. The drill is designed to keep the blocker's feet apart while he is driving. If his feet are too close together, he will step on the board and slip.

As a safety measure, you might consider padding the top of the board, particularly if the drill involves younger players. Doing so will keep your athletes from hurting themselves, if they fall on the edges of the board. Once they understand what they are doing, they usually will not fall or step on the board. This drill can be done with or without pads. You can let the defender hold a dummy or shield, when you first start to use the drill.

There are a number of ways to conduct the drill, from strictly form to full contact. However, you want to remember that this exercise is an offensive drill that is designed to benefit the offensive blocker. If you put the offensive blocker in a full-speed drill against a defender where all he has to do is hold his ground, the defender will probably win. You should incorporate a ballcarrier in all full-contact blocking drills. The ballcarrier will help keep the defender from teeing off on the offensive blocker. A situation in which the defender has to get off a block can make a tremendous difference to an offensive blocker.

The next two drills go hand-in-hand. We start with the "lunge drill" and then continue with the "arm-extension drill." In the lunge drill, the blocker is positioned in a six-point stance. He has his hands, knees, and toes in contact with the ground. The objective of the drill is to lunge out at the defender, while dropping the hips to the ground as he lunges. We want each lineman to extend from his knees into a dummy, fire his head up and through the dummy, and drop his hips to the ground. What we are looking for in the blocker is hip drive. We do not want the blocker to rock back on his heels before he lunges. He should react to the sound and explode into the dummy or sled.

After we master the hip-extension drill, we add the arm extension to the drill. In this drill, the linemen do the same thing that they did in the lunge drill, except they place their hands on the dummy. As they extend their hips, they also extend their arms, as they fall to their stomachs. This drill is a great way to teach the linemen to tuck their hips and extend up and through the block. This drill, which teaches the importance of coming out of the stance, can be done year-round without pads. After the linemen progress in the drill, you can then go to using a three-point stance and do the same thing.

In the "leg-drive drill," the linemen begin in the fitted position. We fit the blocker into a perfect block position on the defender. On the snap, he drives the defender. The defender gives passive pressure on the blocker and moves right and left, as he retreats backward. As the defender moves right and left, the blocker moves to stay in front of the defender.

These four drills teach extension, hip movement, and leg drive. The linemen have to be at least a shoulder-length apart. The entire underlying idea in these drills is to have the linemen stay in front of the defender and stay on their feet. We emphasize the following essential coaching points of the base block.

Coaching Points for the Base Block

- Keep the helmet upward and arch your lower back as you leave your stance.
- Keep your eyes open and locate the defender.
- Work to get the first three steps into the defender, as your forearm rolls forward.
- Maintain your leg drive outside of your shoulders.

The last coaching point refers to the fact that the feet should not be under the shoulders when the blocker is attempting to drive.

The second critical block we teach is the reach. This block is an important block, particularly if you utilize a zone-blocking scheme. If you employ a zone-blocking scheme, the reach block must be coached on a daily basis.

Fundamentals of the Reach Block

- Reach step.
- Utilize proper helmet and hand placement.
- Work for leverage on the defender.
- Teach the reach rule as the linemen learn the fundamentals of the reach block.

We do not position step to try to get into the reach block. Rather, we want to step upfield and gain ground at the defender. As a result, we get more body lean, which aids in getting movement up the field. We want to target the outermost part of the defender and gain ground on the first two steps. The emphasis is to get position and movement on the defender at the same time.

Helmet and hand placement are crucial in executing the reach block. The blockers have to get to the defender's outside armpit and place their hands on their outside shoulder pad. They have to continue to move to the outside, even as the defender starts to widen at impact. If the blockers continue to work for outside leverage, they will gain ground and give the running back an opportunity to cut off their block.

The rule we use in the reach block is to work for outside leverage on the defender. From an outside-leverage position, we continue to work to the head-up position. If we are successful in getting into the head-up position on the defender, we try to work past him and get upfield. The next level is the linebacker level. Our goal is to work past the defender and get a block on a linebacker on the second level.

If you are running a zone-blocking scheme, you have to teach reach blocking daily. You have to drill the fundamentals involved in the reach block to improve the linemen's technique. The primary mistake that younger players make when attempting to execute the reach block is allowing separation from the defender. The defender is trying to keep leverage on the blocker. The lineman has to keep his body in a position relative to the defender's body so they do not separate from each other. If no separation occurs, the blocker will gain ground and give the running back a chance to cut off his block.

A key coaching point with regard to the reach block is for the blocker to not chase the next-level defender if the defender has position on him. As the offensive lineman comes up to the second level, if the linebacker is outside of the blocker, the blocker should turn back and not chase the linebacker. If the blocker chases the linebacker, all that will happen is either a penalty will be called on the blocker or a no-block situation will occur. If the linebacker turns back to the next linebacker, he gives the back a cutback lane, which helps the offensive linemen and gives the back an opportunity to cut back.

The following coaching points of emphasis for the reach block are essential:

- Teach the linemen to gain ground on their first three steps.
- Do not separate from the defender.
- Do not chase linebackers if they already have leverage on the blockers.
- Teach the reach rule to prepare your linemen for everything they might encounter.

The third block we emphasize on an ongoing basis is the gap block. This block involves a frontside, down block. The rule for this block is very simple—the blocker blocks down on the first defender in the inside gap. If there is no one in his inside gap, the lineman blocks the man over the adjacent lineman. If there is no defender in the gap or over the next lineman, the lineman becomes a second-level blocker for the linebacker.

Fundamentals of the Gap Block

- Take a 45-degree step to the inside.
- Use proper helmet placement.
- Utilize proper hand placement.
- Drive the legs.

We use a power block to the inside. As such, the blocker takes a 45-degree angle step to the inside and gets his body and helmet into the defender, with as much power as possible. Ideally, we are trying to knock the defender one man to the inside or one man back. You have to teach your players that this block is a power block. They should get as much force and power on the defender as is humanly possible.

On the gap block, they place the helmet in front of the defender. We do not want to lose the block to the inside. If the defender rolls back to the outside, you stand a better chance of making yards. To get back outside, the defender has to give ground. If the defender penetrates the inside gap on a gap block, the chances are good for a negative play. After the lineman makes contact with the defender, his helmet placement should go inside the defender.

On this block, the lineman should place one hand on the inside part of the defender's body and one on the outside part of his body. That gives the blocker three points of contact on the defender's body. If you are a run-blocking team, your linemen must be able to execute this block. They have to accomplish this block 100 percent of the time. Not only is it the easiest to teach, the rule is the easiest to execute.

You can drill the gap block on the boards (Diagram #3). In this drill, the board should be positioned at the angle at which you want the lineman to come down and let him do the board drill as you did in the drive block.

Another drill you can conduct involves finding the next level in the gap block. The drill can be set up to simulate the down block. Cones can be used to set the aiming point for the down block. The block can be executed against a dummy holder in the backside-linebacker position.

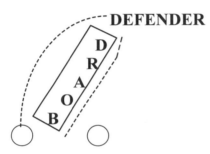

Diagram #3. Angle-Board Drill

As a rule, the defensive players do not stay on the line of scrimmage when the ball is snapped. Rather, they move forward out of their stance. A key teaching point in this regard is that the blocker must not go where the defender lines up. He must go in front of him. That way, he can hit the defender with most of his body. The blocker can always come up to the defender's level if the defender does not move. On the other hand, the blocker cannot prevent penetration by the defender, if the blocker does not start at the proper angle.

The key coaching points of emphasis on the gap block are relatively simple:

- Make the blocking scheme fit the offense.
- Work the gap rule in order to prepare the linemen for everything they might encounter.

The last (and fourth) block we teach our offensive linemen is a backside block we refer to as a cutoff block. The basic rule for the cutoff block requires the linemen to secure everything to their inside, from the next offensive lineman over to the next level. It is a backside block designed to seal the backside for a running lane. It is a hustle block that involves the following fundamentals:

Fundamentals of the Cutoff Block

- Take a flat step.
- Employ proper helmet and shoulder placement.
- Work for leverage on the defender.
- Adhere to the cutoff rule as the fundamentals are learned.

Anyone can be a good cutoff blocker if he wants to hustle. Successfully executing this block is not dependent on ability. Rather, it is the amount of effort the lineman wants to give for the offense. On this block, his first step is a six-inch, flat step, so he can read the next gap to his inside. If the defender is on the line of scrimmage, the blocker's next step is a contact step. If there is no defender to the inside, the blocker climbs to the next level looking for a linebacker. Executing this block properly will create cutback lanes for the ballcarriers.

The backside is sealed and there will be some natural cutback lanes, if the defense over-pursues. This factor is true, regardless if you are a zone or I-formation team. It is important that your linemen are fully aware of and know the key objective of the cutoff block, which is to deny the defender penetration into the offensive line of scrimmage. We teach the cutoff rule in order to prepare the offensive linemen for everything they might encounter.

The aforementioned are the four basic blocks that we teach our offensive linemen. The key to having good offensive linemen is to be mentally prepared to know whom to block. By teaching and re-teaching the same points repeatedly, you can get a greater number of repetitions, which—in turn— can lead to greater confidence. All factors considered, when your linemen are confident about how and whom they are going to block, their execution level is enhanced.

The second most important factor with regard to mental preparation is the fundamental position involved in sound blocking. All of our four basic blocks require proper footwork, which can be worked at any time, with or without pads. Most of the techniques of blocking fundamentals require sound footwork and angles. The physical techniques of blocking are deeply seated in being mentally prepared to execute the fundamental skills that make the various blocking techniques easier to do properly.

If your players are sound fundamentally and mentally, they can perform blocks that are difficult to execute. If your team is going to have success on the offensive side of the ball, your offensive line must be able to block well. The offensive line makes good backs look great and mediocre backs look good. Even great backs may struggle, to a degree, without a good offensive line. On the other hand, if a great back has an extraordinary line, he will be exceptional.

The offensive line is a terrific position to coach. The likelihood that your team will be successful year-in and year-out will be enhanced if your linemen learn how to master the blocks that I have discussed today. Personally, I am lucky to have coached so many good football players. They have been a lot of fun to be around.

If I can help you in any way, please do not hesitate to contact me. Thank you.

Mike Glaser

DRILLS TO DEVELOP OFFENSIVE LINEMEN

St. Xavier High School, Kentucky

It is an honor to be here, and it is a real honor to be talking about offensive-line play. I am going to talk about it based on our philosophy. I do not believe you should do anything without a philosophy. It is what you believe in, and that is what it has to be all about.

Number one, you have to develop each player as an individual. You can build offensive linemen, and you are going to have to because you will be coaching players with the least talent and who are the least strong and the least fast of all of your players. Every day, you have to get them excited about getting better with their feet, their quickness, and everything involved, and then you get them to work as a unit. From day one, your philosophy has to be to bring those guys together. We want them to work as a unit.

Second, fundamentals are the key. Too many coaches just want to scrimmage. As an offensive line coach, you have to believe strongly in fundamentals—in first step, in head placement, and in the eyes. You have to coach the eyes of your offensive linemen. We are going to talk fundamentals every day, and what I hope to do here is just give you a concept of offensive line play.

We have a sign in our locker room that reads: "Do it right! Do it hard! Do it again!" If you are the offensive line coach, you should be making a correction on every single snap. Praise something done well, correct something that needs to be done better, and do it loud so all five linemen can hear it. Make corrections to the whole group, and really emphasize the fundamentals. You can build great linemen.

I want to talk a minute about coaching drills and the accountability that goes with it. You cannot stand back and be a passive coach at the high school level. Have some effort to your coaching. It would also help if you would get in shape yourself, run with your players some, and set an example with energetic work.

Teach and coach your players the knowledge of the game. They need to know more than their assignments. They need to know how plays are designed to work and how their assignments fit together to make them work. Each player should know what we have to get from his assignment.

The last part of the accountability factor is enthusiasm. If you are not enthusiastic as a coach, you should not be coaching. It is as simple as that. Whatever you do in life, have a passion for it.

The next thing about coaching drills is that you have to challenge your players. Do not let players make excuses. They have to be accountable for what they do, but as a coach, you must give them clear directions first, and you have to allow them to ask questions. Once they know what is expected of them, you have to praise them when they do a good job, but you must correct them when they do not. Give them what they need to get better.

I want to speak briefly about drill organization. You need to have a goal for every drill you do, and know what you are trying to accomplish with it. Is it a technique drill or a conditioning drill? It is also important to organize your drills for maximum reps, and then make sure that you have a progression of skills. Think about the skills you are teaching in your drills, and then try to limit successive drills to one, two, certainly no more than three skills each.

It is important to finish what you start. Every drill should have a finish to it, and we have to coach each player to that finish. Every drill we have has to have an end point, and every player has to hustle his tail all the way to that end point and finish the drill.

It is also important to set up drills for success—especially for young offensive linemen who may lack the talent and skills of some of the other players. Put them in a drill where they can experience some success so they will feel good about themselves and want to work to get better. Failure breeds quitting, but success breeds success.

Finally, once your kids experience a little success and develop a little confidence, you need to breed a little competition. Have some drills where competitiveness is the goal, and then let them go at it. Somebody will win, and somebody will lose, and kids do not want to lose—especially when all their peers are watching. If you can breed competition, you are going to have a darn good football team.

You have to instill pride in all of your offensive linemen. In my opinion, the game is won up front, and if we are going to win, it will be with our offensive linemen.

If you platoon, expect the same out of all of your linemen. At our school, our offensive linemen have just the same temperament as our defensive linemen, and they will fight you in a heartbeat. They believe they are just as tough and just as good. Never expect more out of your defensive linemen than you do out of your offensive linemen, and never allow that perception to exist on the team. If those stereotypes exist, you as an offensive line coach have to find a way to break them.

I said before, you have to instill pride in your offensive linemen, and one way to do that is through drills. Be sure you have a clear purpose for each drill, and be sure the player knows what it is. Then, if you are going against the defense, make it clear whether it is an offensive or a defensive drill. Who is the drill designed for?

For example, if it is a competitive pass-rush drill, you have to make sure it is not designed or run in a way that puts your people at a disadvantage. Then, be sure to determine what a win is, and use that as motivation for your guys. There are many ways you can help your offensive linemen to feel good about themselves, and you have to find ways to do that.

Before I get to the specific drills we use, I want to go through some of the concepts that are involved. First, it is important that all drills are done in a progression that will improve movement and confidence. We never time our offensive linemen in the 40-yard dash. None of them are going to be on special teams, and all it will do is frustrate them. We do not care how fast they run the 40. What I care about is how fast they can get from here to there, how fast they can pull and block on a sweep. We like to move our offensive linemen a lot, and that is fun for them, but we are not going to time them in the 40. We want them to be able to move, and we want them to develop confidence.

You will see on the tape later that we do four agility drills every day the exact same way. The drills are for foot movements and to get them to open up their hips. You will all recognize carioca, tapioca, the seat roll, and the seal. The bottom line is that we want them moving. These are to warm them up, but also to condition them. There is going to be rapid fire, about seven going at a time, and there is always a finish point. Those four drills are for conditioning and to get them warmed up.

We try to work on stance every week during the season, all year long. The first couple of weeks, we do it almost every day. We do stance and first step. We teach stance the same way you do, but everything is about hips for us. Our good players are the ones who have done enough squats that they can get down low and sit. When they can break down and be comfortable down low like that, they have a chance to be good linemen.

We do our stance and start drills in seven lines. Later on the film, you will see us do stance and first step drills. We go drive step, reach step, and trap step. Each one is a six-inch jab step. We do a sweep step later. We let them choose whether they want a right-handed stance or a left-handed stance, but we do not let them choose which foot they will step with first. They have to step with the near foot.

On the stance and step drill, we also want them to throw their hands and set their heads and eyes to the aiming point. We go rapid fire with seven lines, and we can get a lot of reps in a short amount of time. Here is the point: do everything in a simple form first. Teach the first step. Then, we can work on the takeoff and the blocks that follow.

I would recommend that you write a drill book for your position. I make our coaches put together a drill book for their position and give me a copy. It will make you think, and it will make you go through the progression of what you want to teach. You will be a much better offensive line coach next year if you will do that.

We do board and chute drills. After the stance and start work, we take our kids on to the board and chute drills. We are going to look at taking off and driving people.

After that, we do the pound steps. You all have done this. We try to pound—boom! boom! boom! boom! —pound them in the ground. If you cannot hear them pounding their feet, then they are not working hard enough on it.

We follow the pound-step drill with a one-step punch drill. Inside hands for linemen are going to win. The offensive or defensive lineman who is low, who has the leverage, and who has his hands inside is going to win the battle. When our hands get inside, we are going to grab you.

We are going to punch first, as hard as we can, we are going to butt you with the helmet, and then we are going to grab you. What we do in the drill is take that six-inch step, shoot those hands, punch with the hands inside, and grab onto you. It just makes common sense that if I make them do that every day, over and over, then when they actually get in a game, they will get their hands inside.

Next, we go to a fit and drive drill. We just fit them into a good blocking position on the defender with their butt down, flat back, and head and eyes up. On "go," the blocker pounds the feet and drives the defender the length of the board. We emphasize a good wide base, and we want the blocker to "climb to the sky."

We finish with a takeoff-on-air drill and a takeoff-versus-defender drill. We try to do board and chute drills every day, all year long. We go right from our agilities, and it is about a 15-minute period overall.

I want to talk about combination blocks. For just line play, you have to do certain blocks. We have two blocking schemes that deal with combination blocks. One is a power-blocking combination that we use in our veer-blocking scheme. We do that every day, and we have drills for it. The bottom line is that we have the power-blocking scheme, and we have a counter-blocking scheme that is essentially the foundation of 14 plays. Two schemes. On the counter scheme, we drive inside gap, pull the guard, and kick out and pull the tackle around. We have six different football plays off that one scheme.

We run a chili drill, which is essentially a two-man explosion drill. We teach a shoulder block. We can use a two-man Crowther sled on the drill, but the players like the chili drill better because they can compete.

In some combination blocks, we have to chip off and up to the linebacker. The key is to keep the shoulders square. In a guard/tackle combo on a 3 technique and an inside linebacker, if the tackle attacks the 3 technique on a straight line, he has lost. The linebacker scrapes and makes the play.

It is the hardest thing to teach offensive linemen to use their eyes. We have to work on it every day. The tackle has to step flat and then come upfield. So, on a combination block where I have a double-team combination from the down lineman to the linebacker, I step flat, and my eyes go up. We do the chili drill on the 3 technique, and the eyes go on up to the linebacker. As soon as he scrapes, I am out there on him. We have to coach that first step, but we also have to teach them how to use their eyes.

Let me touch on pass protection. We teach our pass blocking in a progression of three basic drills. I am not a big passing coach, but we have to do it. First, we do a simple kick drill just to get us out of our stance in a good position. Then, we follow that up with a kick slide drill to develop good footwork.

From there, we do a live pass-rush drill, best-on-best, with the defense, which we call *blood alley*. We align five offensive linemen with proper splits, and we align a defensive lineman in front of each one. We place a stand-up dummy seven yards behind the offense, and we go down the line, one at a time, with the defensive lineman attempting to knock down the dummy.

We do some team offensive drills that are good for our linemen. I think they can help your team. We do a hamburger drill, which is just a 1-on-1 drill with an offensive guy and a defensive guy going live. Sometimes, we put a running back in the drill to run off the blocker. We do it every week, all season long. You have to find a way to have contact in practice and be aggressive, or you are not going to be a real good football team. The 3-on-3 drill is just an extension of the hamburger drill.

These three team drills are good. On team sled, we take our seven-man sled and run plays on it. The five linemen drive the sled, while the skill players execute the play.

On team takeoff, we put the ball on the 20-yard line, and we place five dummies on the goal line. One is in the middle of the field, two on the hashes, and two on the numbers. We run any kind of play. The five offensive linemen block dummies that are right in front of them, and then it is a race by everyone to see who can block the five dummies downfield. Everyone sprints to the goal line.

We do an 11-on-4 drill that we call *team pass*. We bring four defensive linemen down and let them run any kind of rush, while the offense throws against air. It is good for the quarterback to throw while he feels the rush, and of course it is good for all the linemen.

We do a team option drill and some other related drills that I will go over in the drills session. Later, I will show you some of these drills on film.

AGILITY DRILLS

These drills are done in seven lines in an area 15 yards long.

Carioca

- Commands: Breakdown, ready, go
- Procedure: On the breakdown command, the first line of players breaks down.

- On the ready command, the first line of players throws the elbow to turn in the direction designated by the coach on quarter turn from the original position.
- On the go command, the first line of players does the carioca for 15 yards to the other coach. Emphasize low hips, long strides, and fast movement.
- At the end line, they turn forward and break down again until the coach releases them.
- When the first group leaves on the go command, the next group of seven players breaks down automatically.
- There will be no breakdown command after the first group. Repeat the procedure for all lines.
- When all players have done the drill one way, repeat the entire procedure the other direction.
- The players should do the drill moving both right and left.

Tapioca

- Commands: Breakdown, ready, go
- Procedure: Same as carioca, except the players will do very short, fast, choppy steps in place until a second go command releases them.
- They will then sprint to the end line, where the other coach will break them down.

Seat Roll

- Commands: Breakdown, ready, hand signals
- Procedure: On the breakdown command, the front line breaks down.
- On the ready command, they chop their feet.
- On the signal from the coach, the first line dives out onto their bellies into a push-up position with feet chopping.
- The coach points right-left-right, while the players execute a seat roll. Emphasize throwing the elbow of the arm in the direction that they are rolling.
- Also, emphasize rolling on the butt, not the back.
- After the third seat roll, the coach says, "Outta here," and the players sprint to the end line, where the other coach will break them down.

- When the first line exits, the next line automatically dives out onto their bellies and gets ready to do the drill.

Seal

- Commands: Snap count.
- Procedure: The first line gets into good stances with proper splits and alignment.
- On the snap, the players all step flat in the designated direction and throw their elbows.
- They run flat for two positions and then turn upfield. When they turn upfield, they focus their heads and eyes toward the backside of the play.
- They run to the end line, where the other coach will break them down.
- This drill is to simulate the backside blocking technique of option plays.
- This drill is also a good time to work on audibles and freeze-and-go cadence. Have all centers snap a ball in this drill when their line goes.

STANCE AND START DRILLS

These drills are done in seven lines with plenty of spacing between.

Stance

- Commands: Snap count
- Procedure: All players in all lines will get into a good stance as the coach goes through the progression and hold it until the coach releases all players to stand up.
- Stance Progression: Feet should be shoulder-width with toes pointing straight upfield and a toe-to-instep stagger of the right foot.
- Crouch down with elbows on knees, and with head up. Drop the right hand down in line with the right big toe. Fingertips only should be on the ground.
- Very little weight should be forward on the hand. The hand should be able to be knocked away without the player falling forward.
- Place the left elbow on the outside of the left knee with the left hand clenched into a fist. Look through eyebrows at target.
- Back should be flat.

Stance and Step

- Commands: Stance, go
- Procedure: On the stance command, all players in all seven lines will get into a good stance using the progression mentioned in the previous drill.
- On the go command, the players execute the step that the coach has given them. They hold the step until the coach releases them to stand up.
- Get two or three reps with each step and each foot during this period. Go fast (rapid fire).

Steps

- Drive step: Make a six-inch step forward with the called foot. Punch and stay low with chest on thigh.
- Sweep step: Step flat, gaining a little depth off the line. Throw the elbow of the side toward the step. Stay low with chest on thigh.
- Trap step: Make a six-inch step at a 45-degree angle toward the call. Throw the elbow of the side toward the step. This is similar to the sweep step, but is into the line instead of flat.

Stance and Start

- Commands: Snap count
- Procedure: The front line gets into a stance using the progression mentioned previously. On the count, the players take off low and hard with the called foot and sprint for 10 yards. Focus on taking off on the "g" in go or the "h" in hut.

BOARD AND CHUTE DRILLS

Power Steps

- Procedure: Align in a good stance in the chute.
- On the count, take a power step with the assigned foot. This step involves a six-inch drive step while driving the opposite knee to the ground.
- In this drill, the players should actually make contact with the ground with the kneepad of the opposite leg.
- Emphasize pulling the face up on the step and punching with the hands.
- After the power step, they run to the end of the board and go back to the line.

Pound Steps

- Procedure: Align in a good stance in the chute.
- On the count, take a power step with the assigned foot.
- After the first step, the players should travel the length of the board, pounding their feet. The entire foot should pound into the ground, not just the balls of the feet.
- The feet should be pointing slightly out while pounding.
- They should stay low and in a good blocking position while pounding the feet, and their heads should be up.

One-Step Punch

- Procedure: Align in a good stance in the chute. Another player should align in a breakdown position head-up in the chute, no more than a foot from the blocker.
- On the snap, the blockers should take one drive step with the designated foot and punch the defender.
- Emphasize the punch with the thumbs up and the elbows in.
- Do not extend the arms. The face should be within the chest plate of the defender.
- The target of the punch should be the chest plates of the defender's shoulder pads. "Make the knuckles bleed."
- Centers should snap the ball in this drill.

Fit and Drive

- Procedure: Align in the chute in a "fit" position versus a defender in a breakdown position.
- The "fit" is a position that the blocker should be in after making contact on a defender in an actual block.
- The knees should be bent, the head up, and the fists are on the chest of the defender in a good, low blocking position.
- The coach will check to be sure that each blocker is in a good fit position.
- On "go," the blocker will pound the feet to drive the defender the length of the board.

- The defender should give resistance. Emphasize driving with a good wide base.

Takeoff on Air

- Procedure: Align in a good stance in the chute while straddling the board.
- On the snap, step with the designated foot and explode the length of the board low and hard.
- The focus of this drill is an explosive, quick burst off the ball. Anticipate the snap count.
- Move on the "g" in go or the "h" in hut.
- Centers should snap the ball in this drill.

Takeoff Versus Defender

- Procedure: This drill puts the skills of the previous drills together into one movement.
- Align in a good stance in the chute while straddling the board.
- The defender will align in a breakdown position at the midpoint of the board.
- This gives the blocker some room to explode off the ball before making contact.
- On the snap, the blocker explodes off the ball, makes contact with the defender, and drives off the board until the whistle.
- Emphasize explosive takeoff, face and fists in the chest, and a good wide base in the drive. Centers should snap the ball in this drill.

BLOCKING DRILLS

Chili Drill

- Procedure: The players get into two lines shoulder-to-shoulder with one person out front holding a football. He is 10 yards from the two lines.
- The coach is between the two lines and the player lined up 10 yards from the other two.
- On the "ready" command, the first two players in the line sprint out five yards to the coach and get into a good breakdown position with feet chopping.
- When the coach blows the whistle, the player with the football runs between the two other players and tries to split them.

- The other players take one step and deliver a forearm to stop the runner. They are allowed to take one step to deliver this forearm.
- They may not run out and attack the runner. They must deliver a blow in one step.
- They must step with the same foot of the same side they use to deliver the forearm.
- When they make contact, they should roll the hips and pull the head back.
- Emphasize stepping together, delivering a violent blow with the forearm, rolling the hips, and pulling the head back.

Combo Drill

- Procedure: The offensive line aligns in good stances with proper splits.
- Other offensive linemen align as defenders in the front called out by the coach.
- The play will be either 02/03 or 04/05.
- On the snap, the line will block the play.
- Emphasize the combo block of the guard and tackle on 02/03 (Diagram #1) and the combo block of the guard, tackle, and tight end on 04/05 (Diagram #2).

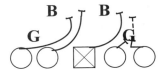

Diagram #1. Guard/Tackle Combo for 02/03

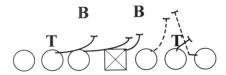

Diagram #2. Tackle/End Combo for 04/05

Also, emphasize the lead zero technique of the center and the seal technique by the backside guard and tackle. Run the same play to the same side several times in a row. Do not mix up plays in this drill. Just get several repetitions of the same play in a row. The coach should stand behind the offense to direct the defense to change alignments and stunts. Offensive linemen should clearly call out the alignments of the defenders on them so that the proper blocks can be executed. Go fast, and get as many quality repetitions as possible in this drill.

PASS PROTECTION DRILL

Blood Alley Drill

- Procedure: Five offensive linemen align with proper splits.
- A defensive lineman aligns on each offensive lineman.
- A stand-up dummy is placed seven yards behind the center.
- The coach stands behind the defense to signal the snap count to the offense.
- Starting with the right tackle, the offensive and defensive linemen engage in a 1-on-1 pass rush/pass protection. The defensive lineman attempts to knock down the dummy.
- The offensive lineman attempts to keep the defense out. This drill is done live with best-on-best (Diagram #3).

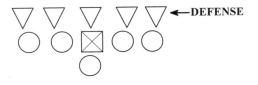

Diagram #3. Blood Alley Drill

TEAM OFFENSIVE DRILLS

Hamburger Drill

- Procedure: One offensive lineman aligns in a five-yard-long chute of dummies.
- One defensive lineman, linebacker, or defensive end aligns head-up on the offensive lineman, leaving enough space between them to simulate the neutral zone.
- A running back aligns three yards deep directly behind the offensive lineman.
- On the snap, the offensive lineman fires off and attempts to drive block the defender.

- The running back fires off and attempts to score through the chute. He must stay in the chute.

- The defender attempts to shed the block of the offensive lineman and tackle the running back before he crosses the line at the end of the chute.

- This drill is done at maximum intensity in a highly competitive environment.

- This drill should be done with best-on-best (Diagram #4).

- Usually, seven chutes are set up side-by-side. However, only one chute goes at a time.

- When a center blocks, he should snap the ball to a quarterback, who then hands off to the running back.

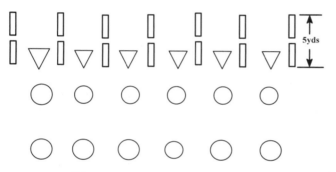

Diagram #4. Hamburger Drill

Three-on-Three Drill

- Procedure: A chute of dummies 10 yards long is formed.

- The drill begins with the ball at the beginning of the chute.

- Three offensive linemen, two running backs, and a quarterback go against three defenders. The defenders can be defensive linemen, linebackers, or defensive ends.

- The objective of the offense is to gain 10 yards in four plays or less, while the defense tries to stop them.

- The offense may only run 12 or 13 yards. The offense will huddle between each play.

This is a highly competitive drill. There should be some sort of penalty for the side of the ball that loses the drill. The players should be assigned "best-on-best."

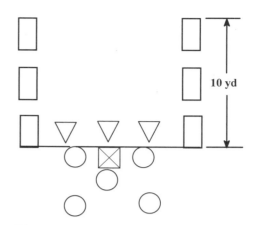

Diagram #5. Three-on-Three Drill

Team Sled Drill

- Procedure: Three offensive teams will huddle behind the five-man sled, usually green, gold, and N groups (Diagram #6).

- One team will call a play in the huddle, then sprint to the sled to align in the called formation.

- On the snap, the offense will run the called play, while the five interior linemen drive block the sled.

- All other offensive blockers will block "air."

- On the whistle, the offense will exit the sled to the direction of the play. If the play runs to the right, the offense exits right.

- When the players exit, they will sprint downfield to the coach, who will then break them down once every player has arrived.

- After they break down, that group will run back around behind the sled.

The tempo of this drill should be very fast. As soon as one group exits the sled, the next group should be calling their play.

In this drill, only off-tackle or outside plays should be run in order to keep the running backs from running into the sled. Emphasize takeoff and hustle. This drill is done primarily to teach and establish takeoff and a rapid-fire tempo.

Team Takeoff

- Procedure: Three offensive teams will huddle, usually green, gold, and JV groups.

- A defensive front with linebackers aligns in a designated front.

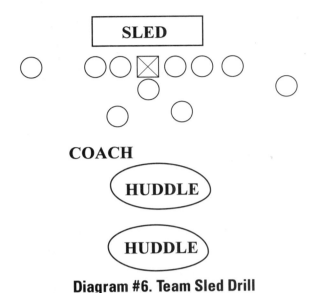

Diagram #6. Team Sled Drill

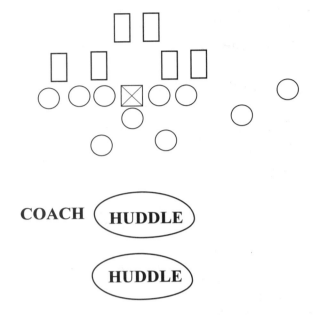

Diagram #7. Team Takeoff Drill

- The first team will call a play and sprint to the line of scrimmage.
- On the snap, the offense will fire off and execute the play versus the dummy defense.
- On the whistle, the offense sprints downfield to break down on the coach. After the breakdown, they run around to the offensive side of the ball.
- The tempo of this drill should be very fast.
- As soon as one group exits, the next group should be calling their play.
- The pace of this drill should be fast.
- Takeoff, tempo, hustle, and perfect execution should be emphasized.

Team Pass

- Procedure: Two offensive teams huddle behind the line of scrimmage.
- One group will call a pass play and sprint to the line.
- On the snap, the offense executes the pass play.
- This is either done on air or against a defensive front with no secondary. Perfect execution and 100-percent completions should be emphasized.
- The ball should be rotated from hash mark to hash mark, and occasionally to the middle of the field.

- As soon as the first group finishes the play, the next group should be calling their play.
- Try to get as many quality repetitions as possible in this drill.
- If new teaching or demonstration needs to be done, try to do it at the beginning of the drill.

Team Option

- Procedure: This is a live drill with an offense versus a defense.
- Only option plays are run, with an occasional play-action pass.
- This drill may be either a green-on-gold, or a green-on-green/gold-on-gold drill.
- Each unit runs six to eight plays before rotating.
- Emphasize takeoff, perfect execution, and proper audibles.

Pass Skelly

- Procedure: Offensive backs, receivers and a quarterback face the defensive ends, linebackers, and secondary.
- The offense runs its pass plays against the defensive coverages.

- Emphasize receiver releases off the line of scrimmage, reading coverages, and the quarterback's passing progression.

Team Rules

- Procedure: This is a pre-practice drill.
- One offensive team huddles, while other offensive players align in an opponent's defense.
- The offense runs the plays of particular emphasis for that day. Run the same play back-to-back each direction.
- The play should be run at full speed to work on proper timing, but the defense should give with the blocks.
- After four to six plays, another offensive team runs the plays.

What It Takes to Be a Lineman

- The lineman is an individual who must want satisfaction from personal accomplishment on the field.
- He will only be recognized through consistent effort.
- A football team is like a machine or a carpenter's toolbox—each part is vital to the accomplishment of the job.
- If you want to be a lineman, you must have an instinct to achieve goals.
- The offensive lineman must take pride in himself and keep in mind what is necessary in order to accomplish team goals.
- He must want to have a high percentage of blocking efficiency.
- He must want to dominate the defensive player in the offensive running and passing game.
- He must never miss an assignment and make key blocks to spring the ballcarrier for long gains.
- These are the goals an offensive lineman must set for himself.

That about covers it, men. If I can help you in any way, just let me know. Thank you.

DEFENDING THE WING-T AND DOUBLE WING

Southington High School, Connecticut

When you think about defending the wing-T offense, you must know what type of wing-T it is. You must know if your opponents are a fullback or sweep team and the types of formations you will see. You will face some coaches who like to run the jet sweep and the buck sweep. They run the trap-influence and waggle. You will also encounter teams that like to run the fullback belly and trap plays. The belly play is the wing-T version of the isolation play in the I-formation. The trap can be run both ways—the belly pass and counter.

My experience at defending the wing-T indicates to me that the aforementioned are the only two types of coaches. Some coaches take their best wingbacks and move them to the fullback, because that is where they want to concentrate the offense. Other coaches want the fullback there to keep the defense honest and work with their speed on the edge. The teams that really give you problems are the ones that have their primary runner at the quarterback. On those teams, the waggle passes and bootlegs become running plays for the running quarterbacks.

Next, I would like to discuss formations with you. I'll use terms that we employ in our terminology (Diagram #1). Our first formation is called "brown." It is a split-end wing set with a halfback set in the backfield. This formation is the most popular set for wing-T teams. It involves a power side, with the tight end and wing, and the fullback game in the middle. Diagram #1 illustrates motion movement in the brown formation. We term it "north" motion, when it goes back into backfield and "east" motion when it goes flat to the line of scrimmage.

In the "gold" formation, the halfback moves to a wing position outside the tackle into the split-end

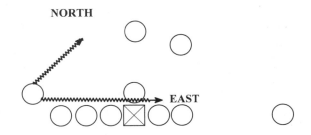

Diagram #1. Brown Set/North-East Motion

side (Diagram #2). This alignment results in a double-wing type of formation. The motion shown in Diagram #2 is "south" motion, which is the opposite of north in the first diagram. This motion goes back into the backfield. The "west" motion is the type of motion that is used with the jet sweep.

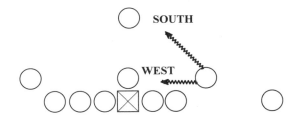

Diagram #2. Gold Set/South-West Motion

In the "blue" formation, the wing moves to the split-end side (Diagram #3). This set is like the "brown" formation, except the wing is on the other side of the formation into the split end. This alignment gives the offense a numbers advantage if the defense does not adjust.

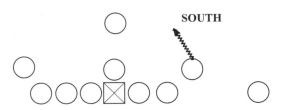

Diagram #3. Blue Set

The wing-T offense signals what they are going to do by the motions they employ. Our terms for motion are north, south, east, and west. From each of these motions, there is a limited amount of things the offense can do.

In "north" motion, the wingback aligns to the tight-end side of the formation. This type of motion goes back into the backfield. "South" motion involves motion by the wingback into the split-end side of the formation. This motion goes back into the backfield, similar to north motion. "East" motion is jet motion by the wingback on the tight-end side. If there is no tight end in the game, it is jet motion to the right of the defense. Jet motion is flat motion across the formation. "West" motion is motion by the wingback toward the tight-end side. Examples of these motions are shown in Diagrams #1 and #2.

With jet motion, the defense should think jet sweep or jet trap. With north motion, the wingback goes into the backfield. The defense should think belly play. When teams use the north and south motions, the quarterback opens to the fullback, and the halfback becomes the lead blocker. With south motion, you get heavy tight-end sweep, with buck action or the bootleg to the backside. When the offense uses south motion, they are trying to get back to the brown set. With east or west motion, the defense should think jet sweep, trap back to the tight end, or jet pass.

If an offense aligns in brown and uses west motion, they are going to a blue formation. The way we align to those formations is the way we adjust to the motions from those sets.

"Cyclone" is the defense we play against the aforementioned types of formations (Diagram #4). In this defense, we play our "anchor" end in a 4i technique. He keys the ball and gets penetration through the B-gap. The nose aligns in a 2i technique. He keys the ball and gets penetration in the A-gap. The defensive end plays in the B-gap to the split-end side in a 3 technique on the outside shoulder of the guard. He keys the ball and gets penetration. The "bantam" is in a loose alignment on the offensive tackle. We call it a 9 technique on the

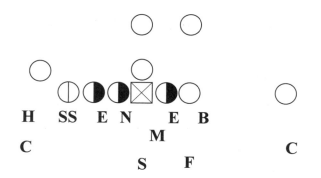

Diagram #4. Cyclone

ghost of the tight end. He is not touching the offensive tackle at any point in his alignment.

The corner to the split end is in press alignment and has him in man-to-man coverage. The strong safety aligns head-up the tight end and has him in man-to-man coverage. The Mike linebacker aligns in the open side A-gap, with his toes at the heels of the defensive line. He keys the fullback and looks for the trap. The Sam linebacker is five yards off the ball over the center. The free safety aligns five yards off the line of scrimmage on the outside shoulder of the tackle to the split-end side. The strong corner aligns head-up the wingback five yards off the line of scrimmage and is responsible for the wing, man-to-man. The "hawk" plays on the wingback and blitzes through him. He contains and looks for the counter and waggle.

The two ends and nose get as close to the ball as they can. Their job is to get penetration through their gaps and cause chaos in the backfield. Because of the 4i and 2i alignments, the offense will have trouble running the buck sweep. If they try to pull the guard, the center is the only lineman who can block the 2i defender. The tackle cannot close with an inside alignment on him. If the center tries to get to the callside, the defense will turn the Mike linebacker loose.

The "hawk" aligns on the outside shoulder of the wingback to the tight-end side. If the hawk gets east motion toward him, he gets upfield for containment and turns everything inside. On this motion, he looks for waggle or counter. If the motion goes away from him, he goes upfield and looks inside. He is looking for someone pulling on him. If he gets the pulling guard, he keeps him on his inside shoulder and makes him stay on the inside. The "bantam" gets up the field and plays the same as the "hawk."

The Mike linebacker plays in the A-gap and creates chaos and confusion. He creates a problem for the center. If the offense wants to pull the backside guard, the center has to cutoff for the guard. If he blocks the guard, the Mike linebacker is free. If he blocks the Mike linebacker, there is no one to block the 3-technique defender.

The Sam linebacker in the middle of the defense has no one who can block him. He keys the fullback. He will make the plays in the C-gap to the tight end. The guard and tackle have inside defenders, while the tight end has the strong safety over his nose. There is no one left to block the Sam linebacker, who plays inside out to the ball and makes the plays.

He has an I/O technique, which he plays with the free safety on the two backs in the backfield (Diagram #5). The I/O means inside/outside technique on the backs. The free safety keys the halfback, and the Sam linebacker keys the fullback. If the halfback aligns in the wing position and goes in south motion back into the backfield, the Sam linebacker has that motion if it comes out to the tight-end side. The free safety's eyes go to the fullback and plays him if he comes to his side.

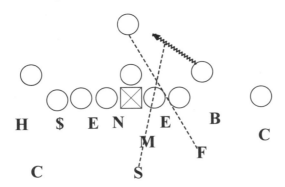

Diagram #5. I/O Technique

The free safety aligns five yards off the line of scrimmage and matches his alignment with the halfback. If the halfback is in the halfback position, the free safety aligns over him. If the halfback aligns

in the wing outside the tackle, the free safety aligns over that position. The free safety has an I/O technique with the Sam linebacker. If he gets south motion, his eyes go to the fullback, and he starts to think waggle pass. He plays run support from the inside out with the bantam.

The strong safety is head-up the tight end and has no run responsibility. He is man-to-man on the tight end. In high school football, we want a wrestler playing this position, someone who can beat up the tight end. The youth level is also a good place to put the defense's most physical player.

The tight corner is man-to-man on the wing. If the wing goes in east or north motion, the corner goes with him. This defender has to make sure he goes behind the linebackers as he comes across the set. It is important that his movement does not get in the way of their reads. The split corner is pressed or off the split end. He is man-to-man on the split end and can expect to get limited routes. On the waggle pass, the split end runs the comeback and post corner. In practice, we try to show the corner what the offense will run and let him work against those routes.

If you have a good man-coverage defender, you can press the receiver. However, if you are nervous about the coverage played off this coverage, you should have him play with inside leverage.

The Sam linebacker and free safety cover the motion going to the tight end by the halfback. As the motion goes to the tight end, the Sam linebacker stays on the motion. When the motion starts, the free safety's eyes lock on the fullback. The Sam linebacker moves with the motion, and the free safety sits on the backside, waiting for the fullback in the waggle scheme. If the offense executes the waggle, the fullback runs right to the free safety. He plays the waggle and the belly coming right at him.

If the formation is a gold formation, we have a big bubble in the defense on the split end side in the C-gap. If the offense employs north motion (Diagram #6), they have to run the sweep to the split-end side. We have a 2i and 3 technique on the pulling guards. There is no one to block the Mike linebacker. If the offense tries to block the belly play, there is no one to block the Sam linebacker. They can block the 2i and 3 techniques with the guards, and the center can block the Mike linebacker. However, there is no one to block the Sam linebacker. If they try to run the belly pass, they had better throw the ball quickly, because the hawk is coming off the tight-end side and has no one to block him. His technique is to blitz, when he gets motion away from him.

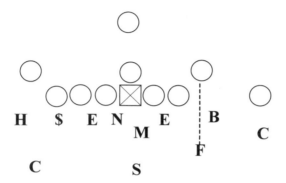

Diagram #6. Gold Alignment

In the "blue" formation, the offense is unbalanced in the backfield (Diagram #7). They have the wing and the halfback to the same side. The corner comes over and aligns on the wing in the slot, and the free safety is aligned on the back in the backfield. We are sound with the number of defenders we have on that side.

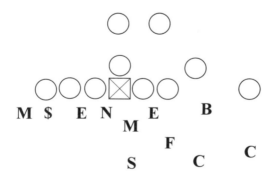

Diagram #7. Blue Alignment

If the offense goes unbalanced in the offensive line by bringing the split end to the wingback side, we have the same basic front (Diagram #8). The corner comes over with the split end and aligns as he did on the other side. When the split end aligns on

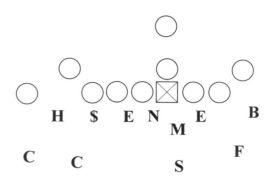

Diagram #8. Unbalanced Line Alignment

the line of scrimmage, the tight end is ineligible. We do not shift the front. We adjust with the secondary.

In this defense, the hawk and bantam have to be players. They need to be the best players on the defense. They have to scream up the field and make it difficult for the offense to block them. They have to make plays on the quarterback. If the defense can get lined up to the formation, that is half the battle. The problem with this defense involves the inside/out technique played by the Sam linebacker and the free safety. These two defenders have a tendency to want to do too much. As such, they need to be patient in their play. They have to realize that they have time because of what is going on in the wing-T offense. If they do not overreact, things will come to them.

The hawk aligns on the wingback. If the wing goes in north motion, his rule is to blitz upfield, looking to the inside for a pulling guard. If there is no guard coming, he knows it is the belly pass and attacks the quarterback. In the same situation, if he sees the pulling guard coming to the outside, he goes and meets the guard. He squeezes the play and makes the quarterback pull up. If he can make the quarterback pull up, there is pressure coming off the backside.

The open-side corner does not have to be Deon Sanders. All he has to do is knock the ball down and get us to the next down. On the other hand, if he has a chance to make a pick, he should try to catch the ball.

This defense is sound against everything the wing-T does. The only problem the defense has involves option responsibilities. The defense has to be tweaked to handle the belly option. The problem is the option to the tight end and wing side. It is a long way for the free safety to get to the pitch.

Next, I'd like to discuss the Mike linebacker. The Mike does not play like a traditional linebacker. If the seams in front of him open up, he takes them and penetrates the offense. If the offense tries to pull guards and block back with the center, he has to shoot the gaps when the offense does not block him.

Before discussing the double-wing set, I would like to reiterate the following points concerning defending the wing-T:

- Penetrate with the front
- Apply outside linebacker pressure on the quarterback
- See the formation and get lined up
- Do your job
- Work hard on the I/O scheme

Understanding how to defend the double wing involves addressing several questions, similar to like you did with the wing-T. For example, what type of motion does the offense employ in their attack? Who is the fullback? Is the fullback a running back or a glorified guard put in the backfield to block? There was a team that won the state championship two years ago that played with a 6'-3" 267-pound fullback. His job was to kick-out the outside linebacker. He did not carry the ball. Who runs the ball? Do they give it to the halfback or the motion man, or does the quarterback carry it?

We use a "cat" defense against the double-wing set (Diagram #9). In this defense, the defensive end to the hawk side aligns in a 5 technique on the outside shoulder of the tackle and is a C-gap player. The nose aligns in a 2i on the guard and serves as an A-gap defender. The defensive end to the Sam-linebacker side is in a 3 technqiue and plays the B-gap. The bantam plays in a 5 technique and is the C-gap defender.

The defensive line in this defense can play two different ways. The defensive linemen can play low in a root-hog technique, where they stay low and hold their ground or they can try to penetrate. The

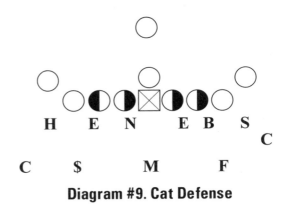

Diagram #9. Cat Defense

defensive line can be shaded any way you want to slide them. You must, however, make sure to leave the center uncovered. The defensive lineman wants to make contact with the offensive lineman in front of him and be as physical as he can with him.

The hawk and Sam linebacker are the cats in this defense. They align in a 9-technique position in a three-point stance and tilt in at a 45-degree angle. Their inside hand should be on the ground and their outside hand up. They should key the football. On the snap of the ball, their mission is to crash inside and come under any blocker who is coming at them.

The defensive linemen should come off the ball as if they were running a hundred yard dash. They should drive their outside arm through the down block of the wingback. They should penetrate all the way to the B-gap. They should create a pile in the B-gap. They crash between the wing and the tight end. They have to be fast enough to beat the down block of the wing.

We rotate three to four players in that position in order to keep them fresh. If you keep fresh players making big hits, as the game wears on, these players will begin to make even more plays.

The Mike linebacker plays a 0 technique on the center. He reads the center and goes opposite his block, if he blocks one way or the other. He has to play the trap. Leaving the center uncovered gives the Mike a good read on which way the play is going. The Mike linebacker plays from the A-gap to the B-gap.

The corners are five yards deep and outside the wing to their side and are cocked in so they can see the opposite wingback (Diagram #10). They should key the opposite wing to the wing on their side. The corner is looking for motion from the opposite wingback. If he does not see motion coming to him, he knows that his wing is going the other way. At that point, he takes a step in toward the tight end, locks in on him, and gets ready to play football. If he gets opposite motion coming at him, he comes up for contain.

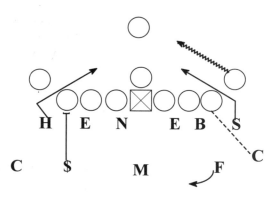

Diagram #10. Motion Adjustment—Corner

The safeties are the two most important players in this defense. If you are playing a double-wing team and have four defensive backs in the secondary, you may consider taking the corners out of the game. In their place, you can substitute another safety or linebacker (Diagram #11). The safeties align five yards deep, head-up the tight ends, keying the opposite wingbacks. If the safety gets motion to him, he comes down and runs through the face of the tight end. He wants to be as physical as possible.

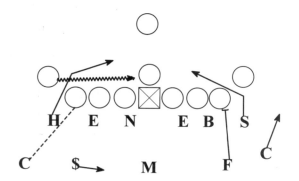

Diagram #11. Motion Adjustment—Free Safety

The outside linebacker crashing to the inside knocks the wingback and end off their blocks. He is creating a pile behind the B-gap. That means the ball will bounce outside the pile. If there is no motion from the opposite wingback, the safety waits for his wingback to clear. He has to be a slow player. If he sees the opposite wingback start to his side after the ball is snapped, he hits the D-gap, because the counter is coming. If he does not see any action coming his way, he pursues to the other side and helps out.

When the outside linebackers are sent inside, the action happens right now. We tell them to trap the trapper. They should try to stay inside and force the ball out.

If the wingback comes in motion and the offense runs the jet sweep, one hell of a collision should occur behind the offensive tackle. If the offense tries to pull the guard, the outside linebacker tracks to the handoff mesh. As the corner sees the opposite back coming in motion, he takes a step to the outside and gets ready to contain. He knows the safety is coming hard on top of the tight end. The Mike linebacker is not going to be a factor on this play until later. He is playing the trap first and pursuing after that. He cannot get in a hurry to get to the outside. We have the corner and safety to play the jet sweep. The guard will not be a factor because he will not get out.

The defensive line's entire job is to hold the line of scrimmage. If the offensive lineman tries to pull, the defensive linemen make contact and penetrate wherever they can.

The following questions reinforce the key points concerning how to play against a double-wing team:

- How much motion do they run?
- Who gets the ball the most?
- Is the fullback a lineman or a true fullback?
- How much does the fullback run the ball?
- Is the quarterback a threat to run the ball?
- From what motion does the play-action pass comes?

Thank you for your attention.

AN UPDATE OF THE BASIC WING-T OFFENSE

Wayne High School, West Virginia

While I am not an expert on all aspects of the game, I am fully aware of what we have done at Wayne High School—and we have had a lot of success with it. In reality, if you are a dyed-in-the-wool, Delaware wing-T man, you may cringe a little at what we do. On the other hand, what I'm going to share with you today is the way we do things. As such, I am a firm believer that you have to have a set number of plays, that you get good at, that complement each other.

Today, I would like to go over our base offense. It probably constitutes about 60-to-70 percent of our attack. We do some other things because as the competition level goes up, teams have a tendency to take away what you do best. The things I will show you today are things we have a hard time running when we get into the playoffs—unless we are really good.

For us, and for most of you, winning the state championship is the ultimate goal, the objective for which we all strive. Someone once said that trying to win a state title is like beating your head against the wall and wondering if it is ever going to end, and then it is that last blow that ends up doing it.

Of course, you have to have good players. To a degree, you also need to have luck on your side—luck always plays a role in winning a state title. In reality, however, you start out wherever you are, and you keep working to get better. In our case, we started out 0-10 in 1997. Over time, we improved ourselves to a point where we finally won the West Virginia state championship. Frankly, I learned the basics of the game that first year. Eventually, we got to where we won most of the time, and when we did not, it usually involved a speed issue. There is no substitute for speed. All factors considered, you'll usually be hurting if you do not have any.

At this point, I would like to go through several factors that I believe are critical to building a sound football program:

- Concentrate on your average players.
- When your players are close to even in their skill level, play them all.
- Never write off your young players.
- Remember that team chemistry is a daily job.
- Begin selling the basic elements of your program to your athletes when your players are young.
- Attend JV and middle school games—both physically and mentally.
- When adversity hits, re-dedicate to the basics of the game.
- Avoid highs and lows—keep the same approach.
- Play your hitters; as early as you can, determine who they are and then back off.
- In crucial times, think of players, not plays.

The following list details a general description of our personnel requirements:

- Quarterback—In our offense, the better the quarterback is, the better our offense is.
- Tailback—Our best player usually plays this position.
- Fullback—Although we have had fat fullbacks on occasion over the years, I really prefer smaller kids in the backfield. The last couple of years, we have gone with our second tailback at fullback.
- Wingback—The wingback must be either quick or a good blocker. If we have a player who is both, he will be really good for us.
- Split end—The split end needs to have good hands, have speed, and be a good blocker.

- Offensive line—We flop our offensive line. We have a skinny side of our line and a bigger side of our line. In addition, we always try to have a sixth offensive lineman, a player who can fill in at any position if someone gets hurt. Having this player keeps me from having to disturb the other guys, by moving somebody around.

We try to determine what our kids do well and what we want at each position. Then, we funnel them into the appropriate positions. We start when our athletes are young, even as early as eighth grade. I would also like to have an idea who my quarterback will be in five years. Things can always change, but that is the way we go about it.

Our base formation is "200 split left," where "200" puts our tailback in the slot, and "split left" tells our split end where to line up (Diagram #1). By changing the call to 400 or 600, we can change our tailback's alignment to either a halfback position or a tailback position. We do that because certain plays work better from certain formations. For example, because we cannot run a dive play out of a 200 set, we get into a 400 set to run the dive. The last couple of years, we had a tailback who ran our off-tackle trap a lot better from the I formation. As a result, we became a predominantly "600" team. It was the same play and the same concept, but different areas in order to be flexible to accommodate the skills and abilities of our players.

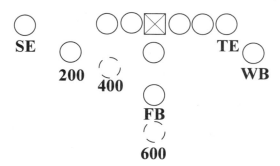

Diagram #1. Base Formation

Our offensive line takes splits of one-to-three feet. In reality, however, we have trouble with this factor. We usually start out with good splits, but as the game wears on, we often find the line positioned almost foot-to-foot.

We try to run a lot of different formations with our five basic running plays and our four pass plays. We can call "200 pro," "200 slot," and all of the unbalanced stuff to give us different looks. We do that to get defenders out of sync and to do different things with them. The problem is, if you do too much of that, you do not know where the defense is lining up. In order to be ready for all of that, there is a lot of preparation involved.

In calling our run plays, our quarterback, tailback, fullback, and wingback are numbered 1, 2, 3, and 4, respectively. We run the middle trap, the off-tackle trap, and the boot. These three plays constitute our trap series. We run a jet sweep, which we call 49G, and a lead play to the same side, which make up our fly series. Those are our five run plays. I will cover our play-action passes in a moment.

When we start a game, we understand that we may not be able to do certain things in our blocking schemes. As a result, we plan to block our five run plays in multiple ways. Although this approach enables us to get a lot of variety in our run game, we prefer that it remain relatively simple for our offensive line. Because we want our kids to be aggressive, we try to keep them from having to think too much. When you have a degree of success, teams will do all kinds of different things to try to stop you. As such, you had better have something basic to rely on.

Our base block rule for our trap series is "gap/backer." Essentially, all that means is that we are going to "meet at the campfire" (Diagram #2). "Trap," for us, means to pull the backside guard and kick out at the point of attack.

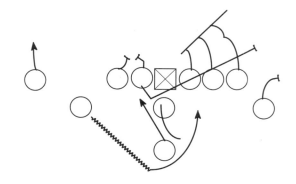

Diagram #2. 26 Trap

We have six different ways that we run a trap. The first, "blast," refers to the fact that the fullback is kick out at the point of attack. If the fullback kicks out and the backside guard runs a "curb," we would call that "blast curb." Turning out at the point of attack, with the backside guard leading up into the hole, is called "turnout." If we call "sweep," that designation refers to both guards pulling, with the playside guard kicking out and the backside guard running the curb. "Trey" means that both the backside guard and backside tackle are up into the hole.

As noted previously, our rule is "gap/backer." We want our kids to be powerful when they explode off the line, rather than their thinking about what they're going to do. Their power step is inside at a 45-degree angle. We block with our shoulder pads. While I know that it is popular in finesse offenses to have offensive linemen get their hands involved in the block, we have our players throw their forearms and try to get people off of the football. If we can get the defenders on skates, then we will work our thumbs up under their shoulder pads. We will also use our hands on blocks at the second level. When it is down in the trenches, however, we are throwing forearms.

On the 26 trap play, we want our line to create a "swinging gate," with no leaks. If it is a fourth-and-two situation and we are running 26 trap, you will hear "nobody leaks!" from the sideline. When we get that nice grading action down in there, good things will happen. Our guard pulls. Our center fills backside. Our fullback comes through and fills in that gap. The backside tackle cleans up. This sequence is our "grader action." If we can run that play and move it on down the line, we will usually have a pretty good year.

We teach our guard to stay tight in the line, be tight to that wall, and then trap out. We teach our backs to stay tight to the down blocks, rather than where the trap is. We want our backs in the hole with their shoulders square. If they turn sideways and run outside, we will play another back, because our big plays happen with overpursuit by the defense. The 26 trap is our base football play.

On the other hand, if we go up against a certain opponent and we want to kick out with our fullback and not pull our guard, we just say 26 blast. If we decide we would rather do it a different way, we can run 26 turnout (Diagram #3). Then, instead of trapping the first person past the 6 hole, we will turn him out. We will still wall the inside and do what we call "rocky block," but in this instance, the wingback becomes the tight end and the guard stays tight to the line, finds the third person in the wall, and leads up through the hole.

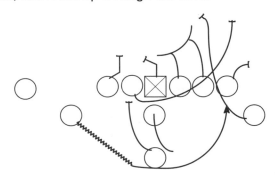

Diagram #3. 26 Turnout

If the base play is not working, we do not give up on it and start throwing the ball all around the field. More simply stated, we do not go crazy, because our base offense is not working. We just go back and do something different. If we still cannot block them, we will try to "formation" them.

The action on this play is designed to make people defend three different areas. We want to make our opponent defend the middle of the formation, the off-tackle area, and the off-tackle area on the other side.

When we run 32 turnout, which is our middle trap play, we want people to respect it. As a result, when we run 26 turnout, we want it to look like 32. I like this approach, particularly because it takes no talent whatsoever to do that. You can always get good at faking. You can be disciplined with the fullback, the tailback, and the quarterback.

Faking forces the defense to "line key." Although defensive players are coached to stay on the guard, they all want to find the football. If we do a nice job of faking, we make the opponent defend the entire tackle-box area.

Although I don't have time to cover the middle trap, I would like to state that if we are having trouble in 32 trap with a 3 technique, we will run 32 turnout (Diagram #4). Then, the pulling guard becomes the other guy in the wall to the backer.

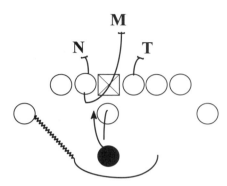

Diagram #4. 32 Turnout

One other factor that I might mention involving the 32 trap play involves running it against an odd front. In this instance, the importance of our "gap/backer" rule must be emphasized (Diagram #5). Any time we get head-ups, we assume they are coming to our inside gap. As a result, we step down as if the noseguard is going to fire that way. If he does not, we stay on our path. We tell the fullback to stay tight to the down block, find the wall, get beyond it, and then get upfield.

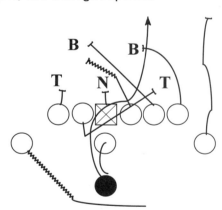

Diagram #5. 32 Trap vs. Odd Front

Next, having discussed trap, sweep, trey, blast, and blast curb, I'd like to go over the fact that we also do all of those things on "boot." After we run 32 and 26, we come back with our boot and try to run it a million different ways.

For years, in many of our wins, that was all we did. We ran the middle trap, the off-tackle, and the boot, and blocked them different ways. Then, a few years ago, we implemented the jet sweep into our offense. We really did not have much luck with this play until we talked to some people and found out what the key to executing it successfully was.

When the wingback comes in full motion and takes the handoff, the key to the whole play is the "clear step." We found that really works well with our 32, 26, and 17 plays, because defensive teams have to have somebody on that backside. If the opponent does not have somebody coming like a banshee off that backside, we will run the jet sweep all day. On the other hand, if they do, that is one less defender for us to deal with on the tight-end side, which is where we want to run the ball anyway.

The jet sweep is a real simple play (Diagram #6). As such, not a lot of coaching is involved in running it. We call our jet sweep play "49-G." On this play, our onside guard pulls. On any 8 or 9 play in our offense, we just reach that way with our playside people. Our split end and tailback communicate concerning who will take the outside player. If the outside defender is coming hard off the edge, the tailback will "stun" him right there. On the other hand, if he is playing off, the split end will "crack" him, and we get our tailback on around.

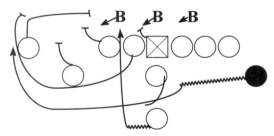

Diagram #6. Jet Sweep

We believe the same way on reaching that we do on other blocks. I do not believe that you should step out and stick your hands out on a reach block. We play teams that do that, and they get their arms broken. When we step, we step and bring a shoulder pad. We try to bring the shoulder pad hard and then work to our hands. At that point, we work our butt off to get to the ballcarrier.

On our jet sweep, the wingback takes his clear step and then, like most people know about the jet sweep, gets it to the hash, the numbers, and the sideline. Common sense will tell him when to cut it up. We want to complement our offense with something that will spread the field a little bit wider—something our opponent has to respect.

It is important that our tailback brings his pads and gets out of the way, while our "G guard" is looking to get up in here and log. Obviously, teams that are good defensively will chase this thing down when the split end goes to crack. On the other hand, we do not tell the guard to go out and trap the defender, because he will go out with the intention of kicking him out. The guard's job is to get out there and log him around. If we can log him around, we will get our wingback on the edge. On the other hand, if the defender comes screaming off the edge, it will be common sense for the guard to trap and for the back to go ahead and cut up.

We run 35 off the same jet-sweep action, giving the ball to the fullback off-tackle to the same side. We block 35 lead four different ways, depending on how the defense lines up. This action is also our iso blocking. If we run straight I-pro, 24-iso right at you, the fullback will be doing the blocking, but on 35 lead, the tailback is the lead blocker.

There are only so many ways for the defense to line up (Diagram #7). We will see a 1 technique and a 5 technique; a 3 technique and a 5 technique whom we block two different ways; and a 1 technique and a 4i technique. Those are essentially the only combinations we will encounter. The next section details how we would block those particular defensive looks.

Our fullback takes a glide step, and it is his responsibility not to run into the wingback. He takes a glide step and just kind of looks. This play may be run in the 3 hole, 5 hole, 7 hole, or anywhere in this area, but it will be run according to where the defense lines up.

The fullback takes his glide step, sees it, and hits it. If we can run the jet sweep pretty well, we will see a lot of flow with the linebackers. As such,

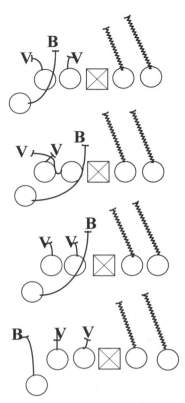

Diagram #7. 35 Lead vs. Four Defenses

our backside people can set a secondary wall if they will hustle off of the football as they should. As the fullback works his way through the hole, he will see the wall, get on the backside of it, and get himself upfield. This scenario is our 35-lead play.

Another key point to note is that we try really hard not to be right-handed. As many times as we run 32 trap, we try to run 33 trap. Because the double wing gives a mirrored offense, you have the ability to run the same plays to either side.

Against good teams, we run our counters a lot. We run a double reverse off our 26 play and block it like the jet sweep. We run an inside reverse and a counter trap back away from jet-sweep action. Another good play for us is the counter dive, off of tailback motion. The tailback motions as if it is 32/26/boot, and then plants, comes back, and runs a quick dive, with the fullback leading through the hole.

In the last few years, we have started to throw the ball more. For example, in several games last year we threw it at least 20 times. In my opinion, it is important that you are able to throw the football.

When you have the aforementioned good run plays, you need to have passes off each of them.

We have two passes off our trap series action. The best play in football is our boot pass, which I will show you how we run (Diagram #8). On the boot pass, the tight end drags, the wingback runs a post, and the split end runs a corner route. The backfield action is 32/26/boot action. The center and fullback block A-gaps, the guards block B-gaps, and the tackles block C-gaps.

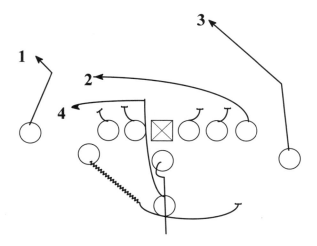

Diagram #8. Boot Pass

As opposed to rolling out, we try to have our quarterback set up in the pocket. We fan around him, and he steps up.

We also have a roll pass (Diagram #9). On this play, the tailback comes in motion and becomes the lead blocker. The wingback runs a wheel route, and the tight end initially reaches for the 9 technique and then works his way into the soft spot. The fullback cheats a little bit and then sprints into the flat to a depth of three yards. As he gets closer to the sideline, he will slow down. From the right hash, he would run it slower, while from the left hash, he would really run it fast.

The whole concept in this instance is that we have a play away from our tailback series action and a play to our tailback series action. Not only does the defense have to defend 32/26/17, they also have to defend the bootleg and the rollout, as well. The aforementioned details five different plays

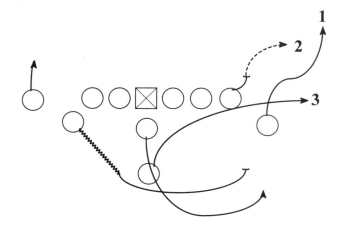

Diagram #9. Roll Pass

from the same exact backfield action, pretty much, which is how we do it.

Finally, from our fly-series action 49/35, we have a waggle pass away from the motion (Diagram #10). On this pass play, the tight end runs a corner route, the tailback runs a drag route, and the split end runs a post route.

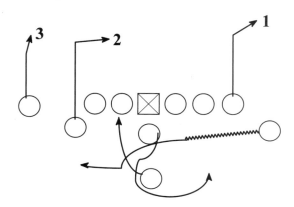

Diagram #10. Waggle Pass

We run our lead pass towards our fly motion, and it is one heck of a play (Diagram #11). On the lead pass play, the tight end runs a post route, the split end runs a takeoff route, and the tailback runs a flat route.

In theory, without much talent our playbook makes the defense defend 49, 35, waggle pass, and lead pass. The way I look at it as a coach, when we get real good at running those nine plays, we need to be as confident running the waggle pass as we are running 26 trap. The ability to execute these nine plays successfully can help get us out of some

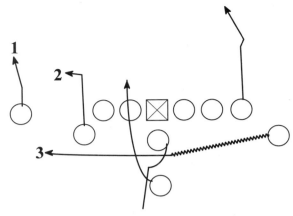

Diagram #11. Lead Pass

binds at some point in a fightly fought game or over the course of the season. Frankly if you have talent, you can do that.

At this point, I would like to show you some film of these plays. Please contact me if you have any questions.

USE OF MULTIPLE OFFENSIVE FORMATIONS

Warren Central High School, Indiana

We have become an offense based on multiple formations. I have become intrigued by shifting formations and motion. We want to make things as difficult as we can for the defense. Shifting and motion are a big part of our scheme. Our goal is to fit those types of ideas into the personality of our talent. The secret is to use word association to keep it simple for the players. When you are simple and the players understand what they are doing, they can execute the scheme better. They can match the intensity of the defense, and your offense will be more productive.

We try to develop our ideas with word association. We want to make it simple for the offense and difficult for the defense. The best example I can give you was our route to the state championship. We were not a multiple talented team. We got great coaching from our assistant coaches, and our players played great football.

We want the defense to adjust to our formations. We played a team in the playoffs that was a good, well-coached team. They ran a strong Bear defense, which was very difficult to run against. We went to a quad-receiver alignment and moved them out of that defense. We want to get the defense out of the front that makes it difficult for us to execute.

On the way to the state championship, we played a team that was a strong man-to-man defense. We had a good game plan to make them get out of that coverage. However, they stayed in the coverage and played their defense the way they had all year. Our good game plan was sound. When they stayed in the man-to-man coverage, we took advantage of it. By using the shifting, motions, and formations, we played very well and defeated them.

On our run to the state championship last year, we were not a multiple talented team. I would like to tell you it was great coaching that lead to the success we had; however, our players played extremely hard and played good football the entire season. I think the thing that allowed them to play that way had to do with the simplicity of the system.

Our back-up safety on that team became our third wide receiver in our open sets in the fourth week of the season. The fifth week of the season, he was the starter. He had no previous offensive background. We felt as if he was a good athlete and one of our better football players. Within a week, he learned our system and became a productive part of our offense.

I made this point to our offensive line coach last week. When we run the zone scheme, there are very few rules that go with that scheme. He is a huge technique coach and wanted to have a rule for everything that could happen on the defense. We do not want to do that. We want to run our offense as opposed to running against a defense that is multifaceted. We have been able to do that because of our formations. Once we find out where the defense will align against our formation, our running game becomes simple.

We do that through game planning. We want to find out in the first two series of a game how the defense is going to align against our formations and motions. We show everything early in the game and watch the adjustments. We want to know if they are adjusting to what we do or trying to maintain their basic approach to their defense. Our game plan is designed to run against the adjustments we think we will get. If they do not move, they are at a disadvantage.

The principle reason we use shifting and motion is to gain an alignment and strength advantage and make the defense feel uncomfortable in their scheme. We want to build doubt and confusion into their thinking. That slows them down and works to our advantage. Every defensive coach will tell you, the defense that is thinking cannot play fast.

Our Goals for Multiple Formations

- Make our offensive scheme as simple as possible to our kids.
- Make our offensive scheme as difficult to defend from a defensive standpoint.

Those are the simple goals we talked about in the introduction. We want to take advantage of our formations.

Advantages to Multiple Formations

- Make the defense play the formation first and the play second
- Make defense prepare for multiple looks.
- Make the defense simplify what they are doing
- Get defenses to change the scheme in their hopes to adapt.

Gentlemen, I want to introduce our offensive coordinator, who will take you through the presentation. He was instrumental in implementing our multiple-formation ideas, which played such a big part in our run to the state championship last year. He is a good coach and my son, Nick Hart.

Nick Hart

Thank you very much; I want to get right into the topic.

A big part of our multiple formations attack is the no-huddle. The no-huddle allows the offense to control the tempo in a game. There is an old adage that says: "Play fast, but do not be in a hurry." We think the exact opposite of that. We believe the no-huddle establishes a tempo for practice as well.

When you use the no-huddle in practice, a two-hour practice can seem like a marathon to your players. It is great conditioning for the players, and it allows you to get many more repetitions in practice. The secret of any offense is being able to repeat a skill over and over correctly. That comes from practicing that skill over and over. The more repetitions you can get in a practice, the more proficient you become as an offense.

In the no-huddle offense, the defenses cannot adapt or get comfortable in their scheme. When you run the no-huddle offense, the offense can change personnel and be at the line of scrimmage before the defense has a chance to react. The defensive coordinator has to have an additional spotter in the booth to see the personnel changes. If he does not, by the time the coordinator in the booth sees the personnel, we are at the line of scrimmage ready to run the play.

The no-huddle gives us the opportunity to use the check-with-me automatics more efficiently. If you are on the line of scrimmage and ready to snap the ball, the defense has to get set in what they intend to play. That gives the quarterback a chance to look to the sidelines for a check-with-me play change. This allows use to restart the offensive sequence and call another play. We can look to the sideline and give a hard cadence, knowing we are not going to snap the ball. That allows us to look to the sideline a second time and restart the sequence without any fear of a delay call. In addition, the hard cadence could incite the defense to jump into the neutral zone.

If you run a multiple-formation scheme, you have to implement the formations. When we go to camp, we install our base formations. We practice those formations and work from them in pre-season camp. Each week, we add another formation, motion, shift, and a play. Fifteen weeks later, we have a complete playbook. We have added 15 formations, 15 motion/shifts, and 15 plays.

During your film study before your upcoming game, you want to find formations that take advantage of the ways the defense aligns. If the opponent did not play well against a 3-by-1, we make sure that is one of our formations. If we do not have that formation in our offense, we add it. You want to find the defense's automatic checks and find a formation to exploit that adjustment.

We script the first 10 plays of every game. That is a big part of our multiple-formations scheme. In those first 10 plays, we want to show at least seven formations. We can deviate from the script if there is an obvious need for another play. If we use a formation in those first 10 plays that gives the defense a problem, we repeat that formation instead of what we may have on the script. The coach in the booth has all the formations we will use in the script drawn up. As we go through the formation, he records how the defense aligned against each formation.

If they made no adjustment to the formations, he makes note of that. If they made some radical adjustment, he makes note of that also. We want to show all of our new formations and shifts in the first 10 plays. This season, we were 13 out of 15 in scoring on the opening drive of a game. We want the defense to see something in the first 10 plays that they have not practiced against.

It gives the defense some problems when they see a formation they have not worked on in practice. The fact that we are no-huddle complicates that situation even further. It makes them scramble and can lead to miscommunications and mistakes. If the defense panics, they will end up in their base defense. They can make an adjustment, but it generally will require a time-out or waiting until after the series. If they wait until after the series, we will be ahead on the scoreboard. We scored 13 times out of 15 weeks on the first series of offense.

This past season, we started practicing our script on Thursday night before the games. In that practice session, the last 10 plays run are the first 10 plays we run on Friday night. That lets our players execute those 10 plays and gets them comfortable and confident with the plays. If there are any problems, you can take care of it on the field on Thursday night instead on the bench on Friday night. When you script those 10 plays, make sure they are your best 10 plays.

In our scheme, we are good at hiding formations. Many of our different looks are a way to disguise our best sets. One of our better sets this year was the bunch scheme. We came up with a multitude of shifts and motions to disguise the set. If you motion into a formation instead of lining up in it, that slows down the defensive reaction.

We want to show a new formation, which the defense has not seen, and motion to the formation they have worked on all week. They have worked on the formation all week, but it looks different to them. They have spent time in practice working on that formation, but they have to move their alignment to get to what they practiced. Those small adjustments take additional thinking and accomplish what our main goal is: we want the defense to think and not play fast.

You need to scout yourself and know your tendencies. I know we have certain tendencies to formations we run. We must know what they are and have counters ready to call with those formations. If you know your tendencies, you can use that to an advantage at the right time. In a big game or big situation, breaking a tendency can lead to a big play. If the defense has prepared plays on third down because that is what you have done 90 percent of the time, they are primed for the play-action.

In our base formations, the double set was our most popular set (Diagram #1). We adapt our offense around the personnel we have, not the other way around. That is the beauty of the multiple schemes in the offense. Two years ago, our best players were our quarterback and the fullback. The formations we used that year were the ones that featured the talents of those two athletes. This year, our best players were our quarterback and the tailback. We used formations that stretched the defense horizontally to make the zone play more effective.

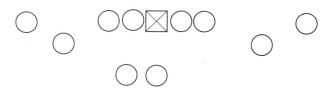

Diagram #1. Double Formation

In the double formation, we want to stretch the defense both horizontally and vertically. We want our wide receivers aligned on the numbers of the field. The slotbacks split the difference between the wide receiver and the tackle. Those splits will vary depending on the hash marks.

If the defense uncovers one of our slot receivers, we want to run the bubble screen as an automatic. Our quarterback is in the shotgun set most of the time. The throw to the left is easier than the throw to the right. To the left, the quarterback's shoulders are pointed that way, and the throw is easy. All he has to do is turn and throw. Going to the right, I tell the quarterback to get his hips around quickly to open them to the target. We do such a good job on these throws that it is almost like a running play. It does not matter what play is called or how many times we have run the bubble screen; if the defense uncovers the receiver, we throw it. In one game this year, we threw the bubble screen 41 times.

The double formation is difficult for the defense to play and keep enough defenders in the box. If there are five defenders in the box, I will get fired if I do not run the football. You have to count the box. We are predominantly a run team. If there are six defenders in the box, we have the ability to run or throw. We have the numbers to run the ball with six defenders in the box. We have five blockers, and they have six defenders; however, we read the backside defensive end on our zone-read play. The quarterback in that situation is blocking one of the defenders by holding him out of the play. He is responsible for the quarterback and is not a factor in the running game. That means we can get a hat on a hat and make yardage.

When we get six in the box, we think we can throw or run in this situation. We like the three-step game. The ball comes out quick and it is pitch and catch for us. The big patterns we like to run in this situation are hitches. If you can be patient enough in throwing the ball, you can march the ball throwing nothing but hitches. Most defensive principles are built with a no-cover zone up to five yards. Those gains are great first-down plays.

If the defense puts seven defenders in the box, we throw the football. Our receivers have to run better than your man-to-man cover defenders, and

they have to make plays. This year, we did not have the athletes to throw the ball down the field, but we did stretch the defense horizontally. We had good receivers, but we did not have the ability to run past defenders in the secondary.

The flexbone is a great set to make the defense play option-responsibility defense (Diagram #2). This formation will always be a staple of the offense. With this formation, you can do many things to hurt the front alignments. When you run this set, the defense has to spend time working on their option responsibilities. This is a good short-yardage formation and is a good set if you have a great fullback. Two years ago, we had a great fullback, and this set was our base formation. This past year, our offense featured our tailback. That meant the play selection required different formations.

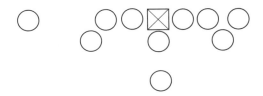

Diagram #2. Flexbone

We put this formation in as part of those first 10 plays. If we do not think the defense is sound, they will see a lot of flexbone that game. We used the flexbone formation along with a diamond formation. Teams that gear up to stop the flexbone cannot match up if we come out in the diamond set. From the flexbone formation, we run the midline option. It is a good play in short yardage, and we use this formation on the goal line. Our fullback this year was not that good, but he still made some big plays from this formation. We use motion with this set most of the time. This set is akin to a wing-T set.

I call the next formation "I formation" but it is an I-open set with no tight end (Diagram #3). This was our I-formation set because our tight end was not effective as a run blocker. We played more with a three-wide-receivers look in this set. Our tight end was better in the slot than on the line of scrimmage. Usually, the tailback is the best athlete on the team. By aligning in the I formation, you guarantee the tailback will get the ball.

Diagram #3. I Formation

If we align in the shotgun, the defense can do things to take the ball out of the tailback's hands. When the offense has a read scheme, the defense can determine who they want to carry the ball. They cannot do that in the I formation.

When we went to the three-wide-receiver look with the I formation, it actually helped our running game. It reduced the number of defenders in the box by a half man, and at times a full man. The defense has to remove another half man from the box to account for the three-receiver coverage. However, when they do that, they open spaces and creases in the defense. They end up with a defender covering grass. We run the lead stretch play, and every good running back becomes all that more difficult to stop when he has space in which to move.

The I formation will keep the quarterback from taking hits. If you have a quarterback who runs the ball, this type of set will give him a play where he can recover from a big hit or a long run. This set is always a good play-action formation. Our best plays out of the I formation were the outside zone and the power pass. The counter and power pass are great play action passes to throw.

The empty set is a great formation to spread the defense and put them in number mismatches with the receivers (Diagram #4). We did not have much speed last year at the receiver position. We did not run the 3-by-1 set much because we did not have enough speed at the single-receiver side. Defenses could man cover the single receiver and take him away from the attack. The empty became a good set for us because it put the tailback into the set as a receiver. We could get the ball to him in space, and it became a great set for us.

In the empty set, if the defense empties the box, the quarterback can run the ball. In our offense,

Diagram #4. Empty Set

we run the quarterback power-O play (Diagram #5). This is a good set to run the bubble screen to either side. We have a play called the "rocket screen," which is good from this set. We also run the jet sweep from this set. We block the play like the stretch play and can run it with the backside read on the defensive end for the quarterback.

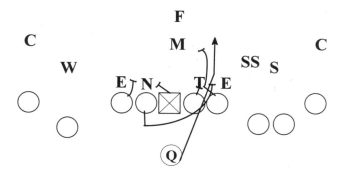

Diagram #5. Quarterback Power-O

There is no learning curve in the empty set. You do not have to teach the set to anyone except the tailback. If we have a better tight end, we like to put a tight end in the set with twin flanker on the outside (Diagram #6). This brings one defender closer to the box, but you can still run the ball. We bring the tight end into this set when we are going to run the ball to the tight end. We know our tendencies, and this becomes a good opportunity to break them and run the ball away from the jet motion on a quarterback sweep.

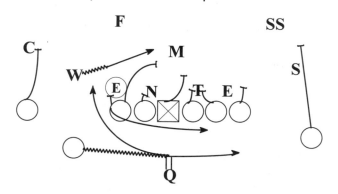

Diagram #6. Quarterback Read

Those are our base formations that we build from. We have double, I, flexbone, and empty. There are other formations you will see on the film. The bunch was a big formation for us this year (Diagram #7). It was a huge part of our offense. This year, we ran it primarily out of the shotgun. We had a great runner at tailback, and we wanted to get the ball in his hands. We could do it out of this set.

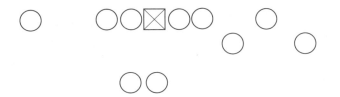

Diagram #7. Bunch Formation

One of the reasons we run the bunch set is to shrink the box. This formation pulls the defenders inside and gives us the opportunity to run to the edge. We ran our quarterback and tailback on sweep plays to the outside. We had a toss sweep we ran for the tailback from the bunch set. We blocked down and kicked out on the edge, or took it to the outside and into the boundary. This became a big running formation for us. We also developed a three-step passing game out of this formation. We became highly successful using this set.

This year, we will have the athlete at the single-receiver position who will make this a lethal formation for us. This set will allow us to develop 1-on-1 moves by the single receiver on the backside.

The stack formation became a huge part of our offense (Diagram #8). In the second week of the season, we played Owensboro Catholic. From the double set, we put in a post-dig combination against their cover 3. The object of the pattern was to read the free safety and linebacker. The inside receiver ran the dig, and the outside receiver ran the post behind him. If the free safety bit up on the dig, the outside receiver kept running to the post. We did not get the field stretched as we wanted. We decided to use the stack formation. From that formation, the post-dig worked great on the vertical stretch.

The post-dig route is a good zone beater as well as a man-to-man beater. Teams played this formation

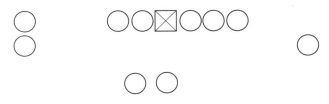

Diagram #8. Stack Formation

in combo coverage with the defenders on the inside and outside of the pattern, waiting for someone to break to them. We ran some great break-out cuts from this formation.

With this formation, we ran a play-action pass with the post-dig on the end of the play. The quarterback faked the zone play to the tailback and started out the backside. The wide receiver came back to the quarterback and faked a reverse. The quarterback turned back after the fake and had a post-dig pattern working in the secondary, which turned out to be a big play.

The *diamond* is a bunch set with the tailback sitting in the rear of the set (Diagram #9). We put this formation in just before the playoffs. We wanted to give people something new to prepare for when they played us. We opened the state championship game with this formation.

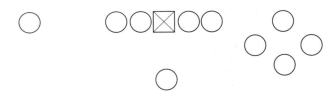

Diagram #9. Diamond Formation

This is an empty set in the backfield. The running back aligns behind the bunch set. We can run break-out patterns to that side. It usually gets teams out of a man-to-man scheme. There are too many picks and natural rubs for the offense.

This set is like the 3-by-1 set. The backside single receiver can create all kinds of problems for a defender. In the state championship game, we ran this set on the first play, and it worked out to be a 1-on-1 play on the backside. Our backside receiver was a good athlete with great leaping ability. He made a big play, which resulted in a touchdown.

BUILDING AND MAINTAINING A PROGRAM

Muskegon Catholic Central High School, Michigan

It is an honor to speak at this clinic. The general essence of my lecture is what we do and how we go about things. Hopefully, you will be able to pick up something that you can use, which is the underlying purpose of the clinic. I would like to start with some background about our system and what we do, and then get into some specifics of what we do.

When you talk about building something, you have to talk about a foundation. Because we're discussing football, there are three things that you have to have—an offense, a defense, and special teams. On the other hand, I believe that a difference exists in the uniqueness of football to my players and to my coaching staff. Understanding the basis of this difference does not involve me standing up here and diagramming my offense. My offense is not going to help you. It might help you if you have to play me, but the reality is that you can win with different offenses. The common thread to the way we view football is that you do have to be fundamentally sound.

I don't know about you, but over the years, we have played people who are not fundamentally sound. When you line up against them, they do not have people in the right position. As a result, you cannot figure out what they are trying to do. Furthermore, more times than not, you are going to win the game simply because you are better organized and are doing things right. The key point is that you just have to be fundamentally sound.

The other key pint that I'd like to emphasize is that you have to be able to attack multiple defenses. While we can draw the various schemes and systems up, you still have to have an offense that enables you to attack the various different defenses. For example, if you are a running team and your opponent stacks the box, you have to have an answer for that. You have to figure out what your offense is, and if you are a young coach, you should start with the offense that you know.

The same factor is true defensively. Your defense has to have enough flexibility to handle an "I" team one week, a wing-T team the next week, and perhaps a spread team after that. If you are not able to do that, you'll have limitations with which you will just have to live.

The same line of reasoning applies to special teams. Regardless of whatever approach to special teams play you employ, it must be fundamentally sound. In fact, I can think of three or four instances in the last few years when a special teams play either gave us the momentum to win the football game or actually won the football game for us.

The bottom line is that you have to be fundamentally sound in all three areas to have a successful program. If you do not have those elements, you are not going to be consistently successful.

The football program at Muskegon Catholic was started in 1972. Four years later, I was hired as a freshman line coach. Eventually, I worked my way up through the program to become the head coach at Muskegon Catholic.

In reality, 95 percent of what we do is what I have kept from the beginning of the program. I have kept it because it has worked for us. While the stuff we run, the terminology we use, and the general organization we utilize has carried over from the beginning, we have continued to build on all of those things.

Next, I would like to discuss our day #1 practice schedule from last year. It is the same practice plan that both our JV and junior high coaches are given. In fact, if you come into our system as a JV or junior high coach, I would hand you a packet of all the practices for the first week of doubles. I would also give you a packet of 10 practices that would include all of the basic run plays and all of the pass plays that would need to be installed and mastered. This step would provide you with a template of how to build the program.

There is a point, however, where you have to be ready to play the first game. Accordingly, you must have a plan for installing your offense and your defense. When you have coached a long time, there is not much difference in what you do in this regard from year to year. In fact, all of this information is on a computer at my home. As such, I develop the next year's plan for day #1 at home. Perhaps the coaches' names will change and maybe some different plays will be added for the first day, but that is basically it.

When we present this material to our athletes on the first day, we adhere to the assumption that our kids have never heard this information before, even though we know they have. Most of these athletes have been in our program since the seventh grade. The seventh and eighth graders play on the same team, while the ninth and tenth graders play on JV together. Then, they all come together on the varsity. The exact same plays, with the exact same terminology, have been used since they've been in the sixth grade. All we try to do is simply build on the number of plays and to perfect the execution of the plays.

We run one week of doubles. The way the system is now, we get one week of practice, then we get a scrimmage week, and then we have to play. As such, we have to figure out how we are going to implement your offense and defense within that time constraint. In that regard, we have a plan that has been successful for us.

Fortunately, over the years, we have had talented players. You obviously have to have talent to be successful. On the other hand, you also have to have both a system and a program that you must be able to implement concerning how to get done what you need to do.

We have had some experience with the playoffs, and it has been easier on us since the playoff system has expanded. In my time since 1988, we have won five state championships and were runners-up in 2001. As such, we have had considerable success during my 20 years at Muskegon Catholic. In fact, we remain competitive, and are going to have our kids ready to play, regardless of the talent level we have.

The bottom line for all coaches is that you have to win if you are going to remain coaching. At this point, however, I'd like to discuss how to maintain your program by developing and adhering to a sound process. Our process has five components that I would like to discuss briefly.

The first component is preparation. You have to prepare properly. If you do not prepare properly, you won't have much of a chance to win. You probably will not even be competitive. As such, preparing your team to win games is absolutely critical.

The second component of the process is that your kids have to have the proper attitude. This factor starts with your attitude as a coach. Sometimes, it can be tough to maintain a positive attitude, and sometimes it can wear on you. You just have to find some way to refresh your energy, because every team needs to have a good attitude, an attribute that starts with the coach.

The third component of the process is player development. You have to develop your players. This factor is a key element in any successful program. From the sixth grade through his senior year, each kid must continue to get better. As such, your program must be designed to help him reach that objective. You have to coach your players every day, every year, so that each athlete has the best year of his playing career as a senior. That is your job.

The fourth component of the process involves relationships. As a coach, you have to get along with the people who are directly or indirectly connected to your program, including the athletics director, the principal, the superintendent, the parents, the fans, and, of course, the kids and the other coaches. You just have to find a way to do that.

The fifth and final component of the process involves being professional. You have a professional obligation to each player to help him succeed to the best of his ability. You have a professional obligation to scout other teams ethically, and you have a professional obligation to grow as a coach. Every coach should work to grow in each of these areas.

A list of the underpinnings of a successful football program would include the following:

- Be fundamentally sound.
- Be prepared; have a sound scouting and practice plan.
- Play great defense.
- Focus on having sound special teams play.
- Exhibit a great work ethic.
- Expect to work hard and to win.

You must also have continuity in your program. As the head coach of a program, you need to have the big picture in mind. As you observe your players coming through your system, you have to help them find where they are best suited to play, a task that can occasionally involve a position change. A kid who is out of position is not going to fit into the big picture eventually. Accordingly, as the leader of the overall program, the head coach sometimes has to step in and make recommendations of position changes at the JV and even the middle-school level.

I am in charge of everything—the varsity, the JV program, and the middle-school program. I am given the opportunity to have considerable input in being able to pick whom the coaches are. As such, I require the coaches at all three levels to run what I want them to run.

My staff has 10 people on it. Four of these coaches work with the varsity, three serve with the JV squad, and three work with the middle-school team. Of the 10 coaches on our staff, seven graduated from Muskegon Catholic Central, and four of them played for me. This factor is crucial, because their background helps them to better understand the determination and effort that it takes to be successful, which they can help instill.

While the JV and middle school coaches can add plays, they must install the base plays. In addition, all terminology is the same at all three competitive levels. Furthermore, I name all new plays. We do it this way so that all aspects of the program are consistent.

Next, I'd like to discuss some specifics on what we do. The first factor is organization. The season starts the Monday after the season ends. Although we do not lift five days a week, our weight room is open five days a week after school. From the time that the football season ends, we do some things with quarterbacks and other positions. On the other hand, every athlete is free to play other sports or engage in some other personal activity, such as getting a job. In reality, it would be nice to see our players occasionally.

To give you an example of how it really is, at our school, we have kids who do not come to our weight room, because they have other proprieties and interests. In those instances, I tell our players to tell those individuals where and when the team is lifting. Seeing how hard the other kids are working can make a difference in the attitude of the kids who are not working out.

We have a meeting in May, in which we have sign-ups for the team. I do not harp on anything involving football until we meet with them in May, although we are lifting weights and trying to get ready physically for the upcoming season.

We run a skills camp in June. With the season getting shorter in terms of a two-week preseason, and only nine days before the first scrimmage, we try to install at least the passing game in the skills camp.

We also have a 7-on-7 that we do in July. We conduct our youth football camp later in the month. In addition, we initiate a night-running program two weeks before we start official practice.

At the May meeting, I hand each kid a detailed schedule to take home with him, which outlines everything we have planned throughout the summer, the beginning of practice, and through the scrimmage week. Since I cannot assume that they will remember everything I tell them, this printed schedule prevents them from having an excuse for not being where they are supposed to be.

To summarize our organization in the fall, our season starts with week one, during which we have doubles. The next week is scrimmage week, which we treat as a non-preparation week for the season. We are simply trying to fine-tune what we are going to show them in the scrimmage. In reality, we are not going to show them anything that they did not already know that we had, and that they may see in our first game.

When the season begins, the focus is on our nine-game schedule. We don't play in a league and don't have an affiliation. As such, we are an independent school. We break our season into three-game groupings. We need to win at least two games each group in order to qualify for the playoffs.

That is all we have. We focus on winning enough games to make the playoffs. We want to be playing in week 10. If we are playing in week 10, whether we win the state championship or not, the season has been a success. We want to be one of the 256 teams that get in.

We also want to be consistent in our summer conditioning program. We start with the night-running two weeks before the season begins. We condition four nights a week for an hour and a half at a time. One year, I tried to have our kids prepare several weeks in the summertime for the night conditioning, in order to be ready for the evening conditioning program. In reality, no matter how much they ran, they were not ready for the night conditioning. This program is not an easy thing to organize and conduct, but it does create the pace and work ethic we desire.

Our night-running schedule for day one, week one involves coming in at 6:30 p.m. and performing drills to loosen up for about 10 minutes. Then, on Mondays and Wednesdays of the first week, we run stations for 12 minutes each, which equates (time-wise) to one quarter of football each. This station-work involves four stations—the weight room, pads/ploys, timed drills, and cones. The athletes perform the 12 minutes, get a two-minute break, do another 12 minutes, get another two-minute break, and so on, until all four stations are completed. Our assistant coaches run the stations.

During station-work, our athletes are constantly on the move, depending on what station they are working. Frankly, I have no idea what they do in the weight room for 12 minutes. I simply walk around the field with a whistle and yell encouragement. We do different things on different days. These activities are not any kind of great undertaking. Our primary goal is to simply have the kids moving for 12 minutes. At the end of those 12 minutes, we want them to be exhausted. Our objective is to get them ready to play our first game. We finish with 10 minutes of team cones, 10 minutes of warm-down stretching, and finally a prayer.

On day two, we change it up a bit. After 15 minutes of calisthenics and agilities, we do a 12-minute run, up, down, and around the bleachers, which again (time-wise) involves the length of one quarter of football. We then do 15 minutes of stride-outs, with the focus on running form, and finish with 10 minutes of timed gassers. Again, we end the session with warm-down stretching and a prayer.

When our actual practice schedule begins, I need to know what plays I will want to run in our first game. I also need to be able to install them in the limited timeframe in which we work. Our coaches may diagram plays for our kids, and I am sure the JV coaches do, but we do not have a playbook. Our coaches and players have to learn our plays and know to execute them. It does not make any difference if how they do that is not exactly the same as last year, just so long as it is perfect this year. Then, we are okay.

Next, I would like to discuss my coaching staff. Our 10 coaches have been together for a while, so we do not have any formal meetings before the season. During the season, we meet every Sunday morning at 9:00 a.m., and the meeting normally goes until 1:00 p.m. If this Sunday meeting goes to 3:00 p.m., I have to buy lunch, a situation that only occurred about twice this past year.

We like to scour our opponent's games. In our meetings, we break down film, looking for every different defense our opponent has run, and sets they like to run them against. We chart every single offensive play our opponent runs, and every formation they utilize. Then, we try to all of that information. We also chart everything our opponent has done with special teams. From all of these breakdowns, we develop our game plan.

Every day, our kids know what we are going to do on that day. Monday is scouting report day. Tuesday is our main offensive day. Wednesday is defensive day. Thursday is pregame work. On Fridays, we have a meeting in the gym to review our game plan. Sometimes, you go places where you have to find a space. We try to make it a habit for us to be able to do things before the game the same way, so the kids have a comfort level. As such, we can remind them of what it is we want them to do and focus on the key things, before we go out and play the game.

You must plan to install your offense, defense, and special teams that you will need for game one. You should prepare knowing that you will see something you had not included in the plan. You have to be able to adjust. Finally, you should not assume too much, and waste time on things you shouldn't have to worry about. If the unexpected does occur, you need to figure it out then.

In summary, you have to start from a foundation and build on it. You have to have continuity in your program, and you have to coach perfection if you are going to be successful. You constantly have to find new things to do and new ways to do them. You need to keep learning. Learning is an ongoing process—attend clinics, read, talk to other people, and always work as hard as you can.

I think that about does it. Thank you very much.

CONVERTING THE 50 DEFENSE TO A 4-3 LOOK

Bethlehem Liberty High School, Pennsylvania

At Liberty High School, we have taken 50 defensive principles, which we use to play a 4-3 scheme. We play different concepts, but our defense is based on 50 defensive principles. I am not going to talk about our huddle procedure, because it is based on a wristband system. We huddle our front seven, with a designated linebacker in front. He takes the signal from the sideline off a wristband and relays it to the huddle. The defensive backs do not huddle. They look to the sideline, get the signal, and check their wristbands for the call. We have as many as 20 numbers on the wristband for a game.

We use base rules to declare the strength of the defense. If the ball is in the middle of the field, we base the strength call on the number of receivers. If the formation is balanced, we make the strength call to the defensive left. If motion changes the strength of the defense, the secondary will role that way, according to the rule for their adjustments. If the ball is on the hash marks, the strength is to the field automatically.

We also make a tight-end call. If there is one tight end in the game, we make the tight call right or left, according to where he lines up. If there are two tight ends, we make the tight call to the strength. If the set is balanced, we call the strength to the defensive left side. If the set is on the hash mark, we make the tight call to the field. If there are no tight ends on the field, we make the tight call to the strength of the formation. If the set is balanced, we make the call to the left.

We number our techniques using the standard technique system. Our gaps are from the inside out by letters. The inside gap is A-gap, while the outside gap is D-gap. We number the shoulders of the offensive linemen. The inside shoulder of the guard is

1, and his outside shoulder is 3. The tackle's inside shoulder is 4, and his outside shoulder is 5. The tight end's inside shoulder is 7, and his outside shoulder is 9.

In our defense, we have taken 50 defensive principles and converted them to a 4-3 scheme. The first factor that I would like to cover is our defensive fronts (Diagram #1). The "tite front," with one tight end, has the defensive end in a 9 technique on the tight end. The tackles align in a 5 technique to the strongside and a 3 technique to the weakside. The nose plays a strong shade on the center, and the Will linebacker plays a ghost 9 technique to the split-end side.

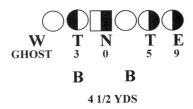

Diagram #1. Tite Right (1 TE)

The defensive linemen are in three-point stances. The 9-technique defensive end is in a three-point stance. The Will linebacker is in a loose technique to the split-end side, on the line of scrimmage in a two-point stance. Any defensive lineman in an odd-shade technique is a spill player. If he gets a down block, he wrong arms everything that comes at him. The inside linebackers align at four and half yards and are on the outside shade of the guards.

If the offense adds a second tight end, the Will linebacker moves to what we call an "ability alignment" 9-technique. The bigger and more physical the tight end, the looser the Will linebacker's alignment becomes. If the tight end is smaller, he can tighten up on him. He is in a shade technique on the tight end and gets in a three-point stance. Since he is an odd-technique player, he spills the ball. That principle is from the 4-3 defense.

If there are no tight ends in the game, both the defensive end and the Will linebacker are in a ghost tight-end alignment, standing up. Anytime they stand up, they play a 50 principle, close the door, and squeeze the ball. They become force players and turn the ball inside. They play two different concepts, depending on whether they are up or down in their alignment.

The defensive end is a bigger player, who is used to playing with his hand in the dirt. When he gets into a stand-up position, we do some things to make him comfortable. The inside linebackers key the guards.

In our "anchor" front, we move the defensive tackles in to an inside technique of the offensive tackles (Diagram #2). That technique is a 4 technique for us. The nose comes back to a 0 technique on the center. We tell him to get up under the chin of the center and replace the center's feet. He wants to create a new line of scrimmage. Our 4 technique players read the guards. If the guard blocks down, the defensive tackles come down on a spill path. If the guard pulls outside, they work across the face of the offensive tackle.

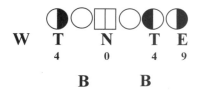

Diagram #2. Anchor Front

We play the same technique with the defensive end. If he aligns in a 7 technique on the tight end, he keys the offensive tackle. If the tackle blocks down, he squeezes to the inside and spills all blocks. The defensive end and linebackers play the "anchor" the same. If the set is a two-tight end set or a no tight end set, the adjustments are the same.

If we add the term "turbo," the defensive tackles align as they did in the anchor alignment (Diagram #3). The difference is they do not read the guards. They are on a pinch slant to the inside. They come down through the ear hole of the helmet of the guard. They still play their spill path. We like this movement against dive-option teams. The linebackers know that they do not have B-gap responsibility. They fill outside the tackles.

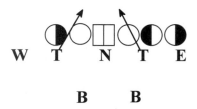

Diagram #3. Turbo Charge

When we go to the "tuff" front, we make a minor adjustment with our defensive tackles and nose. They all go to head-up techniques. We can stem from this front to the tite, anchor, or turbo fronts. We like to get in the "tuff" front, because it disguises our movements. We like to blitz from this front. The technique we play from the "tuff" involves getting the helmet under the chin of the offensive blocker and replace his feet. This is a bull-rush technique in the passing game.

In our secondary shell, we play a lot of "sky" coverage. However, we also play cover 2 and quarters coverage. We put a lot of emphasis on the players making the calls from the game plan.

We have some base rules we apply in our secondary. The corner is aligned at five-to-six yards off the receiver. If the corner has a single receiver with no threat from the number-2 receiver, he has a couple of choices to make. He can make a "hard" or a "change" call. The "hard" call is a cover-2 funnel technique. He funnels the receiver inside, sinks into the coverage, and reacts up on the flat pattern. The corner to the tight-end side has the same call. If both the corners make a "hard" call, the secondary is in true cover 2.

If the corner gives the "change" call, no threat must exist from the number-2 receiver. They have a cover-2 look, but they jump inside, wall the receiver to the outside, and cover him man-to-man, wherever he goes.

The safeties align at 10-12 yards, in a normal cover-2 alignment (Diagram #4). On the hard call, they are at that depth. If the safety gets the change call from the corner, he tightens his depth to eight yards. The safeties play quarters underneath, but are reading the number-2 receiver. The strong safety is reading the tight end. If the tight end blocks down, he reacts to the line of scrimmage and serves as the force player. If the tight end releases to the flat and we have a change call, the safety takes him to the flat, man-to-man.

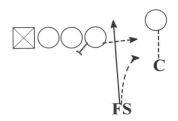

Diagram #4. Change

If the free safety on the other side has a change call, he reads the number-2 receiver in the backfield. If he gets a play-action read, he is the alley runner and cutback player. If he has no release by the number-2 receiver, he is the robber player in the middle and helps the linebackers. If the linebackers get a drag from the tight end, they have trouble covering it. The safety can rob that pattern. In a hard or change call, we still get nine defenders in the box.

We run a couple of corner stunts with the corner. We call this "creep." We bring this stunt off the boundary, because it involves a shorter distance. The corner blitzes off the edge, and the safety plays over the top of the number-1 receiver. If there is a number-2 receiver or the quarterback reads that the corner is coming, the corner may sit in the flat and not blitz. The safety and corner exchange responsibilities.

If we have a twins set, the corner is one yard outside the wide receiver and six yards deep. The safety is two yards inside and eight yards deep on the number-2 receiver (Diagram #5). The corner and safety play "soft" quarter coverage on the two receivers. They play inside/outside, match-up zone

coverage. They take any combination route run by the receivers. If the receivers cross in their pattern, the safety takes the inside route, and the corner takes the outside route.

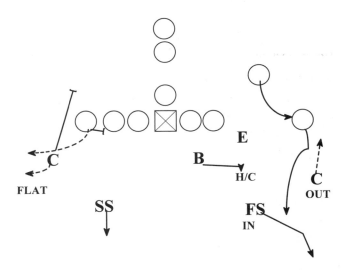

Diagram #5. Quarters

With the twins set to that side, the defensive end walks off, splitting the difference between the tackle and the number-2 receiver. He serves as the run support to that side. However, on a pass, he steps off the line and gets in the throwing lane for the quick pass inside. The inside linebacker has hook-to-curl on that side and reads from the number-2 receiver to the number-1 receiver in his progression.

On the backside of the twins set, we play a "cloud" call. On this call, the corner is four yards outside the tight end and five yards deep. He has the flat on pass and is the support player on run. The safety to that side can cheat over to the tackle's alignment, at a depth of 8-12 yards. He is the half-player to that side. That gives us a soft, hard, cloud, and change adjustment to those sets. In the twins formation, we start out in "soft" coverage to the twin's side and "cloud" coverage to the tight end. If they motion the slot back to the other side, we adjust the coverage to "hard" or "change" to each side. If they motioned the other way, we adjust the coverage to "soft" and "cloud" coverage. In either situation, the run support on the open side of formation does not change. To the tight-end side, we go from "sky" run support to "cloud" support.

If we get trips formation, we can kick the linebackers to the trips side or run a sky call. If we kick the linebackers over to the trips side, the frontside linebacker reads the number-2 receiver to the number-1 receiver. The backside linebacker reads the number-3 receiver to the number-2 receiver (Diagram #6). The strong safety plays over the top in third coverage, and the corner rolls down into flat coverage. To the backside, we play "hard" or "change" with the corner and the free safety. In this coverage, the free safety goes to the middle, and the corner plays man-to-man on the single receiver.

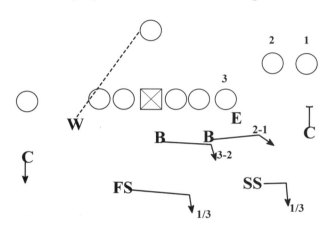

Diagram #6. Kick Adjustment

If we get a double-slot formation, we play soft coverage to both sides. We are backed up and four across in our alignment. If the offense runs four verticals, we are sound in this coverage. Both corners and safeties are playing soft, quarter in/out coverage on the number-1 and number-2 receivers.

If we call "sky" coverage against the trips formation, the strong safety rolls down inside the number-2 receiver (Diagram #7). He is reading his progression from the number-1 receiver to the number-2 receiver. If the offense throws a hitch to the number-1 receiver, the strong safety is in his face.

If the number-1 receiver goes vertical, the strong safety lets him go, focuses on the number-2 receiver, and plays the flat. The corner goes into the outside third, and the free safety is in the middle. The linebackers slide to the trips side. The first linebacker reads the number-2 receiver to the number-1 receiver, while the second linebacker

reads the number-3 receiver to the number-2 receiver. To the backside, the corner has the wide receiver man-to-man, but he can get some help from the Will linebacker. The Will linebacker locks on the remaining back in the backfield. If the back blocks, the Will can give the corner some help on the split receiver.

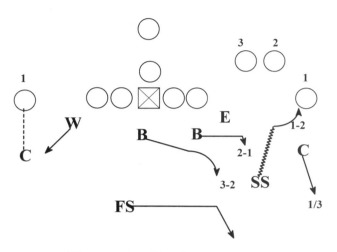

Diagram #7. Sky Cover to Trips

We handle motion by recognizing the set the motion gives us. If we are playing sky coverage against the trips set and soft coverage against the double slot, we play this coverage when the offense motions from one to the other. Motion does not confuse what we want to do. We play the coverage against the set for which we game plan.

We run stunts from this front. In addition to the direction angles and slants, we use twist stunts. Diagram #8 illustrates a "double ex" call. The "E" in the stunt means the ends go first. The defensive end slants into the ear hole of the offensive tackle. The tackle flash steps and loops to the outside around the defensive end. To the other side, the Will linebacker comes tight to the tackle, underneath anything to the inside. The tackle loops tight off the Will linebacker's butt and comes outside.

The companion stunt that goes with the "ex" is "Tex." On "Tex," the defensive tackle goes first, and the defensive end loops behind and penetrates the gap.

In each of the stunts, the strong safety has a "box technique" that he plays. If the strong safety has a "3 box wide" call, he drops down late and is the force on the run. He plays a wide-box technique. On the wide call, he reads the number-2 receiver to the number-1 receiver. If the number-2 receiver goes vertical, he jams him and sits to the inside. If he goes inside, he zones off in the hook-to-curl area. If the number-2 receiver goes out, he moves his coverage to the number-1 receiver who is coming inside.

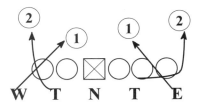

Diagram #8. Double Ex

If he has a "3 box middle" call, he drops down late and plays from the number-3 receiver to the number-2 receiver to that side. If the number-3 receiver runs an outside pattern, he looks for the number-2 receiver coming to the inside. If the number-3 receiver goes vertical, he jams him and sits inside. If the number-3 receiver goes inside, he zones off in the middle low hole.

In every game, we include zone pressure in our game plan. We carry one or two pressures as part of the game plan. We call this zone blitz, "tuff load" (Diagram #9). We run this blitz from the hash mark. We bring the four down linemen, plus one linebacker, on a blitz. We slant into the boundary with the T-N-T (tackle-nose-tackle) linemen. The linebacker runs through the C-gap. The defensive end power rips for outside contain and gets up the field. On this stunt, the strong safety has a "3 box wide" call.

Another zone blitz that we use is "out bomber" (Diagram #10). If we run it from the tuff front, the defensive tackles take a lateral step outside and penetrate the gap. The nose goes opposite the linebackers. The callside linebacker goes first and blitzes his A-gap. The backside linebacker comes second and blitzes the callside B-gap. The defensive end drops to the flat, as does the Will linebacker. On this stunt, the strong safety has a "3 box middle" call.

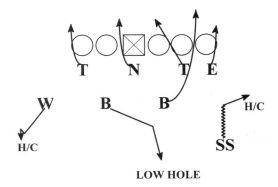

Diagram #9. Tuff Load (3 Box Wide)

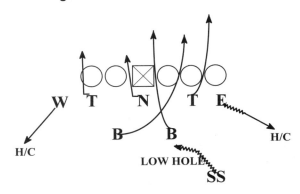

Diagram #10. Tuff Out Bomber (3 Box Middle)

In both of these blitzes, we play cover 3 in the secondary. In this coverage, the strong safety rolls down and applies his box technique. We have three deep defenders and three underneath defenders. In the first blitz, the strong safety is an underneath player to the outside. He reads the tight end and wide receiver to that side. The left linebacker plays the inside hole, while the Will linebacker drops into the boundary flat zone.

In the second blitz, the strong safety drops into the middle low hole. His reads the back in the backfield to the number-2 receiver. The end and Will linebacker play in the flat-to-curl zones on the outside. In all zone blitzes, you have to give up an underneath zone. We try to keep from giving up the same one on every play.

On the "tuff bat," we have a "3 box tite" call for the strong safety. On this call, the callside linebacker blitzes the B-gap to his side (Diagram #11). The tackle read steps and comes around the blitz of the linebacker. The nose and tackle to the backside step into their outside gaps and penetrate.

The defensive end rips outside and contains. The "3 box tite" call brings the strong safety inside the defensive end on the tight end.

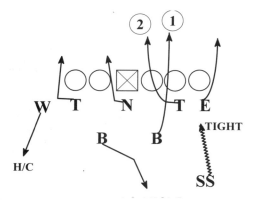

Diagram #11. Tuff Bat (3 Box Tite)

We have blitzes that bring defenders out of the secondary. The "tuff storm" is a wideside blitz by the strong safety off the edge (Diagram #12). On this stunt, we play a cover-2 shell behind the stunt. The defensive line angles to the boundary. We roll the coverage to the wideside of the field. The field corner rolls down and plays a hard corner to the wideside. The free safety comes over the top to the strongside half field. The boundary corner is the weakside half player. The inside linebackers kick their coverage to the strongside. The frontside linebacker plays hook-to-curl to the wideside and the backside linebacker plays the low hole in the middle. The Will linebacker plays the backside hook-to-curl. We give up the backside flat zone.

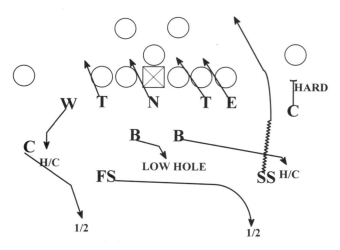

Diagram #12. Tuff Storm Cover 2 Wide

The "tuff comet" comes from the boundary by the corner to that side (Diagram #13). We slant the defensive line to the wideside of the field and bring the corner off the edge. The cover is the same as what we played in the storm blitz, except the strong and free safeties play the half-coverage.

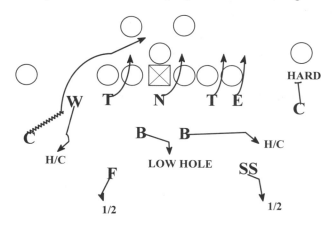

Diagram #13. Tuff Comet Cover 2 Short

When we bring six-man pressure, we play cover 0, which is true man-to-man coverage.

RULES: Cover Zero

- The corners have the #1 receiver to their side.
- The strong safety has the #2 receiver to his side.
- The free safety has the #2 receiver weak (double) or the #3 strong receiver (trips). If two backs are in the backfield, the free safety has the most immediate threat or the dangerous threat. In the I back set, the free safety has the tailback offset I or the far or near back. The free safety has the most immediate threat to go out. He handles any backfield motion.
- Ownership runs with motion.
- Man coverage tagged with flare means we are rushing more than we have to cover. Our outside rushers will play to any flare route by a back.

We bring six rushers, which means we have five defenders to cover. The linebacker who does not blitz gets a fit call. In other words, if we have to two backs in the backfield, the free safety has one, and the linebacker has the other. We fit the coverage to the ability of the receivers. If the fullback is 230 pounds and not so fast, that is the fit we want for the linebacker. The free safety always takes the most dangerous threat. If a defender's man goes in motion, he runs with him. There is no switching or bumping over. That way there are no questions about who was supposed to cover whom.

The stunt we can use with six-man pressure is "double Tex bongo" (Diagram #14). On this stunt, we run the Tex stunt for the tackles and ends. The nose slants into the boundary A-gap, while the boundary inside linebacker blitzes through the fieldside A-gap. Everyone else locks up man-to-man.

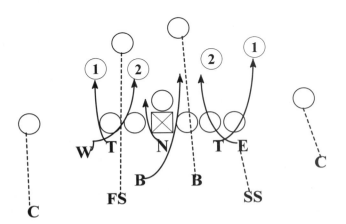

Diagram #14. Double Tex Bongo Cover 0

In our bear front, we move the tackles into 3 techniques on the outside shoulders of the guards. The Will linebacker aligns normally, and the defensive end sets up wider in his alignment (Diagram #15). We bring one of our inside linebackers head-up the tight end and walk the strong safety down into a stack position behind the tackle to the side. The other inside linebacker aligns in a stack position behind the other tackle.

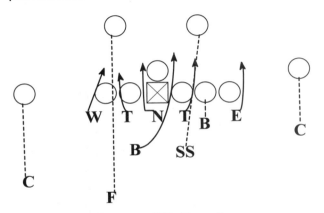

Diagram #15. Bear Bongo

On this stunt, we send four defenders over the middle of the offense. The tackles penetrate their gaps, and the nose penetrates the gap to the linebacker's side. The linebacker blitzes the opposite A-gap. In the secondary, everyone picks up their coverage. The linebacker over the tight end takes him, and the strong safety picks up his man from the backfield.

We employ the "free-check-with-me" call with our bear front. This coverage is dictated according to the formation. We are either in man free, or true man.

BEAR STUNT RULES:

- If we get two backs in the backfield, we are in man free.
- If we get a one-back set, we are in true man.
- The strong safety will always go to the tight-end side in this call, not strength.
- If a single tight end is backside of twins or trips, the corner makes a "rover" call to let everyone know he is going to the other side of formation.
- If there is no tight end, the strong safety will expand and cover the #2 receiver and make a scab call to the linebacker. This call means to replace him in defense.
- The free safety will adjust to all one-back sets and pick up the free man (#2/#3).
- The defense runs with all motion (ownership).

From the same front, we can run "bear under" (Diagram #16). On this call, the linebacker on the tight end aligns in a 7 technique. He read steps and comes under the charge of the tackle to his side. The strong safety picks up the tight end, and the off-linebacker fits on his coverage with the free safety.

When we bring a seven-man blitz, we have to go to "0-flare" coverage (Diagram #17). When we run this blitz, everyone walks up to the line of scrimmage except the splitside linebacker. Everyone rips and gets vertical through their gaps. The splitside linebacker blitzes from his normal position. That gives the blockers time to decide whom to block. The defensive end and the Will linebacker have any remaining receivers. As the defense rushes

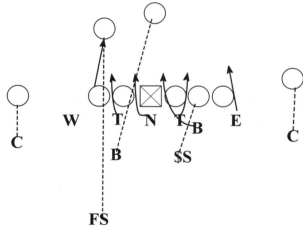

Diagram #16. Bear Under

the passer, if anyone tries to release from the backfield, they pick them up in man coverage.

We run one additional seven-man blitz, which we call "bear balls" (Diagram #18). This blitz is derived from our bear front. We are putting the pressure on the middle of the defense. We want the nose to go right over the top of the center.

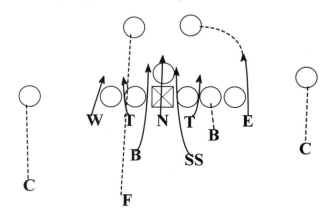

Diagram #18. Bear Balls

At this point, I would like to show you some cut-ups of our game tape. Thank you. It has been a pleasure.

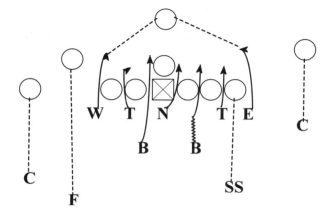

Diagram #17. Tite Blood Up 0-Flare

UTILIZING FIVE-WIDE-RECEIVER CONCEPTS

Robert E. Lee High School, Texas

There are some misconceptions about Texas football. There is a lot of great football in Texas, but there are just as many bad teams. There are good coaches and good programs, but there are more good coaches than there are good programs. Some of the success that exists in some programs is not the coaching. As coaches, we are dependent on our administration for our success. Sometimes, you have good administrators, and sometimes you do not.

At our school, we have access to our players year round. During the day, we have a varsity athlete period and a freshman athlete period. You can do the same thing if you have an administrator who will give you a physical-education period during the day. Our athletic physical education class meets every day. You can sell that idea by getting your parents involved. We tell our parents we can help their sons be more successful in their achievement with these types of programs in place.

To get this type of program established, you have to get all the coaches on board and thinking the same way. In those classes, we do all the drills and weight lifting that makes our players better athletes. In any athletic program, you have to share athletes. If you have the athletic period, it makes that a better situation. If you try to do all the things we do in those classes after school, you interfere with other teams in the school. This is a tremendous aid for us, and you can do it too.

I want to talk about the Raider series. It is our five-wide series and is a great series to run. I have a PowerPoint® presentation and I actually did some of the stuff that is on the program.

Friday Night Lights is not typical in Texas football anymore. That was in the 1980s in West Texas at Odessa Permian High School. They are responsible for some of the rules we now have in Texas. Back in the old days, if your son was a good player, they moved the family and anybody else they wanted into town. They had great teams then. They have not been a factor in Texas football for some time, but they are winning again.

We have a Bayou Bowl that is a Texas-Louisiana All-Star Game. This year, the game was on the NFL network. This will be the sixth year for the game, and I am responsible for it. This year, we are going to Canada to play the game there. Sponsors in Canada were fascinated by the *Friday Night Lights* movie. Therefore, they decided to bring Texas football to Canada. One of the players from Odessa Permian who actually lived what is known as *Friday Night Lights* is going with us. There is tremendous excitement around this game.

In the Raider series, we align in a 3-by-2 or 3-by-1 alignment in some type of five-wide-receiver set. We started doing that because we were fortunate to have good quarterbacks. One of the first quarterbacks we had who ran the system went on to Baylor as a starter and had a career in the Arena League. We had Clint Sterner, who started at Arkansas. He was followed by Eli Roberson, who started at Kansas State. After that came my son, Drew Tate. He started for Iowa for three years and is now in the Canadian League.

My wife knows nothing about football, but every time he got hit, she wanted to know why. I just referred her to the offensive line coach. The quarterback at Utah, Brian Johnson, was one of our quarterbacks. The quarterback from this year's team is going to Army. We had a quarterback named Jeremy Moses, who broke his leg his senior year. He was an undersized player, according to the college recruiters. He went to Stephan F. Austin and started as a freshman. He was 41-58 for 550 yards in one game. That is not a bad outing.

The Raider package gave us an opportunity to compete in our league. We have a lot of speed on our team. Our 400-yard relay team ran 41.7 and did not make it out of the district track meet. We play in the golden triangle, and there is a lot of speed in that area. In our offense, we try to counteract that kind of speed.

Our five-wide series is a no-huddle scheme, and I will talk about that as we go. In our set, we always have three receivers to the field and two receivers to the boundary. We have five plays, and they are memorized. It is the same five plays repeatedly.

I do not want to offend any defensive coaches, and I apologize before I start. It does not matter the order of the plays. We have five plays, numbered 1 through 5. If we want to start out with Raider 3, the count goes 3, 4, 5, 1, and 2. It is not rocket science.

We have five-man protection and always protect the quarterback's backside. The defense will be a 4-2 or 3-2 defensive alignment because of our sets. We will not see too many other defenses beside those. If we see no-blitz types of defenses, we have things built into the offense for those situations. This series has everything built into it. It is a great series and includes our perfect play.

The center identifies the Mike linebacker (Diagram #1). The center and left guard are responsible for the nose and Mike linebacker. The left tackle has the defender aligned on him. The right guard and tackle are single blocking on their defenders.

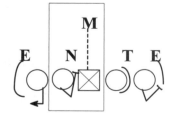

Diagram #1. Protection Scheme

The quarterback knows who can blitz him, but he knows it will come into his face and not his back.

We never want the quarterback hit in the back. If we get someone coming off the edge, we have the ability to slide the defense that way.

We are interested in the tempo, and it comes from the sideline. At times, your players are just walking around on the field. When we see that situation, we want to hurry things up. I watch no-huddle teams signal the plays in, and that is great. However, I have seen no-huddle teams penalized for delay of game. How can that happen? I do not understand that, but it happens.

With the offense, the more complex the system, the more room there is for mistakes. There are teams that are extremely good at what they do. However, you have to make it simple for the players. We are not interested in changing the play and moving around on the field. We are interested in tempo. We want to establish tempo in the game. We do not want to stand there and let the defense align before we go.

We practice the tempo. Raider calls in practice take precedent over everything. I am the head coach and offensive coordinator, and I can say that if I yell, "Raider," our players fly to the ball, and away we go. We run the five plays, and it does not matter whether it is against a defense or against air. The idea is to establish tempo. We want the players to know we are going to run Raider whenever I yell it out. We will run five plays unless I say, "Choke." It does not matter what drill we are in or what we are doing.

If tempo is not good, I yell, "Raider!" We pick the tempo up and the coaches get on their fannies. The receivers' coaches are yelling for them to hustle, get lined up, and get going. As soon as the ball is marked ready for play, we snap it. It is a great thing to see.

We have additional tempo calls. If we yell "NASCAR," we line up and run the play. NASCAR is one of the five plays in the series. If we yell "Indy," we do the same thing. Indy is one of the Raider plays. If I see the defense walking around, we make the call to change the tempo. We may run only the one play.

The first Raider play is NASCAR (Diagram #2). It is a good play, and the defense cannot stop it. It has everything built into it. We practice this in the summer in 7-on-7 camps. We are in a 3-by-2 alignment. We have not changed anything. We got all this stuff from Dennis Erickson, when he was at Washington State. Before he went to the University of Miami, we watched Washington State beat the stew out of the University of Houston in the Aloha Bowl. We called Washington State and asked them to teach us their offense. They told us to go see Mike Heimerdinger at Rice University. He is now with the Tennessee Titans. We went to Rice and saw what they were doing. We went to Miami, met Coach Erickson, and had the opportunity to study their offense.

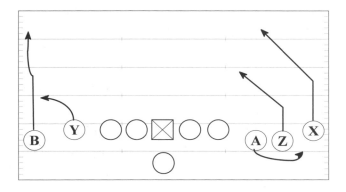

Diagram #2. NASCAR

In this offense, the Y-receiver used to be a tight end. We do not have a tight end in our offense. We did not have a tight end in the program, so out of necessity we went to five wide receivers. What we learned from Coach Erickson was that the Z-receiver is the quickest receiver. The X-receiver is the fastest player. The Y-receiver was the tight-end type of player. The B-receiver is the running back, and the A is the best athlete. We got this in 1988, and we have not changed it. We still use the same terms and letters.

The B-back aligns at the top of the numbers to the shortside of the field. He takes a protection release through the outside shoulder of the outside defender and gets vertical down the field. We want to make sure he releases outside because that is where the quarterback looks as his first read. If we get the vertical route, we take it right now. If we do not get the vertical route, the quarterback looks for the speed-out run by the Y-receiver.

The Y-receiver aligns on the line of scrimmage slightly outside the hash marks. He runs a five-yard speed-out. The A-back aligns outside the hash mark to the wideside of the field. He runs a bubble release. We teach him to take a J-step. He drops his outside leg back and crosses over with the second step. He gains depth and runs to the boundary. The bubble is a pattern you take to the boundary and never stop running the pattern. If they catch the bubble pass, they do not stop and try to juke the defender.

We want a minimum of four yards on the play. We want to catch it and continue to run. It is like a toss sweep. We toss the ball to the back, and he runs his butt to the sideline. Once he gets there, he turns up. The Z-receiver runs a three-step slant to the inside. The X-receiver runs a five-step slant to the inside. We run the double slant at different depths to separate the pattern. If the inside slant is covered, he continues to run, and it opens up the outside slant.

The quarterback works the vertical/speed-out combination first. The quarterback is in the shotgun. He catches the ball and delivers. The Y-pattern is the hot route. He throws vertical, speed-out, and Z-slant. The Z-receiver always has this rule, depending on where the defender aligns on him. If he has a defender inside of him, he takes one step instead of three steps. He flattens his pattern and attacks through the defender's inside shoulder. We want to attack the inside defender on the slant.

If the defender is head-up on the Z-receiver, he still takes one step and attacks him through his inside shoulder. The difference is he is inside the defender and can be a receiver. If the defender aligns outside the Z-receiver, he takes one step at the defender and runs inside. If the defender is inside the Z-receiver, the receiver knows he will not get the ball. The quarterback knows in his pre-snap read who is a viable receiver to the three-receiver side. The defense has to align right away. They do not have time to change and disguise what they are doing.

The second pattern in the Raider series is *Oxford Y-cross* (Diagram #3). This is our crossing package. Oxford tells the outside receivers they run six-yard out patterns. The Y-receiver runs a shallow cross at the heels of the defensive linemen. The A-back runs a 10- to 12-yard in pattern. The Z-receiver runs a skinny post.

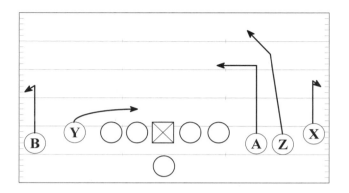

Diagram #3. Oxford Y-Cross

The quarterback reads the out into the sideline first because that is the shortest out pattern. His progression from there is cross, in, and post. He wants to try to throw the out pattern because it is the best look and shortest throw. I talk to our quarterbacks about taking the best look and the shortest throw as their first option.

When we first learned this series from Coach Erickson, he had a passing route tree as a way to teach the routes. In the tree, 0 was a hitch, 1 an out, 2 a slant, and 3 a vertical. We have not changed any of that. We still run the same thing.

How many people know what a protection release is? That is a Utah term, which came from Urban Mayer. A protection release is a release by another receiver to protect the inside receiver. When the B-receiver releases through the outside shoulder of the defender, he protects the inside receiver from getting his butt knocked off.

In Texas high school football, we play by NCAA hash marks on our fields. They are narrower than they used to be. When we starting throwing this pattern, we threw the ball to the old hash marks and that was a long throw. Our receiver got his butt knocked off the first time we threw the hitch, because it took so long for the ball to get there. We learned from that and tightened the splits of our receivers. With the hash marks at the college width, it is not so bad.

The shallow cross by the Y-receiver is at the heels of the defensive linemen. When you practice this, you need to set cones to mark that pattern. If you do not set cones, the receivers will get upfield, and I can guarantee that. They take one step downfield and come across the field. The Y-receiver will never get the ball until he looks for the ball.

We used to key the onside linebacker. If he backed up, we threw the ball to the Y-receiver. We do not do that anymore because the other inside linebacker read the play and killed the Y-receiver. We do not throw the ball to the Y-receiver until he crosses the center box. He is running, but he looks at the linebackers. If they vacate the area, he gets the ball.

The quarterback has a high/low read on the linebacker. If the linebacker comes down on the shallow cross, the quarterback throws the dig behind him. If the linebacker drops into his zone, the quarterback takes the shallow cross.

If the safety comes down on the dig pattern, we have the skinny post going behind him. We have everything handled in the pattern. The thing I like is the patterns are all in the vision of the quarterback. If he does not take the out pattern, the cross, dig, and post are in front of the quarterback at different levels. He does not have to look right or left. They are in front of him. He has to see the linebacker and safety for his read.

The next pattern in the series is Purdue (Diagram #4). It is a layered package. The reason it is such a great pattern is that it is quarterback friendly. The B-back runs a post pattern. The Y-receiver runs a banana route at eight yards. The A-back runs the shallow cross. The Z-receiver runs a banana route at 15 yards, and the X-receiver runs the vertical.

The A-back runs the shallow cross with a one-count delay. He aligns with his outside foot back in his normal stance. He rocks back with his inside foot and gets into the pattern. When the back rocks back with his inside foot, that is the one-count delay. We run the pattern at the heels of the defensive line. If there is blitz coming from that side, he gets the ball immediately.

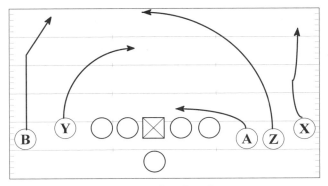

Diagram #4. Purdue

The quarterbacks want to hold the ball and wait on the Z-back to come across at 15 yards. I have to tell them to throw the ball to the shallow cross or the eight-yard banana route and nowhere else. The progression is shallow cross, eight-yard route, 15-yard route, and post. The key to the pattern is for the receiver to keep running. They cannot stop running.

We used to teach receivers to sit down in the zone when they found the window. We want our receiver to keep going. If they do not open in one window, they might find anyone across the field. The routes are layered and they do not stop.

We never tell the X-receiver that he is not a viable option because he could be. The worst thing you can see on tape is a receiver who does not do what he is supposed to do and does not hustle. If the receiver will not hustle or do what he is supposed to do, you may as well sit him down. The defense will cover anyone who is split. It does not matter whether he can catch the ball or not. If the receiver will not hustle, put someone in the game who will. It takes no talent to hustle.

We get all over the receivers if they do not hustle. We want them to do things right. We want a full-speed player, and if he cannot be a full-speed player, he must go take a seat on the bench. When you throw the football, you will have an abundance of receivers. They like that part of the game.

If you do not throw the football, there is something wrong. In the summertime, all your players are playing baseball, basketball, and soccer. There is not a single player who will call another one and tell him to come on over to the school because

we are working on the wishbone mesh today. Who in the hell would do that? You need to get your players involved with a 7-on-7 league in the summer and play football. They like to play pitch and catch.

We also call Purdue by another name. We call it "Indy." If I yell "Purdue," "Indy," or "Raider 3," that is all the same pattern. In practice, if I yell "Raider 3," the sequence of the patterns start at number 3 and run 4, 5, 1, and 2.

The *Purdue whip* is a deviation from the pattern (Diagram #5). The linebacker coach tells his linebacker to hit the crossing pattern and not let them across the formation. They want them to wall the crossing patterns out of the middle. We must have an answer to that strategy of play. The Purdue whip is our answer. This is a game or scouting-report adjustment. The Raider package is in every game plan. It is like our family: it always goes with us. The Y-receiver and A-back start their patterns and come back to the outside.

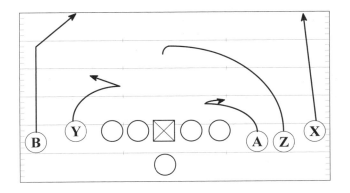

Diagram #5. Purdue Whip

The Y-receiver does not run the eight-yard banana pattern. He runs a whip pattern. We bring the receivers to the tackle box before they start back to the outside. The tackle box is usually where the collisions occur. The receivers come in at their normal depth, stick the outside foot in the ground, pivot, and whip back to the outside. We tell the quarterback we want to work the whip patterns first. The progression is A-whip, Y-whip, Z 12-yard, and the B-post.

The Z-receiver running the 12-yard pattern will open up big time. However, if you have a team that is pressuring you, the whip pattern is where you take the ball. The B-back is way down the list of options. We adjust the Z-receiver's pattern on the whip. Instead of running the banana pattern and continuing to run through the middle of the defense, he settles. He finds the hole in the middle of the defense over center box and settles down. We call it checkdown at 12 yards.

When you run as many crossing patterns as we do, the defense begins to sit on those routes. That is why we have a whip adjustment to this pattern. We add one more tag to the play that gives another option. We can use the term *gig* to give the A-back or Y-receiver an adjusted pattern. This is the Utah pattern. If we call "Purdue whip A gig," the A-back runs the whip route. After he whips outside, he plants and gigs back to the inside. He runs in, out, and back underneath the coverage.

The fourth Raider play is *A sail*. On this pattern, the Y- and X-receivers are the hot reads in the event of blitz (Diagram #6). The first principle that Coach Erickson taught us was the "uncovered principle." You can uncover in many ways. When we first started running this series, we had people who did not line up on the receivers. If that happened, we threw them the ball. You can uncover by movement. If you send a receiver in motion and no one goes with him, he is uncovered. A receiver can uncover by a blitzing defender. If the defender is aligned on the receiver and begins to sneak inside to blitz, the receiver turns and shuffles for a couple of steps.

He does not run up the field. Most of the time, if the defense blitzes, they cover over the top with another defender. If you find two defenders stacked on one receiver, one of them is coming on the blitz. If you release up the field, you release into that coverage. We turn and shuffle for a couple of steps. If we do not get the ball in those steps, we continue up the field with the pattern.

On the sail route, the Y-receiver has a hitch pattern. We want him to find grass, and that means get open. The X-receiver has some choices he can run. He can run a hitch, an out, or an under. He also has what we call "touch me." We tell the receiver if on his release he can touch the defender, he runs by him.

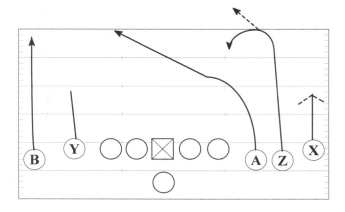

Diagram #6. A Sail

I have a coaching point about choice routes. If you give a player a choice, you cannot chew his butt out for making the wrong choice. If he went out when he should have gone in, that is the way it goes. If you jump him as he comes to the sidelines because the inside was open, that is where he is going on the next choice, regardless of whether the inside is open or not. If you want him to go inside, tell him to go inside. If you want him to go outside, tell him to go outside. In addition, if you want him to make a choice, let him make the choice. Otherwise, he will run what you told him was open, and it may not be open the next time. When you watch the film, he will see what he did wrong and learn.

On the sail, the B-back takes a protection release and gets vertical as quickly as he can. He has to get to the outside. The A-back has the sail route. He releases under the coverage and over the Mike linebacker. When he crosses the center box, he should be 12 yards deep. His aiming point is 22 yards deep at the far sideline. Once he passes the Mike linebacker, he can sit down in any window he finds in the defense.

When you teach this pattern, you must tell him under, over, and out-of-bounds at 22 yards. On his release, he goes under the man covering him. He has to get over the Mike linebacker as he drops. His angle takes him to 12 yards deep over the ball. He continues to run on an angle that would take him out-of-bounds at 22 yards.

The Z-receiver has a post/curl pattern. If the middle of the field has a safety in it, he stops the post and curls. If there is no safety in the middle of the field, he continues his post. Sometimes in a cover 2, that will happen because the other safety picked up the sail and vacated the center.

When we practice the patterns, we have a session we call *routes on air* (Diagram #7). We got this from Hal Mumme, when he was head coach at the University of Kentucky. We use big oil drums in setting up this drill. You can use stand-up dummies. We put the drums in the position of defenders in a cover-2 or cover-3 zone. We run our patterns into the zones of the coverage. We have five quarterbacks and five receivers. All the quarterbacks are bunched together in a line in the center of the field.

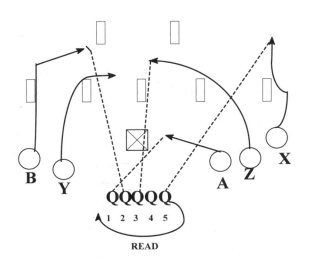

Diagram #7. Routes on Air

We run the same pattern five times. The five quarterbacks are assigned a read. The quarterback on the left end of the line has the first read, and his ball comes out first. After each play, they rotate down the line to the right to change their reads. When he reaches the right end of the line of quarterbacks, he has gone through the progression of the reads for that pattern.

Each quarterback throws a pass on each play to his read receiver. Each receiver catches a pass on every play. The quarterback to the right end goes through his progression and throws the ball to the fifth receiver in the progression. His ball will be the last one to be thrown. The quarterback should look

at each receiver in the progression and not simply throw to his receiver. That way, the balls come out in a staggered pattern and not all thrown at the same time. We get a tremendous amount of reps in a short period of time. If you do not have enough quarterbacks, make one of your coaches throw with them.

The fifth Raider play is *Hawaii* (Diagram #8). The patterns are double out and double slant. The X-receiver runs a protection release and gets vertical. The Z-receiver and A-back run a six-yard out cut. On the backside, we run a double slant by the B-back and Y-receiver.

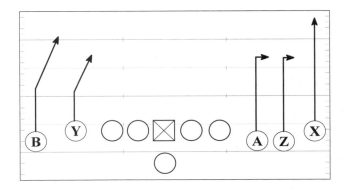

Diagram #8. Hawaii

The quarterback progression for this play is X, Z, A, Y, and B. This is a three-step pattern if the quarterback is under the center. In the shotgun, he catches the ball, gets his feet turned, and throws. If we run patterns with more depth, he drops three steps.

The X-receiver has to get a release and get vertical outside. The coaching point for the A-back is to avoid the coverage. The Z-receiver runs the six-yard out cut to the outside. As the A-back comes down, he cannot run into the flat coverage with his pattern. We tell him to sit down at six yards. It is a stick route. He does not run outside into the flat defender. He also has to be aware of the inside linebacker in coverage.

My favorite route is *Daytona Gander* (Diagram #9). We like to run this against a two-high-safety scheme. You can run it from a 2-by-2 formation, and it is the same route. There are smash concepts in this route. You can do many good things with the smash concept. The B-back runs the hitch pattern, and the Y-receiver runs the corner. From the 20-yard line going out, the aiming point for the corner is the front pylon of the end zone. From the 20-yard line going in, the aiming point is the back pylon of the end zone. The angle of the corner will change, depending on where you are on the field. The quarterback takes care of that adjustment in his throw.

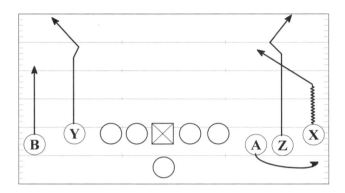

Diagram #9. Daytona Gander

When the defensive coach coaches the corner on this route, they teach him to sink and rally to the flat. The quarterback has to be patient enough to throw the hitch all the time. He never throws the corner route unless the corner sits down on the pattern.

On the backside, the A-back runs the bubble, and the Z-receiver runs the corner. This is the only time the quarterback has to read the safety. The X-receiver runs a slow go pattern. We adapted a name for the slow go route. We call it "Slugo." He comes off the ball slowly. When he gets to a five-yard depth, he sticks the pattern and runs between the safeties in half coverage. He cannot come under the linebacker.

The quarterback takes three steps and looks at the backside patterns. He looks at the Y-corner. He wants to know if the safety to that side is expanding to the corner. If the safety expands with the Y-receiver, the quarterback knows he has the slow go pattern in the middle. If the safety does not expand, he looks to throw the hitch pattern.

If the safety expands, the quarterback looks to the frontside safety. If he has expanded with the Z-corner, there is no one down the middle with the X-receiver. In high school, there is no such thing as

Tampa 2. The Mike linebacker will not be able to match up with the split end. That goes back to the old adage: find the player in the secondary wearing a neck roll and throw at him.

We call that pattern "Gander," "Daytona," or "Slugo" (Diagram #10). If you are in a 2-by-2 formation, the inside receiver to the backside runs a corner and the outside receiver runs a hitch. To the callside, the inside receiver runs the corner, and the outside receiver runs the Slugo route. If we wanted to call it, we'd say, "50 X Smash Z Slugo." The one back in the backfield always swings to the Slugo side.

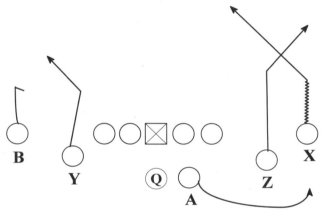

Diagram #10. Gander 2-by-2

The quarterback takes his three-step drop in the shotgun and looks at the weak safety on his way back. If he sees him getting width, he looks at the strong safety. If he gets width, he drills the X-receiver down the middle. If he gets blitz, he goes to the hitch immediately.

The play I showed called A sail is an old play from the Baltimore Colts. Raymond Berry was the great receiver for them. They always ran the play from the right side, and Raymond Berry always ran the play from the left side. Every route that he ran he caught the same way.

If they put him on the other side, his hand position was different, and he did not want to do that. We try to do the same thing. We want to keep our players in the same spots and run the same plays all the time. That is simplicity in an offense.

The one route we do not run enough is the hitch. We are not patient enough to throw it. Everybody wants to throw the big home run ball all the time. We try to throw the ball short as many times as we can.

I want to share one other thought with you. We have only one coach working with the quarterbacks. He needs to have played the position to coach it. If you have three or four coaches talking to the quarterback, you are screwing him up. I am the only quarterback coach at Baytown Lee High School, and no one talks to the quarterbacks but me. None of our assistants talk to other coach's players. If you are the running back coach, you do not make a comment about the offensive line. If you do, you will not have a job long.

Thank you. I appreciate the opportunity for your attention.

THE FIVE-DOWN-LINEMEN ANGLE DEFENSE

Hermitage Middle School, Pennsylvania

I coach kids who are in the seventh and eighth grades and in the age range from 11 to 14 years old. With the angle defense, no one does anything on defense until we teach him how to tackle. We do not start anything until the fundamentals of tackling are covered. Again, we have a wide spectrum of kids, and we feel it is important to teach them the proper techniques of tackling to cut down on injuries.

I have coached at the major college level, the small college level, and I have been a head coach in high school. However, I have really found an environment I enjoy working in. We work the players hard and we get a lot out of them, but we take care of them. It is close to a love relationship that many football coaches experience. The players come to us because we have their attention. We feed them, we clothe them, and we take care of them. We ask a lot from the kids.

Early in working with the younger age groups, I found there are some kids who are always behind the huddle talking and having a good time. They are not too concerned about getting in the game or not. There is a group of kids who want to get better as athletes, and they are going to become your players.

Many times parents cannot un-derstand the things that go on in football. One of the best things I do is have a parent meeting early, and I tell them what our program can do for their sons. We do not play many seventh graders. If a seventh grader is playing, it is either because he is very good or we do not have anyone else to put in that position. We do have several seventh graders on our team so they can learn the work ethic and expectations of our program. I always talk about the TLC in our program. It does not stand for *tender loving care*. We say we

teach expectations, we *look* for performance and the *consequences* of behavior. If a player is not doing what we want them to do, they are not going to play.

I am not big on stats, but at times, we do look at the progress of our team, and that is important. We looked at our stats after the fifth game this past year. I had a staff meeting and discussed the fact that no other team had scored on us, and no one had positive yardage. I had to step back and look at that stat. It would appear that we were doing some good things. In addition, it is a fact that we had some good players.

We start teaching tackling with the angle tackling drill. We are in close quarters. The drill does not have to be full speed. We feel that by not going full speed, we can lower the risk of injures. We step up on the tackle, get an earhole of our helmet across the front of the ballcarrier, strike with the opposite shoulder, wrap him up, and work up the field. We do this drill con-stantly in a walk-through. We do the drill *slow, slow, slow*, every day in practice. I talk to the coaching staff about the progress and how we are improving.

We do other drills to teach tackling. However, I am not a big believer in banging up on teams. We do not need to do a lot of 1-on-1 blocking. We can tell in five minutes if a player is a hitter or not. We set things up in our tackling drills. We never put young kids against the big hitters. We try to match them up to give them the opportunity to learn the fundamentals of tackling.

We used to tackle and put the kids on the ground. We finally got away from that practice because we had kids who went down and could not get up after hitting the ground. What we do now is to carry the man we are tackling. We are very close, and we only carry them a step or two. How many times do you see a player who is knocked down get up and make the tackle? Not very often.

When you look at our philosophy of our angle defense, this is the way we describe it. We are like a *running picket fence*. We are a gap-control defense. And we want to establish our defense as being aggressive.

Here are our defensive alignments. We mirror everything. We label the gaps as most teams do. We have the A, B, C, and D gaps. Everyone is responsible for a gap at the snap of the ball (Diagram #1).

```
 D   C   B   A   A   B   C   D
 TE  T   G   C   G   T   TE
 9 8 7 6 5  43 21012 345  67 89
```

Diagram #1. Defensive Alignments and Gaps

We have a philosophy and we do not want any holes in that picket fence. Everyone is responsible for a gap at the snap of the ball. We say if you can run, you can play defense for us. We do not worry about them being hitters because we can teach them to tackle.

We go over these points repeatedly. We stress these *don'ts* all season.

Defensive Don'ts

- Don't be offside.
- Don't be lazy.
- Don't run around blocks.
- Don't go upfield without a read.
- Don't be a hero.

When we line up on defense, one coach watches the line of scrimmage. We want the kids to be aware of the offside penalty. We keep after them about loafing in practice so we stress, "Don't be lazy." We do not want them to run around their blocks. Your kids will do that. When they run around a block, they open up the gaps. Again, we do not want to leave an opening in the picket fence.

Why Run the Angle?

- Has simple philosophy, techniques, and adjustments
- Provides defensive balance
- Confuses offensive blocking assignments
- Makes the offense prepare for multiple looks

This is what the angle defense allows us to do. Other reasons for the angle defense are that it allows our defensive players to:

- Key the ball
- Read the gap-player
- React to the scheme
- Sprint to the ball

If I were coaching at any other level today, I would do the same things I am doing now. We work on defense to get the players to key the ball. We do not want them to jump offside. We call out the cadence, "Go, go, go," in drills to see if we can get them to jump offside. If they do jump offside, it is TLC. They know what that means. We *teach* expectations, we *look* for performance, and we enforce the *consequences* of behavior. They know they have to do up-downs when they jump offside. They may have to run some sprints or endure some form of punishments.

When we come off the ball, we are looking at the gap, and we are looking at the offensive blocker. We try not to overcoach the players. When I coached at the University of Pittsburgh, we had a player who fumbled the ball several times. The coaches got on him so much he forgot how to run with the ball. I played with Tony Dorsett. Tony took the handoff with his hands open. He did not get his elbow up on the arm next to the ball. He took the ball in an unorthodox manner. However, he was successful. I do not want to overcoach the players.

Hesitation on offense and defense comes from lack of confidence. If they do not know what to do, they are going to have problems.

This is how we line up. We mirror the two sides of our line. To communicate with the players, we label the alignments. This is for communication during the games (Diagram #2).

- *Split defensive end.* Aligns in a 7 technique.
- *Defensive tackles.* Align in a 0 technique on the guards.

147

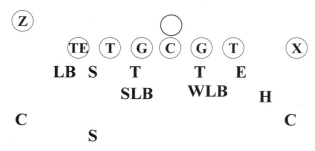

Diagram #2. Angle Defense Alignments

- *Sam linebacker*: Aligns in a 00 technique on the defensive tackle.
- *Will linebacker*: Aligns in a 00 technique on the defensive tackle.
- *Cornerbacks*: Align five to seven yards off the #1 receiver.
- *Safety*: Aligns 8 to 12 yards off the #2 receiver.
- *Stinger*: Always aligns to the tight end in a 9 technique.
- *Hornet*: Always aligns opposite the tight end in a fold technique.

This is how we call the defense. We signal in to the defense the alignment and stunts we want to run.

- The Sam linebacker gets a tight or split signal from the defensive coach.
- The linebacker makes a left or right call indicating the location of the tight end.
- A *Richie* (right) (Diagram #3) or *Louie* (left) (Diagram #4) call will be made directing the slant.

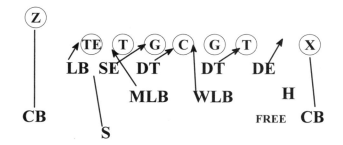

Diagram #3. Split-Right-Richie

The stinger has to find the tight end so he can set the defense. The hornet always goes opposite the tight end. If we get two tight ends, the hornet walks out. On any 00, that means the defender is back off the ball as the linebackers play.

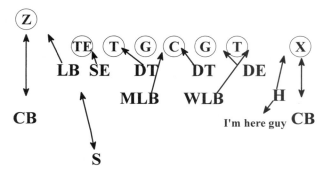

Diagram #4. Tight-Left-Louie

The corner must adjust his depth depending on his speed. The wider the offensive receiver splits, the more the corner must back off the ball. The safety plays 8 to 12 yards deep, depending on the opponent and their offense.

If the defense brings a wing inside, the outside backer cheats outside on him. We are man-to-man in the secondary. If the wing goes in motion, we have to move the linebackers and secondary over, but we must be aware of the reverse or counter.

We designate one of the defenders, usually a linebacker, to signal in the defensive calls. We make the call, such as "split" or "tight." We give the direction we want the angle to slant. The linebacker calls out the direction of the tight end so we can line up.

When the ball snaps, we angle the front line in the direction of the call, and the linebackers cover the opposite of the direction of the angle.

If we see a twins set, we can run our angles either *in* or *out*. We line the hornet on the backside or X-end. The linebacker is on the Z-back. In the *out*, the angle is to the outside (Diagram #5). If we call left, the Mike and Will linebackers are going right.

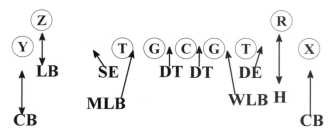

Diagram #5. Twins-Left-Out

If we call the *in* angle, the lines go inside, and the Mike and Will linebackers go outside (Diagram #6). The alignment is the same because it is against the twins set.

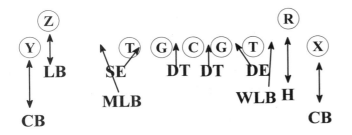

Diagram #6. Twins-Left-In

Next, I want to talk about developing a defensive game plan. We have to answer a few questions about the opponents when we review the films and start planning for the upcoming game.

- Which players make things happen for them?
- What plays must we stop to be successful against them?
- What offensive schemes must we recognize?

In calling the defense, what are the factors we must consider? We base this on the scouting report in some situations, but we use this chart to determine the calls on defense.

- Down-and-distance
- Field position
- Formation
- Personnel combinations
- Certain game situations

Against spread teams, we put the heat on the offense. We mix the calls up, and we pin our ears back and go after the quarterback. We can put the tackles in the A gap and shoot the gaps. We are not just punishing the center, but we are creating havoc.

We have a drill we call *scoop and score*. It is a fun drill. I have a line with six players a few yards from me with their backs turned. I have five other players with shield dummies simulating the offense. We do a lot with shield dummies. We use the shield dummies because some of the kids do not know how to hit, and they cannot take a hit.

I blow the whistle and those six players turn around. I throw the ball to someone or roll it on the ground. The other players must turn and block downfield for the one player who gets the pass or recovers the fumble. They are looking for some people to block. The go and block the five players with the dummies. It is scoop and score.

We do this drill from the sideline to the hash mark. It is a good drill, and we get a lot out of the drill. We allow them to take the ball into the end zone. They score, they get to greet the man who made the score, and they come back to the sideline.

They get conditioning out of the drill, but they are also coached how to scoop the ball up and how to change from defense to offense on the interception or fumble recovery. It is one of our best drills. It is called scoop and score.

I have some film I want to share with you. If you have questions, I will be around. It has been my pleasure to visit with you. Good luck next year, and may you win them all.

SPREAD-GUN WING-T/HIDDEN-HANDOFF DRAW

Thomas Downey High School, California

First, I'd like to thank Coach Earl Browning of the Coach of the Year Clinics and Coach Dave Johnson at the Portland Nike Clinic for the opportunity to speak. I would also like to take a quick moment to thank my outstanding coaching staff who I get to work with on a daily basis, as well as my wife and family who put up with having a coach for a husband and father.

A few years ago, we decided to spice up our traditional wing-T offense with the shotgun and splitting out the tight end. At first, it was a must because we felt like we had no legitimate tight end, two decent wide receiver type of kids, a quarterback who was effective in the shotgun, and an offensive line that was only average. We felt like those elements would have more success in a spread gun type of formation.

The experimentation was a huge success. On top of this offense being unique, we also combined it with a hurry-up/no-huddle approach. As coaches, we really enjoy this offense because it takes the wing-T's blocking schemes and backfield deception and combines it with spread formations that force the defense to defend the entire field. Since going to this offense, we have been at or near the top of our league rankings ever since.

After taking over the program this year at Thomas Downey High School, we used this offense extensively with great results. We coach some great kids with talent, but this year we were without a top recruit to skew our stats. Averaging 58 plays a game utilizing our no-huddle approach, we averaged 450 yards per game (300 of that was rushing), and 33 points per game. We also averaged less than two turnovers a game?a number that is respectable, but, of course, one would like to improve on. Our spread-gun wing-T running attack, along with our hidden-handoff draw, gave us a deadly and diversified ground attack that could attack the entire width of the field.

What are the advantages of running the wing-T from the spread gun?

- Forces the defense to declare its alignment and coverage shell, and the free safety cannot cheat to the tight end/wingside in run support.
- Threatens the width of the field on all plays.
- Allows the tight-end-type kids to play guard or linebacker.
- Easier to open up passing attack, which opens up screen/draw attack.
- *Looks* more exciting and gets more kids to try out for football.

Do not underestimate the power of this *looking more exciting* approach. This offense has allowed us to attract more athletes (from basketball and track)—ones we have not gotten in the past.

The way we go from the traditional wing-T to the spread-gun wing-T is easy (Diagram #1). The tight-end position bounces out to give us a wide receiver on each side. We tell the wide receivers to be in the vicinity of the field numbers, depending on what hash the ball is on. During the game, due to our no-huddle tempo, these kids do not switch sides.

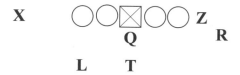

Diagram #1. From Wing-T to Spread-Gun Wing-T

We also have two halfbacks. The traditional dive back moves up into a halfback position, opposite the other halfback (Diagram #2). They are both turned in at a 45-degree angle, and their outside feet are even with the tackle's foot. They should be about five feet from the tackle—just wide enough so they can still down block a defender head-up on the tackle.

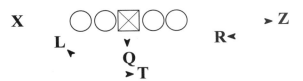

Diagram #2. Traditional Dive Back Moved to Halfback Position

Our offensive linemen are in two-point stances all the time. This is probably a clinic talk by itself. In our offense, we do very little drive blocking. Most of our linemen are down blocking, pass protecting, pulling, or reach blocking. We feel like being in a two-point stance gives us an advantage, but we still emphasize staying down to keep leverage.

If you have a trap chute, it is invaluable throughout the season to reinforce good habits. The guards' and tackles' helmets are even with the hip pads of the center. The guard has a two-foot split from the center, and the tackle has at least a three-foot split from the guard. We like to overemphasize the splits in the spread gun, since a linebacker blitzing through the A gap is less of a threat to the quarterback with him being in the shotgun.

I am asked questions about the shotgun snap technique. My best answer is to not overcoach it. We teach the center to grip the ball like a quarterback and give the quarterback a firm snap to the jersey numbers. We do not want a soft snap, a snap that is a bullet, or a snap with exaggerated spiral. We only want a firm snap with a slight rotation. Three coaching points for the center are:

- He should take a peek at the target on the quarterback, then look up at the defense.

- He should keep his wrist fairly tight throughout the snap. Light spiral is okay, but the faster the spiral, the tougher it is for the quarterback to catch.

- If the snap is getting too high, have the center *sit* over the ball more and straighten his back.

We only had a few bad snaps all season, and we only lost one during the whole season. The shotgun snap seems risky to some, but I would argue that it is not much more risky than the occasional fumble when the quarterback is under center. Lastly, I have found when we try to correct the center too much, it has a negative effect on his confidence, which leads to even worse results. We try to identify our centers in the off-season, and give them plenty of reps in 7-on-7 and throughout practices.

The quarterback puts his toes at three-and-a-half yards behind the ball. His hands should be palms down, thumbs together, even with his jersey numbers. His stance should be loose like a shortstop, always ready to handle a bad snap. In the case of a bad snap, we tell the quarterback to attempt to follow the intended ballcarrier to the line of scrimmage and try to gain at least a yard. We do not practice bad snaps intentionally, but when they do happen in practice, we have to coach the quarterback hard to not quit on the play just because it's practice. We harp on him to follow the intended ballcarrier to the hole. The tailback splits the inside leg of the guard, and his toes are even with the quarterback's heels. His alignment can vary a bit depending on the play.

Our offense uses three basic formations:

- *Red/blue:* Tells our tailback what side of the quarterback to align on. A red call puts the tailback on the right (Diagram #3). A blue call puts the tailback on the left side (Diagram #4).

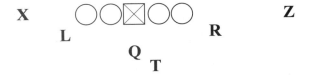

Diagram #3. Red Formation

- *Green/gold:* Is a trips set, and one halfback moves to the other side. The green call moves him to the right side of the quarterback (Diagram #5). If we call gold, he is on the left side of the quarterback formation (Diagram #6).

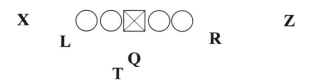

Diagram #4. Blue Formation

Diagram #5. Green Formation

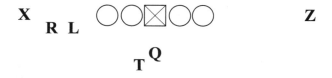

Diagram #6. Gold Formation

- *Empty formations* that we call with one vowel: A, E, I, O, or U. On the A call, we are in a 3 x 2 alignment.

The ease of calling these empty formations helps us to create personnel mismatches, especially when defenses are playing man.

A (left) and *U* (right) puts the tailback between the wide receiver and halfback. Here is the A alignment (Diagram #7). If we call *U*, we switch the formations and have a 2 x 3 alignment (Diagram #8).

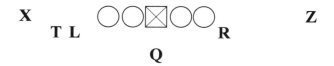

Diagram #7. A Call

Diagram #8. U Call

E (left) and *O* (right) displaces the halfback with the tailback, and the halfback bumps out. If we make an *E* call, the tailback moves inside on the 3 x 2 alignment (Diagram #9). If we call *O*, the formation is switched to the 2 x 3 set, but the tailback is still the inside receiver on the three-man side (Diagram #10).

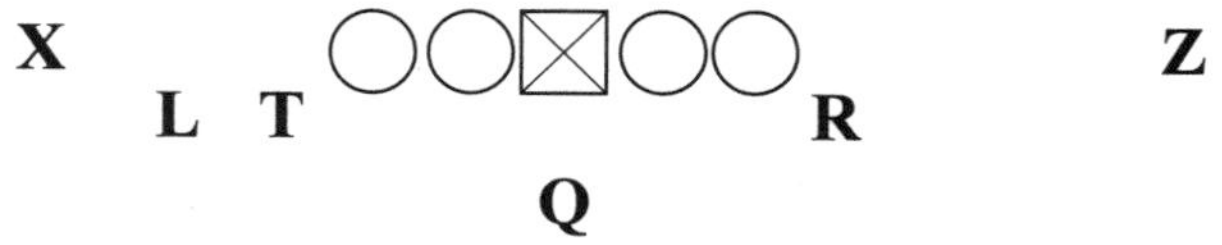

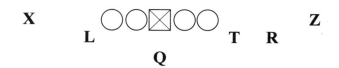

Diagram #9. E Call

Diagram #10. O Call

If we make the *I* call, it puts our tailback behind the center, and the quarterback goes to the wideside of the field. We have the 3 x 2 receivers on the wide side of the field (Diagram #11). If we call *I wide left*, the 3 x 2 receivers' set is to the left side of the formation or on the wide side of the field (Diagram #12).

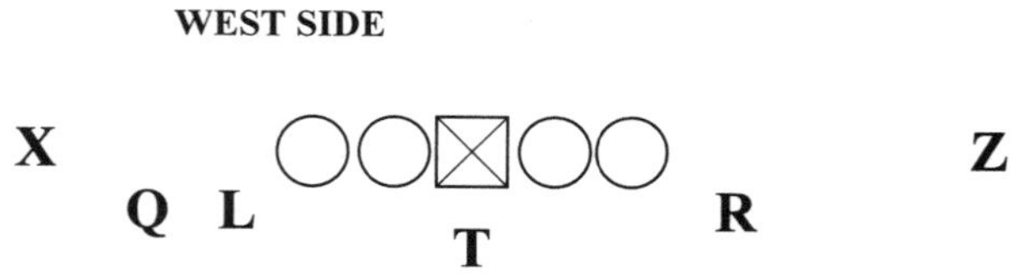

WEST SIDE

Diagram #11. I Call—Wide Right

WEST SIDE

Diagram #12. I Call—Wide Left

We were in the gun 95 percent of the time this season. The only other formation we got into this year was a no-split/double-wing formation. We ran that formation in crucial short-yardage situations—to run sneaks, wedges, and play-action. Those situations were used inside the two-yard line going in or coming out, or on any third or fourth down with less than two yards to go. Other than that, we were in the spread gun using our wing-T principles.

From our base formation of red/blue, running our buck sweep series, we send one of our halfbacks in Liz or Rip motion. Liz/Rip motion for us is a quick three-step motion, which puts the halfback near a traditional dive-back position. This motion must be full speed, and we use the rhythm of our cadence on the play. Our cadence is, "Down, set, hut." Our backs go in motion on *set*, and we snap it on *hut*. For us, Liz tells our left half to go in motion (Diagram #13).

Diagram #13. Liz Motion

Rip tells our right half to go in motion. The motion of one of our halfbacks creates a traditional backfield look from the wing-T.

If we want the wing on the right to go in motion we call *Rip* (Diagram #14). The back goes full speed, and the play is timed so the ball is snapped when the back gets to the original halfback position.

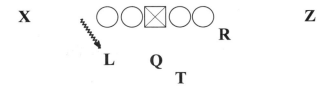

Diagram #14. Rip Motion

In our offense, we utilize two basic series: the buck series and the belly series. Each series consists of an inside run, outside run, counter, and play-action pass. I am often asked if we run a jet series. We did run jet a few times against teams that would stack us inside, and we probably should have run it more.

However, we had some physical backs this year, so keeping it simple was what we did. In addition, since we utilize this running game in a spread gun and combine it with the no-huddle, we feel like it is a little easier to attack a defense's alignment.

As a rule on *all* of our run plays, our playside wide receiver stalk blocks, and our backside wide receiver does a take block.

A *take route* for us is the wide receiver running a straight line pattern between a cover-3 cornerback and a free safety (Diagram #15). By running with speed to threaten their cushion, he effectively blocks two people without touching one of them.

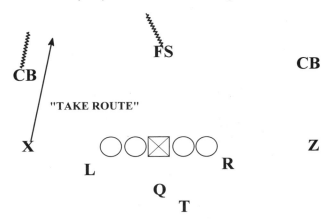

Diagram #15. Take Route

The *take block* for us is when the wide receiver gets to 10 yards, breaks off his route, and looks to shadow the free safety and block him when he turns around (Diagram #16).

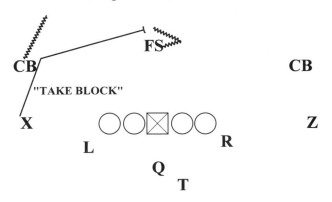

Diagram #16. Take Block

Our buck series contains a three-step motion to start each play. We start with the *trap* (Diagram #17).

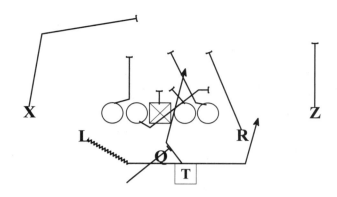

Diagram #17. Trap Right

We saw several 3-3 stack defenses this year, and our trap was great against it.

This was our best play the first half of the season, and it was the first thing the defense tried to take away from us later in the season. We trap the first defender head-up or outside the playside guard. The key coaching point here is the quarterback must step up to give the trap handoff. The tailback takes two steps at the backside hip of the center, and then bends it back playside, reading the block of the playside tackle on the inside linebacker. The slight bend creates a small counter-feel to the play, and is great for setting up our release blocks on the inside linebackers. If we get an A-gap defender at the snap, the playside guard automatically blocks down on him, and we trap the next man to the outside.

Trap Right

BST: Release through B gap to ILB

BSG: Trap first defender head-up or outside PSG

C: On-gap-down

PSG: Gap-down-backer

PST: Release inside to LB

BS HB: Three-step motion, fake sweep

PS HB: Stack backer to safety

TB: Get trap handoff

QB: Step up and give handoff, turn to fake sweep and waggle

The outside play in the buck series is the sweep (Diagram #18). This is the traditional buck sweep without the tight end. It can attack anywhere from off-tackle to the sideline. On the snap, the quarterback turns playside quickly, turning his back to the line of scrimmage, hiding the ball.

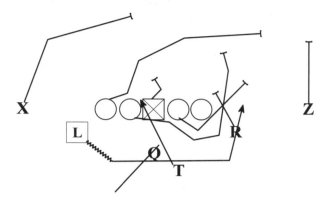

Diagram #18. Sweep Right

The coaching point here is the quarterback does not fake the trap, but the tailback does, creating some deception and confusion to the defense. When the ball is snapped, the tailback fakes hard a trap handoff, and runs through the backside A gap. On our outside run plays, the center is responsible for the playside A gap, and the tailback is responsible for the backside A gap. Note that sometimes we will split the tailback into an empty set, but we can still run the sweep. All we do is lose backside A-gap protection, but because the sweep happens so quickly, we have had linebackers come free and not come close to tackling the ballcarrier.

The playside guard has the key block. He pulls playside and attacks the first defender head-up or outside the playside halfback. Sometimes this kick-out block happens quickly, and sometimes the defender stays off the line of scrimmage and we have to log him. The ballcarrier must anticipate a quick cut if needed, but he can also run to the sideline if we log the contain man. The rest of the play is the traditional buck sweep.

Sweep Right

BST: Release through B gap to super fly

BSG: Pull and plow ILB

C: Fire-on-backer

PSG: Pull and attack OLB

PST: Gap-down-backer

BS HB: Three-step motion, run sweep reading guards

PS HB: Gap-down-backer

TB: Fake trap, fake through backside A gap

QB: Hide ball, give sweep, fake waggle

The counter play we run in the buck series is the *reverse* (Diagram #19). The reverse looks like the buck sweep to start, and then the opposite-side halfback gets the ball and runs outside in the opposite direction. The guards pull playside, but have opposite roles. The playside guard looks to pin a defensive end or plow an inside linebacker. He is actually working together with the playside tackle on an X-change block. The backside guard pulls and looks to attack the outside linebacker.

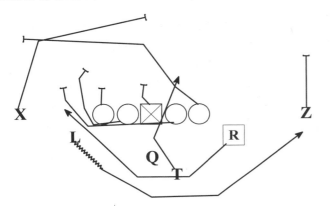

Diagram #19. Buck Series—Reverse

We like to try to pin the outside linebacker if he gets drawn in with the fake, but if he's coming upfield on the snap, we'll kick him out. This is a tough move for the ballcarrier, but if he sees the outside linebacker coming across on the snap, we teach the ballcarrier to make a quick *S-cut* inside the kick-out block, and then get back to the sideline. The faking halfback must get one yard behind the quarterback and be sure not to run into the countering halfback.

The key to this play is a subtle head movement by the quarterback. As the quarterback turns to fake the sweep, he must get his eyes on the faking back quickly. This movement sells the fake on the play. One last note—reverse is the only time we ask our wide receivers to reverse their assignments. So on this play, the playside wide receiver does a take block, and the backside wide receiver does a stalk block.

Reverse Left

BST: Release through B gap to super fly

BSG: Pull and attack OLB

C: Fire-on-backer

PSG: X-change block with PST

PST: On-gap-down (X-change block with PSG)

BS HB: Run behind quarterback, get handoff, read block on OLB

PS HB: Three-step motion, fake handoff one yard deeper, fake sweep

TB: Fake trap, bend and fake through BSG's void

QB: Turn and hide ball, helmet fake sweep, give reverse

The play-action component to this series is waggle (Diagram #20). Waggle starts out looking like the sweep. The quarterback turns, hides the ball, and fakes the sweep. After the fake, he boots out to a spot six yards deep of the playside halfback's original spot. We have our quarterback set up instead of rolling. Also, note the quarterback only fakes sweep, not trap.

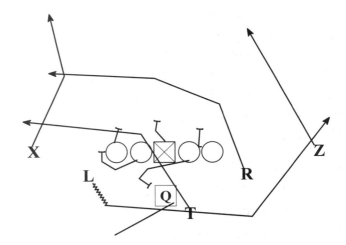

Diagram #20. Waggle Left

Our playside wide receiver runs a take corner. He runs a take route to the hash mark at a depth of 10 yards, and then breaks it deep to a corner route. The backside wide receiver runs a take route. If the free safety leaves the middle of the field open, the take route will be wide open. If we are anticipating no free safety on the play call, we will yell to the quarterback, "Backside," which tells him to fake and pull up quickly, and throw the ball with air for the touchdown.

Something that gets everyone's attention is our backside guard's pull-and-peel block. The backside guard pulls to the playside, but once he crosses the center, he peels back looking for a backside chaser. This turns out to be a nasty block, and sometimes will have a domino effect of actually blocking two defenders. Everything else about the play is traditional.

Waggle Left

BST: Fire-seal backside B gap

BSG: Pull and peel back on chase rusher

C: On-gap-down

PSG: X-change block with PST

PST: On-gap-down (X-change block with PSG)

BS HB: Drag route at 15 yards

PS HB: Three-step motion, fake sweep, swing route backside

TB: Fake trap, get through line of scrimmage, get to playside flat

QB: Fake sweep, boot, and set up; read deep-to-flat

Our second series is the belly series. This series contains no motion. We like to use this series when we see more of an even front. We saw some shade even fronts, so I will draw up this series versus that front. The inside play is belly (Diagram #21). This is a play to the tailback, with the playside halfback lead blocking on the inside linebacker. If we are cross blocking with the playside guard and playside tackle, then the halfback goes over to wall off the inside linebacker.

If the playside guard and playside tackle are *solo* blocking, then the halfback takes a path through the inside hip of the playside tackle and blocks the inside linebacker. The quarterback rides the handoff and lets go, then he fakes to the backside halfback, who is coming around on a *wide* fake. The playside guard and playside tackle do a combination block, working together to open the hole. Our rule is if we see a 2 or 3 technique, we cross block it. If we see an A-gap defender, we solo block him. The guard blocks the A gap, and the tackle blocks out on the defensive end. The center, backside guard, and

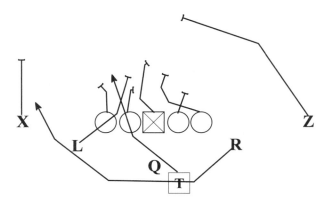

Diagram #21. Belly Left

backside tackle all fire block, but they can combo to scoop block any defensive linemen lined up in a gap.

Belly Left

BST/BSG/C: Fire-on-backer

PSG: Combo/X-block or solo

PST: Combo/X-block or solo

BS HB : Fake wide play

PS HB: Over/under block on   ILB

TB: Belly handoff, read blocks

QB: Ride and give handoff, fake wide, boot opposite way

Our outside run in this series is our wide play, and it is one of our favorites (Diagram #22). The concept of the play is to suck the defense into the belly/trap inside-run threat, and then give it to the wide back at the last possible second, as he is headed outside.

The key coaching point to this play is the ride of the quarterback. We tell him to ride the tailback fake as long as possible, keeping an eye on the wide halfback, giving him the ball at the last possible second. The playside halfback always does an over wall-off block on this play. The line blocks this play exactly like the reverse, so we can limit the amount of line blocks we use.

Wide Left

BST: Release through B gap to super fly

BSG: Pull and attack OLB

C: Fire-on-backer

PSG: X-change with PST

PST: X-change (on-gap-down)

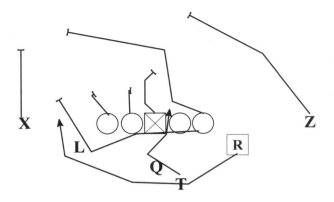

Diagram #22. Wide Left

BS HB : Run wide, get ball

PS HB : Wall off ILB

TB: Fake belly through backside A gap

QB: Ride belly fake, give wide, boot

Our counter play in this series is the belly counter, or backside counter (Diagram #23). We block this play with the traditional wing-T *Sally* concept. This play actually hits opposite the playside call. Our playside guard and tackle block aggressive on the first and second line-of-scrimmage threats. They block from the A gap to the outside. The backside tackle pass blocks and influences the defensive end up the field.

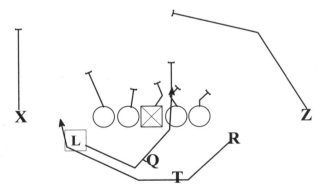

Diagram #23. Backside Counter

The key is the center and backside guard. Together, they each post with the leg nearest the backside A gap. Together, they filter any defenders away from that gap. The center can ride a defender playside, and the backside guard can ride a defender up the field. It is crucial that the area behind the backside A gap be untouched. Between those two linemen, whomever does not have a defender over

him, he six-chop-steps that lineman and goes off to the inside linebacker.

The quarterback fakes the belly, fakes the wide, and turns with the fake. He gives an inside handoff to the playside halfback. We tell the ballcarrier the hole will be anywhere from the backside A gap to the sideline.

BC Left

BST: Pass set and ride upfield

BSG & C: Post to backside A gap, ride the defender upfield or go to ILB on sixth chop step

PSG: Attack #1 from A gap outside

PST: Attack #2

BS HB: Fake wide

PS HB: Delay, take the inside handoff, run to daylight

TB: Fake belly, mirror PS ILB

QB: Fake belly, fake and turn with wide, give inside handoff to PS HB

Our play-action pass in our belly series is *big*. We keep this play very simple and combine it with our route tree, which is another presentation. The numbers we use after the play call dictate who the primary receiver is and the route he runs (Diagram #24). They tell the other halfback or wide receiver to that side, to run a memorized complement route.

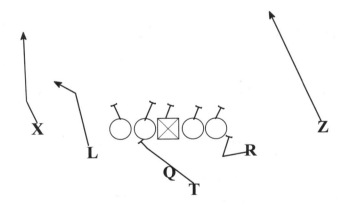

Diagram #24. Big 23

On the opposite side, the halfback protects, and the wide receiver runs a take route. The quarterback rides the tailback, takes one drop-step and two quick steps to throw. The tackles pass protect anyone heads up or outside. The center, guards, and tailback protect the A and B gaps. This play is good for us when we start to get outside linebackers cheating up to the line of scrimmage to stop the run, especially the halfback out route with a wide receiver on a go route.

On top of this base running and play-action game, and since we are in the shotgun, we utilize the passing game, as wells as screens and draws. Our best dropback passing play is our four vertical routes. It is necessary to keep the linebackers loose and the safeties scared of the pass. Our best rollout pass play is a bench route by the outside wide receiver. We run other rollout passes as well, because we feel like our quarterback's completion percentage goes up dramatically at our level when we cut down the field. Best of all, the roll pass also sets up our hidden-handoff draw.

We block the draw play exactly as we block our belly-counter play. Again, this reduces the number of plays the offensive line has to learn. We think that improves their execution by getting more reps of less blocking concepts. Our playside guard and playside tackle block aggressive, our backside tackle rides upfield, and our backside guard and center work the *funnel*. They post into the backside A gap and funnel defenders away from that area.

We have our wide receivers run *hitch* routes and call for the ball. By doing that, it gets the cornerbacks to freeze, and the outside linebackers might drop a little wider. Whether we are in a spread look or a trips look, we have our halfbacks fake our four vertical pass play, and then block when they see the safeties break out of their drop. We call it the *backside counter*.

Draw right means all of the action is going right, but after the hidden handoff, the tailback attacks the backside of the play. The quarterback immediately rolls to the sideline right behind the tailback (Diagram #25). The tailback takes one 45-degree step toward the playside tackle, and then bends over at about 45 degrees. With his back arm, the tailback makes a "bucket" by putting the inside of his hand on his hip pad, creating an opening

between his elbow and side. His inside hand will slide across the front of his body, palms up, and that hand will act as the bottom of the bucket so the ball does not slip through.

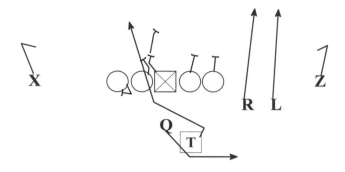

Diagram #25. Draw Right

As the quarterback passes behind the tailback, while his face mask is pointed toward the playside wide receiver, he eyes the ball, jabs the ball, and points down into the bucket with his inside hand. Once the tailback secures the ball, he attacks the backside. The hole will be anywhere from the backside A gap to the sideline. The quarterback continues to roll and fake a throw to the wide receiver.

Draw Right

BST: Pass set and ride upfield

BSG & C: Post to backside A gap,

ride defender upfield or go to ILB on sixth chop step

PSG: Attack #1 from A gap

outside

PST: Attack #2

Both HBs: Run vertical route

TB: One step playside, get hidden handoff, attack backside

QB: Roll playside, jab the handoff, fake throw

I hope this presentation gave you at least one concept you can incorporate into your offensive system. If you would like to see videos of our offense, we have our offensive team and player highlights on our website, which is www.tdfootball.com. If you have any questions, feel free to reach me by e-mail at plaa.j@monet.k12.ca.us.

THE 3-3-5 STACK AND SWARM DEFENSE

Jupiter Christian High School, Florida

Today, I would like to discuss some of the basic reasons why we run the 3-3-5 stack and swarm defense. With regard to the advantages of the defense, we identified seven key points.

WHY THE 3-3-5 DEFENSE?

- Very easy to learn
- Teams have to game plan for it
- Allows smaller, faster athletes to be successful
- Fun for players
- Enables the maximum number of players to be in the box
- Exerts maximum pressure against the pass
- Aggressive, attacking style of play

Our defense had an exceptional season last year. For example, as the statistics indicate, we had a large number of tackles for a loss that came as a result of our stunting, swarming style of play on defense.

2007 DEFENSIVE STATISTICS

- Sacks = 37
- Tackles for loss = 106
- Forced fumbles = 9
- Interceptions = 13

We use a few different key words in our terminology for the different defensive positions. Our secondary consists of two corners and one safety. We call our outside linebackers, Eagles. The down linemen are our e's and nose man. We use a small e to indicate the ends when we diagram the defense. The Eagles are outside-linebacker types. The e's are defensive tackle-type players. We have a strong e and a weak e. Accordingly, one end is the SE, and one is the WE. The inside linebackers are called bullets, while the middle linebacker is the missile backer.

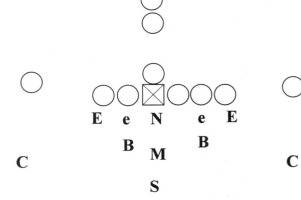

Diagram #1. Personnel

DEFENSIVE LINEMEN/LINEBACKERS

- ❑ Noseguard—Must force double-teams and cause havoc in the backfield.
- ❑ Ends—Should be agile and fast; can substitute size for quickness.
- ❑ Missile linebacker—The quarterback of the defense; must control A-gaps.
- ❑ Bullet linebackers—Typically, the best linebackers; must read nearside the guard to the nearside back.
- ❑ Eagles—Are a combination OLB/DB.

STIMULUS	RESPONSE
❑ Down block—	Eyes up to the near Back.
❑ Out block (pull to)—	Scrape tight.
❑ Pull (pull away) —	Shuffle, shuffle, tight.
❑ Scoop—	Same
❑ Reach—	Gap; if contact, keep the outside shoulder free.
❑ High hat—	Cover the first back to your side, or get to the quarterback.

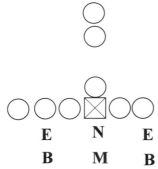

Diagram #2. Defensive Line and Linebackers Base Cover 3 and Cover 2

❑ STRONG END:
- Alignment—Head-up the offensive tackle
- Key—Offensive tackle
- Run to/away—C-gap/ trail/ reverse
- Pass responsibility—TE/OT rush lane

❑ NOSEGUARD:
- Alignment—Head-up the center
- Key—Ball
- Run to/away—C-gap; trail/reverse
- Pass responsibility—Inside rush lane

❑ WEAK END:
- Alignment: Head-up the offensive tackle
- Key—Offensive tackle
- Run to/away—C-gap; backside A
- Pass responsibility—Outside rush lane

❑ BULLETS:
- Alignment—Stack DE's
- Key—Offensive guard/near running back
- Run to/away—Fit
- Pass responsibility—Hash drop

❑ MISSILE:
- Alignment—Stack noseguard
- Key—Fullback/offensive guard
- Run to/away—Fit
- Pass responsibility— Hole drop

POSITION PLAY

❑ NOSEGUARD PLAY:
- Alignment—Nose-to-nose on the center; play as tight as possible and still be able to key and react.
- Key—Movement on the center's hand
- Responsibility—Attack the center and stuff him into the backfield and find the football; wreak havoc.
- Coaching Points:
  - ✓ On a running play, get one-yard deep in the backfield and redirect to the football; hold ground on a double team.
  - ✓ On pass plays, execute a bull rush, rip, or swim move; look for a draw. Get to the quarterback if there's no draw.

❑ DEFENSIVE END PLAY:
- Alignment—Head-up on the offensive tackle; align tight to the line of scrimmage.
- Key—Movement of the offensive tackle's helmet.
- Responsibility—C-gap; make power call; contain the pass rush.
- Coaching Points:
  - ✓ Step flat with the outside foot.
  - ✓ Keep shoulders square.
  - ✓ Attack the outside number of the offensive tackle.
  - ✓ Punch with hands and react to the offensive tackle's first step.
  - ✓ On running plays, get one yard deep, go flat to the ball.
  - ✓ On pass plays, contain and get to the quarterback.

❑ BULLET LINEBACKERS' PLAY:
- Play downhill; get to the football.

STIMULUS	RESPONSE
❑ Down block—	Eyes up to the near back.
❑ Out block (pull to)—	Scrape tight.
❑ Pull (pull away) —	Shuffle, shuffle, fit.
❑ Scoop—	Same
❑ Reach—	B-gap; if contact, keep the outside shoulder free.
❑ High hat—	Cover the first back to his side, or get to the quarterback.

- Alignment/depth—Five yards; make shotgun call

❏ MISSILE LINEBACKER PLAY:
- Play downhill; get to the football.
- Depth—Five yards
- Alignment—Stack behind the noseguard; make the formation call.
- Key—The track of the fullback to the offensive guard.
- Coaching Points:
  - ✓ Go through the blocker.
  - ✓ Look for screens and draws.
  - ✓ Cover the second back out of the backfield.
  - ✓ Continue to the quarterback on pass plays if the back is blocking.

Diagram #3 illustrates our Eagle alignments. First, we go against the pro set-I, with a split end on one side, and a tight end and wide receiver on the same side.

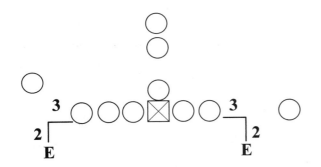

Diagram #3. Eagle vs. Pro I-Set

Diagram #4 shows how we line up against the split end and the slot man to the same side. The tight end is on the opposite side. This is how we line up on the slot and the backside. The following list details the responsibilities of the eagles and defensive backs in this alignment:

❏ EAGLES' RESPONSIBILITIES:
- On the one-receiver side, play downhill; read the last player on the line of scrimmage to the deepest back.

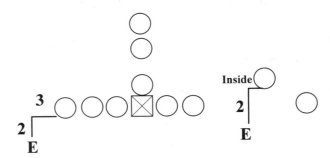

Diagram #4. Eagle vs. Pro I-Set Slot

STIMULUS	RESPONSE
❏ Inside run to—	Stay flat to the line of scrimmage; take away the bounce play.
❏ Inside run away—	Watch for bootleg; take away the cutback.
❏ Outside run to—	Make play; string out to the sideline.
❏ Outside run away—	Watch for a reverse, pursue from the backside.
❏ Pass—	Contain, get to the quarterback.

- If more than one receiver is on his side, cover the number 2 receiver man-to-man; take away the inside route, or play zone coverages (flats).

❏ CORNERBACK'S RESPONSIBILITIES:
- Man-to-man coverage on the number 1 receiver to each side.
- Take away the inside route.
- Disrupt the quarterback/receiver timing.
- Mask the coverage from time to time.
- Cover 2 or cover 3 zone
- Attack the run from an outside-in zone.

❏ SAFETY'S RESPONSIBILITIES:
- Man defense—tight end
- Man free—center field; no one gets behind him.
- Call out motion.
- Cover 2, cover 3 zone
- Run support, inside-out

Next, I would like to cover our 3-3 stack blitzes. First, I would like to review our stunts. Most of the stunts are self-explanatory. The following list details the different stunts and indicates how we determine how we move on the stunts.

- Missile—Weak/strong, right/left
- Bullet—Double, weak/strong, right/left
- Eagle—Double, weak/strong, right/left
- Beast—Double, weak/strong, right/left
- Bam—Double, weak/strong, right/left
- Mean—Double, weak, strong, right/left
- Thunder—Send five linebackers; the three linemen stay at the line of scrimmage.
- Storm—Everyone blitzes, including the three down linemen and the five linebackers.
- Corner or safety—Weak/strong, right/left

Diagram #5 illustrates our missile stunt. The noseguard goes one way, and the missile goes the opposite way.

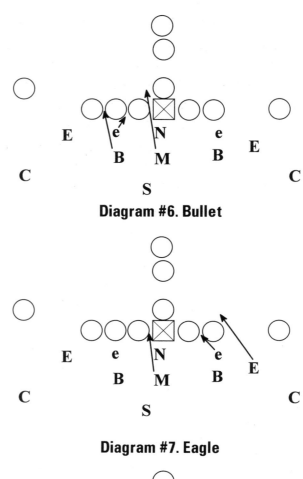

Diagram #6. Bullet

Diagram #7. Eagle

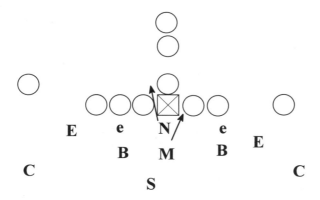

Diagram #5. Missile

On the bullet stunt, we involve four inside players (Diagram #6). The bullet has the C-gap and the missile has the A-gap.

On the eagle stunt, we stunt on the backside (Diagram #7). The eagle on the backside closes in the C-gap. The missile has the strongside A-gap, and the nose has the backside A-gap.

The beast stunt is a backside stunt, with the three outside defenders (Diagram #8). In this stunt, the backer and the end blitz.

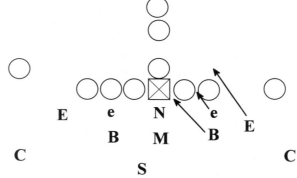

Diagram #8. Beast

When we take the eagle stunt and use it with the missile stunt, we refer to this stunt as the mean stunt (Diagram #9). The difference is the missile has the option to cover either A-gap. The nose man slants left on the mean stunt. The missile reads both A-gaps and fills if the ballcarrier comes to him.

On the thunder stunt, we involve eight players on the call. The ends are coming hard, and the three linebackers blitz (Diagram #10). The down linemen cover for the blitzing linebackers.

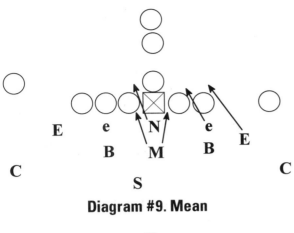

Diagram #9. Mean

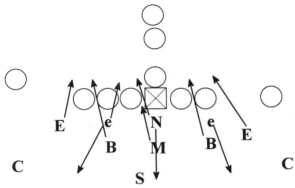

Diagram #10. Thunder

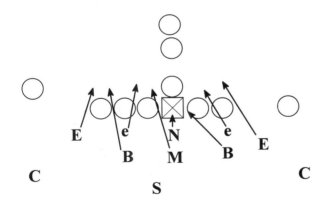

Diagram #11. Storm

On the storm stunt, we send all eight men in the box (Diagram #11). It is an all-out blitz, with the two corners and safety playing the pass.

Next, I would like to cover five different formations and show you how we line up against each of them. I would also like to review the key coaching points for each position in each formation.

The first formation is the I-formation. Diagram #12 illustrates a standard pro right I-set alignment.

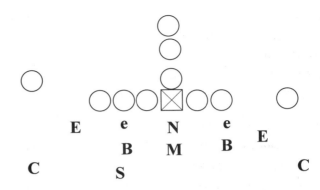

Diagram #12. I-Formation

❑ COACHING POINTS:
- Cornerbacks—Man-to-man pass coverage on the #1 receiver to each side of the line of scrimmage
- Safety—Man-to-man coverage on the tight end
- Eagles—Contain on runs; get to the quarterback on a pass.
- Bullet linebackers—Play downhill; cover the first back out to his side to the quarterback.
- Missile linebacker—Play downhill; cover the second back out to either side to the quarterback.
- Defensive line—Get one-yard deep in the backfield; redirect to the ball on runs; get to the quarterback on a pass.

The next formation I'd like to discuss is the double twins formation. The offense is in a slot on both sides of the formation (Diagram #13). The eagles have to cover the slots man-to-man.

❑ COACHING POINTS:
- Cornerbacks—Man-to-man pass coverage on the #1 receiver to each side of the line of scrimmage; take away the slant pass.
- Safety—Man-to-man to run support
- Bullet linebackers—Play downhill; cover the back if he comes out to his side to the quarterback.
- Missile linebacker—Play downhill and read the quarterback.
- Defensive line—Get one-yard deep in the backfield; redirect to the ball on runs, and get to the quarterback on a pass. The ends take an outside rush.

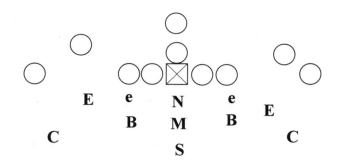

Diagram #13. Double Twins Formation

The third formation is the trips formation. Against trips formation, we adjust with our eagles and bring the safety over to the formation to cover the #3 receiver (Diagram #14). The corners are man-to-man on the outside receivers.

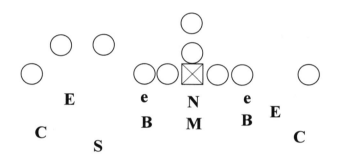

Diagram #14. Trips Formation

❏ COACHING POINTS:
- Cornerbacks—Man-to-man pass coverage on the #1 receiver to each side of the line of scrimmage
- Safety—Man-to-man pass coverage on the #3 receiver
- Eagles—Man-to-man pass coverage on the #2 receiver; come hard at the quarterback; watch for the handoff.
- Bullet linebackers—Play downhill; cover the back who comes out to his side to the quarterback.
- Missile linebacker—Play downhill; read the quarterback.
- Defensive line—Get one-yard deep in the backfield; redirect to the ball on runs and get to the quarterback on a pass. The ends take an outside rush.

The fourth formation is an empty formation. Against the empty formation, we cover the three receivers on one side and two receivers on the backside (Diagram #15). We keep the inside down linemen and linebackers inside.

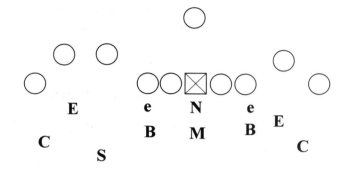

Diagram #15. Empty Formation

❏ COACHING POINTS:
- Cornerbacks—Man-to-man pass coverage on the #1 receiver to each side of the line of scrimmage
- Safety—Man-to-man pass coverage on the #3 receiver
- Eagles—Man-to-man pass coverage on the #2 receiver
- Bullet linebackers—Play downhill; cover the back who comes out to his side to the quarterback.
- Missile linebacker—Play downhill; read the quarterback.
- Defensive line—Get one-yard deep in the backfield; redirect to the ball on runs, and get to the quarterback on a pass. The ends take an outside rush.

The fifth (and final) formation involves playing against short-yardage and goal-line situations. As a rule, we encounter the power stack strong set (Diagram #16). We adjust by bringing the corners in tighter, and we walk up closer to the line of scrimmage.

❏ COACHING POINTS:
- Cornerbacks—Man-to-manpass coverage on the #1 receiver to each side of the line of scrimmage

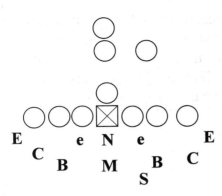

Diagram #16. Short Yardage/Goal Line

- Safety—Man-to-man pass coverage on the power back
- Eagles—Crash hard through the tight end to the quarterback.

- Bullet linebackers—Play downhill, two-to-three yards deep; cover the back who comes out to his side to the football.
- Missile linebacker—Play downhill, two-to-three yards deep; look for the quarterback sneak to the football.
- Defensive ends—Get in a four-point stance; blow in the B-gap.
- Nose—Push the center back, and look for the quarterback sneak.

My time is up. I want to thank you for your attention.

CHANGING THE 5-3 TO THE 3-3 DEFENSE

Beechwood High School, Kentucky

Thank you, it is a pleasure to be here. I do not have much time, so I am going to get right into the topic. My topic today is converting from an eight-man front to a six-man front without changing personnel. However, I will be the first person to tell you, we make many personnel changes in obvious passing situations.

The coach at Dixie Heights emailed me after he saw my name on the speaker list. He wondered after I told you that we take our tackles out and put in two defensive backs, what was I going to do for the next 58 minutes.

I am going to show you a couple of ways you can convert the defense without changing personnel. The first thing you have to look at is the type of personnel you want to use in the 5-3 defense. You have to look at the nose first. People like to play against the big heavyset lineman. The small, quick defenders cause them the most problems. There are some coaches here from northern Kentucky who have played against us. They will tell you that we focus on smaller, quicker defensive linemen in our program.

I am going to show you our base stack and shade alignments. When we align in our 5-3 defense, we play a 4-3 defense on the edge. When I talk about the 4-3 edge, I am referring to the three players in the outside triangle: the linebacker, defensive tackle, and defensive end. They play in the B and C gaps. I will show you who they read and where they look. We play our 5-3 defense like a 4-3 defense.

The defensive end in our 5-3 defense is going to squeeze inside like a 4-3 defense. That lends itself to converting to the 3-3 defense. That is one of the key things in converting to the 3-3 defense. The personnel you play at your nose make the conversion easier.

As far as our personnel arrangements, I will show you how we have done it before and other ways to do it. Fort Thomas Highlands runs the 3-3 defense, but they play their tackles in a 5 technique and the linebacker up close to the line of scrimmage. They call their strong safety players dogs. They play their 3-3 differently than we do.

In the introduction, they read my coaching record. That record comes from having a great coaching staff with a lot of experience and tremendous talent on the field. If I can stay out of the way, we will be fine.

At the nose, we want to play a quick player who can back up and play middle linebacker (Diagram #1). He has to be the type who will draw a double-team block when he plays down. There are times when we get in trouble with this type of scheme. I will not sit here and tell you we do not. In fact, the tape I am going to show you is from a game we lost. I think that will do more to help you understand the concepts.

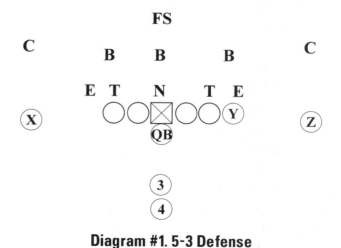

Diagram #1. 5-3 Defense

The tackles are larger, heavier players in comparison to the nose. I replaced Mike Yeagle at Beechwood. I was fortunate to coach with him for a number of years. The 5-3 defense was Mike's baby. In his 5-3 defense, the tackles were two-gap players. They aligned in a 4 technique and played the B gap and spilled into the C gap late. We made the tackles one-gap players and took the defensive ends and played them like the 4-3 concept. In the 4-3, the great players in that defense are the defensive ends. I made the defensive ends two-gap players. That made the tackles more one-dimensional and made it easier on them.

The defensive ends in this defense are the best leverage players on the field. We want the most athletic players at defensive end. He has to be able to wrong arm a kick-out block, play the skate technique on the option, drop into coverage, and rush the passer. If I need him to play on the hash, he could do it. We do not run a lot of zone blitz, but when we do, this player can cover it.

The middle linebacker is a fill-and-plug player. I told our middle linebacker if he could play from C gap to C gap, we would be a 8-2 or 7-3 team. If he could play from D gap to D gap, we would be state power, and if he could play sideline to sideline, we would have a chance to play in the state championship. He has to be a fill-and-plug player and bounce the ball to the outside linebackers.

The outside linebackers must have good feet and must have great football instincts. They have to play downhill and drop into coverage. They play on the edge and play *outside-in* all the time. The reason we won the championship this year was because I had talented players playing on the outside who understood the game.

I do not separate the free and strong safeties. This is the same position for us. We are a 5-3 team, which means we play one defender in the middle of the field. When we go to a 4-3 defense with a cover-2 look, the free safety is a fill downhill type of player. The corners are players with great feet and vision. They are the type of player you want playing corner in this defense.

When we go to the 3-3 defense, we stack the linebacker, and the end is playing on air. You really must have an athletic player to play on air. That is

the position Lawrence Taylor used to play. To play on air and do it well, you have to be a heck of a football player.

I want to show you our base 5-3 defense and some of the concepts that allow us to get into the 3-3 without changing personnel. If the offense gives us two backs in the backfield, we will be in an eight-man front. You have to start with the outside stack in the defense. We call that the *outside triangle*.

To the tight-end side, the defensive end aligns in a 9 technique. If the tight end blocks down, the defensive end closes to the inside (Diagram #2). If the fullback or guard tries to kick-out the defensive end, he puts his face mask on the inside V of the neck of the blocker and bounces the ball outside. I do not like to trade one for one in a blocking scheme. The defensive end plays down inside so the tailback bounces outside, but he becomes a D-gap player late. Initially, he is a C-gap player, but he also helps outside.

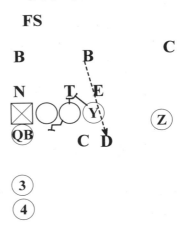

Diagram #2. 5-3 vs. Down Block

The tackle fights the double-team in the best way he can. You have to decide how you want him to play. This year, we had one tackle who grabbed grass and stayed low in the hole. The other tackle got skinny and split the double-team. You have to decide what your personnel can do. The outside linebacker reads the down block by the tight end and becomes the D-gap player.

We have a simple rule for the defensive end on a base block (Diagram #3). We tell the defensive end that if the tight end puts his hand on him, he is a D-gap player. It does not matter what the tight end tries to do. If the tight end tries to arc release, the defensive end fights him outside. If the tight end tries to block the defensive end to the outside, the defensive end is the D-gap player, but he squeezes the tight end back to the inside. He does not run to the outside and open the inside gap. He squeezes and tries to push the tight end back inside.

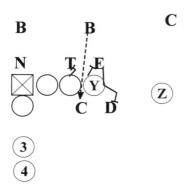

Diagram #3. 5-3 vs. Base Block

When the outside linebacker sees the tight end start to block the defensive end, he becomes the C-gap player. He plays downhill into the C gap as soon as he sees the tight end put his hands on the defensive end. He fills hard the instant he sees it, his eyes go inside, and he plays off what he sees. These techniques lead to the 3-3 defense, which I will get to in a minute.

We have a shade alignment from the 5-3 front (Diagram #4). On the shade, the noseguard moves to the shade alignment on the center, toward the tight end. The backside defensive tackle and end reduce their alignments to the outside shoulder techniques on the offensive tackle and guard. Since the backside reduces down, the outside linebacker (instead of stacking) kicks-out to the outside of the defense. The outside linebacker splits the difference between the offensive tackle and the split end. His rule tells him, with two backs in the backfield, he takes one giant step toward the offensive tackle in his alignment. If there is one back in the backfield, he takes one giant step toward the split end. In the one-back set, he aligns wider because there is one less blocker to that side.

On the split-end side, the read for the defense does not change. They have the same read as to the

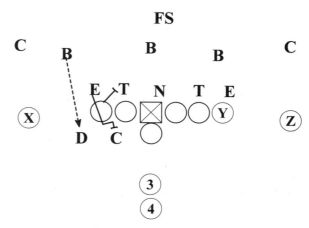

Diagram #4. Shade 5-3 vs. Down Block

tight-end side. If the offensive tackle blocks down on the defensive tackle, the defensive end is the C-gap player and closes to the inside. As you look at the diagram, I know it is actually the B gap, but we still consider that gap the C gap. The outside linebacker on the down block is the D-gap player. If the offensive tackle base blocks on the defensive end, he becomes a D-gap player and plays with his responsibility to the outside, but squeezing to the inside (Diagram #5). The outside linebacker is now the C-gap player and has to get into that gap in a hurry. He is the downhill player looking inside for his next key.

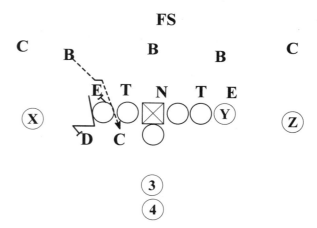

Diagram #5. Shade 5-3 vs. Base Block

If the offense spreads the outside linebacker with an additional receiver to his side, he gives a *tight, tight* call to the defensive end. That tells the defensive end he cannot fill the C gap on a base block from the tackle. Now, the defensive end has to play the C gap, and the linebacker plays the D gap. Those are the basic reads in this defense, and that is where you have to start. It is a 5-3 defense, but it plays like a 4-3 in the triangles on the outside.

When we play the spread offense, the simplest thing to do is leave the tackles in 4 techniques and walk your defensive ends off on the slot receiver (Diagram #6). That alignment looks like the 3-3 defense, except for the two-deep secondary. The flaw of that alignment is you need defensive ends who can play in space. Last year, I played with one defensive end who could not play in space. However, I had one defensive end who could. I will always have one defensive end who can play in space. That is the decision I have to make at the beginning of the year. If I want to be a 3-3 team, I definitely must have at least one defensive end who can play in space. It goes back to what I said at the beginning, the defensive ends have to be great players.

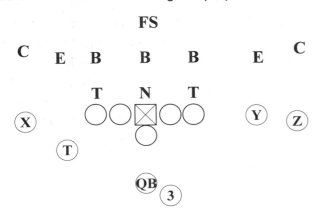

Diagram #6. Adjusted 5-3 to Spread

From this defensive adjustment, we can play cover 3 with no problem. The ends take the flats, the outside linebackers have hook to curl, and the Mike linebacker has the hook zone in the middle. The safety goes to the middle third, and the two corners play the outside thirds.

We can roll the secondary strong or weak from this alignment (Diagram #7). If we roll to the defensive left, the corner and defensive end collide on the outside receiver and slot to prevent them from going deep. The safety plays the deep half behind the left corner, and the right corner plays the weak-half coverage. That leaves us six underneath defenders in five short zones. However, the linebackers will more than likely be in some kind of blitz game.

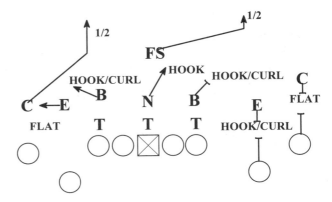

Diagram #7. Cover 2 Left

If the offense is hurting the defense with an option or some kind of wide play, we roll the corner up to get the hard corner. However, we never drop the defensive end into the deep third behind the corner. We have to get from the clinic to the practice field. You cannot give the defensive ends too much to do. You cannot change their reads so that you are coaching them in an entirely new scheme.

The outside linebacker's read in the 3-3 alignment does not change. However, it is opposite. If he gets a down block by the tackle, he fills the C gap. If he gets a base block, he scrapes. He still reads the same way, except now he has flat coverage or hook-to-curl coverage.

One way to get from the 5-3 to the 3-3 is very simple (Diagram #8). You can do all the adjustments from one side of the defense. This makes it simple so you do not have players running all over the field to get into position. You do all the movement from one side. The nose tackle backs off the line of scrimmage and becomes the middle linebacker. The right defensive tackle bumps into the nose-tackle position. The right defensive end becomes the down 4-technique tackle, and the inside and outside linebackers become the outside linebacker and dog player or inside safety. You have to decide which of the linebackers plays better in space and which one is the better run stopper. If your Mike linebacker plays better in space, he could become the outside dog-type player. You have to decide that according to your personnel.

In the defense, one end can play in space and the other is a run stopper kind of player. That is the

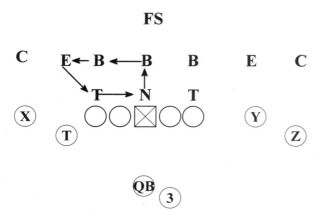

Diagram #8. 5-3 Defense to 3-3 Alignment

same concept of the anchor end and the drop end. We have six players in the box who can do all kinds of things. However, we have seven cover players in this defense. The next thing you have to decide is how to play your second-level defenders. You actually have six defenders in the underneath second level, because one of the corners will drop into deep coverage every time.

We have different ways to align the six underneath defenders. We can align all the second-level players at five yards deep, or they can align in a press-coverage look (Diagram #9). When we align in a press alignment, we bring the outside corners and inside dogs to the line of scrimmage.

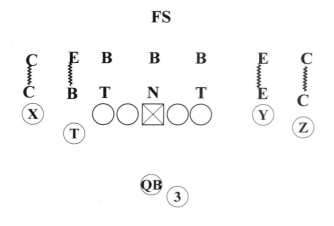

Diagram #9. Press

In our 3-3 alignment, the six inside defenders will never come out of the box. The three down linemen and the three stacked linebackers will always be in the box. What that means is the offensive formation will never cause the inside six players to make an

adjustment outside the box. The offense tries to get the defense to move with their formations. I looked at the Nike notebook they give us each year and it is obsolete. On the pre-drawn formations on the pad, the quarterback is under the center. You never see that anymore. I can call a defense that causes our players to leave the box, but the offense cannot do anything that affects the way we align.

The offense has rules they try to exercise in their play calling. If there are five defenders in the box, they run the ball. If there are seven players in the box, they throw the ball. With six players in the box, the rules are cloudy. If you keep six players in the box, there are so many things you can do. That makes the defense very diverse, without changing a thing from your base teaching. The linebackers and ends are still reading the triangle. If you get a down block, the end squeezes and the linebacker scrapes. If they try to base the end, the linebacker screams into the gap and the end is outside in the D gap with the corner in the wide D gap.

The flat player is a run player first. Whoever is assigned flat coverage is a run player first. We want him to play the run first and recover to the flat. How many teams will try to move the ball down the field throwing to the flat repeatedly? It is too hard of a throw, and most do not have the patience to do it. With high school quarterbacks, it is too much of a risk to dink the ball down the field throwing to the flat. With the high school hash marks, your quarterback has to be good to get the ball outside the numbers into the wide field. We tell our flat players they play *run, run, run,* and get to the flat when they need to get there. If the offense wants to throw the ball into the flat, we come after the quarterback and make him throw the ball over the flat defender.

This past year, Fort Thomas Highland's defensive tackles were amazing. We scrimmage them every year. They play the tackle in a 5 technique on the outside shoulder of the offensive tackle and control the B gap. It looks like a simple play to turn out on the tackle, lead up on the outside linebacker, and have a great play. We have been blessed in that we have some big offensive tackles.

Their defensive tackle pushed our tackle down inside, played over his face, and made the play. They closed on the out block and the lead blocker never got to the linebacker.

We do not have those types of tackles all the time. That is why I like to stack in the 4 technique. We get in a 5 technique, but it is generally in a long-yardage situation. We give the tackle a *jet* call that is a pass-rush mode. They get wider outside in an angled stance and come as hard as they can in a pass rush. If the offense runs the ball, they may get eight or nine yards, but they still have to punt.

In our base defense, our tackles play a 4 technique (Diagram #10). The linebacker reads the guard. I cannot change his rules completely. Because of the size of our school, we are a one-platoon football team. I play seven or eight players both ways. That is a minimum number because some years it is more than that. We do not have that much time during the week to work on our defensive scheme, because our players are involved on both sides of the ball. We have maybe two-and-a-half hours, tops, in any given week to get ready for our next opponent. We do not change reads for any given opponent. If the guard blocks down or up, the outside linebacker fires into the B gap. We do not worry about the offensive tackle reaching the defensive tackle, because the Mike linebacker's alignment is deeper than the other two linebackers are. He plays over the top to the outside and can fit outside the tackle.

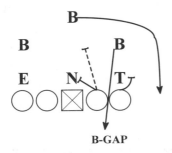

Diagram #10. 4-Technique Stack

The Mike linebacker's alignment is what we call an *inverted wishbone* look. The outside linebackers are in front of the Mike linebacker as far as his depth. I have not talked any pass coverage yet, but I am going to do that next.

If you are thinking about doing something like this, you need to start thinking early about how to get out of the eight-man front into the six-man front. Everyone runs the spread offense, and you have to defend it. I showed you how we do it. However, you may have another way that fits your personnel better. Our way is the way we do it—it is not necessarily the only way.

If you go back 15 years, particularly in single-A football, you saw maybe two teams in the spread. When Hal Mumme came to the University of Kentucky as head football coach, the entire state went to the spread offense and it has not changed since. High school coaches follow what is going on at the state level, which is probably a good thing. When Hal Mumme came through the state, everyone went to the spread and they never looked back.

If you go to the 3-3 defense and someone comes out in the tight-end set, you have to adjust (Diagram #11). One of the ways we adjust is to align the dog (who is a defensive end) on the tight end. The defensive tackle to that side aligns in a 4 technique head-up on the tackle. The reads are the same. If the tight end blocks down on the defensive tackle, the defensive end closes the C gap, and the outside linebacker scrapes into the D gap.

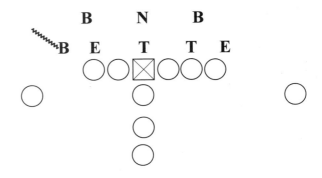

Diagram #11. Adjustment to Tight End

The defensive ends in this defense have to be *special*. We have two outside linebackers and two defensive ends in four positions. In those four positions, you must find two players who are special players. If you look at the 5-3 defense, the Mike linebacker can be an average player. All the pressure is on the perimeter. That is especially true now because teams are not going to run in the A gap, B gap, and C gap as their only offense. They will stretch you laterally and vertically.

When we play 3-3 defense, we play many coverages in man defense. We bring six defenders all the time to rush the quarterback. We play the free safety as a linebacker quite a bit. He is a downhill player.

I want to look at the coverage from the 3-3 defense. When we go to our 3-3 defense, we call it nickel. The reason we call it *nickel* is that we have substituted two defensive backs into the defense. One of our nickel backs is an outside-linebacker type, and the other one is our fourth defensive back. The reason we play those types of players is the rotating coverages we play.

We do not like to take the safety out of the middle (Diagram #12). We use rotation coverage to get the nickel back into the deep outside third. We do not let the defensive end run this type of coverage, but when we substitute the fourth defensive back, we feel comfortable letting him run the third. This coverage is a rotation right. The right corner collisions the wide receiver coming off the line and settles into the flat coverage. The nickel back, who looks like he is playing the flat, retreats into the deep third, and everyone else plays the same.

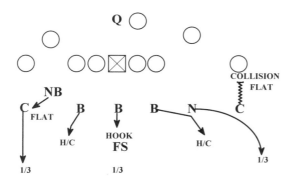

Diagram #12. Cover 3 With Rotation

You can do that a hundred ways, but that requires you to teach all the different techniques to all the players. We are not going to do that. We let the defensive back, who knows how to cover the third, make the adjustment. Remember the rule about the flat player. The flat defender plays the

run first. That, now, is the corner. He reads the offensive tackle block for his key. He collisions the receiver and gets his eyes to the inside.

I tell our third players they should be making tackles on the run four to seven yards down the field. If they are making tackles at the line of scrimmage, we will get beat deep on a pass. Mom will be cheering when he makes the big play. However, she will not take any credit when he gets beat deep. When a player has third responsibility, he has to be late on run support.

If we want to rotate the coverage to the left, the fourth defensive back moves to the left side and runs into the outside third. We never let the linebacker type play a deep third. In their stance, the flat player will have a parallel stance. The third player opens to his third in his stance. He disguises his foot movement to keep from tipping his coverage.

We can go to a *dime* package from this scheme (Diagram #13). When we go to the dime package, the fourth defensive back in the game is now a half player. We have a 3-2 look on the inside, and the outside linebacker moves out to the hook-to-curl area. Both corners roll down into flat coverage. The outside linebackers are the hook-to-curl players, and the inside linebackers cover the middle hooks or come on a blitz. The safety and the fourth defensive back run the hash marks.

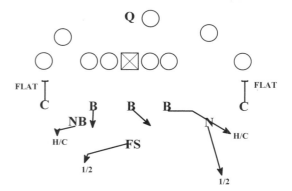

Diagram #13. Dime Coverage

In this coverage, we can never call rotation coverage or dime coverage with the defensive end to the side that has to rotate into a deep zone. We have to be smart enough to keep the defensive end in a hook-to-curl area or a flat zone. He probably could learn how to do it, but when will we find time to teach him.

From our dime coverage we run two under (Diagram #14). The thing we have to do in this coverage is learn how to play man coverage. We play two types of man coverage. We play *outside-over-the-top* or *inside underneath*. We have more trouble teaching inside underneath than we do outside-over-the-top. That type of man coverage is the inside-trail position for the defender. The players understand over-the-top coverage because that is what they play in backyard football. You never play man under with a safety over the top in the backyard.

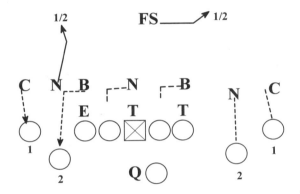

Diagram #14. Man Two Under Dime

The corners' rule is press technique on the #1 receivers to their side. They collide with the receiver, force him outside, and get into trail man coverage under the receiver. The nickel backs play the #2 receivers to their side or the #3 receiver away. They play the same type of press technique as the corner. If the offense is a balanced formation, the corner takes the first receiver and the nickel takes the second receiver.

If the formation is a trips set, the backside end or linebacker has no second receiver to his side (Diagram #15). He comes over and takes the #3 receiver to the trips side. We always want to keep the end or linebacker on the #3 receiver. If the fourth defensive back has an away #3 receiver, he comes over, takes the #2 receiver, and puts the linebacker on the #3 receiver. We want our defensive end on the worst receiver. We do that by

the scouting report. We played one team that played a trips formation all the time but had only thrown to the third receiver five times the entire season. We want our linebacker/defensive end type of player to cover that receiver.

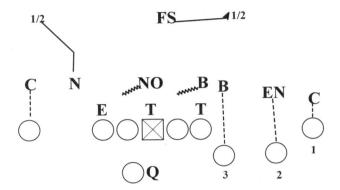

Diagram #15. Trips Formation

We like to play press coverage because you can play zone out of the press technique (Diagram #16). We bring our defenders down into press coverage, which looks like man coverage. When they snap the ball, the defender collides with the receiver and drops into his zone. As soon as the quarterback starts the cadence, the nickel and linebacker covering the #2 receivers peek in at the tackle to see what he is doing. When they get their hands on the receiver, they look at the tackle to see what he is doing. If he pops up in pass protection, the defender goes to his zone responsibility. If the tackle shows a run-blocking mode, the defender gets into his run support responsibility.

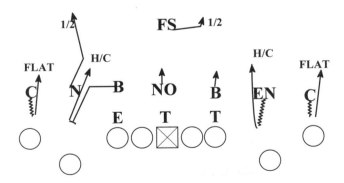

Diagram #16. Press Cover 2

We can play cover 3 out of the press alignment (Diagram #17). The only thing you must have is proper footwork. The trick is the corner in press alignment bailing out into his third coverage.

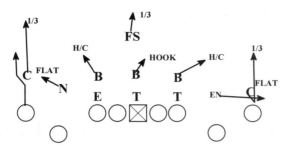

Diagram #17. Press Cover 3

I have one last thing I will talk about. We call it *spy 0*. The corners have the #1 receivers to their side in man-to-man coverage. The nickel backs have the #2 receivers to their side or the #3 receiver away. They are in man coverage, but there is no help deep. They must play over-the-top man coverage because there is no help deep. They stay on top of the receiver and keep him in front of them. The safety lines up seven to eight yards deep and spies a particular back or the quarterback. This is a game plan type of coverage. We can account for the running quarterback or a back trying to take advantage of a mismatch with a defender. We can also blitz the safety out of this coverage.

Coaches, I will stick around as long as you want to talk. I hope that I was helpful to you. I appreciate your attendance and your patience with me. I will answer any questions you have. Thank you very much.

TWO-PLATOON FOOTBALL IN HIGH SCHOOL

Garnet Valley High School, Pennsylvania

First, I want to give you a quick rundown on the history of the Garnet Valley football program. When we first started coaching in 1986, we were one of smallest AA schools in the state of Pennsylvania. In fact, at the Unionville High School homecoming game in 1990, we dressed 23 players from grades 9 through 12. During the late 1990s and early 2000s, we were the fastest growing district in the state of Pennsylvania. We have a strong history of family, selflessness, and a working-class program. Today, we are getting more and more kids out for football.

Let me give you some reasons why we wanted to go to two-platoon football in high school:

- It provided more accountability in the weight room.
- We wanted to get more players on the field. We wanted more players to take ownership of the program.
- We felt like a rested, well-coached, second-level player would play as well as a first-level player, especially when factoring in ownership.
- We thought practice would be much better, and it would be more competition in practice and at game speed, etc.
- We wanted to develop depth. If a star player who only goes one way is injured, there is less impact of loss.

What are the advantages of playing two-platoon football in high school? First, I want to discuss the advantages we felt we would gain in practices:

- We would be able to get all kids involved in all practices.
- It would be more fun. We would have fewer "walking wounded" in practice.

- We would be able to have 100 percent attendance at practice.
- Any kid who missed practice because he was sick, etc., had to call us or email his coach.
- We felt the players would be more adherent to fundamentals.
- It would allow for teaching with much more detail for both individual and team periods.

On defense, we saw several advantages as well. It would help our defense with the development of pursuit and tackling.

On offense, it would provide us with some advantages that would make us a better offensive football team. We could develop our offense to the fullest by running the midline and triple option. We could add more reps, and that would provide us the opportunity for better execution of our offense. We could cut down on the mistakes on our offense with very few assignment mistakes. The by-product of this factor would help our offense develop confidence.

There were other factors that two-platoon football would help us in our offensive, defensive, and special teams. We could spend more time for special teams in practice and place more emphasis on our special teams.

We saw advantages in developing a program that would involve more competition in practice. We could have our first offense against our first defense, and our second offense against our second defense during team practice. In addition, we could scrimmage starters versus starters at any time in our 7-on-7, etc.—at game speed.

Our junior varsity players could be coached for a 20- to 25-minute team period *every* day. It would allow for offense, defense, and special teams "team meetings" before or after practice. During the playoffs, we would be able to coach our scout team to perform better during practice.

We listed advantages we would gain in the games as well. Several of these points carried over from the advantages of practicing in a two-platoon system:

- We would be able to communicate with all players throughout the game and after every series.
- We would have players that were fresh by playing more individuals. (We had players tell us, "Coach, I do not even feel like I played a game." However, we won several games in the second half.)
- We experienced fewer injuries from the game by having fresh players in the game.
- We could increase playing time for both varsity and junior varsity. More playing time equals more opportunities to evaluate players.
- Young players on special teams would get real and meaningful varsity-game experience, which develops depth and prepares them for the future.
- All of our players would be better prepared going into games. They would work the whole week of offensive or defensive time versus one-day-and-a-half the old way. This was very evident during playoffs.

We also saw several off-season advantages by playing two-platoon football:

- We would have more players with something at stake by playing football. They would feel as if they have a vital role on the team.
- We believed two-platoon football would lead to more purposeful, focused, intense, and team-oriented workouts.

Our attendance at our off-season workouts averages about 95 percent or higher.

Our players also benefited in our two-platoon football system and demonstrated an attitude that they were having fun playing football:

- All players were willing to take team ownership.
- There was more fun—loving competition involved throughout practice and in games.
- With two-platoon football, we had 22 starters. We had 22 more on special teams. We had 66 players who knew they were starting, or they were a play away from starting (11 on offense, 11 on defense, and 11 on special teams, with the same number of backups and special-teams players.)
- We found it was easier for players to focus on their individual responsibilities. As a result, we had fewer mental mistakes.

We listed the advantages for the coaching staff by going to a two-platoon football system:

- Coaches are able to develop even closer relationships with the players.
- Coaches become better coaches by knowing their positions better and by knowing that their contributions are meaningful and crucial to the success of the team.
- Most coaches want more responsibility within the team framework. When they are given the opportunity, most will do a good job.

When we started talking about going to a two-platoon football system, we had a good idea of how it would affect the players and coaches, but we were not sure how the parents and community would react to the new system. We found a great deal of parent/community support by going to the two-platoon system.

The parents absolutely love it. The community/school support intensifies because more of the kids feel like a *real* part of the team. This all equals more outsiders interested in football, and it equals more kids coming out for the team.

After installing the two-platoon system, we have concluded several interesting results from this decision. Players love it, and they are more motivated and work harder than in the old system.

Practicing 1s versus 1s makes both groups better. Practice is at game speed. Mistakes cannot be hidden and masked. Competition is fierce for each practice.

The simpler we are in our approach to offense, defense, and the kicking game, the better we are. Many people thought we were better because we have more time, and we could run more plays, and have a more complicated defensive system with the two-platoon system. They felt we could do *more* in the two-platoon system.

Our philosophy is exactly the opposite. We did even less on offense, defense, and the kicking game. The fact is we committed ourselves to getting better in those areas and at becoming good at what we did do.

We found out the two-platoon system builds pride in the offense, defense, and the special teams. The groups do not want to let each other down.

Here are some additional things we found out with the new system:

- It develops confidence.
- It allows quicker catch-up for lack of experience. For instance, if a player has to move from inside linebacker to guard from his junior to senior year, he gets twice the reps in practice and the ability to know exactly what he is doing.
- The weight room provided outstanding results.
- Players feel prepared with a knowledge of assignments?they feel fresh and technically sound.
- We found we need to identify our best 22 football players and figure out how to get them on the field.
- It results in fewer injuries.
- Community/parental/school support is phenomenal.
- We had more players come out for the football team.

We found it best to train players in just one position. Our initial plan was to take one day per week and train each player in an opposite position. For us, it didn't work. We found it better to select two to four players whom we felt most realistically might have to play both ways. We trained them during individual drills one day per week and during opposite team times.

We have listed the *musts* to be a success with the two-platoon system:

- Communication is key. We must be able to get everyone on the same page to be successful. Everyone must understand what we are trying to accomplish and what is involved in two-platoon football.
- We must have organized, efficient practices.
- Honesty is necessary. We must be honest with players, coaches, and parents. We let the players, coaches, and parents know what is expected of them in all phases of the program.
- Everyone must be committed to two-platoon football. We cannot tell players, "We're going to run this system," and then stop because we are afraid it will not work. We told our players, "If we get attendance in the weight room, we will commit to two-platoon football."
- Keep things simple. If we have to move a player from offense to defense or vice versa, it is an easier transition.
- A staff of eight coaches is ideal for a two-platoon football program. We have been fortunate at Garnet Valley because we have a number of outstanding assistant coaches.

I have a couple of practice schedules that represent our practices for our two-platoon football system. The bold sections on the schedule are for the defense. Some areas apply for both the offense and defense.

PRACTICE ONE

2:30   Junior varsity jags lift
3:00   Pre-practice (on field)
3:30   Dynamic warm-up
3:35   Competitive conditioning
3:45   Individuals
4:00   Team triple and midline
         Tackling
4:10   1s versus 1s
4:20   Punt individuals
         Punt return individuals (extra point)

4:25 Punt
Punt return (extra point)

4:30 Punt versus scout
Punt return versus scout (extra point)

4:35 Group pass (versus junior varsity defense)
Formation recognition/favorite play (junior varsity offense)

4:45 7-on-7
7-on-7

4:55 **Goal line—live**

5:00 **Team defense**

5:20 Team offense

5:40 Finish up

PRACTICE TWO

3:00 Pre-practice (offense and **defense**—film review in classrooms)

3:30 Dynamic warm-up

3:35 Team midline
Individuals

3:45 Team triple
Tackle

3:55 Team counter
Team versus sweep

4:05 Punt individuals/punt

4:15 Team belly
Team versus jet

4:25 Team toss
Team versus pass

4:35 Team play-action
Team versus counter/counter XX

4:45 Team three-step
Team versus I-toss

4:55 Team offense (no-huddle)
Team versus pass

5:05 **Mix it up**

5:15 **Team defense versus two huddles**

5:35 Extra point and quick conditioning

5:45 Finish up

I see my time is up. Thank you for your attention.

Frank Rocco

MULTIPLE FORMATIONS AND PERSONNEL GROUPS

Liberty Christian Academy, Virginia

It is a pleasure for me to be here to talk about some of the things we do with our offensive scheme. You know, we all have people who have influenced us in our lives and in our coaching careers. My father was my high school coach, and there is a lot of what I do today that I derived from my father as I was growing up. I went on to Penn State and played for Coach Joe Paterno and his staff, so a little bit of Penn State is in what we do right now. Then, in my coaching background, there are a number of significant coaches who have put things in my brain, and from all of that I have pieced together what our package is today.

When I first coached in high school, we were a one-back, multi-formation offense. We were successful, but it still was a little bit piecemeal. When I moved back into college coaching at Liberty University, I was forced to learn that offense the way the head coach wanted it taught, and it got me out of my comfort zone a bit. I had to learn the same offense, but I had to learn new terminology and some concepts that made things even better than what I was already doing. What we are doing today at Liberty Christian Academy is the result of piecing all those things together.

First, I want to show you how we have pieced our package together to get to where we are today. In the second part of the lecture, I want to show you things we do in the play-action passing game. This is high school now, but it was what we did at the college level at Liberty University. In summary, I want to talk about the multi-formations and personnel concepts, and a simple way to put formations together without a lot of verbiage. Then, I want to finish with some of the play-action stuff we do.

I want to start with personnel groups. There are several reasons why we use them at the high school level. They provide multiplicity, they allow you to get into more offense, and they affect the defense in many different ways. You can give more kids playing time, which (among other things) makes a lot of moms, dads, and boosters happy. It also allows you to get more of your best athletes on the field at the same time.

Personnel groups allow us to create favorable match-ups. We may run from four wideouts on third down, to three tight ends and one wide receiver on fourth down. It provides deception. You can give a heavy-run look, and with a real good play-action fake and an aggressive blocking scheme up front, you can get tight-end verticals downfield and have home-run balls on what looks to be a run formation.

I want to get into what we call *formation strength*. As we put our package together over the years, we built up a rather large glossary of terms as the system expanded. It became hard to remember all of that, so we developed a very simple way to get the job done with all of these 20 or more formation names and personnel groupings. We condensed them down to five, maybe even four.

When we talk about a formation, we talk about formation strength. Some coaches designate strength with *right* or *left* but we simply use *zero* or *one*. We yell our plays out sometimes, and I think that our way is a little bit more deceptive.

Our base is a 2 x 2 set, and we label our receivers *Y, Z, H,* and *X* (Diagram #1). In a zero formation, Z is wide right, and Y is the second receiver, while on the left, X is wide, and H is the slot receiver. We have those people take on those letters no matter what the formation is.

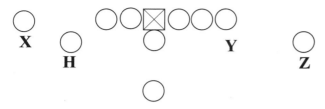

Diagram #1. Zero Formation

I want to get into personnel groups. In Diagram #1, we are in ace personnel. It is one tight end and three wide receivers.

Let us look at the way our system works. We have a coach on the sideline with all of our *messenger* players with him. We can go anywhere from three tight ends and one wide out, to four wideouts and sometimes even five, but we are going to just work with four today.

As we line up on first down, we may be in ace personnel and zero formation. That is what is on the field. Suppose we gain six yards on first down. Now, we are looking at second-and-four. I want to go with deuce personnel (Diagram #2). I tell my sideline coach and he puts two hands up in the air. Our second tight end, whom we call our *big H*, will go running onto the field with two hands up in the air. Our *little H*, who is the slot receiver, will come off the field.

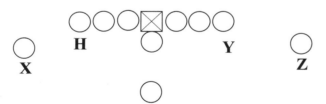

Diagram #2. Zero Deuce Personnel

They get in the huddle, and then from the sideline we call the play. For example, zero, 14, zone or whatever it might be. Now, we are in deuce personnel, and it looks different to the defense. It is a longer front. It is two tight ends on the field with the Z-receiver to the right and the X-receiver to the left because it is a zero formation. We have not changed anything except one player, but it is a big difference along the front.

Suppose we gain three yards on that play, we are down to third-and-one, and I want to get *jacks* personnel onto the field (Diagram #3). My sideline

coach puts his thumb up in the air and our third tight end, who is our jacks tight end, runs onto the field, and our Z-receiver comes off. Our jacks tight end positions himself in a 1 x 1 wing position off our Y receiver. Anytime two tight ends are side by side, they automatically come in to a wing relationship like that.

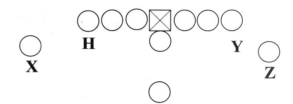

Diagram #3. Zero Jacks Personnel

Now, we have a wing who gives us a lot of run possibilities and several play-action possibilities. We also have a tight end back to the backside with a wide out that will pull the corner out and create more space there. Just by alignment, it gives us a lot more possibilities and it gives the defense a lot more to defend.

If we get the first down, we may want to take a shot downfield or maybe try to throw something underneath, so we may want to go with four wideouts. The sideline coach will put up four fingers, which is the signal for our *flush* personnel, and all three tight ends will come off the field, replaced by three wide receivers (Diagram #4). Now, we are in a zero-flush formation.

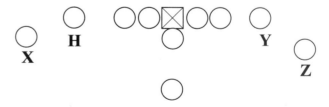

Diagram #4. Zero-Flush Formation

Every formation grouping I have described to you is a zero formation. We do not have to say zero wing, zero wide, or zero double tight. We just say zero, and the personnel group gives you what you want by the alignment rules that are in our system.

I do not know how you call your formations or groupings, and this may be something you already do, but it was a revelation to me. It made everything simpler. It was simpler for the kids to learn and for our staff to put together packages.

Everything I have talked about to this point is a one-back set. We are a one-back, multi-formational offense. We use personnel groups and motions to create mismatches. We may use more two-back stuff this coming year. In the two-back set, the personnel group is just regular for us, so the H-receiver comes off the field and is replaced by a fullback type of player.

We have five different looks, five different right-handed formations that give us something different every time we come up to the ball. The defense has to adjust to each one, and all we have done is call zero in the huddle. If we call one, it just flips over and we have five the other way.

Placements is a tag word that we add to the formation strength call to create a 3 x 1 formation. Everything I have shown so far has been 2 x 2 balanced sets, five to the right and five to the left, and all we have had to call in the huddle has been a zero or a one. To change to a 3 x 1 set, we use a couple of tag words, which we refer to as placements.

Trey terms are for the H-receiver. If we go with zero out of ace personnel, but we call zero trey in the huddle, nobody has to know anything but zero, except the little H (Diagram #5). Trey tells him we line up in a 3 x 1 look. We have a tight end, slot, and a Z-receiver to the right, and we have a split end to the weakside.

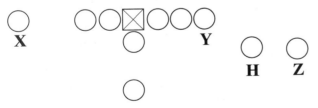

Diagram #5. Zero Trey Out of Ace Personnel

If we are in deuce personnel, we have two tights and two wideouts on the field, and the second tight end is our big H. If we call zero trey, the trey tells H to align in a 3 x 1 look, and our side-by-side rule for tight ends tells him to create a wing off of Y (Diagram #6). All we are doing is calling zero trey, but it is something totally different to the defense.

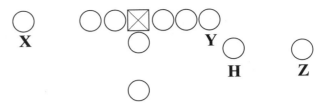

Diagram #6. Zero Trey Out of Deuce Personnel

Let us go to jacks personnel. We have three tight ends on the field, and trey puts H to the #3-receiver side with the other two tight ends, but tight ends together always line up in a wing set (Diagram #7). That means that H is in a 1 x 1 wing position off Y, and Z, who is also a tight end in this personnel group, in a tight double-wing position off H.

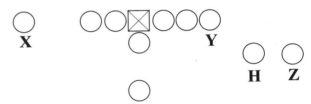

Diagram #7. Zero Trey Out of Jacks Personnel

You see a lot of the NFL teams run this type of set. It gets us heavy on the edge and allows us to do creative things with it. We have great angles to run a pitch, and we have many possibilities in the play-action game. That is zero trey with jacks personnel.

Finally, we want to get a 3 x 1 set with flush (Diagram #8). Flush is four wide receivers, so if we call zero trey in that personnel group, Y goes right because it is zero, but he is a slot. The H comes over, X moves up on the line, and we have zero trey out of flush personnel.

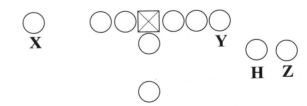

Diagram #8. Zero Trey Out of Flush Personnel

My point now is that I just showed you four completely different formations, each of which requires a little different defensive adjustment, and all we did in each case was just call zero trey. Then again, obviously, we can flip them all over by calling one trey.

In the same way that trey talks to H and tells him to go over to the other side of the formation, trips refers to Z and tells him to do the same thing to the opposite side. That means we can get any of those four personnel groups in the huddle and, just by calling zero trips, we can create four different 3 x 1 sets by bringing Z over to the other side of the formation.

I want to just briefly go through them with you, and I will do all four out of a zero formation. If we have ace personnel in the huddle, the quarterback calls zero trips, and Z lines up between X and H on the left side (Diagram #9). We now have a 3 x 1 set to the left, with Y tight on the right side.

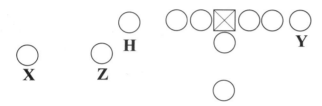

Diagram #9. Zero Trips Out of Ace Personnel

If we have deuce personnel in the huddle, the quarterback again calls zero trips, and Z, again, lines up between X and H, but now, H is a second tight end (Diagram #10). We are in a 3 x 1 set, but it is an entirely different look for the defense.

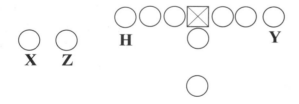

Diagram #10. Zero Trips Out of Deuce Personnel

If we have jacks personnel in the huddle, the quarterback calls zero trips, and Z, who is now a third tight end, gets in a wing position off of H, who is the second tight end (Diagram #11). Now, as you learn more about your offense and the things that you do, that can mean something. We do a lot of max protection, which keeps the tight end in to block. Well, by formation we can get that Y to be to the right or to the left, and that means something in how we set up our offense.

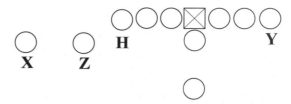

Diagram #11. Zero Trips Out of Jacks Personnel

Finally, if we have flush personnel in the huddle, the quarterback calls zero trips, and Z again comes over and lines up between X and H, but now Y splits as a single receiver on the other side (Diagram #12). We have a 3 x 1 set with three wides to one side and a single wide to the other side.

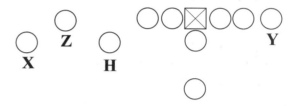

Diagram #12. Zero Trips Out of Flush Personnel

We are still just calling one formation, zero trips, but it looks entirely different—four different times—just by the built-in rules that personnel groups give us.

There is one more term I want to share with you that we use a lot. We have a set that we call *flipper*, which is essentially a wing set. We do it always out of deuce personnel. I will draw it out of a zero formation, so this is zero deuce. Instead of turning it into a 3 x 1 set, we want to change the receivers' alignment and stay in a 2 x 2 set, and create a wing set to the strength.

Where trey is for H and trips refers to Z, the term *flipper* speaks to both of them, so both Z and H flip (Diagram #13). The Z goes left and lines up in the slot position, but H is a tight end in deuce personnel, so he aligns in a wing position off of Y.

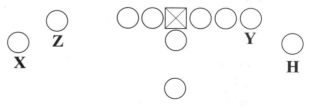

**Diagram #13. Zero Flipper
Out of Deuce Personnel**

That is called *zero flipper*. We have a wing set on the right and a twins look over on the backside. If we called one flipper, that flips the other way.

We showed five different formations, right and left, out of just a 2 x 2 set. Then, we showed you four different formations that a trey tag can give us, right and left. Then we showed you four different formations that a trips tag can give us, right and left, and with the flipper set added in, we are talking about 22 different formations. For all of that, all we said was zero or one, zero trey or one trey, zero trips or one trips, or zero flipper or one flipper. We made four calls to encompass 22 different formations.

The sideline coach sends in the subs and the quarterback gets the play from me. As he steps into the huddle, he sees what personnel he has. There is nothing else for him to call.

There is one small coaching point I want to mention. Our run-blocking scheme is essentially a zone scheme, and the offensive linemen work together on it using calls to coordinate them. For that reason, our tackles need to know early on if they have a tight end or split end to their side. We accommodate them by having our tight ends always "check in" with them when they arrive in the huddle. That is important to us in the way we do things.

We are not a huge motion team, but we do use it. Simply put, if you can just think about what we just talked about with the trey and trips calls, we can go H zero trey. We line up in just balanced zero, and then H motions over to trey. We can go Z zero trips, line up in regular zero, and then Z motions over to trips.

Just by saying the letter, we tell the man tagged to go in motion and create the formation we are calling for on the other side. We can also go the other way with it. We could call Z zero, and Z would line up in trips, and then motion back across to create a balanced zero set. That is how we do motion.

I want to show you three of our play-action passes. First, I want to talk about why we believe in our play-action passing game. We believe that it obviously has an effect on linebackers and safeties, and makes them indecisive. It gets them to bite, and

it makes them tentative. If they get tentative, they are less apt to come and plug in the run game, and in the pass game they do not want to run out too quick.

It slows down the rush. Sometimes, unfortunately, we do not block a soul, but a good fake by the quarterback and he can set and throw the ball.

With our play-action package, we can make the fake, set, and throw, or we can move the pocket, come outside, and throw. This is hard to believe, but in our four years at the school, we gave up two sacks the entire first season, the second year we gave up one, the third year we gave up three or four, and this year we gave up six or seven. We have never given up double-digit sacks. The main reason for that is that we do not do a lot of dropback passing. We want to run the ball, and then fake it, pull it out, and get rid of it quickly.

The last reason we believe in our play-action game, and the thing that is most exciting, is that it gives us home-run opportunities. We like to get the safety biting up and then throw it over his head. We can throw play-action passes, get the ball out in 1.8 to 2.2 seconds, and get long gains.

The first play is our pass *38 free go*. It comes off our 38 running play, and it gives us many home-run opportunities. On the 38 play, we get a down block at the point of attack and we are pulling one of the linemen, either for a kick-out or a lead-up on a linebacker (Diagram #14).

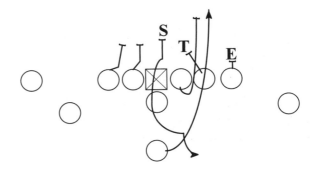

Diagram #14. Zero 38 Out of Ace Personnel

This is against a 3 technique, a 9 technique, and an inside linebacker. When we have this look, our linemen make a *tag* call. The tackle blocks down, the guard is around, and the tight end stretches the end as if it is a zone play.

The running back opens, plants, crosses over, and hits the inside leg of that tackle. The quarterback reverses out and shows the ball. The ball is a magnet, and we want to cause the defense to flow, so we will show the ball. This would be zero 38 out of ace personnel. We see the 3 and 9 techniques and we call tag. We get the down block by the tackle, we get the guard pulling up on the linebacker, and we get the end stretching. The quarterback is reversing out and showing the ball right now to get linebackers to try to hit the point of attack.

On the backside, we call it *dancing bears*. Everyone just takes a flat gap-protection step, and then they get square and work up to the next level. If someone engages them, they engage right back, and if not, they work up to the linebacker level. That is how we block the backside.

We have different calls against different fronts, but I want to emphasize the tackle blocking down, the guard violently pulling around, the quarterback showing the ball, and the back hitting the hole as I described. That is the essential action of the running play.

Now, we call pass 38 free go (Diagram #15). The linemen hear pass, but they have to stay down and give that first snapshot to the defense that we are running 38, which happens to be our best running play. We are telling the tight end that he is free to go, so he cannot reach the 9 technique. He takes the best release he can get and then works to his four-verticals landmark.

We have a 2 x 2 set here, and let us say the ball is in the middle of the field. We tell our inside verticals to be two yards outside a college hash, and we tell our outside guys to be at the bottom of the numbers.

Here is the beauty of this play. Back in the day, we used to all run the veer and throw the dump pass to the tight end. He was always open, but the safety would tackle him for an 8- or 10-yard gain. It

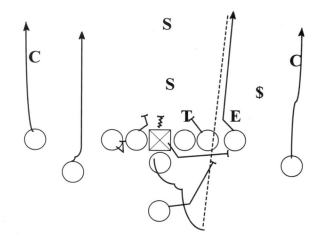

Diagram #15. Pass 38 Free Go

was very productive, but it did not give us the home-run opportunity. Now, if you take that concept and put it into the 38 free go play-action, you have the four verticals. The quarterback reverses out, shows the ball, brings it back to the running back, makes a great fake, sets up on the inside leg of the tackle at about six yards, hits and throws. The ball is thrown in 1.8 seconds.

Once the running back runs over the mesh, we nod our head and our shoulders. We show the ball and we take it away.

The pulling guard replaces the tight end on his block. He opens, goes aggressively, and puts his helmet under the chin of the 9 technique. It has to be aggressive.

Since the quarterback is reversing out, the pre-snap read is very important. If it is a single high safety, the quarterback thinks he will be going to one of the two inside seams. Because of the play-action, the safety may be covering more to the tight end, so the backside seam may be the route that becomes open more. The ball is caught at 18 to 20 yards.

If a team is more of a cover-2 team, we have a very good situation. We will get them into that flipper look, and we run 38 repeatedly. The H tight end is releasing and hitting the corner in the mouth, repeatedly. We are blocking the tag scheme inside and the whole deal.

The corner is seeing the same action repeatedly, and starts overreacting to the running play, and we have them set up. We will come back with zero flipper pass 38 free go (Diagram #16). The quarterback reverses out, shows the ball, pulls it out, sticks, and throws. The H tight end now runs over the outside shoulder of the corner and catches the ball right down the sideline.

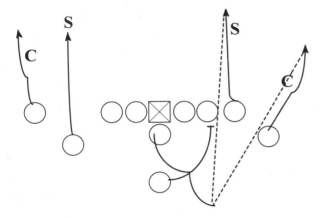

Diagram #16. Zero Flipper Pass 38 Free Go vs. Cover 2

It is free go against double safeties now, so the Y end takes his easiest release and runs right through his landmark, holding the strong safety. We hit the wing 99 percent of the time, but if the safety happens to play off the hash, we will stick the Y end right down the hash mark.

The fun thing is to take every one of those personnel groups and different formations and run pass 38 free go, and you hit it from every different way. For example, picture us in zero trey out of deuce. Z is wide, and a Y and an H tight end are in a wing, with a split end on the backside. We can almost count on some kind of cover 3 or single high type of cover.

Y would work across to the backside hash mark, H would run right down the near hash mark, and Z is running down the outside. We are stretching that safety again, we have the linebackers biting up, and the quarterback is just pulling it out and sticking it. The beauty is taking all those formations and running that one play, and all it is is four verticals. It has been our biggest one play and we scored many touchdowns with it.

The last two plays are *15 throwback* and *15 boot*. Everyone runs some sort of a boot. We do it off our

zone play. We fake 15, which is a zone play, and run boot to the right. That way, off a play-action, we can affect the flow of the defense, and we can move the pocket.

On the 15 throwback, we pull up right behind the center, but on boot, we are getting out on the edge. In play-action, we can change up our launch points, and you know that quarterbacks do not want to always stand and throw from the same position.

On 15 boot right, we are faking 15, and the line is blocking inside zone left (Diagram #17). The quarterback opens up and shows the ball. He goes to the mesh point, pulls the ball away, and nods. He sticks his outside foot in the ground, boots outside, and picks up whoever is the outside contain man right now. It could be an end or an outside backer, but the quarterback wants to get out on the edge. If he is a running threat, it is what we want.

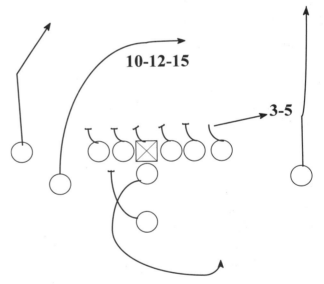

Diagram #17. 15 Boot Right

Our wide receiver runs them off, and it is key for him to run through the outside shoulder of the defender and get his eyes turned outside. That is important because we have our tight end running into the flat. Our tight end shows as if he is blocking zone and then he is out in the flat. The tight end is only wrong when he is not selling it enough to influence the contain guy.

The slot receiver is the crosser and we try to create a stairstep. The flat man should be three, climbing to five yards, and the crosser is 10 to 12, climbing to 15 yards. The backside runs a post.

If the quarterback can get on the edge and tuck the ball, then we want him to go. If he gets on the edge and somebody contains him late, he is looking for the flat man first every time. If they adjust and cover the flat man, he hits the crosser.

We can run boot right or boot left, and we can run it off most any of our run plays, even the counter.

Let me show you our 15 throwback, and then we will show you this tape (Diagram #18). It is off 15, and now the quarterback is setting up almost directly behind the center, but it might be more of the guard area to get a little pull on the defense.

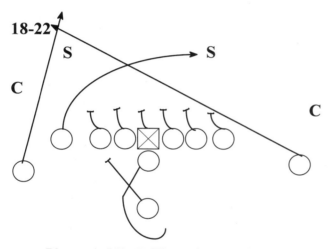

Diagram #18. 15 Throwback Z Cross

We call 15 throwback Z cross, and the linemen are blocking the run 15 zone. The quarterback shows the ball, meshes, pulls it away and nods, sets up, and takes a shot down the field. It is another home-run ball. We are trying to create a high-low on the safety.

The Z runs a cross at 18 to 22 yards and climbing to whatever depth he can get. The H receiver runs under the Mike linebacker and over the Sam linebacker and continues on the route that he runs on the boot. It will look like 15 boot right with the action by H and the quarterback.

Our X-receiver runs a speed post route, coming right out of his stance on an angle to split the two nearest defensive backs, the corner and the safety. Once he gets to the same level as the safety, he will take it to the near upright.

Our quarterback will pre-snap read the coverage. He is thinking he will get a high-low stretch on the safety. If the safety bails with the speed post, he looks for the crosser underneath. If he is going to bite up on the crosser, we will take a home-run shot at the speed post.

We have three cut-ups of each one of these play-action passes. I want to show them on film.

Thank you, guys. I appreciate your attention.

THE OFF-SEASON TRAINING PROGRAM

Steubenville High School, Ohio

Most coaches that I know understand that strength, speed, and quickness are essential parts of the game of football. Coaches should also be aware that the mental aspect of the game is a critical factor of the game. This mental aspect manifests itself in a player's attitude—his basic level of toughness. In my opinion, without attitude, you have nothing.

This time of year is when you win football games. The time between January and July will tell you if you will have a winning season or not in the upcoming year.

I have been married for 38 years and have been coaching for 37 years. All I know is family and football, and, regrettably, it has not always been in that order.

To most coaches, however, football is more than a job. Your whole community is involved with what you are doing and depending on you. I have never seen anyone in our town rally around anything like they rally around our football team. It is the greatest sport, and I am honored to be a part of it.

My topic today is centered on developing speed, strength, and mental toughness. The key factor in football, however, is not Xs and Os, offense, defense, lifting, running, recruiting, having a camp, conducting or attending a clinic, or any of those things. Rather, in my opinion, it is the attitude with which you do those things. You can learn anything, but knowing it is not the important factor. It is how you present it to your players that can make the biggest difference.

To a degree, almost every team does the same drills, engages in the running program, and devotes essentially the same effort to preparing their teams. The difference in winning and losing is often how you get your players mentally prepared to do something they do not normally do.

Football is getting players who are "poor" to get along with the ones who are "rich." It is getting players who are black to get along with players who are white. It is getting players who are Italian to get along with players who are Greek. It is getting your players to love the game and making playing football the greatest experience they will ever have in high school.

Those are my goals. I want my players to thoroughly enjoy the experience of playing high school football. If every teacher taught with that attitude, we would have a better school system. I want this to be the greatest time of their lives. If I were coaching or teaching something else, I undoubtedly would want the same thing.

Football is a great team sport. I tell my players during summer workouts that the sun hates everybody. It does not pick out individuals. You cannot treat all your players the same, but you can treat them all fairly. You cannot treat everyone equal, because everyone does not deserve to be treated equally. However, everyone deserves to be treated fairly.

Yesterday, before Coach Tressel spoke, a marine spoke. He talked about how hard it was to be a marine. Hell, it is hard to be anything good. It is hard to be a good coach, priest, janitor, parent, or bus driver. The key word is good. It is difficult to be anything good. Anybody can have a team, but it is hard to have a good team. Attitude plays a critical role in what you are going to do.

I have seen players who could lift a building and bend steel with their bare hands, but they never got in the game, because they would not hit anyone and did not have the proper attitude to play. In reality, it is not hard to get on a strength-training bench and push a weight up. It can be hard, however, to transfer the performance in a weight room to the field.

I have seen 4.5 and 4.6 players play like 5.2 players when they snap the ball. I have also seen players who are 5.2 players who look like 4.1 players when the ball is snapped. In this regard, the key point is it does not matter what your speed is. What matters is what your football speed is and the attitude at which you are playing.

Football speed is getting to the ball in a bad mood—getting to the ball and wanting to make the hit. The following list details ways to improve a player's field speed:

Steps to Improve Speed on the Field

- Stay simple
- Study film
- Scouting report
- Master the plant-and-point technique

The first thing you have to do is keep what you are doing relatively simple. As such, the alignment, assignment, and adjustments for your players should be straightforward. All factors considered, if a player knows his alignment and assignment, he will get there quicker than the player who does not.

Football is a simple game. As such, coaches should not try to make it difficult. Film study is important in high school football. In that regard, it takes less than 20 minutes to make 10 DVDs, which the players take home with them. Watching these DVDs can help players prepare. The more your players know about their opponent, the quicker they will do what they have to do.

Coaches should give their players a scouting report and talk about it. Rather than just handing them a sheet of paper, coaches should discuss key factors involving the next opponent, such as down-and-distance. In reality, if your players are going to come to see you every day in school, you should let them have a question for you.

Master the technique of plant-and-point. One of the biggest assets in football is the ability to change directions. This factor can play a big part in both offense and defense. You must be able to plant your foot in the ground and point to where you are going. When you talk to a guard about pulling, you must talk to him about pointing his foot to his target. Improving your athlete's plant-and-point technique on the field will develop their ability to get to a particular point faster. People who can run straight lines run the shortest distances.

Football Strength

- Out rep
- Heart
- Never quit

Football strength is not a one-lift repetition. Your team may out bench press us, but we will out rep you every time. You might be able to lift 330 pounds in the bench, but we will lift 275 pounds a thousand times. Football is not a one-play game, nor is it a one-quarter game. All factors considered, football is not one game. Football is one season long. As such, football is spending the time and doing whatever is necessary to win.

Frankly, we don't know the number of times a player has to line-up in a 3 technique and come off the ball. The only thing I can tell him is that every time he lines up, he has to be ready to go for six seconds. As such, we are preparing the players from December to August to play two hours of football; that is if they are going both ways. If they are playing on only one side of the ball, they will play an hour. To a degree, everything that they do in the off-season is designed to prepare them to play one hour of football.

Both players and coaches must b able to play and coach every play from the heart. In reality, coaches often come off the field more fatigued than their players, because they are pushing their players—both mentally and physically. Every coach has to believe what he is doing is right and push his players to do what is asked of them. A player can never quit. Every player should be coached that way. Players should never be allowed to quit at anything.

Football is not Xs and Os. Nor is it the Willies and the Joes. Rather, it is getting your players to play their butts off for the full 48 minutes. Whatever it takes to do that is our primary job as coaches. You have to get the best out of every player. Accordingly, you should treat every player on the team as if he is your son. Coach every kid on your team as if he has a bag over his head. It should not matter to the coach who the player is. All that should matter is to "coach him up." That philosophy underscores how I feel about the game. If we coach it like that, we cannot go wrong.

After the 1998 season, we were 4-6. It is the only losing season we have had in 25 years. We were winning every game at the half or were ahead in the second half. We vowed as a coaching staff never to let that happen again. However, those are only words. What could we do to help our program?

Our physical-education program includes a weight-training class. Our players sign up for those classes. Three days a week, we also have fitness workouts after school. As a staff, we decided to get better on the field, we had to add something to our efforts to improve. As a result, we incorporated plyo boxes, ladders, change of directions, dots, hurdles, and all the kinds of stuff that many of you people currently do now. We also added mental toughness to our program.

Our (Big Red) off-season program is a mind game. We are trying to get in our players' minds. We want our players to know this program will be the toughest thing they will ever have to go through. However, if they successfully make it through the program, it will be worthwhile.

When I first became a head coach, size, speed, and strength were important to me. While they certainly are essential, nothing is more important than "football character." Today, we believe that football character is the most important part of our football program. You can talk about grades and good students, and we have good students. You can also discuss having jerks, and we have them too. Similarly, you can talk about having good kids and bad kids. In our case, we even have kids you could water, because they are so much like plants.

The point I am trying to make is that, to a degree, it does not matter whether a player is a 4.0 student or a 1.0 student. It is the character, dependability, and performance on the field that matter. While I would like to have those 4.0 students, there are many 4.0s in prison, just as there are many 4.0s who are a pain in the butt. As such, grade-point average has nothing to do with how you play football. The team has to buy into "we" or "us"—not "I," "me," or "mine." In other words, the name on the front of the jersey has to be more important than the name on the back of the jersey.

Football Character

- Play with pain
- Refuse to lose
- Will to win
- Leave it on the field
- Better average players

"Football character" reflects what you do in the weight room and on the field every day. It has nothing to do with you being a future astronaut. We want the player who wants to play football. I do not care if he is going to be an astronaut or a janitor. Football character is the ability to "play with pain." I want the guys who have a sore elbow or ankle and still play.

Football character involves having a "refuse-to-lose" attitude. It is not the fact that this player comes from a good family or his dad was a great player. What I want to know is will this player give up a vacation so he can participate in a team activity? Does this player miss school for a legitimate reason, but hustle back for weight lifting? Will this player come to school on a snow day to lift weights? Football character is having the "will to win."

Don't get me wrong, I want good players just as you do. Great kids are always happy. On the other hand, we have some players on our team who have had a tough life. Coaches should not put their players in their place, until they have been in their place. Coaches should talk to their players who are more fortunate. They have to let their fortunate kids know what is going on. The only thing they know is what their parents tell them. As such, coaches should make their fortunate kids know what is going on and let them see the world.

I want my players to leave everything on the field. As such, if you expect your players to play every play from the heart and with the passion that it takes to win, you had better coach every game from the heart and have even a greater level of passion.

I want our average players to think that they can kick your average player's butt. If they can do that, we will win the game. Regardless of the competitive level, that happens with every team. Although every team has its stars, in reality, there are more average players on those teams than stars. As such, I want to convince my average players they are better than they are. If I can do that, we'll win the game.

I want my players to feel honored to be on the field wearing their school colors. I want them to know I am honored to be their coach.

True Success

- Compete
- Great teammate
- Pride
- Do not pout
- Force discipline

Consistency is the truest part of our program. Over the years, we have been 219-31 in the regular season and 39-14 in the playoffs. The regular season in Ohio is immaterial; it is what you do in the playoffs as to how you are measured. That is when you play better opponents. You have to prepare your team for the second season.

True success is your ability to perform every day, year-in and year-out. We maintain our traditions with or without great players. Although players graduate, traditions never graduate. You may be sitting there wondering what this has to do with speed, toughness, and character.

As previously noted, football is all a mind game. We want our players to go through our off-season exercise and workout program to become mentally tough.

You do not need great talent to teach your players to compete. it is the greatest feeling, as a coach, to see your team out on the field competing and fighting. They may get beat, but they are competing. They are competing on the field, because they competed every day in the weight room.

The greatest thing a player can be called is a great teammate. If you are a great teammate, you have it all. When I die, I hope the players I played with and the players I coached will consider me a great teammate. You cannot take anything for granted. If you are not ready every day, something will jump up and bite you.

Coaches and players should take pride in everything they do because their name is on it. If they get beat, they should not pout about it. They can be upset and mad, but they should not pout. Their so-called friends are glad that they have something to pout about. Everyone should learn from a loss and do something for themself every day that gets them mentally prepared.

Football games are different than other games. It is not the best two out of three games. Football is a one-game season. You can beat anybody one time. If your rival comes in to play you, all you have to do is beat them that one time, and you do not have to play them again until next year.

A player's attitude will tell you what his altitude will be. You have to remember that forced discipline leads to self-discipline, and no discipline leads to destruction. Accordingly, you should do whatever you have to do to have discipline on your team, staff, and yourself.

People say that kids are not like they used to be. That is bullcrap. I played in the 60s. We started football in August, and it was over by November. Over the winter, we played basketball, and in the spring we played baseball. We took the summer off and started again in August. The kids we have today go year-round in our program. Today, we have to deal with all kinds of multiple fronts and formations.

However, the aforementioned are not the biggest factors with which we have to deal. In reality, the biggest obstacles we encounter on an ongoing basis are the drugs, alcohol, parents from Woodstock, lawyers, and an administrator who never won a game as a coach. It is also video games and kids in time-out, instead of on the field getting their butts beat.

One key question that you and your players have to ask yourselves is, "How much are you willing to sacrifice to prepare to win?" It should be noted that the question does not refer to winning; instead, it is to prepare to win. As such, everyone should be aware of the fact that what we are doing in the weight room, in our conditioning drills, and during our agility drills is preparing our team to win.

Your players have to transfer the things they do in your off-season program to the field next fall. You do not have to be 6-2 and 250 pounds to be mentally tough. Mental toughness is not lying on the couch, visualizing being tough. Mental toughness in the quarterback, for example, is being able to play the next play, regardless of what happened on the previous one. The tailback has a different type of mental toughness. He wants the ball again, when he just was lit up. The defenders have to think, "Run at me." The offensive lineman is thinking, "Run behind me, and we will get the first down."

If you want to read a hell of a good book, I recommend John C. Maxwell's text, *Seventeen Indisputable Laws of Teamwork*. If you read this book, it will help you coach your butt off. This is a great book. To win in football, you must have strong work ethic. While team chemistry is very important, it is somewhat hard to explain. If we could explain what it is and manufacture it, we would have it every year.

When you lose a game, you often think, "If I only had two more good players, we would win." You can make two more good players. The thing you must remember is that while there are coaches who lose with good players, you cannot win with bad players.

Everything costs money. We built our own plyometric boxes. We have two 30-inch boxes, one 28-inch box, one 36-inch box, and one 42-inch box. When we start our conditioning regimen, we get loosened up. The players step up on the box with their right foot. They try to get their foot flat on the top of the box. We want them driving their right arm up, as they lift their foot. Once we get to the top of the box, we step down and use the left foot to step on the box.

We do some of this conditioning work before we lift. When you are doing a conditioning drill, you should not worry about strict adherence to the exercise techniques. In reality, what you really want to do is get your athletes' heart rate up and get them to a point where they want to quit. At that point, you can push them further. If you are working on something to get better at, this is when you work on technique.

After we do the one-step drill, we then jump on top of the box. We spring off the ground with both feet and land on top of the box. Not only do we want them to explode off the ground, we also want them to explode down with their feet and plant them on top of the box. We want to see their elbows drive down through the box. When we jump to the tops of the boxes, we do not jump down. We step down from one box to the next box. We may jump down every other week. If you jump down from the boxes, it exerts load forces on your hips and ankles.

The next exercise we perform is the hurdle drill. In this drill, we step over the first hurdle, go under the next one, and step over the third one. This exercise is designed to enhance hip flexibility. Coaches should make sure that when their athletes step over the hurdle, they do not get their foot outside the hurdle. If they do, we turn them around and make them go over the hurdle going sideways. We also put the hurdles against a wall to prevent the players from going around them. As a result, they have to step over them. We want our players to lift their legs and get them as close to their nose as they can.

The next exercise we do is the ladder drill. We are not trying to develop quickness on the ladder. Instead, we are working for explosion. We pound the feet in the openings. We concentrate on the hands in this drill to get their feet moving faster. The faster the hands move, the faster the feet move. We do all kinds of patterns with our foot movement. When we perform these drills, we want them to stay as close to the rope as they can. We do not want them lifting their feet off the ground too much.

The next drill we do is one they do at the NFL combines—a change of direction drill. In this drill, we emphasize the plant-and-point technique.

From that drill, we go to the four-cones-in-a-square drill. In this drill, you sprint forward, shuffle to the next cone, backpedal to the next cone, and sprint through the finish. In reality, however, you can invent whatever type of agility exercise you would like to use.

Next, we go to the weight room. In the weight room, we use a three-exercise rotation at each station. The first station includes the bench press, bentover rowing, and spotting. The player does the bench first. His second exercise is bent over rowing. After he completes those two exercises, he becomes a spotter.

When the player starts his first exercise, the coach starts the count. He counts to 12. In that time, the player initially performs 12 reps on the bench press and then goes to the bentover row station. He does three sets of each exercise. On the first set, he does 12 reps. On his second set, he does 10 reps and on the third set he does maximum reps to fatigue. He alternates between the bench press and the bentover rowing. When he finishes doing the exercises, the next player rotates into the exercises. The coach should employ voice inflections to regulate the speed of the repetition. On the bench press he says, "Do-wwwwwwwww-n-up." The player brings the bar down to match the voice inflection. At the bottom of the exercise, the coach says, "Up." The player explodes the weights up. On the bentover row exercise, the coach says "Up-dowwwwwn." We do that for 12 reps. On the third set, the coach says, "Up-down, up-down, up-down." Since we are maxing out to fatigue, we go rapidly. The spotters have to be alert in the maximum set. We want the slow movement on the recovery and the explosion on the push.

From that station, we move to the next station, which includes the military press, upright row, and spotting. Our players do the same routine on these upper-shoulder exercises.

The third station involves the triceps group. This station includes skull crushers, or triceps pullovers, chair dips, and spotting. When you do the straight-bar triceps pullovers, you have to spot your players. From there, we go to the bicep station and do curls.

At the other end of our weight room, we have a fake sandbox. When we feel a player is not working hard enough, we tell him to go down and play in the sandbox.

All factors considered, players will work for you. By the same token, the better relationship you have with your players, the more you can treat them like crap. While each one of your players is not going to love you, they are going to love playing football. They will do whatever it takes to get on the field. If they have to put up with me, they will do that to play. The same factor goes for me. I do not love all of our players, but I respect them for what they go through to play. I tell them that every day. I tell them that I like some players better than others, simply because they work harder.

We call the last part of our conditioning program "death row." This segment is a 12-minute burn-out at the end of the program. We do it every Friday. Death row involves a line of stations. The first station is a bench press area that entails having our players exercise with 50 percent of their weight. The next station is a bench, with two 35-pound plates on each side. The third bench station has only an Olympic bar. Next in line is the upright-rowing station, followed by a station where 80 pound dumbbell- fly exercises are performed. Next, we have bentover rowing in the line. Subsequently, we have curls, lat pulls, and an assorted number of weight-lifting exercises. A coach is positioned at each station.

Fortunately for my staff, I take all the jerks. My goal is to make them quit, while their goal is to make it through. You can be as tough on them as you want.

The first player starts on the first bench press, where he remains until he does as many repetitions as he can. He then moves to the next station and starts over until he maxs out. He goes down the line of exercise stations, working the different muscle groups. At every station, there is a coach urging him to do one more repetition and challenging him to do one more. You can choose the weight exercises you want, but the emphasis should be on safety. As such, the workout should not include military presses or squats. When we work legs, we work on weight sleds or leg-press machines. Because these players are going to work to fatigue, they would not be able to handle free weights. Coaches should allow their players to lift anything over their heads or to be in any situation where they could get hurt.

While we also do traditional lifting, today I have discussed our conditioning program and gut-check drills. As I stated before, football strength and speed involves more than being strong and fast. They also require toughness and the ability to perform when it counts and where it counts. Hopefully, I hope you got something out of my presentation today that you can use. Thanks a lot.

INSTALLING THE 4-4 DEFENSIVE SYSTEM

Chartiers Valley High School, Pennsylvania

This clinic is one of my favorite weekends of the year. I have always appreciated and enjoyed coming to the high-school sessions and listening to my peers. I have always been able to take things from them and apply them to our program. Hopefully, we will go over some things today that will be of value to you that you can take back to your program.

I would like to go through the development of our 4-4 defense. I personally will cover the organizational part of it and how we develop it, starting in January and going all the way through the season until we get to game week. Then, I will to bring up our defensive specialists, and they will talk about the implementation aspect.

We are in a AAA football conference. We have taken a program that traditionally has struggled and have gotten it to where it is at a very competitive level. We are not an elite program. We have no championships to boast of, but we have gotten ourselves to a point where football in our school and in our community is very important.

We are coming off the best four-year span at our school in the last quarter century. An integral part of our success during that period was a very strong defense. We do not have all the answers, and today my approach is to share ideas, information, and insights with you.

Our philosophy is very simple. We have built our program on the principles of pride, character, love, and respect. We believe in pride. We try to emphasize and talk to our kids about pride. Our coaches are all good role models, and in everything we do, we try to do with pride. We also believe in character. We believe that winning is certainly not the most important thing. We want to teach our young men character and help build young men by giving them skills that can be applied in life. Finally, we believe in love and respect. These factors involve a three-way deal—from coaches to players, players to players, and hopefully, players back to coaches. Everything we do in our coaching and teaching is undertaken in a loving and respectful way.

We are a public school. We do not recruit, and do not have significant numbers of families moving into our community. We deal with the kids that we have. We try to groom our kids, create enthusiasm in our community, and work with what our community provides. We have not had a bunch of great players, but we have had a bunch of good, disciplined kids who play well as a team.

Whatever personnel we get, we want to make sure we utilize it properly. We want to make sure we are sound as football coaches, and that we are prepared for everything that we face.

At this point, I would like to get into our game planning a little bit, and talk about how we try to get ourselves and our kids prepared. Certainly, execution, and specifically what happens on Friday night, is critical, and accountability is something that I review with all of our coaches at the beginning of every season. We have to take responsibility as coaches for taking every kid we have and doing everything we can to help to develop him. We have to be accountable for that. Finally, we perpetually evaluate what we do as coaches, and I will say more about that as we go along.

We have already started developing our defense for 2008. Right now our kids are in the weight room, where they work out two days a week. Our emphasis at this time of year is on strength, speed, and athleticism. We are trying to develop our athletes and come together as a team. Our staff attends the Nike Coach of the Year Clinic every year and makes a couple of spring visits to colleges. We try to improve our staff every year at this time.

As we start our April staff meetings, we put together a coverage contingency chart to guide us in developing a base defensive plan. We list every possible formation we might see down the left side of the chart, and list our four primary coverages across the top. Then, by checking the preferred coverage against each offensive set, we can put together our basic coverage package. We make copies of the chart and get them to our kids as soon as possible. We want them to be familiar with what our base adjustment is to all situations.

In May, we are getting ready for our passing camp, holding our staff meetings, and developing our coverage package installation plan. In June and July, we conduct our passing camps. We do competitive 7-on-7s, and then we attend a team camp as well. It gives us a chance to compete against some good programs, and it gives us a chance to get a little bit of work done as a football team.

By the time our passing camp stuff is completed, we think we have done about everything we are going to do in terms of pass coverage. In addition, our offensive passing stuff is all in by then too. When August comes, practically all of our entire offensive and defensive packages are in, and we are ready to go.

Next, I would like to discuss our game-week preparation, which starts for us immediately after our game on Friday night. After the game, whether home or away, we let the kids clear out of the locker room. At that point, we deal with any administrative issues we may have. We also do a quick post-game review of the film. We start our computer input, which involves utilizing two different software systems. Our offensive stuff is going on to the Landrum system, while our defensive stuff is going into the Apex system. It takes a while to get all that stuff digitized, so we start that immediately after the game. We work through it as a staff, in kind of an informal watch, and we are in the office for about an hour after each game.

We come in Saturday morning at 7:00 a.m. and begin copying our scouting tapes for Sunday. The Apex is voice activated, so one coach begins to put all of our opponent's plays and information in there. All the other coaches start to grade our players.

We score our players on a four-point system that resembles a GPA schedule, because it is something with which our kids are familiar. Basically, a 4 is an A, a 3 is a B, a 2 is a C, a 1 is a D, and a 0 is an F—just like our players are used to in the classroom. We score every single play that is possible to score, and then add up the scores, and divide the total by the number of plays scored. That gives the player his "football GPA."

All of that takes us probably an hour and a half on Saturday morning. We post the defensive GPA list, and it is the first thing the kids look at when they come in on Saturday morning. We also make copies and distribute them to each of the players for the video analysis.

The players report at 8:30 a.m. The JVs play all of their games on Saturdays, and I will take the varsity kids down to the weight room. Then, we go up and break down the films. We have four offensive coaches and three defensive coaches. The offensive coaches go in and watch film for about an hour, and then the defensive coaches come up. Meanwhile, the other staff is working. The players are out of there by 11:00 a.m. Usually, they then go check out the second half of the JV game.

At the point when the players leave is when our defensive plan starts to come together. We have pretty much wiped away everything from Friday night at this point. Of course, there are factors that must be fixed, and we will address those things in Monday's practice. But at this point, we are making the transition to next Friday night. By this point, we have four hours in on the computers, and most of our opponent's tendencies are coming together. We have down-and-distance, field position, personnel groupings, and opponent player evaluations, and are starting to print out all of our tendency charts.

This schedule and plan gives us a chance to get to know our opponents. We put together an opponent player board. We score each player we expect to see on Friday night on the same four-point scale that we use with our players.

A 4.0 player is a D-1 kind of kid. He is what we would consider a difference-maker. An all-conference caliber player would be a 3.0, an average AAA athlete would be a 2.0, and 1.0 is a weak link. We put the player names on the board by position, with height, weight, and talent score. We circle the two-way players, and then add up the talent scores to get an overall team value. All this goes up on the opponent white board.

This undertaking has made us better evaluators of players and has given us a better idea of what we are up against. We follow it up by rescoring our guys. Sometimes, our opinions of our kids may change a bit, there may be a kid who is hurt, or, perhaps, there is going to be a lineup change, but we will always look at our score against the score of our opponent. It gives us a good idea of where we stand. It helps us do a better job of analyzing matchups, identifying problem areas, and devising attack strategies.

By 4:00 p.m. on Saturday, we start to put together a tentative game plan and prepare our game-week schedule for Monday through Thursday. When all that gets done, we clear out of there for Sunday. I have been on staffs that work all seven days, but we take Sunday off.

While I believe in getting away from the office for a day, we make up for it throughout the week, particularly on Saturdays and on Monday nights. All of our coaches take tape home, and I put in multiple hours watching film on Sundays, but all of that is on an individual basis. This way, we get a chance to let the game plan settle a little bit, and we can get out any of the feelings that may be left over from Friday night. It allows us to really focus in on the new task at hand.

Monday is a fundamental practice. When we go out on Monday, we have not finalized our game plan. We tell our players this is a day when we are going to focus on our stuff. We are going to look back at Friday night, go back and fix things that need our attention, and focus most of that practice on our stuff. We work fundamentally on those things we have to do to get better as a football team.

We schedule a time where we get our defense and talk about the opponent and about what we expect. The players know that we will meet Monday night to finalize our game plan.

Tuesday is an installation day. It is a minor team day. We videotape all of our group and team stuff on Tuesdays and Wednesdays and watch it as coaches after practice both offensively and defensively. Practice includes an individual period, an inside-run period, a 7-on-7 pass skeleton, and a brief team period.

Wednesday is our team day. Most of our defensive work is in a team situation. By this time, we have had a chance to look at some things, fix or adjust some of our game plan, and do our goal-line work. On Wednesday night, our staff analyzes it all on video, and gets a better picture of how we are handling the game plan.

We try to make Thursday as light as possible, and we try to make it fun. Of course, we watch some opponent video as a team, and I review the Friday protocol with our players and staff. I want no surprises on Friday. I talk about the bus ride, the color of the opponent's uniform, the kind of stadium we will play in, the kind of fans they have, what kind of atmosphere we are going into, and every possible situation that might otherwise arise.

We put together a game-situation script that is essentially our Thursday practice. We start with the kickoff. We walk our captains out for a coin toss. Then, the script covers practically every situation we might encounter during a football game. Doing so allows us to work through substitution changes, on and off the field, sudden change, and all other change situations. As such, out kids really like it. As we move through it, we run three play drives when the offense goes out, and three three-and–outs when the defense goes out, occasionally reviewing specific factors involved in the game plan.

Friday is our game day. At 6:00 p.m. we will have a defensive captain meeting that usually involves the defensive coordinator, the defensive position coaches, a linebacker, and the free safety. Essentially, it would be the guys who are essential in getting our defense into the right position.

On game night, we do an individual warm-up, and all of the kids get a final opportunity to meet with their position coaches and re-establish goals. I believe that our kids find that comforting.

For game communication, our defensive coordinator is on the field, and our signals are called by two coaches in the box. We split up at halftime and analyze the first half. Depending on the situation, the offense or the defense may go first, whoever is ready. We discuss any necessary adjustments, re-establish goals and mission, and point out the fact that we have 24 minutes of football left.

Next, I would like to focus on our defensive stuff. In my personal philosophy, if we can stay in 4-4 cover 3 the entire game, I would be as happy as can be. If we are a better football team and we can contain another team through that, then that is what I want to do. We have been very multiple at times and have done different things, but the 4-4 cover 3 is our defense.

We use the standard Bear Bryant technique numbering system (Diagram #1). Although we have only used it for four or five years, I cannot imagine coaching football without using this communication system. This tool has made us better as coaches. It has also made our players more aware, and has greatly enhanced the level of feedback we get from them during the game. I strongly recommend this system.

Diagram #1. Techniques

When we communicate with our defense, we state the front and any variation involved, then we call any stunt or blitz, and finally we call the coverage. For example, our "storm" is our base defense. If we call "storm crush cover 3," the base front is storm, the stunt is crush, and the coverage

is cover 3. As such, our system of communicating is relatively simple.

I want to start with our base alignment (Diagram #2). If we can stay in that throughout the game, then we will. To be honest with you, there was probably only one game that we did that last year, but this is our basic defense.

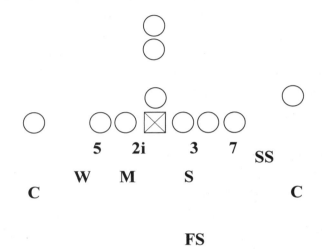

Diagram #2. Storm Cover 3

In our packet we hand out, we have a chart that provides an outline of all the core responsibilities. It includes alignment, assignment, "run-to" responsibility, "run-away" responsibility, plus the option responsibility, and our pass responsibility. Notice that our strongside end is "horse," and our other end is "pony." The other position names are standard.

At this point, I am going to turn this presentation over to our defensive coaches. Matt Swift is going to do our defensive line presentation, while Phil Donofrio will do our defensive backfield presentation.

COACH MATT SWIFT—Defensive Line

Thank you. I coach our defensive line. Going back to the previous diagram, I want to discuss our base alignment real quickly. The definition of a storm implies something that is violent and something that is attacking, which is how we want our defense to play. While we want to be under control, we also want to be violent and want to attack.

At this point, I would like to discuss our front. Our base front is a 32i, with a 5 technique. We have played around with tilting our 5 technique to squeeze the line a little more. It was helpful for us this year. We move our tackles around a little bit, anywhere from the stack technique, which we call "22," to 3 techniques, which we call "33," or even 2i's, depending upon the situation. We stem to the different alignments.

With our defensive line, I want the kids to know where I am coming from, and what my expectations are of them. Our relationship is based on love, respect, trust, and communication.

I want to communicate to them as much as I can. I will give feedback after something is done right and after something is done wrong, not with yelling, but always on the go. Fortunately, we went to a split staff, after which, we split our practices up offensively and defensively, so it seems like we are gaining more time.

We want to give our kids ownership of their positions—even on defense. Eventually, things might evolve to where we might tag a blitz after someone, and the kid's eyes just light up when he knows he is coming on a blitz.

We look for certain characteristics in our defensive linemen. Every kid wants to play defense. However, athletically, not all of them can. We are looking for good footwork. We want a fast, aggressive defense, and we want kids who are self-sacrificing. Defensive linemen have to know that they might have to occupy two blockers, so our linebackers can run free. They have to have that mindset.

They must be coachable, aggressive, and, obviously, be physically fit. You have to be in shape to play defense. Defensive players are going to take a beating and are going to get knocked down some. As a result, they have to be mentally and physically tough enough to keep getting up, and to keep playing hard.

We want risk-takers, and we want resilient players who have short memories—players who can stay focused on the present.

I want things to be as simple as possible, so our kids can turn loose and play, but our players also have to learn what to do and be able to apply that learning quickly.

Finally, whether a kid is a starter or a substitute, he must be an active participant. Whatever we are working on, he has to be mentally and physically in it, with the proper attitude and with full effort. That starts in practice and obviously translates to the games.

We talk to our players about the scope of their position. We want each player to do his one-eleventh—to know his alignment and assignment and do his job. We talk about owning the line of scrimmage, fighting pressure, stopping the run, and pressuring the quarterback.

We stress exerting great effort on pursuit, making sound tackling, and creating turnovers or a change of possession. In that regard, we want them to understand the *sudden change* situation. We will build that situation into our practice schedule.

Our staff believes in building up kids and developing them as players. We try to integrate skill development and personal development. We want them to react in a positive manner to adversity. We want our kids to have fun, relax, and do their jobs. Of course, we are going to teach and emphasize fundamentals every chance we get. We will be specific and detailed, and will provide constant feedback.

It is also very important to evaluate and explain any breakdowns that might have occurred during the game. We want our players to understand whether a breakdown was the result of a structural weakness, bad execution, or simply a missed tackle. Helping kids understand what happened when something went wrong will help build confidence and strengthen our defense.

Next, I would like to briefly review what we emphasize with stance and start. The defensive lineman's down hand should be on his fingertips and his off hand in front and ready. We want his feet at shoulder-width, with his toes pointing straight ahead. His butt should be slightly elevated in a sprinter's stance, crowding the ball. He should be able to move full-speed forward at the snap. We teach players to react to the ball, penetrate to the heels of the offensive line, fight to stay square, and be able to move laterally. We drill hard on all of these factors.

We perform a lot of bag drills and cone drills to improve agility. We try to make them game-applicable, and we emphasize athletic posture throughout. We want the defensive lineman's hips down, his chest and eyes up, his shoulders square, and quick foot movement. In all of these drills, we emphasize attitude and focus, and never going through the motions.

Our main point of emphasis in tackling is to never lead with the head—safety first. Then, we teach the standard coaching points: stay square; chest to chest; eyes open; head up—bite the ball; rip arms up and through—wrap up; run through the ballcarrier—step on toes—keep feet moving; first man secure the tackle; and second man strip the ball. Because we work hard on tackling, our kids are good tacklers.

We have to be able to defeat run blocks. In that regard, we work against base blocks, double-team blocks, down blocks, and trap blocks. We want to engage with the hands and facemask, with the thumbs up at the numbers. In addition, we want to stay low, bring our feet, and stay square to the line of scrimmage.

We teach our players to fight pressure. In this regard, the coaching point we use is "hips to the heat." We react to both visual keys and pressure keys. In addition, we have started "wrong-arming" the trap block and the kickout block, particularly with our 5 technique. Finally, after we defeat the block, we want to create separation, get off the block, and get to the football. We do not allow our kids to use offensive holding as an excuse for not getting off a block.

We also have to be able to defeat the pass block. We always talk about defeating half the man. We never want to run straight over a pass blocker. Because we are usually in a shaded technique, we attack half of the man. We want to close distance quickly and keep the blocker's hands off. Then, we want to create separation and get to the hip. If we can get to the hip, we have him beat. At the same time, we have to stay in our rush lane and get no deeper than the quarterback. We teach a bull rush, a rip, and a swim. On the other hand, we only allow certain athletes to use a spin technique, which is something that most kids cannot do well.

Finally, we teach a mindset for our kids when they go into action. When we say, "take the field," they know that we want them to go with an attitude and set the tone. Whether it is going from drills to breaks or breaks to drills in practice, or a change of possession in a game, or a sudden change in a game, we want a mindset of shifting gears and getting it going.

Finally, even though Coach Saluga went over the weekly schedule earlier, I would like to emphasize what we do as a defensive line on Mondays. First, we address areas of concern—focusing on fundamentals and spending 30-to-40 minutes in individual drills. Then, we spend five-to-ten minutes on the game plan, and go over the individual personnel of the opponent. Our kids really want to know about the player they will be matched up with and what his strengths and weaknesses are. We tell them what they will be up against. As such, they usually rise to the challenge.

Next, I would like to turn it over to Coach Phil Donofrio, who coaches our defensive backs.

PHIL DONOFRIO—Defensive Backs

Thank you. It is exciting for me to be here, and I am glad to be able to do this. I give our kids a packet at the start of each year. The first page has our defensive-secondary objectives, which are standard coaching points for defensive backs anywhere. They include playing fundamentally sound, eliminating long passes, being mentally sharp, attempting to create turnovers, disrupting by disguise, tackling in a sound manner, and playing together.

The second page of the handout lists the defensive back requirements and briefly explains each one. They include the ability to move, exhibiting physical and mental toughness, and the ability to concentrate.

Next, we list and explain our principles of defensive-secondary play. The first three involve always knowing the call, always having proper alignment, and always lining up in a good stance. The next two have to do with executing the backpedal technique or the "shuffle and bail," and knowing how to play the ball. Finally, every defensive back must be able to recognize run or pass, and must carry out his assignment.

Every day in practice, we practice getting off blocks, work on tackling, and do a variety of ball drills. Next, we perform group drills. Finally, we install the game plan. I prepare a handout for our kids that includes the game plan and I will include statements about each player we will face. Our kids really look forward to that. I also put together game film for each player to watch.

We teach our defensive backs to read the quarterback's pass indicators—eyes; front shoulder; long arm; and ball release. We want them to get an early break on the ball.

We also try to teach them to be aware of wide receivers who tip plays. In this regard, we utilize our wide receiver checklist. For example, we look at the receiver's eyes to see if he is looking at the sticks, looking for an upfield aiming point, looking in at a crackback target, or looking at the defensive back against whom he is going to run a route. We also look at his split to get an indication of whether the pass route involves an inside pattern or an outside pattern. In addition, we watch him out of the huddle to see if his body language tips his assignment.

We tell our defensive backs that some things are just common sense. For example, it is common sense to avoid foolish penalties, be a good tackler, think turnovers, make good judgments, do the little things, play with pads over toes, and know the kinds of situations when it is likely that the next play will be a pass.

Our basic coverages are cover 1 man, cover 1 off-man, cover 2 zone, cover 3 zone, and cover zero man.

Our coverage rules for each type are fairly straightforward.

In cover 1, our corners always have the number one receiver, and they have to take way the inside (Diagram #3). The free safety is in the middle, 10-to-12 yards deep, aligned over the strong guard. If the offensive formation is trips, he aligns over the strong tackle.

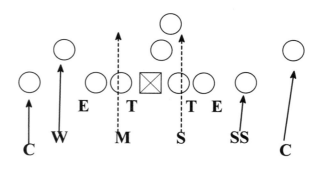

Diagram #3. Cover 1 Man

How tight the corner plays depends on the kid. Our defensive backs are told to never take their eyes off the receiver. Our Will and strong safety cover the number two receivers, and Mike and Sam cover the back out to their side. When we play this coverage, we are usually bringing five.

In cover 1 off-man, the corners start at five yards, and then come up and take the number one receiver. It is essentially the same for everyone else. The only difference is that the corners are giving a different look.

In cover 2, the corners funnel the number one receiver to the inside, and keep their hands on him until they see the number two receiver (Diagram #4). If no one shows, they stay with number one. The safeties will line up on the hashes at 10-to-12 yards deep. Their alignments depend on the game plan that week. The linebackers play their underneath zones.

In cover 3, the corners are in a tilt technique at seven yards (Diagram #5). They then take their read steps and bail to cover their deep third. The free safety aligns at 10-to-12 yards over the guard to the field, and the linebackers, as in cover 2 zone, cover the underneath zones.

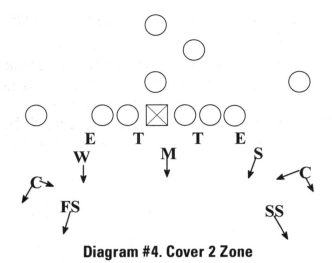

Diagram #4. Cover 2 Zone

Although we play cover zero man, when we call it, I get a little tight, because we have no one in the middle to guard the field (Diagram #6). The corners play the same as cover 1. They cover the number one receiver and take away the inside. The Will linebacker covers number 2 weak, and the free safety takes number 2 strong. The strong safety takes number 3 strong. A blitz always accompanies this coverage.

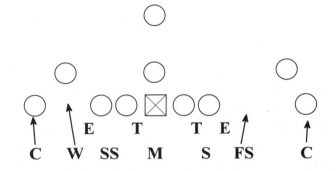

Diagram #6. Cover Zero Man

That is about it for the defensive backs. Thank you for your attention. I think Coach Saluga wants to show you some film of our defense.

That concludes our presentation. Thanks a lot, guys.

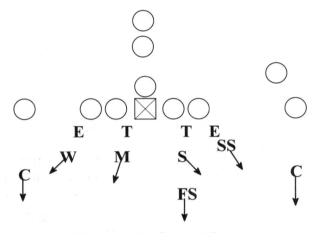

Diagram #5. Cover 3 Zone

PLANNING AND COACHING RESPONSIBILITIES

Central High School, Kentucky

First, I want to thank Nike and the clinic staff for allowing me to speak. Nike is a great organization, and this is a great clinic. I hope that I will be able to give you one or two ideas that we do in our program that will allow you to take back to your team and become a better team as well. There are some coaches present today who have helped me in many ways, and I would like to thank those coaches for being in attendance.

I have really been blessed—in life, as well as in coaching. Since we won the State Championship, I have had the opportunity to give a lot of speeches. But by far, this is the largest coaching clinic at which I have spoken. Most everyone in this room probably knows more football than I do.

At this point, I would like to give you a quick background on my career. I have been a head coach for six years. In reality, there are many coaches who are currently in this room who have been coaching longer than I have been playing and coaching.

As such, I do not have all of the answers. I plan to share with you want we do at Central High School from one Friday to the next Friday in our game planning efforts.

If I go over something that you want to know more about, you can email and I will send it to you. In my opinion, you will not have to write a lot of the information that I discuss down today. Hopefully, this session will be to ask questions and talk football.

What I'm going to cover today is what we do at Central High School. One point that I'd like to address is the fact that I periodically remind all of our coaches of one saying that I feel is very true in football: *"Fail to Prepare, Prepare to Fail."* As such, I stress to the staff we must be willing to put in the time to prepare the best we can in order to be fair to the team.

I believe it is the responsibility of the head coach to write down the coaching responsibilities for each coach on his staff. Every coach needs to know what his responsibilities and duties are for a team to be successful. If he does not have the responsibilities spelled out for him, he may leave practice, without doing the things he should be doing, such as checking films. Later, that same coach might want to know why he does not have input into the game for Friday night. The pint I'd like to make is that coaches should give member of their staff something meaningful to do and make it their individual responsibility.

My advice to every head coach in this room is that when dealing with assistant coaches, let them coach their position. They are dedicated individuals who are not being paid a lot of money. Coaches should not try to micromanage their assistants. For example, I do not attend all of the defensive meetings. Instead, they give me the necessary paperwork as they leave the locker room. While I visit with the defensive coordinator during the week, I let the assistant coaches coach. I also let each coach know that there are certain things he has to do before the week is up.

Next, I want to go through the coaching responsibilities for our staff. The following sections detail how we break up the responsibilities for our staff:

Quarterbacks Coach

Basic Responsibilities:

- Make sure all other offensive coaches are up to speed on all details and changes.
- Help with game planning for the week.
- Help with lining the game and practice field.
- Give a report on any quarterback problems or concerns.

- Conduct weekly meetings with the quarterbacks.
- Help with the game planning and practice efforts of the quarterbacks.
- Develop a grade report on the quarterbacks.
- Run the scout team's offense during the defensive period.
- Call the plays in the JV games.
- Help and evaluate youth-league players.

Game-Day Responsibilities:
- Inform the head coach and all other offensive coaches of any game-planning situations.
- Make sure the stat book, team roster, and filming equipment are ready and loaded on bus, if necessary.
- Ride the first bus with the other offensive coaches.
- Keep all coaches off the field during the game.
- Check the game balls—obtain a new ball each Thursday.

Offensive Line Coach

Basic Responsibilities:
- Obtain the weather report (trust UPS).
- Hold offensive-line meetings and report any problems or concerns.
- Grade the report on the offensive line.
- Supervise the equipment room.
- Help game-plan with other offensive coaches.
- Open (unlock) the equipment shed.
- Help with lining the game field.
- Help and evaluate youth-league players.

Game-Day Responsibilities:
- Help set up the game field.
- Obtain the weather report.
- Obtain any towels and plastic bags that are needed.
- Bring a dry-erase board and pens to the game.
- Help the coach with game plans.
- Meet with the offensive line while the defense is on the field.
- Ride the first bus with the other offensive coaches.

Wide Receivers Coach

Basic Responsibilities:
- Conduct meetings with the wide receivers and report any problems or concerns.
- Work with kick-returners.
- Help game-plan with the other offensive coaches.
- Grade-out the wide receivers.
- Help with lining the field.
- Help with the scout team's offense.
- Help and evaluate youth-league players.
- Write down all plays for the week.

Game-Day Responsibilities:
- Help set up the game field.
- Keep the players behind the cones.
- Inform coaches of any players who will not be able to participate, for example, because of an injury.
- Make sure players clean up the locker room as they leave.
- Be an eye in the sky (i.e., check out the other team on injuries and other helpful information involving the opponent).
- Ride the first bus with the other offensive coaches.

Running Backs Coach

Basic Responsibilities:
- Conduct running backs' meetings and report any problems or concerns.
- Call plays in the freshmen games.
- Give a report to the head coach about any problems involving the freshmen players.
- Help the coach give out JV and freshmen game jerseys.
- Be on the sideline during JV games.
- Line the practice field.
- Help with lining the game field.
- Grade out the running backs.
- Help and evaluate youth-league players.

Game-Day Responsibilities:
- Help set up the game field.

- Make sure tables are available.
- Keep the players off the head coach's nerves (i.e., we dress a lot of freshmen; they can get restless, and get on my nerves at times).
- Help with control of the locker room before and after the game.
- Make sure that small cones are available and placed 4.5 yards back off the sideline.
- Set and break down the game field.

Director of Football Operations

Basic Responsibilities:
- Collect fundraiser money with the head coach (the job involves a lot of paperwork).
- Collect spirit pack money with the head coach.
- Help monitor and supervise the equipment room.
- Get things ready for the JV and freshmen games.
- Attend all freshmen and JV games.
- Watch game film and help develop a game plan every week.
- Coordinate picking up game uniforms.
- Help with lining the game field.

Game-Day Responsibilities
- Help set up the game field.
- Help the coach with game plans.
- Double-check and make sure everything that needs to be available is available.
- Make sure the headsets are loaded (batteries).
- Ride the first bus with the other offensive coaches.
- Serve as an eye in the sky.
- Bring down the halftime stats to the head coach.
- Call in game stats to the media.

Defensive Coordinator

Basic Responsibilities:
- Lead the defensive meetings on Sunday and any other time they are scheduled.
- Make sure all other defensive coaches are up to speed on all details and changes.
- Game plan for the week.
- Give a report on any problems or concerns.

- Conduct weekly meetings with the head coach on any concerns.
- Grade-out the linebackers' play.
- Conduct the linebackers meeting and report any problems and concerns.
- Help with lining the game and practice field.
- Help and evaluate youth-league players.

Game-Day Responsibilities:
- Inform the head coach and all other defensive coaches of any game-planning situations.
- Take care of all equipment problems.
- Ride the second bus with the other defensive coaches.
- Help keep all coaches off the field during the game.

Defensive Line Coach

Basic Responsibilities:
- Grade-out the play of the defensive line.
- Conduct the defensive line meeting and report any problems and concerns.
- Help with the scout team's defense during offensive periods.
- Watch game film and help come up with a plan to stop the opponent.
- Attend all JV and freshmen games.
- Help with lining the game field.
- Call the defense for the freshmen games.
- Make sure tees, balls, and net are available for the JV and freshmen games.
- Help and evaluate youth-league players.

Game-Day Responsibilities:
- Help out in the locker room, before and after the game.
- Make sure the kicking game equipment is available (net and tees).
- Know where the tees are during the game.
- Film trade with the other team (ONLY IF WE GET OUR FILM BACK).
- Help keep the players behind the cones.
- Help break down the film.
- Ride the second bus with the other defensive coaches.

Corners Coach

Basic Responsibilities:
- Conduct defensive back meetings and report any problems or concerns.
- Grade-out the defensive backs.
- Attend all freshmen and JV games.
- Call the defense for the JV games.
- Help with the scout team's defense during offensive periods.
- Watch game film and help develop a game plan every week.
- Help with lining the game field.
- Help and evaluate youth-league players.

Game-Day Responsibilities:
- Help the coach with game plans.
- Double check and make sure everything is available and all windows are locked.
- Make sure headsets are loaded (batteries).
- Ride the first bus with the other defensive coaches.
- Help break down the field.

Safeties Coach

Basic Responsibilities:
- Grade-out the play of the safeties.
- Conduct meetings with the safeties and report any problems and concerns.
- Watch game film and help come up with a plan to stop the opponent.
- Attend all JV and freshmen games.
- Help coach both the JV and freshmen games.
- Supervise the equipment manager.
- Help with lining the game field.
- Help and evaluate youth-league players; serve as the youth-league coordinator.

Game-Day Responsibilities:
- Help out in the locker room, before and after the game.
- Supervise the equipment manager; make sure the equipment box is loaded on the bus.
- Make sure that the press-box phones are loaded.
- Help break down the film.
- Ride the second bus with the other defensive coaches.

FRESHMEN COACHES

Basic Responsibilities:
- Line the practice field for the freshmen.
- Keep the players off the head coach's nerves.
- Make sure the freshmen set up and break down the practice field.
- Make sure the equipment box, kicking tees, footballs, and water are at the JV and freshmen games.
- Help run the freshmen program
- Evaluate youth-league players; ID players that should be observed in all leagues.

Game-Day Responsibilities:
- Keep game stats.
- Keep the players off the head coach's nerves.
- Help with lining the game field.
- Ride the game bus for the JV and freshmen games.
- Make sure all players represent Central football in a positive way.
- Keep the players behind the cones, off the fence talking to fans, and stay involved in the game.
- Help set up and break down the game field.
- Make sure the kicking game equipment is loaded (net and tees).
- Know where the tees are during the game.
- Give suggestions at the appropriate times.
- Make sure that a dry-erase board and pens are available.
- Make sure all players keep their jerseys tucked in.
- Be involved on Friday nights.
- Leave with the set-up crew.

Central Yellowjacket's Five-Step Phases to Success

"Out-coach your opponents before you get to game day."

Friday night is the show. It is too late if you have not planned and prepared your team for what is to take place when the whistle blows. In this regard, we adhere to the following plan for success:

- Film session—We dissect our opponents and how we think that they are going to play us.
- Game plans—This is not the final plan, but we put something together on paper that we think will enable us to beat our opponent.
- Practice—Next, we work on the things we covered in the game plan for three days.
- Game plans—We then come back to the game plan and finalize it and refine it to do the things that we feel give us the best chance to win the game.
- Play the game according to our game plan—There are times when we will get off the script. If we are playing a team that is giving us something we were not prepared for, we may adjust what we are doing. However, most of the time we are going to stick with the game plan that we worked on all week.

The following schedule illustrates what we do to prepare for a game during the week:

❏ SATURDAY:
- This is a day off for our players, except during the playoffs. Once the playoffs start, we practice every Saturday.
- The head coach trades film and makes multiple copies of the film for the staff meeting.
- This is also primarily a day off for the staff.
- The coaches individually responsible for picking up Friday night's game film and grading out their positions perform their duties.
- The grade sheet is due when the coach who is responsible for filling out the sheet arrives at the Sunday meeting.
- All coaches take individual accountability and ownership of their responsibilities.

❏ SUNDAY:
- Staff meetings are from 9:00 AM to 12ish or so, before the NFL games start.

- Coaches get their concerns off their chest. This occurs with the door shut. Everyone expresses their views.
- The staff talk about Friday night's game (highlights, bad and good).

PHASE #1:
- Watch the opponent of the week.
- Each position coach must give me their scout sheets before they leave.
- I want to know:
  ✓ The jersey numbers for all starters and a brief comment about each starter.
  ✓ What defense/offense the opponent runs.
  ✓ What the opponent does in down-and-distance situations.
  ✓ Our personnel changes, if any.

PHASE #2
- Game-plan sheets and openers are started on (we write down 10 plays that we feel we can run successfully against our next opponent).
- Each coach leaves with a DVD of the opponent and turns in Friday night's copy of the game.
- Each coordinator must submit their game plans by noon on Monday.
- We select a few plays for our opening plays for each game.

We write everything down, including the plays we can run from each formation and the plays we can run with motion. We do the same with the defense. We want to know what we feel will work best against the opponent's offense. We write it down. We do not run all of the plays and formations we have listed. Eventually, we determine six or seven of the things that we have written down on our opponents that are most appropriate for our use.

❏ MONDAY:
PHASE #3
- Practice schedules are set for the week.
- The game plan is typed and copied (the final draft for the offense and defense will be on my computer at 12 noon).

- The scouting report is typed and copied.
- Study hall is conducted.
- Last Friday's game evaluation and the first half of the report on the upcoming opponent are reviewed.
- Practice—the wide receivers coach brings the play sheet to practice.
- We practice all of our offense on Monday.

❏ TUESDAY:
- Study hall is conducted.
- Defensive practice—we primarily practice defense and some offense. The offense never leaves the field without practicing some plays.
- Weights—we do four drills and get in and out in a reasonable time.

❏ WEDNESDAY:
- Study hall is conducted.
- The offense and defense practice.
- Weights

PHASE #4
- The coaches meet to finalize the game plan. We delete the plays we decide are inappropriate for our needs as the game plan is finalized.
- Game situations—first-and-long, second-and-short, etc.—are reviewed.

❏ THURSDAY:
- Team FCA is conducted (no more than 30 minutes).
- Study hall is held.

- Film—during the season, this is when the team watches film. During the playoffs, the team watches films every day.
- Practice—we go back to our game plan and put everything together that we plan to run.

❏ FRIDAY:
PHASE #5
- We print out the final game plan.
- A team meal is held.
- Travel or dress policies are reviewed.
- Players' meetings
- Pre-game
- Game
- Coaches' meeting
- The coaches go out to eat.
- The head coach copies the game-film DVD to trade with opponents and for viewing by our assistant coaches.

Contact Offer

If you want any of the materials I have discussed today, or if you just want to talk about the things I touched on, you can contact me any time or email me:

Ty Scroggins, Head Coach; Central High School; 1130 West Chestnut Street; Louisville, KY 40203; 502-485-8226
Tyrran.Scroggins@jefferson.kyschools.us

My presentation has focused on Central High School football. In closing, I would like to remind all of our coaches of one saying that I mentioned earlier. I feel this is very true in football in all programs and at all competitive levels: *"Fail to Prepare, Prepare to Fail."*

THE DOUBLE-WING POWER OFFENSE

Joliet Catholic Academy, Illinois

Today, I hope I will be able to give you something you can take back to your program. Joliet Catholic is a power football team on offense, and we have been so for several years. We have used this offense for years, and we have enjoyed success with this system. The formation I will be covering today enables us to do what we do better (Diagram #1). In our double-wing set, we have always run the cross buck and sweep plays.

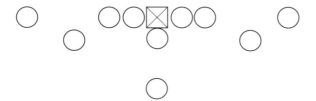

Diagram #1. Double-Wing Formation

Most coaches who talk about their philosophies on offense reflect their views in the formations they run. We are the same way. We do what we do. What you see is what you get with us. I am going to show you the one formation and what we do from that formation.

I want to give you a history of the double-wing offense. Back in the 1970s, Woody Gillespie started a four-year run of state championships by running the power-I formation. That is when Joliet was considered a power-type team.

In the early 1980s, they went to the T formation with the backs in the slot going in motion. Coach Gillespie wanted to balance the formation. We ran the counters and cross bucks. Then, he split the ends out wide and ran the passing game.

When we went to St. Francis College, we brought the ends back inside and started running the ball more. The reason behind this formation was

to outnumber the defense at the point of attack and to gain leverage on the outside.

We want to force the defense to align to give us leverage at the point of attack. We use the wingback and end to wall off inside and to seal down to the inside so we can run the power play, or cross-buck play. We use the triangle blocking of the tackle, the flex end, and wingback to block down inside (Diagram #2). We are going to outflank the defense.

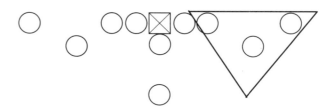

Diagram #2. Triangle Blocking Angles

What the defense does to adjust on the triangle determines what we do on offense. We want to know what the defense does to adjust to our slot set. They may use their linemen or linebackers to take away that leverage. If they do that, we have created the second phase of this formation where we can stretch the defense. We are going to open up some A-gap and B-gap holes if the defense adjusts the linemen outside to cover the slot. We bring our uncontested linemen down inside on the linebackers.

Today, many teams are in the *spread* formation on offense. That is not us. We are in the stretch formation. We are going to *stretch* the defense. We are going to create 10 gaps along the line of scrimmage. From the outside of the flex end to the other flex end, we have five gaps on each side of the center (Diagram #3).

Eight-man-front teams are going to widen their ends. That is when we run the A or B gaps. They

Diagram #3. Create 10 Gaps

may roll their corners up. That allows the corners to give run support. When we block the end outside, they fill the alley with the corner.

If the defense does not use linebackers and linemen to take away the leverage, they can use the secondary to take away that leverage. They may play with four defenders across the back and funnel one of the safeties down hard inside against our motion. They can keep the safeties deep and bring the corners down outside the force.

The defense can go to a nine-man front. If the defense does that, we have put them in a new coverage. There are going to be some holes in that new coverage.

This is the basic philosophy of the formation. We want to gain leverage on the edge. We want to outnumber the defenses at the point of attack.

If we want to run off-tackle, we are going to wall down and kick out. If we want to run the option, we can outnumber a team. We want to know how the defense is going to drop in their adjustments.

We run what we want to run. If we want to run the power play, we have the leverage. We have eight or nine adjustments on offense. We do not see other teams running this formation very often. In our scouting report, we list the basic defenses we expect to see against each team each week.

We list three or four things they can do to us in this formation. Our adjustments are made based on the defensive fronts. In a game, if we recognize a different defensive front, we have an automatic adjustment that we make. There are certain things the defense can do out of each front, and we work on the front we expect to face.

We are using the *Lombardi theory*—we have one sound formation that we can run many different plays from. Teams will see us in the double wing or the wing-T over 75 percent of the time. We do run

some wide formations, but this is the formation we use the most.

We know how defensive teams are going to align, and we know how we are going to attack them. The formation is a balanced set. We know if we are going to play geography, we have leverage to the sideline.

We have had a lot of success with this formation. I ran this offense when I was the head coach 11 years ago, and it was good for us then. Last year was one of the best years we have had with this formation. We ended up with 6,651 total yards on offense. We averaged 475 yards per game. We averaged 46 points per game. All three backs gained over 1,000 yards. Our left wingback had 174 carries, the right wing had 172 carries, the fullback had 160 carries (and he missed one game because of an injury). Our balance comes with our running game. All three of our backs are involved in our offense.

Look at our splits for the ends. We would like them to split four to six yards from the tackle—reality is two to six yards on their splits (Diagram #4). We do adjust these splits depending on our personnel and the scouting reports.

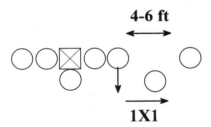

Diagram #4. Split of Flex End

Our wingbacks are one yard off the line of scrimmage, and one yard outside the tackles. We angle the halfback at a 45-degree angle. We do not get into a three-point stance, we are in a two-point stance. There are a couple of reasons for this. First, it allows the halfback to move in any direction. It also allows the wingback to attack on the down block and our double-team chip blocks.

Another reason we like the stance for the wingbacks is that we face teams that stem and move their line just before the snap. By being in the two-point upright stance, the wingback can see the entire defensive front. He can see where the holes are in the defense. He can see the open area without tipping off our opponent. If he is in a three-point stance, he cannot see the stemming and movement in the defensive line.

Depending on how quick the fullbacks are, we line them up between four and five yards deep. It depends on personnel and the plays we are running.

Our line splits are as follows: The guard is 30 inches from the center, and the tackles are 36 inches or more from the guard.

We are very dedicated to our techniques. We want to stretch the defense. By stretching the defense, we get the big plays in the middle of the formation. We want to force the defense to align their defense, and then we are going to try to outnumber them.

The other aspect of the double-wing formation is the motioning involved. We run one- or two-quick-steps motion to get to the normal running back's position. We do not run the motion to get depth as much as we run it to get the quick start. By doing this, we have flow right away. It is very difficult for the defense to stem to the quick motion.

To adjust to our quick motion, defensive teams will slant their lines, and slide their linebackers. By doing this, the defense is subject to the misdirection and counter plays.

Again, we want to be able to beat the defense at the point of attack and outnumber the defense at the flank. We can use the front of flat motion with the wingback. By flat motion, the halfback goes along the line of scrimmage. By going in flat motion, we can end up in a trip formation where we can flood the zones.

We can run a *wham* package with the wingback as well. If we have a big wingback who is a good blocker, we can have him on the kick-out block, or he can lead the play back inside with wham blocking.

We can use motion to throw the play-action pass. If we see teams that allow their secondary to overreact to motion, we use the play-action game against them.

The next area of the double-wing formation is the personnel. Earlier, one of the speakers was talking about their *20 personnel*. We might say we are a *42 personnel*. That is because all four of our backs are runners, and they all four carry the ball. We spread the ball out with all four backs.

Our wingbacks or our halfbacks run the sweep plays and cross bucks, and they run the inside game. The fullback runs in the gaps along the line of scrimmage. The quarterback carries on the bootleg, power play, and certain misdirection plays. All of our backs are involved in carrying the ball, but more important, they are also involved in blocking. To be a good wingback in our system, the wingback has to be a "Walter Payton" type of player. He has to be multitalented. He must be able to run well. He must be able to carry the football. Our kids enjoy blocking, and they really take pride in blocking.

We tell the wingbacks this: If one of them is running the ball, the defense has 11 players who are trying to knock his head off. The least he can do when he is not carrying the ball and he is blocking is to knock the crap out of one of the defenders.

Our wingbacks are also our leading receivers. They are in the tight slots coming out on their routes. Sometimes, they are a flanker, and, at times, they are a second receiver. They become our leading receivers. They are usually our best athletes.

By running this formation, we open up the offense to threaten with four potential deep receivers. This can be productive for our passing game.

The fullback must be a good inside runner and he must be a good, hard-nosed blocker. He must be able to pass block on the dropback game.

Our ends are a mix-and-match set. We may play a tight-end type of player at one end, and a smaller-type split end at the other end position. If we have a big wingback, we will put him to the side of the smaller end. We take our smaller wingback and place him on the side with the big tight end.

This gives us the chance to adjust, and we still can go big-on-big if we need to. Usually, the right wingback is the big back, and the left wingback is our tailback-type player.

We can adjust the end any way we choose. If we move the tight end to the left and call *Liz*, we can move the tight end inside next to the tackle (Diagram #5).

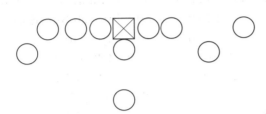

Diagram #5. Liz (Wing/Tight-End Set)

We still have the same set to the right, but now we have our tight end working off the defensive end on the left side. If we call *Rip*, the tight end goes to the right side.

Most defenses treat the tight end as the strength of the formation. Teams shift their lines to the tight-end side. However, we are still balanced, and we are just as strong blocking to the flex-end side of the formation.

That is our I-front formation. I want to give you a look at the defenses we see the most. We see the odd front with a 5-2 look or a 3-4 look (Diagram #6). What happens is determined by how the defender who is over the slot aligns. Is he playing over the slot or on the inside shade to take away the corner? If he is taking away the corner, we still have leverage. Our leverage is still sound, and we can combo-block down inside and kick out the end.

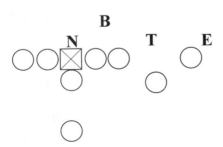

Diagram #6. Adjustments

What if the defense brings the safety up and drops the corner off? We are in a position to block the safety. We still have the double-team block, and

we have the kick-out block at the point of attack. We have some options on ways we can block each play. We can do several different things on each block.

Many times the defensive end is working hand in hand in the B gap. If he works outside, our tackle goes down on the linebacker. Our wingback and end work together on the slot defender. The center and playside guard work on the nose man and offside linebacker.

We have our ends in a three-point stance. We feel they can get off the line better that way. It gives them a better release from that position. If we split them wide, they are in a two-point stance.

If the defense shifts to the slotside of the formation, it ends up as an eight-man front (Diagram #7). Now, we are going to stretch the formation. We can run to the inside gaps. We can run our trapping game. We go down on the linebacker, and we trap the noseguard. We still have good leverage. We have angle blocks inside.

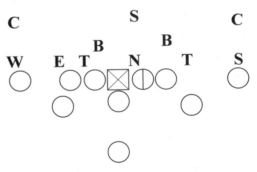

Diagram #7. Eight-Man Front

We can use the wingback to block down, or he can kick out the end. He could come inside for the inside linebacker. We are always looking for the angles and for the numbers.

To the other side, we still have the angles. The wingback and end are accountable for the end and linebacker inside. We kick out the safety that has contain to that side of the formation. Even against the eight-man front, it has opened up some of the gaps inside.

The way the even-front defenses play us is in a 4-3 or 6-1 look (Diagram #8). We need to see what

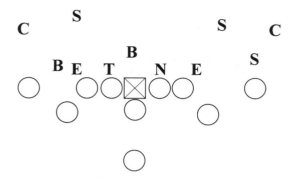

Diagram #8. Even-Front Defense—4-3 or 6-1 Look

adjustments the defense makes to stop the off-tackle play.

If the defense widens the C gap to stop the off-tackle play, we still have great leverage. If the defense has a piece of our tackle, we bring the wingback down on the double-team. The end releases inside and blocks the safety.

If the defense widens the tackle outside of our tackle, the slot and end double-team him. If the defense offsets, our tackle has to come down inside.

One of the most defensive sets we see is the 4-4 or 6-2 even-front set. It is the same situation as the eight-man front (Diagram #9). We can run our A gap, B gap, and our trapping game inside. We can run our fullback up in the B gap, and we can run the counter-trey up in the B gap. We still have good leverage.

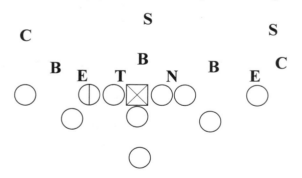

Diagram #9. Even-Front Defense—4-4 or 6-2 Set

This gives us the combination block with our guard and tackle. We can block 4-on-2 here if we want.

We see the defensive line shift against our formation. When they shift to the wideside of the field, we run to the backside A gap and B gap, and we are solid on the backside.

We do spend a lot of time on our timing with our backs. We work hard on timing motion. We run our plays against air for conditioning. On rainy days, we go inside and work on speed in the gym. We run the players through the cone drills. We put the defense in front of the defense with the hand-shield type of dummies. They step to the position where the defensive man is going to be as the ball is snapped.

We break our practice down where we have individual improvement periods. We work on individual skills at that time. The wingbacks work on their running, pass catching, and blocking skills. The flex ends work on their blocking. They work on the double-team block with the wingback. Also, they work on their receiving techniques.

The linemen work on all of their blocking combinations. We may bring the wingbacks and ends to work with the guards and tackles on their combination blocks. The linemen work on their pulling skills, and they work on their pass protection skills. All of this is in our individual practice sessions.

Our cadence is: ready, set, go. We must figure out where the ball needs to be snapped when the wingback is in motion. It is the responsibility of the wingback to know where he needs to be when we snap the ball. The quarterback has to know how long to hold the cadence to make sure the wingback gets to where he needs to be.

We do have a *quick package* where we snap the ball on a quick sound. This will help keep the defense honest, and it allows us to run the motion with timing on the regular cadence.

I want to show you the film so you can see what we have been talking about. It is much better when you can see what we are doing as opposed to me telling you what we are doing.

I appreciate your attention. Thank you.

DEVELOPING SPEED AND STRENGTH

Bluefield High School, West Virginia

It is good to be here today. I have been the head coach at Bluefield High School for 22 years, and the longer I am in the game, the more fun I am having. However, every head coach has to deal with the everyday problems that go with a high school program. We had a problem this year that reflects how the attitudes of head coaches are changing. I did not dress everyone for all of our games. We played an away game, and I felt like if we did not take everybody, the team could focus better. Two of our players who did not dress showed up at the game. They approached one of our coaches and asked if they could pass out Gatorade® at halftime because they cared about our team and wanted to be involved.

On Sunday, the coaches came to our coaches meeting and wanted to talk to me. They felt those players worked hard and needed to dress. I thought about it and agreed with them. That was the last time I did not dress everyone on the team for a game. I have learned that players today will not stay out for the team if they do not get some kind of reward. They are out there getting their butts knocked off and deserve to dress.

We had another situation this year that required a lot of thought. We had a senior running back who came to talk to the coaches. He wanted the opportunity to carry the ball in short-yardage situations. He felt we were not giving him a chance to run the ball in those situations.

My son is the offensive coordinator. He told the player that the reason he did not get the ball was because he would turn the ball inside and then bounce it outside every time. He told us if we would give him a chance, he would run it inside hard. In the next game, the opportunity arose and the back hit the ball inside with a great deal of authority. If that had happened when I was playing, my coach would have kicked me out of the office. Things have changed. I am willing to communicate with players as long as they are coolheaded and I trust them.

In coaching, you surround yourself with winners. One of my assistant coaches played on the 1997 Bluefield championship team, he works at the bank as a vice president, and he helps me every afternoon. I have several coaches like that. These coaches care about the players as much as I do. We are not worried about backstabbing or people talking trash about us. We are trying to make sure we teach our players the fundamentals of the game. We want them to know how to treat each other.

We have a great time. In the last five years, I have had as much fun as I did in high school and college. I think that is how it should be. It may not always be that way, but now it is great.

The weight program has changed in the last 22 years. That is how long I have been the head coach at Bluefield High School. We have to coach football, teach, and take care of the weight program year-round. We are not like most colleges that have a weight-training coach on staff. We have to do it all.

You have to develop a program to condition athletes that uses every phase of available techniques and training. You have to use speed programs, lateral speed work, plyometrics, weights, core work, and balance training. You never allow the athlete to get out of shape. We have problems with our middle school kids. Some of them do not do anything to get in shape. They come to high school at 5' 8" and 250 pounds, and it takes us three years to get them close to being in shape.

I wish physical education was taught every day and the administration made kids take it. You have to use current research to enhance your program. I am constantly trying to find something that will help our players get better. If you can find ways to make your players better and not bore them, that is what you need to use. You still need the squat, bench, and power clean, but if you can find something that is not the same old thing, it helps.

We try to combine the terminology we use in the weight room with that we use on the football field. We *train to win*. We may not win the 40- or 100-yard race, but we will win the five-yard race—and we will focus on it.

In our objective, we want to teach our athletes how to bend. I refer to bend as load.

Accomplish Bend

- *Power:* Angles to straight lines
- *Foundations:* Eyes and feet, shoulders and hips
- *Arch:* Eyes up, deep breath, tighten core
- *Angle:* Back and hips, knees, over ankles

My terminology to the players is *load* instead of *bend*. They know what I mean by that. When they do a squat in the weight room, they have to have a good foundation. I tell them their foundation is their eyes and feet. On the squat, the feet are a little wider than the hips, with their toes out for balance and their eyes straight ahead. That is their foundation. If I am a defensive lineman, I will have one foot up in the stance with my eyes in at the football. That is the stance and the foundation.

When I tell the players to *arch angle*, they take a deep breath and arch their lower back while angling down on the squat. I tell them to do the same thing on a sprint start we do. In the stance, at times we have the right foot up, and at other times the left foot is up. To win the five-yard race, you have to push off different feet. They cannot go with one foot all the time—they have to switch their feet. After we take a deep breath, we start angling down. It does not matter if it is a stance or a squat exercise.

The second objective is to teach the *power source*. You have to teach the athlete how to start and explode. The explosion comes from the lower back, glutes, and hamstrings. We teach those things in sequence. We teach foundation, arch angle, load, and power source. We constantly work on coming off the ball or starting from a stance. We do the same thing in squatting in the weight program. We get under the bar, establish our foundation, get the correct arch angle, load, and explode up with the weights.

After we teach that aspect to the athlete, we teach them to run. We work with their arm techniques and leg movement. We spend time working on form running. What is often overlooked is deceleration. I do not tell our players to go out on the field and hit someone. If a player is not in a proper position, he cannot tackle. You cannot expect a player to make tackles if they are not in a position to tackle. We teach our players how to decelerate and reload. That technique is involved in the trap block, stalk block, or the tackle.

The next thing we teach is *eyes to mind, mind to muscle*, and *muscle to heart*. The eyes to mind part is the thought process that goes into making a tackle. The mind to muscle part is the technique you use to perform the tackle.

The third part needs a little more explaining. Three times a year, I sit down with our players. Those times mark the three segments of our program. The first stage is January to March, the second is April to May, and the third is June to August. Since we do not have all our coaches in the building every day, I have to do most of the grading. I see my players every day in school. I sit down with the players, which takes three to four minutes per player. I ask the players to grade themselves. When it is all said and done it will spell out *heart*.

I tell our players, if our grade is 80 percent or better as a team, we have a chance to win the state championship. Without that kind of percentage, I do not think we do. What I do is hard work because it requires record keeping.

If one of our players misses one day of the off-season program without an excuse, they get a minus. There are exceptions to every rule. If we have a player who signs out of school sick, I make a judgment call on that situation. We lift at least three days a week but, on occasion, it is four or five days a week. We start in January and we do not finish until practice starts in August.

The second part of the grade is enthusiasm. If we are supposed to do 10 reps on a certain day and the player does eight and loafs on them, I tell him he did eight reps instead of 10. I do not say anything else, but when I sit down to grade him, he gets a minus grade in enthusiasm. If they bust their butts and do a good job, they get a plus and they deserve it. In these meetings, I ask them what they think they deserve. I want to hear what they have to say.

The next area includes attitude, ability, and grades. Attitude is the best support for achievement and the best *ability* is *dependability*. If they are coming every day, they are enthusiastic, and they are working their butts off, they get a plus in that category. If they do not have at least a 2.0 grade point average, I do not let them participate in the program. When they get the 2.0, I let them come back into the program.

I want to know what type of respect they show others in their lives. I look at the respect they have for the teachers, our staff members, other players on the team, and me. If we have a player who needs help on his technique with the power clean, I want to see which player helps him. That is respect to me.

The last thing is team. There is no *I* in team. If we ask a player to change his position, it is the team we have in mind. He should have the team in mind also. The team comes before any individual.

If you put all those things together, it spells out the word *heart*. If we have *H*ard work, *E*nthusiasm, good *A*ttitudes, *R*espect for others, and belief in the *T*eam, that spells *heart*. If the team has a grade of 80 percent or better, we have a chance to win the state championship.

That gives me a two-way conversation with every player on our team about our weight program. We are not doing the weight program just to have a program. We are going to the weight room to get better.

Part of our evaluation of our off-season program is testing. We test all of our players. We test them so we can maximize the player's performance. This allows us to assess possible goals they want to achieve. The testing allows the athlete to monitor his progress. Testing provides a monitoring system to ensure the weight program is working. It helps to identify past, present, and future trends in our weight program. It motivates the athlete. If they see they have tested well and have visible progress, they will improve their work habits. Working hard to achieve positive results always works.

In any testing system, the testing must be reliable. The testing order will always be the same. We test in the same areas and have the same people who monitor in those areas do the testing. We do not hedge on the scoring. If our players are not getting below parallel on the squat, is does not count. I have to see that move. Our goal is to increase our speed. It is not to squat 500 pounds by going down two inches and coming back up. I am strict on them because the only way to develop speed is to get your knee bend parallel to the floor.

We test three to four times a year and no more. We have an "Iron Beaver" club in our weight-lifting program. We have a point total assigned to different exercises, runs, or skills in the off-season program. If a player squats 180 pounds, he gets one point. If he squats 425 pounds, he gets 24 points. When a player gets 110 points, he joins the Iron Beaver club. Last year we had 10 players who got into the Iron Beaver club. They battle like crazy because they want to get into that club. We take pictures of every player who makes the Iron Beaver club, and we put them in the program. I used to put a picture of the player who had the most points in the program, but I do not do that anymore. That does not feature the team?it makes it about an individual.

We test an exercise on Monday, with something different on Tuesday, and something else on Wednesday. We use Thursday and Friday for make-up days if we need them.

The first part of our workout is getting our vocabulary and terminology consistent to our teaching. We lift during the season, but we do not perform the same exercises that we do in the weight program.

When we start an off-season program, we have to get in the room and teach them. When we teach the power squat, we use our terminology. We talk about foundation, arch angle, load, and power source. When the player does not get down as far as he needs to in the squat, I instruct him to load. He understands what that means.

We use hurdles to warm our players up before we lift. This is a way to get our players stretched out. They step over the top of the first hurdle, walk under the next hurdle, and alternate the activities down the row of hurdles. We run them sideways and do the same thing. They step over the first hurdle and go under the second hurdle. This teaches them how to stretch their legs and how to bend properly. We are not big physically as a team, but we work hard.

The next thing we do is a sprint, teaching them how to decelerate and reload. We throttle down the run, get under control, gather, and get ready to repeat the elements of bending. When we gather, we get the foundation, arch angle, load, and explosion into their target.

We go through mat drills with our players in their position groups. They work on the techniques that go with their positions. We start our defensive players pushing on an offensive linemen, concentrating on the same elements of explosion. We work on the reads they will have as defenders. We work on pulls toward and away, down blocks, and situations that affect the way they play. In all the drills, we have one central theme. We want to bend and stay loaded with a good base and explosion. We are transferring our vocabulary from the weight room to the football field.

We do front squats as part of the lifting program. Front squats have the weights in a power-clean position in front of the body. They should have it on the shoulders behind the head. We want the elbow up and the bar across the front of the shoulders and chest. It is the power-clean position,

and it requires balance and good posture to do the squat exercise.

Our basic lifts are squats, bench, dead lift, front squats, and hamstring exercises on the leg machine. We do single-leg step-ups on the plyometric boxes and all kinds of dumbbell exercises. We do body-resistance exercises like pull-ups. We do different angled push-ups with the hands in different positions to change the muscle groups. We use a VertiMax® machine that works on vertical jump and explosion. We also do standing presses, which I think are great.

We do single-arm bench presses with dumbbells, which are great for the core muscles and especially our offensive linemen. In pass blocking, offensive linemen have to use one arm in a slightly different position to fend off the defender. This is great for that type of situation. There are two ways to do it. With dumbbells in both hands, you can move both dumbbells up simultaneously or alternate one and then the other.

We have adjustable benches in our weight room that allow you to do incline bench presses as well as regular presses. We use dumbbell exercises for extensions using both hands as opposed to one hand. That uses the muscle groups differently. I try to use double-set exercises to work the opposing muscle. If I have a pulling exercise, I also want a pushing exercise. You do not want to strengthen one group of muscles while neglecting the opposing group.

We use *kettle-bell* lifts as well as the dumbbell exercises. By using the kettle bells, you strengthen the hands as well. We curl, press, work the triceps, do military presses and power pushes. Our kettle bells run from 15 pounds up to 100 pounds, however, we do not have too many players who can handle the 100 pounders.

In our power-clean stations we work on power cleans, push jerks, power-clean full squats, and power-clean push jerks. Power cleans snap the weight to the clean position repeatedly. Push jerks take the weight from the clean position to an over-the-head-lock-out position repeatedly. I have already talked about front squats. The power-clean push jerks are taking the weight from the floor to the clean position and jerking it into an overhead position repeatedly.

In our function exercises, we use medicine balls. This is a nice change-up from weight training. These types of exercises work the core muscle in the areas where you change direction. Instead of doing a sit-up, we work our core with a change-of-direction movement. The first one is a chopping action type of movement. As the player does a sit-up, he brings the ball down in a chopping action.

The next one is an uppercut throw. The player throws the ball over his right shoulder or left shoulder. This works on change-of-direction movement and core muscles. This may sound easy, but it is not. It gets your heart rate up and wears you down.

The next exercise we do is with the resistant ball. We do hip rolls and shoulder rolls, which works on their hamstring strength. In the crunch position, we use hip twisters with the medicine ball. We move the ball to the opposite knee on each repetition. We use this alternative exercise as part of a circuit with weight-lifting exercises, sprinting, or ladder-speed work. These exercises are done in about an hour. It is not like the college scenes. Our players have to go to school, work out, and go home after practice. This is what we do in our program. You can do any type of exercise that you can dream up.

We use a balance ball, which is a resistance ball with some of the air removed. We do push-ups on it, and we can stand on it and do knee bends. It is a way to work on balance. We get the players to tip the ball, and we throw a medicine ball to them. They have to catch the ball and maintain balance. We also do the *Superman* to improve balance and leg strength. The Superman is a simulation where the athlete lies facedown with his body extended across the ball, while he maintains balance with all his limbs off the floor. He poses as Superman with his arms extended and his legs spread.

We use the VertiMax machine and bungee cords to help with vertical leap. We use all kinds of exercises with the elastic bands. We work on hamstrings and do other movements. These are great for rehabbing injuries and using as preventive measures.

We work on a speed ladder and do all the movements that go with football skills. We run forward and backward, tapping in and out of different areas. Any drill you can do in running ropes, you can do on the ladder, except it is faster.

We had a couple of players tear an ACL several years ago. When they were rehabbing, the therapist put them on a slide board. It is like using a rubber band. This board is flat with foot stops on the outside of the board. The player slides to a foot stop on one side of the board, pushes off, and then slides to the other foot stop on the other side of the board. These exercises are good for rehabbing injuries and injury prevention. I went out and bought my own, and we use it to work on our lateral movement. It works on knee movement and balance. It works the players, and it is not something we are doing for fun.

When you use these devices, you have to teach the proper use of them. After you teach them, all you have to do is watch and correct. They will get the work done.

We have a drill we call *wheel extender*. It pushes and extends the feet off at angles in what I call the *spokes of a wheel*. If his power source is his left foot, he pushes off his left foot at a different angle. That gets him used to foot movement at different angles than what he uses in games. He alternates from his left foot to his right foot.

We use a weight sled, however, I do not run with them. I do marching action and maybe skipping (high-knee) action with them. We load them with the amount of weight dictated by the exercise we are using. We want to load as much weight as they can handle and keep their technique correct. If the player cannot do his technique correctly, he has too much weight on the sled. We have a hallway outside of our rooms, in which we work with the sleds and on sprinting drills.

I am old-school, and it is a constant battle with the players to get that idea over to them. We want them to respect their opponents, the officials, and their teammates. We want them to hand the ball to the referee when they score. We want them to keep their mouths shut and play football. It is not easy with today's players, especially when the pro players they watch every Sunday get by with the behavior and conduct they display.

One of our players reflected the personality of our football team. He collapsed in practice one day, and the doctors diagnosed him with a heart ailment that took him out of football. He could not play again. He could not practice or play, but he came to practice every day. He helped us whenever we needed help. He showed up for every weight-lifting session last year and helped his teammates with their technique and behavior. He showed up for every practice this year, and I made him an honorary captain. He would have been a starter for us. He showed his unselfishness and exemplified the idea of a teammate. I want you to know how proud I am of that player.

Our players work like dogs all year long. If they do not, they do not play for us. If a player is involved with another sport, we do not pressure him to make a choice between sports. That is a selfish attitude by any coach who does that. We want them playing other sports. If they play other sports, they are probably good athletes, and we want them involved with our program. I tell them to try to get to the weight room two days a week on the days we power clean, squat, and incline press. That is all I can do. They only live once, and I cannot tell them they cannot play. We do not have a problem with that.

This statement pulls all of what we do together: "Many have the will to win, but few have the will to train to win! Those that do are the champions." We push "team" as our concept.

I appreciate the opportunity to speak at this clinic. Thank you for your attention.

ZONE CONCEPTS IN THE 3-3 DEFENSE

St. Xavier High School, Ohio

I am an odd-front defensive coach. When I became the head coach, I struggled with trying to teach coverage drops to the players. I could not figure out how to teach them to drop to space. We put up the cones and taught them to drop to spots. We coached them well. They knew how to get to those spots even if the quarterback was in a full sprint the other way. As a result, we came up with a matching-zone concept. It is like a match-up zone in basketball.

Every scheme in football works. It is only a matter of what you believe in. You have to develop a defensive philosophy so your players know what you hang your hat on. They have to believe you have a system and a plan. They must know that in a crunch time we will run this system.

We are an odd front, but we are more of a read scheme now. In the past, we were more aggressive, but we have developed into more of a read scheme. We were always in a three-deep matching-zone concept until this year. Teams that we played began to catch up with what we were doing. We went to some different concepts of two-deep. We also ran some quarter coverage this year. We had 10 returning starters on defense, and four of them were three-year starters. We could do more with that personnel and we did a lot.

The defensive scheme boils down to how it fits your personnel. In 1999, we started running some odd-principled defenses. We started playing smaller defensive linemen. What happened in our progression was that our big safeties became linebackers. The linebackers became defensive linemen, and the old defensive linemen became offensive guards.

I like the balanced front because it does not give the offense a bubble to check to. That is especially true of option teams. Against option teams, if we stay in an odd front, they do not have anything to check to. We can disguise our reduction and slant and angle on the snap. That gives us an advantage.

We run a multiple matching-zone concept. When we play three-deep, it gives us an additional man in the box. When we go to the two-deep scheme, we play a funnel-trail technique and a funnel-flat technique with our corners. The last thing we play is what we call *alert* and *siren*. Those adjustments are a combination coverage, depending on the formation.

I like the matching zone because it restricts our players from covering air. It gives us the ability to play seam and hole defenders. We went to the 3-3-5 defense because of the spread offense. We got more speed on the field. We got rid of the big outside linebackers who were a little stiff in their drops. We struggled with linebackers playing slot receivers. We needed to get more defensive backs on the field.

We can adjust to motion and formations quickly. We have one defender who makes all the adjustments. We call him *the adjuster*. He is the player who has to think. Outside of him, we only have two players who have to adjust to what the offense gives us. That enables our players to play faster. Once we hear the call, eight of our defenders are playing the call, no matter what happens before they snap the ball. We have three players who have to check somewhat.

Everything we accomplished is still available for us. We still have the balanced front, and we can disguise by reducing at the snap. It gives quarterbacks problems.

We have many options to disguise what we are doing. We have multiple options we call *falcon*, *sparrow*, and *ninja*. In our base alignment, the defensive ends are in a 4 technique on the offensive tackles, and the nose aligns in a 0 technique on the center (Diagram #1). The stacked linebackers are stacked behind them at three to four-and-a-half yards. The jet linebacker is the strongside linebacker. The Sam linebacker is the middle linebacker, and the Will is the weakside linebacker. We may cheat them closer against some option teams, and we have gotten deeper against some teams in passing situations.

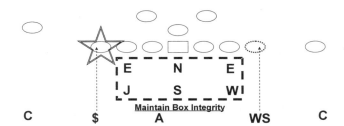

Diagram #1. Base Defensive Alignment

We want to maintain the box integrity as much as we possibly can. We played 15 games this year, and 13 times we played some sort of spread offense. Those offensive coaches always look at the number of defenders in the box. We want to keep six in the box as many times as we can. The safeties play seven yards deep on the outside shade of the tight end or an imaginary tight end. If they are over a slot receiver, they stay at seven yards on their depth and move to an inside shade on the slot. The hash rule for the boundary hash is never go more than three yards inside the hash mark. That alignment can vary according to the game plan.

The corners align in an outside shade of the #1 receivers at four to seven yards deep. They have a six-yard sideline rule. They are never closer than six yards from the sideline.

The key to the defense was the player we called the *adjuster*. He was a three-year starter, and next year he is going to Stanford. He was a great player, and we could do many things with him. This position is designed for the most complete football player on

our team. He may not be the *best* player, but he is the most *complete* player because we do so much with him.

The two biggest keys to what we do defensively are our jet backer and the adjuster. The jet backer is the strongside linebacker. The adjuster will normally align at seven yards over the strongside guard. However, that alignment will vary according to game plan. If we need to get someone over the tight end, we can adjust down and cover him. However, it has been better for us to keep defenders back at seven yards.

We found we played the run better because the tight end had to block someone in space. He blocked down on the defensive tackle, the linebacker, or someone in space. It was difficult to block our safety in space. In the scheme, if the tight end blocks down on the tackle, that makes our adjustments easier.

If we get a double set and teams start to spread us, we do not adjust too much. The safeties widen but still maintain their inside shade of the slot receivers. The box remains intact and the bonus player is still in the middle of the field over the guard.

If the offense gives us a 3 x 1 set, we adjust somewhat (Diagram #2). The strong safety plays on the inside shoulder of the #2 receiver in the set. The strong linebacker moves out into a position, splitting the distance between the #3 receiver and the offensive tackle. The adjuster moves to an inside shade on the #3 receiver. The bonus player is the weakside safety because he has no one in the set to match. We always match defenders. That is the basic alignment in our five-across look.

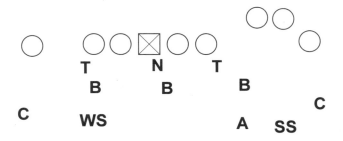

Diagram #2. Base Alignment vs. Trips

We have four fronts that we play with some regularity. We have *spread*, *falcon*, *bluff*, and *ninja* fronts. In the spread front, we walk our outside linebacker up on the line of scrimmage (Diagram #3). The secondary does not move on this adjustment.

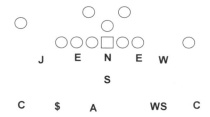

Diagram #3. Spread Front

The falcon and ninja fronts are almost the same. On the falcon front, the strong safety walks down into the box on the tight end. In all of these adjustments, the defender doing the adjusting is 3 x 3 on the tight end or ghost tight end. In the ninja front, the weak safety walks down into the box. If we run the bluff front, both the strong and weak safeties are down in the box (Diagram #4). In the diagram, the bluff front is shown. The position played by the safeties in the falcon and ninja are the same as the bluff front, except that in each front only one of the safeties is down in the box. The problem with the falcon, bluff, and ninja is that we have a two-deep look in the defense instead of a closed look.

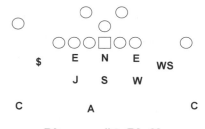

Diagram #4. Bluff

We can combine the fronts by adding a tag to them. If we want to play the spread front, both outside linebackers give to the line of scrimmage (Diagram #5). If we add a bluff tag to the call, that brings both safeties down in the box at 3 x 3 outside the tight end and ghost. This gives the defense a 5-3 look. We can call spread and add a falcon or ninja call and get a different look. We are getting into multiple looks and using tags to move the players. That is the concept of the defense.

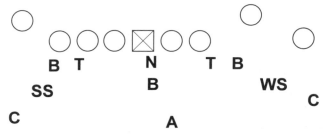

Diagram #5. Spread Tag Bluff

At the beginning of every year, we want to decide how many techniques we can teach our players. You can see we have many things going on within the defense. With 10 starters returning this year, we did most of the things in these fronts. Our adjuster played six different techniques. Normally, we do not put that much on one player. If we get more than two techniques, I start to get nervous. We have to sit down in the off-season and decide. Whatever we teach, we have to get good at it. In the secondary, we teach our *storm* and *fire* concepts most of the time.

The first matching-zone concept is the fire-and-storm concept. These are two separate coverages that allow us to play tighter outside man leverage on the wide receivers while playing match-up zone underneath. It enables us to get additional pressure on the quarterback without putting the secondary defenders on an island. You can play this coverage and not give up the pick routes to the offense. If you play teams that run rub and pick plays, this works well against that scheme. This enables us to run a five-man fire-zone package.

High school quarterbacks do not like to throw to receivers who they feel are covered. They want to throw to spots in the defense. They like zone-drop teams. We were able to play tighter coverage while maintaining our philosophy in the coverage. It also enables us to adapt to virtually any coverage scheme. We can change our deep-coverage scheme while the underneath scheme stays the same.

To run this coverage, you must have two corners who can effectively match up with two speed receivers. At the beginning of the year, every skilled player in our program is a corner. We find the two best players to play corner and build from there. We must have safeties and outside linebackers who can run with slot receivers for 15 yards. That is asking a lot from those players.

It is imperative for us to disrupt and reroute all inside receivers. The underneath defenders have to understand progression reads. We mix and match our underneath defenders with tags. *Fire zones* are five-man pattern blitzes. A four-man pattern blitz with a spy is *fire-zone coverage*. Any four-man pattern blitzes are *storm coverage*.

On fire-zone coverage, we have rules and responsibilities (Diagram #6). The corners play outside leverage on the #1 receiver. He plays him all over the field, and we hope we can effectively erase those receivers and play 9-on-9 with the rest of the defense.

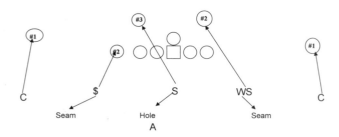

Diagram #6. Fire-Zone Coverage

We number the receivers because our seam defenders have to understand how they are going to match up in this zone. The seam defenders are generally an outside linebacker or a safety. Since this is fire-zone coverage, the seam players are the safeties.

Rules for Seam Defenders

- Read #2 to #3 route progression.
- If no immediate threat, get under #1.
- #2 vertical—collision outside in.
- Know where help is (safety inside).
- Carry to 16 yards unless #3 threatens the flat, then play flat man. Read quarterback outside-in and release late. Give up shallow.
- If #2 tries to fight to corner, maintain outside leverage and take away the corner route.
- #2 cross—carry the cross and deliver to hole.
- Look up #3 out of backfield.
- If no #3, think crossing route coming back (dig).

The progression for the seam player is the #2 receiver to the #3 receiver. That is generally a slot receiver or a back in the backfield. If he is on a single-receiver side, the #2 receiver is in the backfield. There is no immediate threat to the defender. In that situation, he plays underneath the wide receiver to that side. The corner has him man-to-man, and he helps him on inside moves.

If the #2 receiver runs to the flat, he takes him. If the receiver runs a wheel pattern, he runs with him. He has that man on any pattern he runs.

In the pattern, if the #2 receiver runs a vertical route, the defender collisions him from an outside-in leverage. He has help to the inside and wants to force the receiver that way. We want to squeeze everyone to the middle.

The defender carries the #2 receiver for 16 yards unless there is a threat to the flat. If the #3 receiver runs to the flat, he becomes the #2 receiver. The seam defender reacts back to the flat and arrives late. We give up all shallow routes.

The route that concerns us is the *smash* concept. If the safety feels the receiver is trying to get to the corner, he fights him and runs with him to the corner, trying to maintain his outside leverage. He tries to wall the receiver off the corner route.

If #2 runs a cross to the inside, we have to work in tandem with the hole defender. He calls, "Cross, cross," and squeezes the receiver and delivers him to the hole defender. He works outside and helps on the dig route or crossing route coming from the other side.

Rules for the Hole Defender

- Read #3 to #2 route progression.
- Always step with #3, sink 10 to 12 yards.
- #3 flat—deliver to seam and look up #2 on quick cross.
- Carry the cross and deliver to seam.
- #3 vertical—collision and sink to 15 yards.
- Keep eyes back on quarterback, expecting underneath threat.

The hole defender reads opposite the seam defender. He reads from the #3 receiver to the #2 receiver. That generally is the back in the backfield and the slot receiver. However, it can be the third receiver in a trips formation to that side. If the #3 receiver goes flat, he knows there is an outside receiver coming inside. He delivers the flat route to the seam defender and looks up the #2 receiver coming back inside. If a receiver vacates a zone, there will be a receiver coming back into the zone.

The second read is a vertical by the #3 receiver. We do not see this pattern much from the backfield. We see this pattern from a 3 x 1 set. He collisions the receiver and sinks to 15 yards. We tell him to sink to 15 yards, but he will never get there. For a high school player, if we can get him to 10 yards, we are happy. He sinks with the vertical and waits for someone to come back underneath. The two-seam players and the hold player work as a synchronized unit in the underneath coverage.

Storm coverage is the same premise and has been good for us (Diagram #7). It is a nice change-up. The five-zone coverage has only one hole defender in the middle. It is a five-man pressure scheme. Two defenders are involved in a blitz or spy technique, and that leaves only one defender in the low hole. In storm coverage, we bring four-man pressure, and we have two hole players in the middle. The seam defender reads the same as they did in the fire zone. The difference is on the crossing route. The seam defender passes the cross off. However, instead of reacting back outside, he drops back and sits on the dig route.

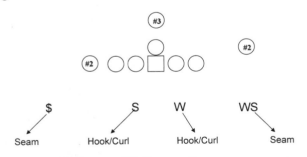

Diagram #7. Storm Coverage

Since there are two linebackers in the middle, they can jump the #3 receiver going to the flat. With two linebackers, there is always someone to take the cross pattern. If the #3 receiver blocks, the linebacker should expect a check release by the back. His depth should not be as deep as normal.

This is an adjustment to a simple stunt in a 3 x 1 set. The stunt is a strong-edge stunt (Diagram #8). It is a four-man pressure scheme. The jet linebacker drops down and comes off the edge to the #3-receiver side. We want to match and collision every receiver in that formation. To match every receiver in this set, we have to *sling* the coverage. We have no trouble matching the #1 and #2 receivers. The corner and strong safety can match them. I do not like the Sam linebacker in the middle having to match on the tight end, and worse, a slot receiver. That is a mismatch.

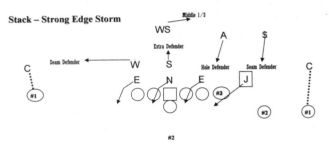

Diagram #8. Adjustment to 3 x 1

Sling Rules

- Strong safety rolls to seam defender.
- Adjuster automatically rolls into low hole.
- Weak safety rolls to deep middle.
- Will linebacker plays backside seam.

We sling the coverage and bring the adjuster down into the box, and he takes the coverage on the #3 receiver.

Coverage Scheme

- The weak safety slides to the trips side and plays the middle third.
- The strong safety slides to the trips side and plays the seam #2 to #3.
- The Will linebacker to the single side looks up #1 and gets under slant or plays #2 to #3 in seam.
- The Sam linebacker is an extra defender and can spy quarterback or deep drop.
- The adjuster replaces stunt to trips and plays hole.
- The corners play loose man on #1.

The Will linebacker and the corner to the backside bracket the wide receiver. The adjuster drops down in the box and does the adjusting to take the position of the jet linebacker who is on the edge stunt. Any sling adjustment tells the adjuster he is the hole defender. Every receiver is matched with a defender. We have a bonus defender (Sam) in the middle of the field.

We had to make a change in our 2 x 2 coverage to take away four verticals (Diagram #9). If we run the same edge stunt, the secondary plays what we call a *three match*. The strong safety replaces the jet linebacker and is the seam defender playing #2 to #3, which is no change for him. The weak safety is still the seam defender, and that is no change. However, he has to match any vertical from the #2 receiver—any other move by the #2 receiver, he plays normal. The Sam and Will linebackers play hook to curl and read #3 to #2.

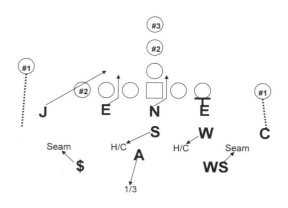

Diagram #9. 2 x 2 Adjustments

The adjuster plays the middle third unless he gets a release by the #2 receiver to the side of the blitz. In this case, to the jet linebacker side he matches the vertical by the #2 receiver. That is our answer to four verticals in a three-deep look. Before we put in this adjustment, teams tried to exploit us with the four-vertical scheme. The corners are playing loose man coverage on the #1 receivers.

Three-Match Rules

- The weak safety matches any vertical from #2 (seam).

- The strong safety matches any vertical from #2 (middle third).

- Everyone else plays their normal responsibilities.

Our cover 2 concept is not that far away from what we do in our fire-and-storm coverage. Those coverages are good for our corners to press and take away the quick routes. If teams start using the three-step quick game, we can go to our cover-2 coverage. We are not going to have to teach everyone. We do not want to give the players too much to play. If you play too much, they will be thinking and not playing fast. You have to decide how much is enough.

Cover 2 can take away the short game, but it also can take away the intermediate routes (Diagram #10). In cover 2, nothing changes for the seam/hole defenders except that we teach funnel-trail and half-coverage techniques. The corner and safeties have to learn a new technique, but the underneath coverage is almost the same.

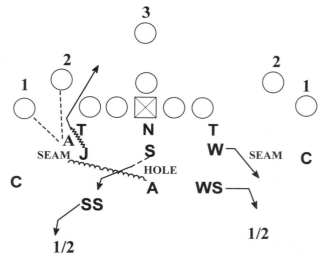

Diagram #10. Cover 2

The key to the coverage is route disruption of the #1 receivers. We need athletic safeties who can run with the slots, play a good trail technique, and cover half the field. The variation we use for the corner is a bail technique—a cross-corner scheme—and we will play sparrow in this coverage.

The seam defenders play the same coverage they played in the fire coverage. The hole defenders have the same technique as the fire coverage, and nothing has changed. The safeties play deep halves of the field. We teach them to read from the #2 to #1 receiver. If #2 goes to the flat, they find out what #1 is doing. They will have help underneath their coverage.

The change-up is in the technique played by the corner. The corners funnel everything to their help in the middle of the field. They are going to play physical and collision the receivers. If they get the fade route, they open to the receiver and force him wide. Regardless of what happens, they assume a trail technique. If the receiver releases inside, the corner uses an offhand jam, gets up underneath him, and trails him on whatever route he runs. It is the same technique used in the fire-and-storm coverage, except it is from a press alignment. The corner knows he has help over the top from the safety and underneath from the three inside linebackers.

We do not worry about landmarks in our coverage. We worry about where the receiver is aligned.

Our *ice* coverage is a little different in our matching-zone philosophy. When we go into the football season, we always run the storm and fire concepts. This year, because we were so experienced, we went to a different type of zone match-up out of the cover 2. We try to stay ahead of the curve, and teams are beginning to catch up to what we are doing.

Ice coverage is a solid change up to our three-deep matching-zone concept (Diagram #11). This coverage enables us to get into a much tighter underneath matching zone with two safeties over the top to take away deeper routes. The match-ups change considerably, which gives the quarterback more to think about, yet remains relatively simple for the underneath coverage players. Unlike fire/storm, this coverage enables the underneath defenders to take away the quick game by pressing all receivers knowing they have help over the top. Because of the fact that we sacrifice run support in this coverage, we mostly run it in passing situations. However, we are able to better disguise our three-deep matching-zone concepts by giving the two-deep illusion and bringing our pressure packages off the look. Although we run this concept out of an odd stack, the matching-zone concept can be adapted to any defensive system.

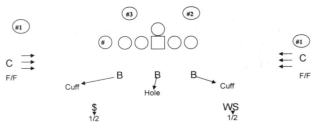

Diagram #11. Ice Coverage

This gives us a way to play pass coverage and shut down the short passing game inside and outside.

Keys to Successful Coverage

- Great funnel on the #1 receivers
- Good collisions on all inside receivers—route disruption
- Quick, deep drops by both one-half defenders
- Deeper drop by the remaining hole defender when he is not threatened

Calls/Variations

- Three-man game with a spy
- Four-man games
- Sparrow/falcon

We number the receivers as we did in the other schemes. The funnel/corner plays the same funnel technique but does not trail the #1 receiver. They funnel the #1 receiver but play a flat defender after that. They read #1 to #2 receivers. If we get the flat-fade combination by the receiver, the corner carries #1 to the sideline for seven yards and comes off looking for the #2 receiver. He rallies back to the flat, late. We give up the shallow pass and force them to move it down the field a little at a time—if they have the patience to do it.

Funnel Flat Defenders

- Read #1 to #2 route progression.

Press Alignment

- Collision and route disrupt everything from #1 outside/in.
- If #1 releases wide, carry to the sideline for seven yards before opening to #2. Rally late to anything in the flat.
- If no flat threat, carry underneath #1.

The cuff defenders can be linebackers or safeties. Their progression read is from #2 to #1. If there is no immediate threat by the #2 receiver, they get underneath the #1 receiver. If #2 goes to the flat, they run and give the illusion they are going to be the seam defender. They invite the curl route by widening. They sink under the curl and play a robber technique on the curl. They can be a factor on the dig and skinny post inside.

Cuff Defenders

- Read #2 to #1 route progressions. If no immediate threat, think #1.
- #2 flat—widen and rob #1 (curl/dig post).
- #2 vertical—collision inside/out—squeeze the release of #1 and #2.
- Look for #1 coming back underneath.
- Know where help is (safety over the top).
- #2 crosses—widen and gain depth—deliver to the hole defender.
- Get underneath #1 and rob curl/dig/post (follow flat read).
- Rally up on shallow crossing routes.

If the #2 receiver goes vertical, the cuff defender collisions the receiver and squeezes him using inside-out leverage. The corner squeezes the #1 receiver outside-in. They funnel the receivers into the half safety. After the collision on the #2 receiver, they get their eyes back to the #1 receiver. If that receiver comes back underneath, the cuff defender works back up late on him. If #2 crosses, he widens and gains depth. They still have the hole defender in the middle to help them. They deliver the cross to the hole defender and read the quarterback's eyes. The hole defender and half safety do the same thing. Their technique does not change.

Hole Defender

- Read #3 to #2 route progression—follow normal hole rules.

Half (1/2) Safeties

- Follow cover 2 rules for half coverage.

This defense worked well for us this year but we had an experienced group that could play the coverage. We had a couple of combination coverages we ran. We ran alert and siren.

Alert is coverage that is dependent on the offensive formation. This coverage enables us to get into the matching-zone coverage. They defend what the offense likes to do out of 2 x 2 sets and a 3 x 1 set. We have used this concept primarily against spread offenses that like to isolate the #1 receiver backside while running concept routes to the #3-receiver side. Our matching-zone principles apply to this coverage. The coverage is dictated by the offensive set (Diagram #12).

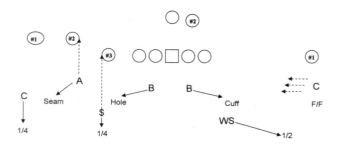

Diagram #12. Alert

Versus 2 x 2 balanced sets, we check to our cover-2 matching zone (Zorro) while a 3 x 1 set will jump to our cover-4 matching zone (thunder). The premise behind the coverage is to outman the offensive formation by at least one defender. We are able to double-team the isolated receiver with a bump-and-run corner, with safety help over the top and backer help underneath while maintaining a 4 to 3 ratio with the receiver set.

Keys to Successful Coverage

- Formation recognition and quick check to make sure everyone is on the same page
- Physical play on the isolated receiver by the cornerback
- Route disruption
- Quick progression reads by the seam and hole defenders
- Disguise scheme and mix and match safeties

Calls/Variations

- Field/strong stunts
- Key stunts

We want the corner to press or bail and give the illusion we are in cover 2. He plays quarter coverage.

Corner

- Play quarter coverage out of press/bail alignment (read #2 to #1).
- Vertical release by #1—lock on—outside/in.
- Quick cross by #1—sink and look for #2 on a vertical seam or skinny post.
- Hitch by #1—think corner by #2—rally up to #1.

The adjuster comes down in a falcon alignment and is a seam defender. He reads #2 to #3 defender and rallies to any kind of smash concept.

Adjuster

- Shift to an inside shade of #2.

Seam (4) Defender

- Read #2 to #3. Think smash concept off vertical release. Get underneath #1. (This is the only change from normal seam coverage.)

The strong safety shades the outside of the #3 receiver. That is the mismatch in this coverage because we have a linebacker on the slot receiver. We want the strong safety to help him on a vertical by the #3 receiver.

Strong Safety

- Outside shade of #3—quarter coverage (read #3 to #2).
- Vertical release from #3—lock on—outside/in.
- Shallow cross or flat from #3—sink and look up vertical (to skinny post) from #2.

The jet or Sam linebacker will be the hole defender and play his normal progression.

Jet/Sam Backer

- Hole defender (read #3 to #2). Normal hole progression reads.

The isolated receiver to the backside is the object of this coverage. We want to press him with the corner.

Corner

- Pressed coverage—cover 2 technique (funnel flat)—trail technique to the isolated receiver.

Backer

- Seam defender (get underneath #1).
- Flat release from running back—release to corner and rob #1 (curl/dig/post).
- Cross away/block away—look up #3 coming back from the concept side.
- Vertical collision inside/out and restrict passing lane for weak safety.

In this coverage, we have mixed and matched our fire and storm concepts with the ice concepts. We are playing the cuff backside and the seam and hole defenders to the strongside.

If we play the alert in a 2 x 2 set, the corners play their ice coverage (Diagram #13). The adjuster comes down in a falcon position and plays a cuff defender. The backside linebacker plays a cuff defender with normal progression read.

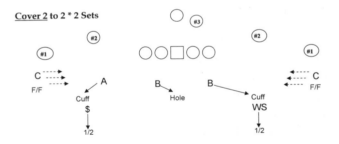

Diagram #13. Alert vs. 2 x 2

Alert Coverage Rules and Responsibilities

Corners: Pressed coverage—cover 2 technique (funnel flat). Normal progression rules for cover 2 corner

Adjuster/Weakside Backer: Shift to an outside shade of #2—cuff defenders (read #2 to #3). Think curl by #1. Normal progression rules for cuff defender.

Strong Safety/Weak Safety: Half coverage (read #2 to #1). Normal progression rules for deep one-half defender.

Backer: Hole defender (read #3 to #2). Normal progression rules for deep one-half defender.

That is our combination coverage we use against these sets. We decide at the beginning of the year who is the default. This year it was our adjuster in the falcon position. He has graduated now, and we have to find out who that player is going to be. In other years, the adjuster was more of a pass defender than a box player. In that case, sparrow was our default formation because the weak safety could play in the box.

Here is my email address on the screen. If you want to come visit our coaches, they know the defense a lot better than I do. Come see us?we are always open.

Steve Specht
600 North Bend Road
Cincinnati, OH 45224
(513) 761-7600
sspecht@stxavier.org

ADJUSTMENTS IN THE 3-4 DEFENSIVE FRONTS

Arrowhead High School, Wisconsin

It is an honor to speak at this year's clinic. I have been a big fan of Earl Browning and his *Coach of the Year Clinics Football Manual*. In fact, my collection of these clinic manuals dates back to 1977.

For the past 26 years, I have been the head football coach and defensive coordinator at Arrowhead High School in Hartland, Wisconsin. Hartland is a town located 20 miles west of Milwaukee on the road to Madison. Arrowhead is one of the largest public high schools in Wisconsin.

This fall, we won the 2007 Division I state football championship with a perfect 14-0 record. During the past 15 years, we have set a state record in Division I football by playing in eight state championship games. We have won four state football championships, and we have four state runner-up places to our credit. In addition, we have produced a large number of major college football players, including the 2007 University of Wisconsin quarterback Tyler Donovan, their offensive MVP who was one of three former Arrowhead football players to start this year in the Big Ten Conference.

We have run the 3-4 defense at Arrowhead for all 26 of my years there. We believe in the 3-4 defense and feel that it is a great defensive scheme for all levels of football, from the NFL to the lowest-level youth program.

I first learned the 3-4 defense from my college football coach, Dave Hochtritt, who now works in the Canadian Football League. Over the years, a great number of outstanding college football coaches have shared their ideas on the 3-4 defense with us. I would like to credit Ken Donahue, Gary Moeller, Lloyd Carr, Greg Mattison, Charlie McBride, Bob Elliott, Barry Alvarez, and Bret Bielema for their help in building our defensive package.

We love the 3-4 defense for the following reasons:

- It is extremely flexible.
- It is sound versus all offensive schemes.
- It is simple to teach.
- Most high school football players can master it.
- It is easy to align properly on every play.
- You get your best athletes on the field.
- You get more speed on the field.
- Size, up front, is nice but not required.
- You can easily play multiple secondary coverages.
- It has stood the test of time.

This clinic talk will pertain to the front seven players in our 3-4 defense. I realize that time constraints do not allow me to go into our secondary-coverage package, but you can use any and all secondary coverages with the 3-4 defense. The reason for this is that both outside linebackers must have the ability to pass drop. This certainly adds to your defensive flexibility.

We begin each football season by lining up our 3-4 defense against two tight ends. We use a very simple call system that works like this (Diagram #1). First, we use a color to call the secondary coverage. Then, we use a number to describe the defensive front alignment, and then we tag the stunt if we have a stunt called. An example might be *red 70*.

In this defense, everyone lines up nose-to-nose and toes-to-toes. The outside linebackers align in a tight 6 technique, the defensive tackles align in a 4 technique, the noseguard plays a 0 technique, and the two inside linebackers align in a 20 technique four yards off the ball. This gives us a great starting point in which we begin to play three basic blocks regardless of the backfield set. These three blocks

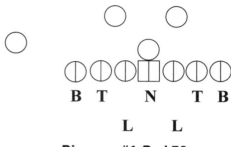

Diagram #1. Red 70

will dominate our initial practice segments all year. These blocks are:

- Hook block
- Down block
- Base block

We feel if we can play these three blocks well, up front, that we will win a lot of football games.

We believe if we are effective in our base 70 odd-man front, we have the potential to be a great defensive football team because we could play this defense against everything our opponent has. The key to this call is having a great two-gap noseguard. Nick Hayden, a 6'5", 275 pound, U.S. Army All American for us in 2003 was that kind of player. He became a three-year starter for the Wisconsin Badgers and should be drafted this spring into the NFL. The trouble is that you do not get too many U.S. Army All Americans, so you have to adjust your base package.

The way we begin to adjust our 70 package is to add the word *tight* to the call, making the call 70 tight (Diagram #2). The word *tight* tells the defensive tackles to shade their alignments to the inside of the offensive tackle and take responsibility for the B gap.

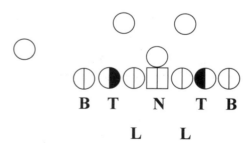

Diagram #2. Red 70 Tight

All other alignments remain the same. The inside linebackers are now responsible for the C gaps. The 70 tight is a great defensive call to protect your inside linebackers and control the inside run game.

Once we have mastered these two basic front calls, we begin to introduce the angle defense into our 3-4 package. This is our movement package, and the linemen love it. They get to run around blocks now. Instead of being hit, they can really hit the gaps with their quickness. The front seven alignments remain the same. We just call it *70 angle* (Diagram #3). We can angle wherever we want. If the code call is 72, we will angle the front right.

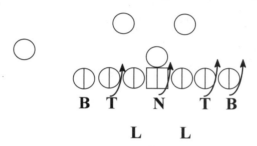

Diagram #3. 72 Angle Right

The important thing to remember is that by the code, we can angle anywhere and everywhere we want to angle our front. This was a big part of this year's defensive package. We were smaller and quicker than usual.

Combining the 70, 70 tight, and 70 angle calls gives you a great defensive package against any offensive scheme. It is sound versus the spread, excellent against the power I, great against the wing-T shifts. We simply teach fundamentally-sound football each week and improve our basic 3-4 defense that way.

Now that the basic package is in, we begin to add the extras for the future playoff run. We start outside in. Sometimes our front seven need to play a wider shade alignment rather than the tighter head-up base alignment (Diagram #4). We get to that part of our 3-4 defense by making a *50 call*.

Now, the defensive tackles move out into wider 5-technique alignments, and the outside linebackers move out to wide 9-technique alignments. We are

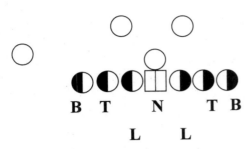

Diagram #4. 50 Call

weaker up the middle but have great outside-in leverage on the ball. This call is also sound regardless of the offensive formation your opponent presents you with.

The next adjustment we make is to call 50 eagle (Diagram #5). This is the most common odd-man front defense used today. What we do is reduce the front to the split-end side and play the basic 50 front to the tight-end side.

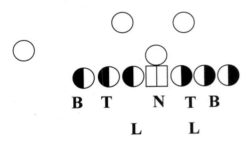

Diagram #5. 50 Eagle

By reducing the split-end side, we cover up the weakside inside linebacker, and with the proper secondary call, we can make him a fast-flow runner to the tight-end side. Reverse the secondary-support call and the tight-end side inside linebacker can become a fast-flow runner to the split-end side. Either way, you have given the offense a problem without much expense to the defense.

If offensive teams are able to split out an end and still hurt you with the inside run game, we make a *70 tight eagle* call (Diagram #6). Now, we combine a couple of previous calls to get into a loaded inside-run defense. We reduce the split-end side defense to a 2i-technique defensive tackle and a 5-technique outside linebacker.

To the tight-end side, we play a 4i defensive tackle and a 6-technique outside linebacker. We are

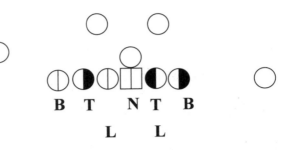

Diagram #6. 70 Tight Eagle

extremely strong up the middle and our inside linebackers are very well-protected.

When teams are very balanced in their ability to run the ball to both the tight-end side or the split-end side with equal success (which I have found over the years to be very rare), we run our 50 stack package (Diagram #7). In this package, we take our splitside outside linebacker and stack him over their offensive tackle.

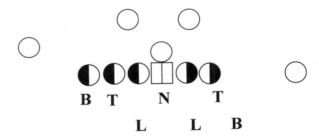

Diagram #7. 50 Stack

This alignment makes it almost impossible to run the ball inside to the split-end side. You have to either take the ball outside with the option or run the ball to the tight-end side. The problem for the offense in this case is that the splitside inside linebacker is a fast-flow runner on run to the tight-end side. He is very hard to nearly impossible to cut off on running plays to the tight-end side.

So in review, we have built a multiple 3-4 defensive package with just a few slight adjustments up front. The great thing about this defensive package is that nobody up front moved his alignment more than one man over. We now have an excellent two-tight-end defensive package that can also adjust quickly and effortlessly to a wide-open spread offense. In fact, that is exactly what happened to us in our 2007 state championship game.

Now that we have the basic 3-4 front packages installed, we can begin to add stunts to our fronts. Having run the same defensive package for so many years, we have about a hundred different stunts that we have tags for, and we can select from all of them. I will show you a couple outside and a couple inside stunts that we use.

Lloyd Carr once told me the best stunt in football and the hardest stunt to protect against is to have the openside 9-technique outside linebacker who has been pass dropping all day to rush (Diagram #8). We call this stunt *70 knife*.

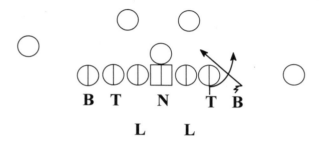

Diagram #8. 70 Knife

We love this stunt out of our 70 package because the offensive tackle never knows if the 4-technique defensive tackle is going inside or outside of him because of our angle defense.

We charge the outside linebacker hard at the quarterback's shoulder as he drops back to pass. We like to look for the blindside strip if we can get it. Either way, we like to hit the quarterback high and hard. The defensive tackle is slow out of his stance and loops behind the outside linebacker to provide containment.

The complementary stunt to 70 knife is *50 Texas* (Diagram #9). In the stunt, we jet rush the 5-technique defensive tackle upfield hard and he provides outside containment for the quarterback.

Once he goes, we bring the outside linebacker right under his hard upfield charge. This stunt is great versus a reach-and-pick protection type of blocking scheme.

I will show you a couple of great inside linebacker stunts out of our 50-eagle reduction package that really hurt the tight-end side run or

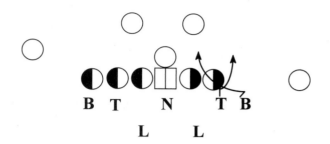

Diagram #9. 50 Texas

pass game. The first is quite simple and involves a gap exchange between the inside linebacker and the noseguard (Diagram #10). We call it 50 eagle X. It is a great stunt versus full-zone scheme offenses. This stunt normally frees up the crossing inside linebacker more often than not.

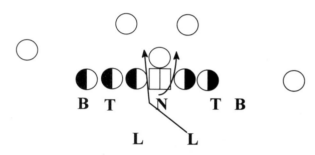

Diagram #10. 50 Eagle X

We also stunt both inside linebackers if need be to the tight-end side of the offense by calling 50 eagle bang (Diagram #11).

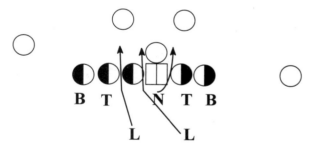

Diagram #11. 50 Eagle Bang

I could go on for hours talking football with you, but my time is almost up and I would really like to thank you for taking the time out of your day to attend this clinic. Football is a great game, and I appreciate all of you for your efforts in helping the youth of America enjoy football as we do. Thank you.

Jason Vandermaas

THE SIMPLICITY OF THE 3-5 DEFENSE

Carman-Ainsworth High School, Michigan

I want to give you a quick overview of some of the things we do at Carman-Ainsworth, and then I am going to let my defensive coordinator, David Johnson, come up and talk about the details of the 3-5 defense.

I have been a head coach for six years. The last five years, I was at Croswell-Lexington, and this past year, I got the job at Carman-Ainsworth. I was hired late in the year, so we had a tough time installing everything. We struggled to a 2-7 record, but it was not because of our defense, which actually played very, very well. We do have some work to do on offense.

We had success with our 3-5 defense this past year and the year before at Croswell-Lexington where we originated our scheme. Our defensive coordinator over there was Rick Patterson who is here today, and he will answer some of your questions. Rick really instituted the defense. We had five shutouts with it that year, and our kids had a lot of fun playing it.

If you ask any kid why he plays football in high school, he will say he plays because it is fun. The majority of players want to have fun, and I think that is what you should base your program on. Certainly, having fun can mean winning football games.

When I first started coaching, I tried to coach like somebody else. I tried to copy what I saw other coaches doing, thinking that must be the right way to do things. But I have come to realize that is not the way to go about it. I think that you have to stay true to your beliefs and coach your personality. When you coach like someone else, your kids will read through that.

As part of my basic philosophy, I believe that you have to find out what your kids do well. We only have

a small amount of time to really work with them, so why not take advantage of what they do well?

Also, everyone knows that KISS means to *Keep It Simple, Stupid*, but I think you have to find a happy medium in that. You cannot keep things too simple, but you can also lose games by outthinking yourself.

Especially in the things we are trying to do, fundamentals are extremely important. Every day you need to work on fundamentals and be willing to sacrifice a win or two at the freshman level, if necessary, to become fundamentally sound. The coaches at that level cannot focus on winning to the extent that time is not spent on blocking drills and tackling drills. You can win a freshman game at our school by running a reverse because we have some speed, but that is not going to necessarily give you success when those kids get to the varsity level. We have to remember that the whole goal of the program is for success on Friday nights, and if you can get everybody to buy into that, you will be successful much sooner.

In the off-season, we will have staff meetings periodically, but I try to have a seniors meeting at least once a month. That meeting is just with me and the seniors, and it is kind of an open forum. I buy them breakfast, and they come in and I can find out what they are thinking. We bounce ideas off each other and think about ways we can improve the program.

In the off-season, we will lift Monday through Thursday. We do a lot of Olympic lifts and multipoint lifts. We do not focus on a lot of the old traditional lifts that people have done in the past.

It is important to get the kids started young. A lot of young kids, especially freshman, are intimidated about coming into the weight room, particularly when the seniors are lifting a lot more than they can lift. We might have a different lifting session for those kids this summer so they can get more acquainted. We might bring some older kids in and let them get more comfortable so we can get them in earlier.

During the summer, we will run a team camp. We will bring three or four teams in and really get a lot done in two or three days. By the way, we still have one opening for this summer if any of you are interested.

Fundraising is a necessary evil that every coach has to work on, especially in today's climate of insufficient school funds. I have had a number of different things that have worked, and each coach has to find out what will work best in his school community. There are a number of programs out there, including cards, mailings, and other such things that we have had success with, but it is something that everybody needs to do, and you just have to find out what works for you.

At Croswell-Lexington, college coaches were not exactly knocking down the door at such a small farming community, so I did not have to deal with recruiting issues there. Carman-Ainsworth, however, is a little bit different. Because of the expectations and some of the things that come up, I have to have a plan for dealing with recruiting and with college recruiters.

Every kid wants a personal highlight film now, so we try to put that together for them. We now have a spring meeting with incoming freshmen and all of our parents to discuss the recruiting process. All of that is necessary, but it takes a lot of time too, and we have to have a plan going into it.

Now, I want to get into today's topic. Our 3-5 defense has its origins at Croswell-Lexington. Three years ago, we were running a 50 defense and going from a 5-3 to a 5-2. We were having a lot of trouble stopping people, and we were involved in a lot of high-scoring games.

Going into 2006, we had a lot of linebacker, "tweener" type of kids. We did not have a lot of defensive linemen and we did not have a lot of size, but we did have a lot of athletes. We discussed our situation, talked about the 3-5 defense, and then tried it out at camp.

We really liked what was happening. The kids were having a lot of fun with it, and that was what was most important to me. They were encouraged by it, and it was a pretty easy learning process, so we became a 3-5 team.

We like the defense because it lets you take advantage of your athletes. It allows you to put your best players on the field. We already wanted to do that on offense, so it matched our philosophy there. It puts your best players in a place where they can be successful. They can be aggressive, and they do not need to think a lot.

It was simple to implement. We sat down and applied some of the things we knew and just plugged in our own terminology. We started it out as a gap-control system, and then we evolved from there to use a few different wrinkles.

Each year, we have to evaluate what worked well and what did not, and then change things up to better meet the athletes that we have. We always want to put the kids we have into the best position to be successful.

Now, I want to bring up our defensive coordinator, David Johnson, and let him discuss the details of our 3-5 defense. Also, when we finish, we will stick around and make ourselves available to answer any questions that you may have.

David Johnson

Thank you, Coach. I believe you have to have a passion for what you are doing. When we implemented the defense, it was something simple, the kids picked it up, they understood it, and they were excited about it. When they saw how simple it was, they felt they could really get into it—they could let their athleticism and abilities show and be successful in it. That is what we wanted the defense to do.

Our defensive philosophy is centered around constantly and consistently attacking the offense.

We want to make sure that the offense cannot get a good read on what we are doing. Some people say that we live and die with the blitz, but it is not always a blitz.

We have our front three coming, and then there is always a fourth. We want to make sure we are getting pressure on the quarterback and on the running game, and with three guys coming every time, it is not going to happen. Three against five or three against six puts you at a disadvantage, so if we can line it up and have that fourth person coming, that is just a four-man front coming at you from different angles.

Of course, we are going to have two or three more guys coming from other positions on the field, and that would be a blitz. So when you hear *live and die with the blitz*, it is not always a blitz that is coming—it is just that fourth person.

It is a point of emphasis with our players that they have to be extremely aggressive. We are going to go a hundred miles an hour. If our guys know it is simple and they know what their responsibilities are, then they can be expected to do that without worrying about complicated responsibilities. This is an aggressive attack defense.

Players are to get to their responsibilities immediately, without being tied down by too much thinking. They come hard to their gap read, but after that first step, they just play ball. They take that first step, but once they see the play, they just react from there. It is all about the attitude and confidence with which they play.

In our 3-5 concept, we want to eliminate reading and reacting. We could line up in a head-up position and think two gaps, but we do not want to play two gaps. As Coach Vandermaas pointed out, it is a one-gap responsibility, so each player is responsible for just one gap, and they have to trust each other and play as a team. In the film, you will see that even when a player makes a bad read and goes to the wrong gap, the player behind him sees it and covers it up.

This defense is going to set the tempo for the game. Many of our opponents will script their offensive plays to start the game. After seeing us on film, they get an idea of what they are going to see, but starting with our first play, we are going to come out and put real pressure on them. In our 3-5 set, we will have someone coming from somewhere that they do not know about, so then we feel that we have evened the field.

The offense knows exactly what they want to do. The receivers, running backs, and linemen know exactly where they have to go to block. The defense really is reacting. If we sit and have to think about it, rather than simply react, that can be the difference between a one-, two-, or three-yard gain. On the other hand, when we know which gap we are attacking, and we know the player behind us will cover for us, then we can set the tempo, make a play, cause a pile, or create some kind of advantage for our defense.

We want to make sure the offense is adjusting to us. When the offense first sees a 3-5 front, they may think they can run all over it because they see only three down linemen, but once the ball is snapped and we get our guys moving, the offense may get a little confused. They do not know who is backing off and who is coming, so now, they have to go through the first series, make sure the headphones are working with the coaches upstairs, and ask a lot of questions. We want to be able to force the offense to adjust to our defense.

We know that mistakes will be made, but we sell our kids on the belief that we will be okay as long as we are playing hard. As long as we play hard, we have the capacity to cover for each other and still make plays.

We will not harp on and scream at players who make mistakes because that tends to intimidate them, and it destroys their confidence. We try to eliminate all the pressure and just let them play and have fun with it.

Now, this is a flexible defense, and it can easily be converted into different sets. It is essentially a 50 front in which you take the ends and step them back, put them in space, and give them the opportunity to make plays. By moving people around just a little, we can easily give a 4-4 look, a 4-3 look, or a 3-4 look as well.

In selecting personnel, we want to put emphasis on speed over size. Size is great, but the kids we get here are a little quicker, a little faster, and not so big, so we want a defense that will allow us to make speed one of our strengths.

We took a running back who stood 5'4" and put him at one of our *dog* positions, which is like a strong safety in most defenses. He was an aggressive hitter, he was fast, and he was smart, so the move worked to our advantage.

We had a very strong linebacker who put on a little weight, and we ended up moving him to defensive tackle. He became an outstanding player for us. These are just two examples of our being able to utilize the "tweener" type of kids in our 3-5 package.

This defense gives us the ability to have multiple personnel groupings for various defensive packages. With us, we can match offensive personnel groupings, either by substitution or by moving individuals around within the grouping that is on the field, without making substitutions. That gives us an advantage in the game. Because of the versatility of our players, we can make adjustments by moving kids within the defense rather than bringing different players into the game, and thereby tipping our hand about what kind of defense we are going to be in.

Of course, we look for certain characteristics in players at each position. With our nose man, we want to have one of two types of players, and if you have them both, it is great because you can mix it up and wear a team down with them. We either want a big kid who is a two-gap player and will demand a double-team block, or we can play with that small, quick, wrestler type of player?a guy who understands he has to stay low and move because he is small. He will command the double-team block because he is able to shoot through the gap. The smaller nose man can disrupt an offense, while the bigger, stronger nose man is more of an anchor point type of guy.

Our tackles are what you might call "typical" defensive linemen. They are strong guys. They have to be able to recognize the run when it is directed at them and take on blocks. They have to be able to hold their gap versus the double-team block. Some people teach their tackles to sit down when they are double-teamed, but we do not teach that. You cannot make plays when you are on the ground, so we try to fight harder, push back out, and hold our gap. We can still make a play even if we do not make the tackle.

Our tackles must also recognize passing situations and be able to force the pocket if a pass develops, but they can still react to draw plays or runs if they develop instead. They might not always make the tackle, but they might still make the play.

We want to have a tackle on the weakside who is strong enough to win in a 1-on-1 situation, and we expect a lot of pressure from that position. The linebacker we moved to tackle is a good example of the type of player we need on the weakside.

Our Will linebacker normally lines up on the weakside, but we can change that up if we want him playing to the wideside. He needs to be a sure tackler. He must also be a strong kid who can take on a lead block, but fast enough to cover a #3 receiver in man coverage.

Our Mike linebacker is bigger and stronger, and he has to stop the middle. He has to meet things head on, and be able to attack the line of scrimmage. We did a lot of things with him—including a lot of blitz stuff—but his main responsibility is to come downhill from tackle to tackle and make plays.

His gap responsibility is determined by the defense called, but he never thinks to drop back in pass unless there is nobody in the backfield and he does not have a stunt called. He would step down and look for draw first, and then he would drop back in the middle, looking for any crosses. Mostly, he runs stunts with the tackles and the nose, and he is a run stopper.

The Sam linebacker definitely aligns to the strongside, and he is our best tackler. He is strong enough to step up in the hole and take on pulling guards. He is the one who will come clean because of what our line does in front of him. They should keep him clean so he can scrape and flow to the ball.

Our dog linebackers line up out in the flat at a depth of five yards. They are four yards off the line of scrimmage, unless you have a twins or trips set. At that point, we will put them maybe two yards inside of their receivers.

Their responsibility is run. They are that extra man for the run coming that way, but they also have to be able to recognize the pass. They are the strong safety/linebacker type of players. The guys who play the position for us are often the "tweeners" who really want to play, are sure tacklers, and are able to recognize quickly whether it is run or pass. The size of the player is not a limiting factor at this position.

In the secondary, we coach our cornerbacks to play both sides. We want each guy to be a complete corner, which means being able to cover the pass, support the run, and tackle. It also helps if he can catch the football.

In zone coverage, our corners line up with the outside foot up so they can see the zone, but if it is man-to-man, we teach inside foot up, because now we are focused on the man. For corners, it is pass first and run second, and they must have enough discipline to stay focused during the whole game.

Our linebackers stunt a lot and have a lot of fun while all the cornerbacks do is cover, so they might tend to get a little bored back there. They have to stay focused and disciplined enough to play man when it is man and zone when it is zone.

The free safety is probably going to be the smartest kid in our secondary. He is a good tackler and a kid who can recognize a play as it is developing. He is back 10 to 12 yards, and he is reading the quarterback. He is to the strength in certain defenses, and if we have a two roll where it is two over weak, he will line up on the weakside, but he is always able to read the quarterback.

He should be the second wave of defense right behind our linebackers. On sweeps, he should fill the alley immediately and get into position to help the picket fence and help control the gaps. He has to be a good tackler.

Our base coverage is cover 3. Our corners and safety are deep, our dogs are in the flat, and our backers are underneath in the windows.

In cover 2, we implement our 3-4 look up front. Both dogs become the rolled-up corners, the safety takes one side, and one of the backers that stepped out is a safety on the other. So now, you have your 3-4 cover 2 look.

Our 3-5 cover 2 over is what we call the *roll*. We will line up in a 3-5 for the quarterback to get his pre-snap read, and then we will roll the safety over to one side. The corner on that side will now sit and take the flat, and the safety will roll over top of him.

The backside corner takes the backside half, and the dog up on the line becomes the flat player. We have three down linemen, three linebackers, two dogs, and the corners and safety rolled to one side. That is our 3-5 cover 2 over.

The one thing we want to do is give you the same look on each play. That is part of our masking of the defense—part of our surprise. Part of our aggression is giving you the same look so you do not know what to expect from your pre-snap read. When the ball is snapped, that is when everything happens. Complete confusion gives us an opportunity to level the playing field.

Our cover 2 spy is what some people call the *robber*. Both corners will drop and cover halves, the safety steps down, spies any digs or runs, and takes away any mid-level route. Both dogs then become our flat players. That is cover 2 spy.

Cover 1 is man-to-man. Against twins, the dog covers #2, the corner covers #1, and the safety is free. Against trips, the dog covers #2, the corner covers #1, and the safety can roll over on #3, or the Will linebacker can cover #3 so the safety can still be free. That is our choice, but we really prefer to cover #3 with Will and keep our safety in the middle.

Cover 0 is pure man, and our kids love it. Everybody has a man, and those who do not are able to blitz. Against a pro set, the corners cover the wides, the safety covers the tight end, and everybody else can blitz. The only thing is, if a back flares out to your side when you are coming, you have to pick him up. Our kids want to run cover 0 every time.

Now, I want to draw up a couple of sets against different formations so you can understand some of the things I was talking about. We will start by looking at what we call twins (Diagram #1). The backers are five yards off, and they are almost in a stack. I labeled them all as backers and not as Sam and Will because we have not dictated where the strength is. Normally, if we are looking at it like this, our strength would be to the left side because a lot of teams we play have right-handed quarterbacks.

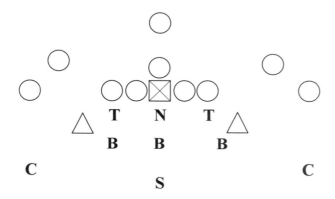

Diagram #1. 3-5 Defense vs. Twins

The corners are at seven yards deep in an outside shade if this is cover 3. Our dogs are normally at five and four off the last man on the line of scrimmage, but because we have twins out here, we will put them at five and one or five and two on the inside, looking for the quick slant. The quick slant normally comes from the split end with the slot running on out.

The quarterback will read the dog, and the minute he drops off, he will hit the slant in the seam and he is gone. So, when we say look for the quick slant, we mean to look for the #1 receiver. The inside slant will be picked up by the backer. This is our base defense versus the twins formation.

If we are going to line it up versus trips, the safety will shade that way (Diagram #2). The bigger

threat is the three receivers to one side. On the backside, this corner is still an outside shade in our cover 3, but he will be able to squeeze this a little bit more because the safety is helping over here.

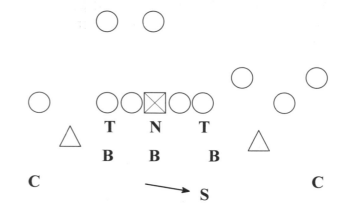

Diagram #2. 3-5 Defense vs. Trips

Also, this Sam backer will be able to help underneath. It is his responsibility to get out there and recognize the quick slant. The strong corner is in an outside shade, and the dog is on the inside of the #2 receiver.

Now, this will set up the offense to say we can *run the quick bubble screen*. Our backer is always looking at #3, so when he flares, he is ready to go right now. The safety helps over top, and we still have four versus three.

That backer to the trips side is always going to help with the quick slant from here to here and with any runs going that way. This is our help, but we can send the Sam backer and cover with Mike. We are not going to give away anything. When you step out to see us, everything looks the same. We can also get in an *over* look, especially if the ball is on the hash, because we really do not like cover 3 against trips in that situation.

I want to draw up a stunt or two before I finish. We run a pinch, a slant, an angle, and a pinch out. When they hear that, the linemen know automatically where they are going, and the backers know what gap they have. This is a gap-controlled offense, so in our base defense, he will go outside, and the nose can go to strength or he can go opposite (Diagram #3). We were set on going to strength every time, but then Coach noticed that when we called this, the nose would go to strength every time. That is a tendency he picked up on, so now you can switch it up, and we did. We went with *base opposite*, so then the nose would go opposite. Our dogs have outside, and you can see our gap responsibility.

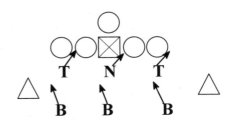

Diagram #3. 3-5 Defense Base Stunts

If we go to a pinch defense, these guys will pinch to the inside, and then the backers will go to the outside. If strength is to the right, our nose goes to the right, and the middle backer goes to the left.

On the slant and angle stunts, we slant everybody one way, and the backers are responsible for the opposite gaps. It is a gap-control defense.

We ended up running gaps with double dogs and cover 1. The defensive linemen are stepping down for their gaps, and the inside linebackers are stepping back for pass. We can call slant double-dog cover 1 or slant weak-dog Sam fire, and every gap is still accounted for. As I said before, it is a gap-control defense. Now, I want to show you some film.

That about does it. We will be around to answer any questions. Thank you.

THE SUPER POWER RUNNING GAME

Wilmington Area High School, Pennsylvania

Today, I plan to show you the main series that we run out of the wing-T, which we call the *super power series*. To begin with, we believe in multiple formations. Years back, we ran the wing-T, but you probably could not have identified it as the wing-T. We were basic—out of one formation?and although we did well then, I do not think we could get away with that today. We are now a multiple-formation offense, but we run the same plays.

Today, especially with the wing-T, you need something different, and that is what we want to show you today. You do not often see people that run the wing-T running this little toss power play that we have. Furthermore, the other series is somewhat different than the way I have seen anybody else run the buck series.

What I want to start with are some of the formations we use. We will run the slot to one side, with a tight end and wing on the other side. *Red* means tight end right, and *blue* means tight end left. We also love to run two tight ends and two wings to balance things out, and we can run a double-slot look. As long as we have one slot, one wing, or one man in the backfield, we can run this play. Coach Copper is going to go over the main play, which is what we call super power, and then I will come in and go over a few of the counter plays off it.

You need to realize that this is just one play. Now, defenses can stop any one play, but in doing so, they may not be able to stop the counters off it or the other plays that complement it. Keep that in mind. We run all kinds of different formations and several different things, but we still run this one play.

We even run the play from the shotgun set. I believe that as long as you have the fundamentals and the blocking is the same, you can do many

different things. We have done that over the years. Obviously, you have to have some athletes, but I think you can still beat some of the better teams when you are just an average team if you have a good program, and that is what I think the wing-T is.

Now, Coach Copper will go over the super power play with you, and then I will come back up and show you how we block some of the counters off it.

Coach Copper

Super power, for us, is our number-one play. It is our bread-and-butter play. We have an attitude about it, and we impress that upon our kids—all the way down to the junior high level. We are determined that we can make it work in any situation. Our kids believe that it does not matter what the situation, super power will get us out of trouble and, as coaches, we take that seriously too.

We are flexible with our formations that we can run the play from. We are only going to show it to you out of our red formation, but we can run it from essentially every formation we have (Diagram #1). There are many options for us as far as formations go. It does not really change a lot of the blocking for the kids, so it is not that tough.

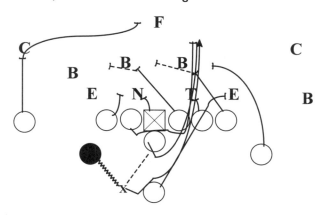

Diagram #1. Red 32 Super Power vs. Even Front

I am showing it first to the tight-end side versus an even look, and as I draw it, I want to point out the details of the assignments. Starting with the center and going all the way out to the wing, the basic blocking rule is simply one word: *down*. It is not that simple, and I will explain, but they are all down.

We have a 1 technique, and our center blocks back on him. The guard has the same rule, but the nose man is not exactly down from him, so we want him to take a path. We are not telling him to take a man, but we want him to take a path so if the nose stunts to his side of the center, he will pick him up. He is not actually going for him, but as he takes that path down, if the nose shows or a backer blitzes through and comes onto his path, he picks him up. That is really the idea for all of these blockers.

Our tackle comes down on the defensive tackle because he is down from him, but the tight end has the same thing as the guard. He is coming down and taking a path that, if that tackle slants out and crosses his path, he picks him up.

Here is one of those little things that some people may overlook when running this play. If the defensive tackle is able to shed our tackle, we do not want our tight end going for the playside backer. This play is a pitch, and maybe that action makes the defense think we are going outside, but the backers are going to be moving, and our tight end would probably not get the playside backer anyway. The pulling people coming through are the ones who will probably end up on him. We want the tight end to help with the tackle if needed. However, if the tackle does not come on his path, he continues to the backside, looking for the backside backer.

The wingback comes down also, as tight as possible off the defensive end, and he will probably get that playside backer. We do not want him to go inside of the end because we are going to be kicking him out. The defensive end is probably going to close down because the tight end in front of him went down, so he is probably not going to be there anyway. But you will see a couple of plays on the film where the defensive end just stood there, and our wingback ended up blocking inside of him. Normally, that will not be the case.

We have a kick-out on that end with our fullback. That will occur more to the inside because that end should be closing down. However, having said that, the kick-out is not what opens up the hole. We are expecting the kick-out block will occur more to the inside of the defensive end's alignment, so the hole is opened by the down blocks.

We have to move the inside people. We are not expecting the fullback to bury an end if he is closing down like he is supposed to be doing. If they do not close their ends, they will not stop the play anyway. Against teams that are good, they will close it down, and we have to get the movement on the tackle. The play opens by controlling the front four, not by blocking the linebackers. The backers usually take themselves out of the play, and they are not our primary concern.

The guard is pulling, and he is coming up through the hole—inside the kick-out block. He is told to go up inside through the first hole that he sees, and that might not necessarily be the hole that the ballcarrier will come through. Usually it is, but the pulling player really needs to get up in the hole and get out of the way of the ballcarrier. If he cannot find somebody to block, he should just keep running, but get off the tracks.

We send our back in motion, and we get our pitch. It is important that the back cannot come back too far because the backside defensive end would have a chance to run him down from behind. We have our tackle pull-checking for the pulling guard, which means that he turns his shoulders too, comes down the line, and cuts off anything coming inside where that pulling guard left. That means that the defensive end could conceivably come off the edge and catch our back from behind if he gets too deep on his motion. That did not happen one time this year because our kids were getting back to about three-and-a-half yards, getting that ball, planting, and going straight up into the hole.

After the quarterback pitches the ball, he is also pulling and getting up through the hole. We have run the play for about 10 years, and we have never had a quarterback get hurt leading up through the hole. He really does not have to knock anybody down. What he has to do is get up through the hole and get in the way. It is kind of like a wedge off-tackle, and if there are bodies in the way, you cannot make a play, and we will let our back figure that out.

The last thing I would point out about the running back involves the plant. He is coming in motion back to about three-and-a-half yards, he is planting, and he is coming up to the line. Where? We really do not know. It is a big mess in there, but the cutback is huge on this play.

Everybody is going to the right for us, and the backers are on the move. That is why we do not want the tight end picking up the linebacker. He is going to be moving, and the backside linebacker is going to be moving, and there is not much left. We tell our kids to always look for the cutback.

We do not want them to round it off as they make the catch. When they catch the ball, we want them to plant, and then head straight up the hole. When we show the film, you will get the idea of how quickly these players are getting up there, and they will never be caught by that end.

Now, the next one I am going to show you is against the same look, but now, we are going to the shortside (Diagram #2). This is 38 super power, and although we have lost one of our down blockers because we are going away from the tight end, we are gaining an extra puller because we are going to pull the guard and the tackle from the backside.

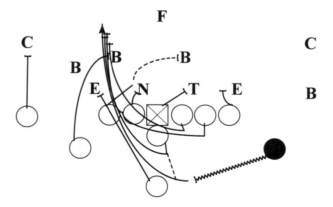

Diagram #2. Red 38 Super Power vs. Even Front

The center blocks back. He has further to go this time to get to the 3 technique, but that is where his rule takes him. The guard blocks down on the nose, and we have the same idea with the tackle where he is taking a path down that will pick up the nose if he gets into that path. This is the key block on the play: *blocking inside movement*.

Now, on the kick-out block by the fullback, we have to move the nose man. That is how the hole opens. If the guard gets the nose blocked without any help, the tackle continues on to the backside. Again, he is not heading for the playside backer because he will probably be running, and the pulling people will get him.

It is the same idea with the wing. He comes tight off the defensive end and inside to the first thing that shows in his path. The backside guard pulls up through the hole and blocks the first wrong-colored jersey. The backside tackle also pulls up through the hole, and he blocks the first guy he comes to.

By pulling two from the backside, we leave a good hole so the tight end has to pull-check from his position all the way down to the center. That leaves the only problem being the outside linebacker, who could get up on the line and time his blitz to get to the back. Our backs have to do a good job with their motion, not get too deep, plant, and get up in the hole.

The fullback does his kick-out on the defensive end, and the quarterback will pitch, turn, get up through the hole, and find somebody. That covers the play run both ways against the even front.

I want to show you what this looks like against the odd front because that does change things a little (Diagram #3). Our tackle and end are a lot closer to each other. I want to point that out first.

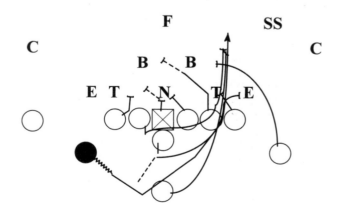

Diagram #3. Red 32 Super Power vs. Odd Front

First, the center has to bump the nose man. His rule is down, but we want him to bump that nose man first. The guard comes down, and he is ultimately responsible for that nose, but if we get penetration from the nose man, our pulling guard is done. That is why we tell the center before he blocks down that he has to check that nose man. He steps off, gets a piece of the nose, and then blocks down. It could be the backer coming through, but otherwise, it is all the way back to that tackle. If the backer walks up on the line and shows blitz, then the center makes a call that lets the guard know the center cannot help him now, and the guard is on his own.

It is the same exact idea with the tackle. He is going to bump, which is not his rule. His rule is down, but the tight end is coming down on the defensive tackle. The perfect scenario would be for the tight end to wash the tackle down alone. However, that is not always going to happen, and it is the block that matters.

The tackle has to move. If he does not, we do not have a play. We tell our tackle not to get off the block until that kid starts moving. I hope that we can get him moving and we will chip off.

It is the same assignment for the wing. He comes tight off the end inside. It is the same for our fullback with his kick-out block on the end, and it is the same for the guard who is pulling and getting up through. There is a big gap between the nose and the tackle. There is a good chance there will be an open window there.

The backside tackle has a pull-check, more than likely on the defensive tackle, but we do not tell him he has a certain man.

The back comes in motion. The quarterback pitches and gets up through that hole. The back plants, and he gets up through the hole.

The last set I will show you is red 38 super power against the odd front (Diagram #4). There are several changes on this play. We do different things to block it than we do on any other play.

Everybody's rule is down, but since it is a 50, the center will bump the nose man before he blocks his rule. The left guard is coming down. Ideally, our left

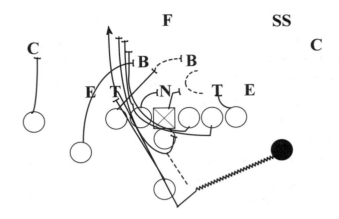

Diagram #4. Red 38 Super Power Short vs. Odd Front

tackle is also coming down and blocking inside on the backer, and we could just send our wing down on that tackle. That is not a very good match-up, so the tackle will help him, and it will be a double-team block if we are going to do it this way.

We might choose instead to *on* block, which means our tackle single blocks the tackle, and the wing will forget trying to help on him and block down inside. Everybody will then on block on the other side, and we still kick-out the end.

We can also forget kicking out the end, and, instead, bring the fullback to kick-out the tackle. We would call that 38 super power short. We have probably done it that way the most, and we have had success doing it that way.

Those are two examples of ways to change up the blocking for us. You can see that they are all the same ideas, we just tinker with a couple of things here or there, and it really helps us out.

The standard way to run it would be to double the tackle—hopefully moving him out—and still get the kick-out with the end, two pullers, and a pull-check by the tight end. All the rest is the same.

We are going to make this play go in every game, and our kids have an attitude about it. Of course, we do have counters to it, and that is what Coach Verrelli is going to talk about now.

Coach Verrelli

The first counter that we like to use to balance off our super power play is what we call *Sally*. Now, when Delaware runs the play, they pass block. They step back and do all that, but that never worked for us. College teams pass a lot, and they are all geared up to rush the passer. I tried that years ago and nobody rushed. We were pass blocking, and nobody rushed. Obviously, it was not a good play for us, so we decided to use the same type of blocking. We decided to use the same rule that we used on super power and just block down.

We come with the motion as if we are running super power, which is what everybody is expecting, and we are actually coming back to where the motion came from with our counter (Diagram #5). The center and guard will block using their down rules. As the tackle comes down, he is checking the guard, and if the nose loops, spins, or whatever, he helps the guard get him out of the way. If that does not develop, he continues on his path, probably to the backside linebacker.

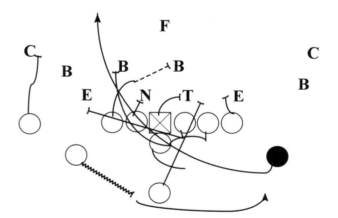

Diagram #5. Red 31 Sally at 7 vs. Even Front

The fullback comes over and fills for the pullers, and in Sally blocking, the guard has to kick out in his place. He cannot lead up through the hole as he does on super power. So everything is super-power blocking except for the fullback and the pulling guard.

The tackle pulls and leads up in the hole, and the tight end has a pull-check. The quarterback turns around, fakes the pitch, keeps moving, and then hands off to the wing coming back through. It is an inside handoff.

It is a simple counter that many teams run, but what makes it go is not necessarily how we are

blocking it. It is the play defenses are worried about the most. If the backers do not run, we do not need to run anything but super power, but if they do run, they become vulnerable to the counter.

Against the 50 look, it would be no different from what Coach Cooper was showing you on play 38 (Diagram #6). We really do not want to double that defensive tackle anyway. The rules say to block down, and the 50 tackles that we see have no respect for our tackles coming down—they just blow upfield. That is the technique they are coached to use against the run, and that is fine.

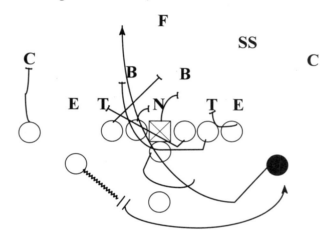

Diagram #6. Red 31 Sally at 7 vs. Odd Front

We are going to be sure to move the nose, allow no penetration, trap the tackle, and pull our tackle up through the hole. The rest of it is the same.

The other play that is on the handout is our outside super power play, which we call *31*. If people want to stop our 32 play with an even front, they have to bring that defensive end down inside. When our tight end blocks down to the inside, they have to really bring that guy down or they have a problem.

When they realize that bringing the slot in motion means we are probably running super power, they will put people in there and try to fill to our tight-end side, so we are going to run outside super power (Diagram #7). We call it 31 because of the way we number the holes.

In this case, the tight end is going to go down. That is what he does on super power, and the end usually gets kicked out. The end is tired of getting kicked out so he is closing, so then our wing comes down on him. It does not take much of a block. The hardest thing for the wing sometimes is just trying to catch him because he closes so hard.

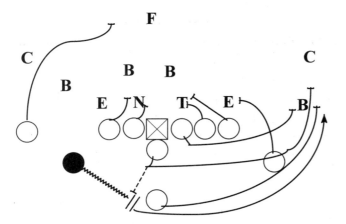

Diagram #7. Red 31 Super Power vs. Even Front

We pull the guard around the corner, and we can pull the tackle as well if there is no penetration threat. We pitch it like we do on the inside super power. The fullback is around the corner, the quarterback is around the corner, and all the backside men are fire blocking to the inside shoulders of the defensive men in their areas.

The backers will run, but they are running down the line. When we turn the corner, the hole could be anywhere. This is just another one of those plays that hurts people because they are too conscious to the inside, as we will show you on film. Thank you for your attention.

THE MULTIPLE 4-4 REDUCTION DEFENSE

Legacy High School, Colorado

I am going to give you our version of the multiple 4-4 reduction defense. I played this defense, and I have coached it for 15 years. To be successful over time, we agreed as a staff on these principles of defensive football: We needed to be committed to the scheme, and we had to decide to win *now* or prepare for the future. We made the decision to go to the multiple reduction scheme. It provides us with many looks, and it is hard to prepare for. It is flexible, and we can adjust to the different offenses. It is simple for athletes to learn and understand. This is the base for everything we do on defense.

- We must maintain gap control until the ball is no longer a threat to it.
- We aggressively read the defensive blocking schemes and patterns.
- We read guards with our linebackers, and we read blocking schemes with our defensive linemen.

Multiple Zone Coverage

- Supports run defense
- Allows the free safety to be part of the run game
- Prevents big plays
- Disguises coverage

Stop Big Plays

- Make offense sustain drives—bend but not break.

Frank Beamer says that the scoring percentage for touchdowns is related to field position. He breaks down the field and the percentages in the following manner:

- If a team takes over on their own 20-yard line, they have 1 out of 30 chances of scoring.

- If a team takes over on their own 20- to 40-yard line, they have 1 chance in 12 of scoring.
- If you move the possession up to the 50-yard line, the percentage becomes 1 out of 5 chances to score.
- If a team takes over on the opponent's 40-yard line, the chance of scoring is 1 out of 4.
- If a team takes over on the opponent's 10-yard line, the chance of scoring is 1 out of 2.

As you can see, if we can get 10 more yards on the punt return and start at the 50-yard line, our chance of scoring improves to 1 out of 5.

Jimmy Johnson says that scoring percentages of both touchdowns and field goals are:

- < -25 = 7 percent
- -25 to 50 = 25 percent
- 50 to $+25$ = 45 percent
- $+25$ to $+15$ = 60 percent
- $+10 >$ = 80 percent

With this information, we can stress the importance of stopping the big plays. We want to stop big plays because that allows us to cause turnovers and to win the physical battle.

Let me mention our huddle. Several points are worth mentioning. The huddle is important to use for the purpose of communication.

Huddle

- Everyone on the field needs to be on the same page
- Down-and-distance (drop linebacker)
- Front, stunt, blitz, coverage (I or E linebacker)

After Huddle Breaks

- Set defense (whoever makes the call)

- Backfield formation (other I linebacker)
- Pre-snap calls (defensive line red and purple)

We use the same gap/numbering system that others use (Diagram #1). We label the gaps inside out, and we number the techniques from the inside out.

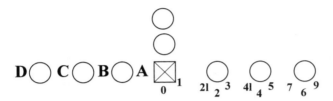

Diagram #1. Gap/Alignment System

We separate our defensive players into three groups:

- Reduction (R, T, bolt, eagle)
- Okie (N, 5, drop, inside)
- Secondary (corners/free safety)

The reduction side of our defense will go to the call. The Okie side will go away from the call.

Player Terminology

- R=Rush end (7 technique to callside)
- T=Reduced tackle (3 technique to callside)
- N=Nose tackle (1 or 2i away from call)
- 5=5 technique (away from call)
- E=Eagle linebacker (callside A gap)
- I=Inside linebacker (Okie-side B gap)
- D=Drop linebacker (9 technique to tight end away from call)
- SS=Strong safety to callside
- FS=Free safety
- C=Cornerback

Basic Front Calls

- Strong (receiver strength)
- Weak (away from receiver strength)
- Tight (to the tight end)
- Split (away from the tight end)
- Field (to field)
- Short (to boundary)

With the time allotment, I am going to show the 10 adjustments we make on the formations we see. We will cover the actual defense in action when we show the film.

First is our traditional Oklahoma 50 alignment (Diagram #2).

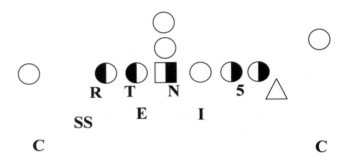

Diagram #2. Traditional Oklahoma 50

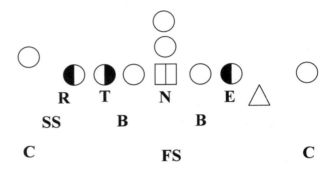

Diagram #3. Split 3 Deep vs. I Pro

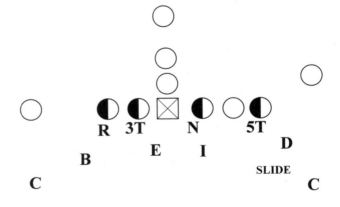

Diagram #4. Split 3 Deep vs. I Pro (Check Slide)

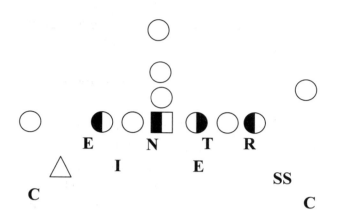

Diagram #5. Strong 3 Deep vs. I Pro

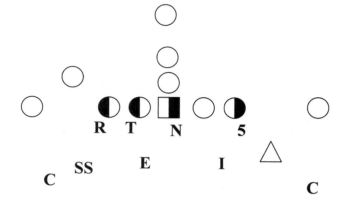

Diagram #8. Strong 3 Deep vs. Cincinnati

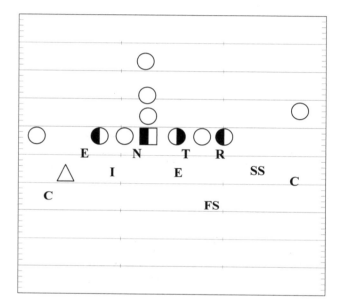

Diagram #6. Field 3 Deep vs. I Pro

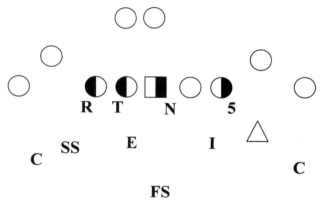

Diagram #9. Strong 3 Deep vs. Shotgun Spread

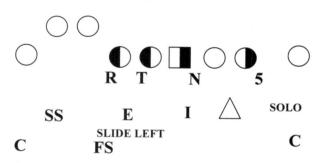

Diagram #10. Strong 3 Deep vs. Shotgun 3 x 1

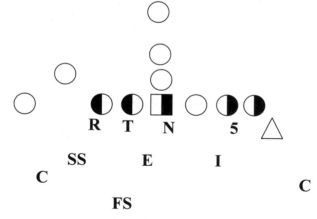

Diagram #7. Strong 3 Deep vs. Pro I Twins

Next, I want to move on to *team pursuit*. We want to be sound in our flow to the ball. To teach team pursuit, there are some points we feel we must coach.

- In our defense, it is essential to have excellent pursuit angles and exertion.

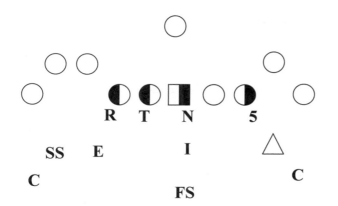

Diagram #11. Strong 3 Deep vs. Empty

- We have identified with the 959 philosophy, which puts nine of our guys within five yards of the football—at the time of the whistle?90 percent of the time.

Marvin Lewis of the Cincinnati Bengals said, "Playing defense in the NFL is pretty easy if you can get all 11 players running to the ball every play." That is what we would like to do every play.

To coach team pursuit, we have developed basic words to assist us in communicating with the players. This is the pursuit terminology we use with this defense.

Force: Primary contain on flow to him

- Attack all lead blocks/outside in.
- Squeeze the running lane, trying to stay square to the line of scrimmage.
- Never give the outside arm and leg up.

Secondary Contain: Run support after threat of pass is eliminated

Protect sideline:

- Replace force if cracked
- Play halfback pass
- Alley: Playside linebacker
- Play downhill (toward ball)
- Stay square and attack ball
- Inside-out——one step behind

Inside-out/fill (free safety in three-deep):

- Pass first
- Inside-out leverage on ball

No cutbacks:

- Backside/leverage: cutback/counter
- Shuffle when flow goes away
- Secure cutback/counter gaps
- Get to pursuit angles

Touchdown saver (backside corner):

- Keep everything in front
- Play throwback, counter, reverse
- Stop the score (at all costs)

This is what the flow to reduction looks like on the field (Diagram #12). The secondary contain is by the corner on the flowside. The touchdown saver is the backside corner away from the flow. Our free safety fills in the alley.

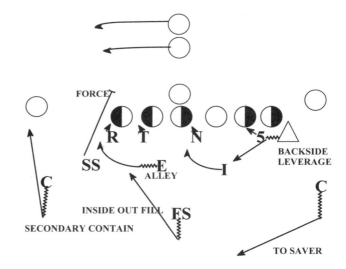

Diagram #12. Team Pursuit Flow to Reduction

This is the team pursuit flow to the Okie side. It is just the reverse of the reduction flow. The force comes from the tight-end side (Diagram #13). The rush end, strong safety, and corner have the responsibility on the bootleg, counter, and reverse on flow away.

In closing, I want to take a few minutes to talk about a program that we are involved with in Denver. It is the NFL High School Player Development program. You may have seen the logo we use for the program. Those of you from areas where the NFL is located should know about this program. We have the program at Legacy High School in May, and we go from 5:30 p.m. to 7:30 p.m.

I want to explain the program, and if you are interested in knowing more, you can contact me at the numbers I have listed at the end of this lecture.

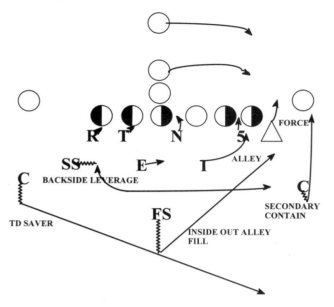

Diagram #13. Team Pursuit Flow to Okie Side

The NFL High School Player Development program is designed to address the issues that face high school football programs in communities in need. Urban-based high school coaches, college football recruiters, collegiate coaches (Divisions I, II, and III), NFL general managers, and player personnel directors have all identified a core group of common issues.

Key Issues and Observations From Football Community

- Lack of feeder systems (no introduction to the game) results in decreased interest in playing high school football.
- Players of today are deficient in the fundamentals of the game.
- Academics are disqualifying many football players.
- NFL High School Player Development provides incoming fall-season sophomores through seniors a program that focuses academic counseling and specific football skill training by position.
- Each participant gains a full awareness of what is necessary to become a successful high school and collegiate student-athlete, along with the resources and information to meet the NCAA clearinghouse requirements.

If you have questions, I will be glad to talk more with you. If others are interested in the program, please email or call. Thank you for your attention.

Wayne.voorhees@adams12.org

- 720-972-6876 (work)
- 303-601-9171 (cell)

Rob Younger

BUILDING CHARACTER THROUGH PRACTICE

Sweet Home High School, Oregon

I want to thank the Oregon Athletic Coaches Association and the Nike Coach of the Year Football Clinics for this special opportunity to speak today. I remember the first football clinic I attended in 1976. I was awestruck by the idea that I was going to be able to listen to and learn from great coaches like Bud Wilkinson, Duffy Daugherty, and Bear Bryant. I have long since lost my notes from that clinic, but I still remember today something that Coach Bryant emphasized. Coach Bryant said, "If you get one thing from any clinic you attend that can help your program, then it is time well spent." So, my goal today is to be able to share with you something that you can use and implement into your program.

I have two handouts that you need. The green cover has the PowerPoint notes from today's presentation. You can just add your own notes as we go. The yellow cover has 20 pages of ideas, stories, and activities that we use to help develop character and attitude in our players. If you would like me to send you a copy of either, please contact me at my email address, given at the end of this lecture.

Today's topic is on the importance of and the strategies to help develop *character* in your players. I will share with you how we incorporate weekly and daily character lessons in our practice schedule. We have come to learn that our players' character traits are the foundation to our success.

I umpire baseball in the spring and summer. I have had the opportunity to work in the Pac-10, and now enjoy working high school and legion games. Anyone who has played or umpired baseball can attest to the fact that you cannot tell a baseball by its cover, and it is what is inside that counts. It does not matter if it is a cheap $4 ball, or a more expensive ball—both look very much alike. On the outside, they look very much alike, but baseball coaches and players know they are very different. The core of the baseballs and the material used in winding the inside of the baseballs differs greatly. You could not tell by looking on the outside or at the cover, but get inside and the truth will be made clear.

What is true for baseballs is true for coaches. As coaches, we can make some changes in how we look. However, over a season, and particularly when we face adversity and difficult times, the truth of who we are and what we believe in comes out. We want to develop our players on the inside, even more than we want to develop them on the outside. An example we want to teach our players is, "*Respond* to adversity, don't *react*!"

This past fall, I completed my 33rd year coaching high school football. I have coached the last 28 years at Sweet Home High School, the first eight as the defensive coordinator, and the past 20 as head coach. Sweet Home is a logging community. In 1980, we had eight mills in the surrounding area. Today, we have one. Our school has about 750 students, and many come from lower socioeconomic families. This past fall, less than 20 percent of the players in our football program lived with both their biological parents.

Even in families that are intact, parents spend 40 percent less time with their children than they did a generation ago. With the decline of the family unit in our culture today, a coach becomes an even greater influence in the lives of the young people of their community. The breakdown of families has contributed to a deterioration of character in today's society. Today's student-athlete is different than the ones I began working with over 30 years ago. As I have interacted with our players and listened to their problems, I am convinced of the importance of teaching character and values that were once commonly accepted and taught. Today's players need to be taught how to be successful—how to be leaders and productive teammates.

At the beginning of each season, only 8 to 10 football teams in each classification possess the *tradition*, the *coaching*, and the *talent* to win a state championship. The differences among those 8 to 10 teams are very slight. Often the factor that determines who finishes first, fourth, or tenth is a matter of character. Championship teams develop a unique chemistry based on several elements: honesty, hard work, self-sacrifice, faith, and loyalty. Good coaches understand the game. Great coaches understand the game and their athletes—and how to teach both of them. Football gives you the opportunity to teach and learn the following:

- Confidence
- Courage
- Poise
- Discipline
- Perseverance
- How to win and lose with dignity
- Teamwork
- How to be a great competitor
- Sportsmanship
- Integrity

A team's character and chemistry are the keys to being successful. Talent just gives you a chance to win. Following is a list of our season records, league records, and our success in the state playoffs over the last six years. Our short-term success (season and league records) may differ from year to year, but the lasting lifelong experiences that a player takes from our program should never be dependent on what our record was that year. Another trait we want to teach our players is, "The way you do *anything*, is the way you do *everything*!" Often times, when you have student-athletes who are successful in the classroom, they will also be successful on the field.

Sweet Home Football Records

- 2002: 8-2, 5-0, state quarterfinals (3.35 GPA)
- 2003: 10-1, 5-0, state quarterfinals (3.25 GPA)
- 2004: 9-3, 5-0, state semifinals (3.32 GPA)
- 2005: 5-5, 4-1, state playoffs second round (2.76 GPA)
- 2006: 4-6, 3-2, state playoffs first round (2.90 GPA)
- 2007: 5-5, 3-2 (3.12 GPA)

We want to teach life lessons, values, and character within our weekly game preparation. This is what they will take with them years after playing football.

In our first team meeting in the fall, prior to our first practice, we want to explain to our team how we will become a successful team. We want to start the season thinking like champions. How you think will determine the choices you make—choices that you make on things that you have control over such as effort, attitude, and character. The following are topics we want to cover:

- Attitude and chemistry are the keys to winning
- Trust and respect
  - ✓ Accept differences between teammates
- Importance of character/foundation for past team's success
- Player ownership
  - ✓ Individual improvement
  - ✓ Leadership
  - ✓ Role models
  - ✓ Level of expectations
- Accountability and responsibility
- Sense of family
  - ✓ Brothers
  - ✓ Each player/coach has a role
- Introduce team pledge
- Locker room posters
  - ✓ Poster of schedule
  - ✓ State championship history
  - ✓ Capital conference championship history

The team pledge is something that we got from the University of Oregon. We place the pledge in the middle of a poster board. We discuss the different promises during daily doubles, and then we have a signing party on the last day of doubles. By signing the team pledge, you (meaning the players and coaches) are committing yourself to something bigger than yourself. It has also been a very positive step in working with discipline problems as they arise during the season.

During this initial meeting, we also discuss the four posters that will be in our team room the entire season.

This was first introduced to us by the University of Colorado staff. The first poster is our schedule of games for that season printed from bottom to top. The first game on our schedule is printed on the bottom, the second game is the second from the bottom, and on up the schedule. Our schedule goes all the way through the state playoffs, concluding with the date and site of the state championship game at the top.

We color code our pre-conference, conference, and state playoff games. This poster shows our players the necessary succession of events that will lead us to having the kind of success we all want. We develop goals for each section of our season—pre-conference games, conference games, and the state playoffs. It has been very beneficial to keep us focused on the big picture and the many components within that big picture. We put a big red square around the November games along with the motto, "Games played in November are games you will remember!" The key to the poster is in the preparation it takes to be playing games in November. After each game, we post the score after the opponent's name and discuss what was accomplished that past week.

The other posters, our state championship history (quarterfinals or better), our state playoff history, and our conference championship history, help our players understand past traditions and previous teams' commitment and leadership that lead to their success. I post the years that our past teams have accomplished each of those goals, with the present year having a question mark behind it. The players see these four posters every day of the season.

One of the most valuable things we do is systematically discuss values and character as they relate to our weekly football preparation. During the season, we focus on and develop our weekly preparation and game planning around a specialized quality or "theme of the week." These are themes that teach lessons on attitudes in honesty, loyalty, courage, unselfishness, work ethic, discipline, confidence, leadership, teamwork, mental toughness, handling adversity, perseverance, accountability, service, pride, humility, integrity, responsibility, and family relationships. We want to teach positive lessons that our players will take with them and use to become successful and productive husbands, fathers, and members of their communities.

We discuss and incorporate our weekly theme into our team meetings, position meetings, and it is usually part of our pre-game talk. Throughout the week, we may also reinforce the theme by having guest speakers come in and address our team. Coaches from other sports, alumni, staff, and community members are some examples of who we have used in the past. Some of our best presentations have been from teachers in our building. Once they take part in our program, they become some of our best supporters.

Other ways we reinforce our theme during the week is with inspirational quotes and messages. Each daily practice plan will contain a thought for the day, which we ask the players to relate to our team and the game of football. Examples might be:

- "Life is 10 percent what happens to you and 90 percent how you respond to it."
- "Good thoughts bear good fruit, bad thoughts bear bad fruit, and man is his own gardener."

Each week we give our players a *ready sheet* that is a summary of goals we want to accomplish and information regarding our upcoming opponent. The ready sheet is a big part of our players learning to take ownership of our success through individual preparation and improvement. We also incorporate character development throughout the ready sheet. On the cover sheet, we include thoughts for the week and discuss qualities leading to successful individuals and championship teams. Our coaching staff also includes the theme of the week into their ready sheet pages that discuss our offense, defense, and special teams preparation. The fifth page of our ready sheet is a story or message centered around our theme that week. I have included 20 examples of different stories/messages we have used in the second yellow handout. If you did not get one, you can email me and I will send you one.

The sixth page of our ready sheet is a worksheet that our players are responsible for completing and returning prior to our Tuesday practice. Again, the emphasis is player ownership and character development. The first question on the worksheet each week is:

- What is an area *you* want to improve on this week in practice?
  - ✓ Offense:
  - ✓ Defense:
  - ✓ Special teams:

This allows the players to take responsibility toward their own improvement each week. We believe that the more ownership you give them, the more motivated the players become. Many of the questions on the worksheet deal with information from our staff that we want our players getting from the ready sheet concerning our upcoming game. We complete the worksheet with questions like the following three that deal with individual and character development:

- What is one idea/concept that you are going to do differently that will make us play better on the road?
- As you reflect on the championship team quality this week, "The brothers stay focused on what is really important," how can you apply that to yourself and our team?

- As you read the poem, *The Man in the Mirror*, how do you apply it to yourself and the game of football?

We want to constantly reward players who show outstanding character and qualities that make teams successful. One way we do this is with our *Black Lion* award. This is a very special award sponsored by Jerry Farnsworth (SHHS, class of 1987). Jerry is a West Point graduate and is still serving our country in the military. Following is a description of the award:

Dedicated to the memory of Don Holleder and the men of the 28th Infantry. The Black Lions who gave their lives for their country in the Battle of Ong Thanh, Vietnam, on October 17, 1967. This award is presented to the football player who best exemplifies the character of Don Holleder: leadership, courage, and devotion to duty, self-sacrifice, and, above all, an unselfish concern for his team ahead of himself.

Don Holleder, as a West Point cadet, was an All-American end as a junior, and he was sure to repeat as a senior. But duty called and before his senior year, he was asked by his coach to change positions and sacrifice any further personal glory for the sake of his team. He did so willingly and unquestioningly. He made no All-American teams, and, in fact, he was often criticized, but thanks to his unselfishness, his courage, and his leadership, his underdog Army team upset mighty Navy.

As an Army officer in Vietnam while charging into the jungle to rescue injured comrades, Major Donald W. Holleder was struck and killed by a sniper's bullet. He gave his life for his team and for his teammates.

Each week we select Black Lion award winners. They are given a black practice jersey with *Black Lion* printed on the back. They wear the jersey that week in practice. A Black Lion helmet sticker is also awarded. This is a great way to honor special players who might not play in the games but are critical to your success as scout-team players. We often say how important these players are to our success, but how often do we reward their efforts? A team is only as good as its weakest link.

We also give an annual Black Lion award that has become the most highly coveted award we give. Our players and coaches consider this a very prestigious award due to the commitment to their teammates that it takes and the many sacrifices that the winner must make.

To conclude my presentation, I would like to give you some "food for thought" from my 33 years of working with high school football teams.

Qualities of Great Teams

- Leadership
  - ✓ Leaders of great teams develop loyalty.
  - ✓ Leaders must see the big picture.
  - ✓ Leaders focus on the things that need to be done, and they do them.
  - ✓ Leadership needs to be positive.
  - ✓ Leaders go the extra mile.
- Guiding principles
  - ✓ Enthusiasm
  - ✓ Work habits
  - ✓ Team-first attitude (servant hood attitude)
- Pride
- Communication
- Motivation
- Persistence
- Have players who understand and accept their roles
- Positive attitude

Develop Traditions

- Husky walk—"Be worthy as you run upon this hallowed sod, for you dare to tread where champions have trod."
- F.I.S.T

Create a Sense of Identity

- If you turn out young men of character and loyalty with a devotion to family, then you have succeeded.
- Winning a few football games is just a bonus.

"Winning on the professional level is required. Winning on the collegiate level has become expected. Winning on the high school level should be a pleasant by-product of what you're really supposed to be doing, which is developing young people into men and women of character." —Bob Kanaby, NFHS director

Some people spend an entire lifetime wondering if they have made a difference. Coaches don't have that problem.

I have included a letter from an ex-player, Ernie Oar, in the second handout. I do so only as an example of what all of us can do in the lives of the players we are entrusted with. The greatest compliment that I have ever received was from a player I coached 20 years ago. Recently, he told me how much he was enjoying teaching his son the character traits that he had learned by playing football for Sweet Home High School. It does not get any better than that.

I would like to finish my presentation with a short story about Abraham Lincoln. In 1863, President Lincoln and an aide attended a Sunday morning church service. Leaving church, the aide asked President Lincoln what he thought of the pastor's message. President Lincoln responded by saying the message was well thought out, and his presentation was good. But the pastor had failed because he did not challenge us to do something great.

I would like to challenge you to coach your players and lead your staff by making life-long differences in their lives on your way to winning a championship. Within your daily and weekly game planning, teach them qualities and character traits that will influence them for a lifetime.

Thank you for this great opportunity to present today. If I can ever be of further assistance or if you need any of the handouts, please contact me: rob.younger@sweethome.k12.or.us.